Sun® Certified Enterprise Architect for J2EE Study Guide

(Exam 310-051)

Sun® Certified Enterprise Architect for J2EE Study Guide

(Exam 310-051)

Paul R. Allen,
Joseph J. Bambara

McGraw-Hill/Osborne

New York   Chicago   San Francisco   Lisbon   London   Madrid
Mexico City   Milan   New Delhi   San Juan   Seoul   Singapore   Sydney   Toronto

The McGraw·Hill Companies

McGraw-Hill/Osborne
2100 Powell St., Floor 10
Emeryville, CA 94608
U.S.A.

To arrange bulk purchase discounts for sales promotions, premiums, or fund-raisers, please contact **McGraw-Hill**/Osborne at the above address. For information on translations or book distributors outside the U.S.A., please see the International Contact Information page immediately following the index of this book.

Sun® Certified Enterprise Architect for J2EE Study Guide (Exam 310-051)

 234567890 CUS CUS 019876543

Book p/n 0-07-222688-9 and CD p/n 0-07-222689-7
parts of ISBN 0-07-222687-0

Publisher Brandon A. Nordin	**Acquisitions Coordinator** Jessica Wilson	**Computer Designers** George Toma Charbak, John Patrus
Vice President & **Associate Publisher** Scott Rogers	**Technical Editor** Charles Medley	**Illustrators** Melinda Moore Lytle,
	Copy Editor Lisa Theobald	Michael Mueller, Jackie Sieben, Lyssa Wald
Acquisitions Editor Timothy Green	**Proofreader** Pat Mannion	**Series Design** Roberta Steele
Senior Project Editor LeeAnn Pickrell		
	Indexer David Heiret	

This book was composed with Corel VENTURA™ Publisher.

About the Authors

Paul R. Allen is with UCNY, Inc., an international consulting firm that helps Fortune 500 companies improve operations through the use of database and object technology. His e-mail address is *pallen@ucny.com*. He has over 15 years of experience developing applications systems. He has been developing database applications for the last eight years using Weblogic, WebSphere, and SilverStream, and for the past three years, he has used Java for web development. He is a Certified Weblogic, WebSphere, and SilverStream Trainer, Developer, and FAE. His industry experience includes financial, brokerage, pharmaceutical, and manufacturing, and he specializes in transitioning clients to web-based, object-oriented database technology. In addition to teaching numerous courses in computing at Columbia University in New York, he has co-authored the following books: *PowerBuilder: A Guide To Developing Client/Server Applications* (McGraw-Hill, 1995), *Informix: Client /Server Application Development* (McGraw-Hill, 1997), *Informix: Universal Data Option* (McGraw-Hill, 1998), *SQL Server 7 Developer's Guide* (IDG, 1999), and *J2EE Unleashed* (SAMS, 2002). Over the past seven years, he has presented numerous courses and presentations on computing in several cities and countries, including Los Angeles, Vienna, Paris, Berlin, Orlando, Nashville, New York, Washington, D.C., Copenhagen, Oslo, and Stockholm.

Joseph J. Bambara is a principal of UCNY, Inc., an international consulting firm that helps Fortune 500 companies improve operations through the use of database and object technology. His e-mail address is *jbambara@ucny.com*. He has been developing applications systems for over 25 years, including relational database development for the last 15 years and Java application server for web development for the past four years. He is a Certified Trainer and Developer. His industry experience includes financial, brokerage, manufacturing, medical, and entertainment. Mr. Bambara has a Bachelor's and a Master's degree in Computer Science, and he also holds a Juris Doctorate in Law and is a member of the New York Bar. In addition to teaching various computer courses for CCNY's School of Engineering, he has co-authored the following books: *PowerBuilder: A Guide To Developing Client/Server Applications*

(McGraw-Hill, 1995), *Informix: Client /Server Application Development* (McGraw-Hill, 1997), *Informix: Universal Server* (McGraw-Hill, 1998), *Informix: Universal Data Option* (McGraw-Hill, 1998), *SQL Server 7 Developer's Guide* (IDG, 2000), and *J2EE Unleashed* (SAMS, 2002). Over the past seven years, he has presented numerous courses and presentations for Weblogic, WebSphere, SilverStream, and Sybase in several cities and countries, including Los Angeles, Vienna, Paris, Berlin, Orlando, Nashville, New York, Copenhagen, Oslo, and Stockholm.

About the Technical Editor

Charles "Flip" Medley currently works as a Senior Principal Consultant for Dante Consulting in Arlington, Virginia, on behalf of clients such as PriceWaterhouse Coopers and Riggs National Bank. Prior to that, he worked for Sun Microsystems for four years, immersing himself in Java and J2EE technologies and was regarded as one of Sun's top Java instructors.

To my family
—Paul R. Allen

To Thomas A. Casoria (FDNY) who died a hero on September 11, 2001
—Joseph J. Bambara

CONTENTS AT A GLANCE

CONTENTS

3 Object-Oriented Analysis and Design 79

4 Applicability of J2EE Technology 121

5 Design Patterns 201

6 Legacy Connectivity 301

ACKNOWLEDGMENTS

We would like to acknowledge all the incredibly hard-working folks at McGraw-Hill/ Osborne: Tim Green, Jessica Wilson, LeeAnn Pickrell, Wendy Rinaldi, and Flip Medley for their help in preparing this book and for being solid team players.

—Paul R. Allen and Joseph J. Bambara

Very special thanks to my co-author, Joseph J. Bambara, especially for his encouragement, strength, and perseverance, which make it possible to succeed at all of our endeavors. Thanks to my family who are always there when I need them.

—Paul R. Allen
New York, New York

A very special thanks to my co-author Paul R. Allen, especially for his friendship and for being a great partner no matter what we try. Thanks to my family who are always there when I need them.

—Joseph J. Bambara
Greenvale, New York

PREFACE

Because of the complexities involved in enterprise application development, it is becoming increasingly important for Information Technology architects to become certified as Sun Certified Enterprise Architect (SCEA) for the Java 2 Platform, Enterprise Edition (J2EE) technology. This certification is the highest in Sun Microsystems Java technology. Certification in Java technology will improve your career potential, provide credibility and respect, and increase job security. With certification, you prove that you are qualified to architect J2EE applications, which increases your opportunities for professional advancement.

The SCEA for J2EE exam is the ultimate test in the Sun series. The series presently includes the following certifications:

- Sun Certified Java Programmer (SCJP)
- Sun Certified Web Component Developer (SCWCD)
- Sun Certified Java Developer (SCJD)
- Sun Certified Enterprise Architect (SCEA)

The SCEA for J2EE exam tests the concepts you've gained as a professional architect. These concepts are typically gained in a career that spans ten or more years and includes diverse languages and technology beyond Java. The exam tests your ability to produce an enterprise architecture using J2EE. Chapter 1 provides a detailed overview of the exam and the objectives along with test-taking tips. We will cover all of the objectives in the book's chapters.

In This Book

Sun Certified Enterprise Architect for J2EE Study Guide (Exam 310-051)) is organized in such a way as to serve as an in-depth review for the exam for everyone from experienced J2EE architects, professionals, developers, and even newcomers to J2EE and related technologies. Each chapter covers a major aspect of the exam, with an emphasis on the "why" as well as the "how to" of working with and supporting J2EE-based applications and related enterprise technologies.

On the CD

For more information on the CD-ROM, please see Appendix A.

In Every Chapter

We've created a set of chapter components that call your attention to important items, reinforce important points, and provide helpful exam-taking hints. Take a look at what you'll find in every chapter:

- Every chapter begins with the **Certification Objectives**—what you need to know in order to pass the section on the exam dealing with the chapter topic. The Objective headings identify the objectives within the chapter, so you'll always know an objective when you see it!

- **Exam Watch** notes call attention to information about, and potential pitfalls in, the exam. These helpful hints are written by authors who have taken the exams and received their certification—who better to tell you what to worry about? They know what you're about to go through!

- **Practice Exercises** are interspersed throughout the chapters. These exercises help you master skills that are likely to be an area of focus on the exam and give you practice for SCEA Part 3, the essay portion of the certification exam. Don't just read through the exercises; they are hands-on practice that you should be comfortable completing. Learning by doing is an effective way to increase your competency with a product.

- **On The Job** notes describe the issues that come up most often in real-world settings. They provide a valuable perspective on certification- and product-related topics. They point out common mistakes and address questions that have arisen from on the job discussions and experience.

- **Scenario and Solutions** sections lay out potential problems and solutions in a quick-to-read format:

SCENARIO & SOLUTION

You need to maintain non-enterprise data across method invocations for the duration of a session. What kind of EJB would you use?	You should use a session bean, an EJB that is created by a client and usually exists only for the duration of a single client-server session.
You need to create an EJB to represent enterprise data. What kind of EJB should you use?	You should use an entity bean, which is an object representation of persistent data maintained in a permanent data store such as a database.

■ The **Certification Summary** is a succinct review of the chapter and a restatement of salient points regarding the exam.

 ■ The **Two-Minute Drill** at the end of every chapter is a checklist of the main points of the chapter. It can be used for last-minute review.

 ■ The **Self Test** offers questions similar to those found on the certification exams. The answers to these questions, as well as explanations of the answers, can be found at the end of each chapter. By taking the Self Test after completing each chapter, you'll reinforce what you've learned from that chapter while becoming familiar with the structure of the exam questions.

Some Pointers

Once you've finished reading this book, set aside some time to do a thorough review. You might want to return to the book several times and make use of all the methods it offers for reviewing the material:

1. *Re-read all the Two-Minute Drills,* or have someone quiz you. You also can use the drills as a way to do a quick cram before the exam. You might want to make some flash cards out of 3×5 index cards that have the Two-Minute Drill material on them.

2. *Re-read all the Exam Watch notes.* Remember that these notes are written by authors who have taken the exam and passed. They know what you should expect—and what you should be on the lookout for.

3. *Review all the S&S sections* for quick problem solving.

4. *Re-take the Self Tests.* Taking the tests right after you've read the chapter is a good idea, because the questions help reinforce what you've just learned. However, it's an even better idea to go back later and do all the questions in the book in one sitting. Pretend that you're taking the live exam. (When you go through the questions the first time, you should mark your answers on a separate piece of paper. That way, you can run through the questions as many times as you need to until you feel comfortable with the material.)

5. *Complete the Exercises.* Did you do the exercises when you read through each chapter? If not, do them! These exercises are designed to cover exam topics, and there's no better way to get to know this material than by practicing. If there is something you are not clear on, re-read that section in the chapter.

INTRODUCTION

Sun's most advanced certification program in Java technology is the Sun Certified Enterprise Architect ("SCEA") for Java 2 Platform. This book, the *Sun Certified Enterprise Architect for J2EE Study Guide (Exam 310-051)*, provides all the information that you may need to prepare for the SCEA. It has detailed chapters and a CD covering all the topics of the SCEA exam. To pass the certification, the candidate should be familiar with the fundamentals of Java applications programming and should have skill in Java programming. Additionally, there are some specific technologies that the candidate should know well. These topical areas are as follows:

- Basic principles of enterprise architectures
- Object-oriented design using UML
- Two-tier, three-tier, and N-tier common architectures
- Legacy connectivity
- EJB and container models
- Protocols (HTTP, HTTPS, IIOP, JRMP)
- Applicability of J2EE
- Design patterns
- Messaging
- Internationalization
- Security

The final chapter is an enterprise architecture case study (using UML), which will help you prepare for Part 2 of the SCEA exam, an architecture and design project.

I

Sun Certification for Enterprise Architect

Sun's most advanced certification program in Java technology is the Sun Certified Enterprise Architect for Java 2 Platform (SCEA). This book provides information that you will need to prepare for the SCEA exam. To pass the certification exam, you should be familiar with the fundamentals of applications programming and should have some proficiency in Java programming. Additionally, you should know specific enterprise technologies. All of these topics are covered in the book's chapters and on the CD accompanying the book:

- Basic principles of enterprise architectures
- Object-oriented design using UML
- Two-tier, three-tier, and n-tier common architectures
- Legacy connectivity
- EJB and container models
- Protocols (HTTP, HTTPS, IIOP, JRMP)
- Applicability of J2EE
- Design patterns
- Messaging
- Internationalization
- Security
- Enterprise Architecture case study (using UML)

Seven-plus years into its life, Java is now the acceptable and mature technology most commonly used behind the strategic scenes for an enterprise. After years in which Java development seemed to be reserved primarily for Internet applications, larger firms in the corporate world are using Java as the language of choice over C and COBOL for most of their new development, including but not limited to messaging, back-end night cycle functions such as database repair and warehousing, and data capture from external data feeds.

Java's appeal lies not only in its affinity for network and distributed computing (although intranet, extranet, and Internet applications remain the major focus of Java development) but also in Java's other qualities, such as ease of programming and cross-platform capabilities—the "write once, run anywhere" promise.

Widespread Capabilities for Application Development

A large portion of the appeal of Java is the ease with which it allows the creation of web-based, self-service applications that enable customers to do their work and perform other tasks over the Internet through a browser. Most applications are HTML on the web server front end with Java servlets on the application server back end that run on the company's web server. Figure 1-1 shows the application server hierarchy.

Java isn't just for e-business. Many organizations with large user bases are reengineering their client-server configurations because the deployment and distribution of this design is cumbersome and expensive. Some are developing Java applications for internal use, occasionally deploying Java clients to employee desktops.

Still, many issues stand in the way of Java 2 Enterprise Edition (J2EE) adoption by corporate application development groups. These include concerns about the development environment, the need to locate or train Java developers, the complexity of Enterprise JavaBeans (EJB), and the need to upgrade to the new generation of J2EE application servers to take full advantage of the technology. This is where the J2EE architect is most needed. The right architect can step into the enterprise to resolve these issues and make the dream of a J2EE-based enterprise a reality.

FIGURE 1-1   The J2EE application server is the focal point.

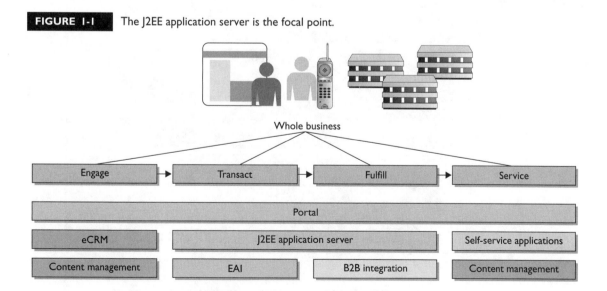

An undercurrent of concern also exists about what Microsoft is doing with its .NET initiative and what impact, if any, those actions will have on a development group's Java plans.

Judging from the J2EE application server market, however, Java and J2EE are here to stay. At the time of this writing, research leader Giga Information Group projects the application server market that was $1.64 billion in 2000 will be $9 billion by the end of 2003, which is up from about $585 million in 1999.

Java Is the Glue That Binds the Application Development Process

J2EE application servers are key to developing and deploying scalable enterprise Java applications. Application servers provide the infrastructure to execute and maintain business-critical applications, especially e-business applications. J2EE defines the programming model and provides underlying services such as security, transaction management, and messaging to enable developers to build networked Java applications quickly and deploy them effectively in the distributed world. Figure 1-2 shows the multiple functions of the J2EE application server.

FIGURE 1-2

J2EE application server is multi-functional.

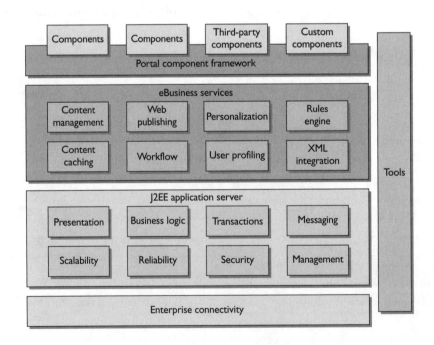

A rush to deploy the latest J2EE application servers in the business environment is fueling growth. Perhaps 200 application servers are being offered on the market today, with more appearing weekly. However, only a few dominate the market. Three companies—BEA Systems, IBM, and Sun—each claim 20 percent or more of the market, and several other vendors that specialize in market niches claim less than 10 percent each. The J2EE application servers that are on top are BEA Systems WebLogic, IBM WebSphere, and Sun iPlanet. More specialized players include Iona Technologies, which provides a J2EE application server with Common Object Request Broker (CORBA) capabilities.

The application server has emerged as the focal point of the new distributed, networked, corporate development. The application server acts as middleware, making the necessary back-end connections, running business logic and messaging, and managing functions such as transaction management and security. The latest application servers are adding support for wireless computing and integrated Extensible Markup Language (XML) capabilities.

You can create distributed applications without an application server, but you'll end up having to build from scratch much of the functionality the application server provides—such as database connection pooling. For example, one of our UCNY, Inc., (*www.ucny.com*) clients uses Lotus Domino as its web server and does not use an application server. "We've already built a lot of the functionality we'd get in an application server," reasoned the application manager. Long story short, the company is now in the process of porting its applications to IBM's WebSphere J2EE application server.

Companies Increasingly Need the Internet to Compete

Through the next decade, many, if not most, business transaction will be conducted over the Internet. To make this work on a grand scale, standards will be critical. The success of J2EE is important, because it will ensure that the Internet is the most cost-effective media to use for promoting the services of a business. Conducting business with a user-friendly, reliable, speedy, and attractive set of web pages supported by reliable back-end business logic will make the difference between success and failure in the enterprise business.

The entire business must be Internet-enabled. The business site must engage the customers and enable them to conduct transactions without the necessity of human interaction. Moreover, it will feed the organization's "fulfillment" engine as well as provide a place to go for post-transaction services.

Corporations will need architects to anchor development standards such as J2EE to facilitate the construction of web sites. These sites will communicate the business objectives of their clients, whether they want to direct functionality to local, national, or international markets.

Roles are now more important than ever. The architect, along with other technical and graphic design personnel, must work together to ensure that the web pages not only meet the business's needs but that they also maintain a perfect balance between performance and professional graphics work. The design of each component must follow a standard such as J2EE to ensure that the end product looks professional, loads faster, and effectively communicates the company's business objectives to the world.

Challenges of Application Development for the Enterprise

Timing has always been a critical factor for adopting new technologies, but the accelerated pace inherent in a virtual, information-driven business model has put even greater emphasis on response times. To leverage Internet economics, it is imperative that the architect not only project, build, and display enterprise systems, but that he or she does so repeatedly and in a timely manner, with frequent updates to both information and services. Just as the SQL standard facilitated data access, widespread acceptance and inherited experience with the J2EE standard will make it easier for architects to construct enterprise systems. The architect's principal challenge is one of keeping up with the Internet's hyper-competitive pace while maintaining and leveraging the value of existing business systems.

In this economic environment, timeliness is critical in gaining and maintaining a competitive edge. A number of factors can enhance or impede an organization's ability to deliver custom enterprise applications quickly and to maximize their value over their lifetime. Hopefully, architecture and ensuing development with J2EE will progress quickly so that the rapid application development (RAD) ability we grew fond of in the client-server architecture model will be present for the Internet.

Increasing Programmer Productivity

The ability to develop and deploy applications is a key to success in the information economy. Applications must go quickly from prototype to production, and they must continue evolving even after they have been deployed. Productivity, therefore, is vital to responsive application development. J2EE provides application development teams with a set of standard application programming interfaces (APIs)—that is, the means to access the services required by multi-tier applications and standard ways to support a variety of clients. This can contribute to both responsiveness and flexibility.

In contrast to data access that is standardized and stabilized by SQL, a destabilizing factor in Internet and other distributed computing applications is the divergence of programming models. Historically (in web terms), technologies such as Hypertext Markup Language (HTML) and Common Gateway Interface (CGI) have provided a front-end mechanism for distributing dynamic content, while back-end systems such as transaction processors are based on IBM Customer Information Control System (CICS), Tuxedo, IBM Message Queuing (MQ), Lotus Notes, and other data access systems. These technologies present a diversity of nonstandard programming models based on proprietary architectures.

With no single standard for application models, it is difficult for architecture, development, and production teams to communicate application requirements effectively and productively. As a result, the process of architecting applications is extremely complex. What's more, the skill sets required to integrate these technologies is not organized well for an effective division of labor.

Another complicating factor in application development time is the client type. Although many applications can be distributed to web browser clients through static or dynamically generated HTML, others may need to support a specific type of client or several types of clients simultaneously (for example, WAP, or Wireless Application Protocol). The programming model should support a variety of client configurations with minimal consequence to basic application architecture or the core business logic of the application.

J2EE enables development to be role oriented. Components are architected by one group, developed and assembled by another, and deployed by still another.

J2EE Architecture Must Respond to Consumer Demand

Imagine a multi-location retail business trying to increase its customer base by a factor of 10. How much time and effort would be expended on remodeling storefronts, building new warehouses, and so on, to keep up? Realistically, constant rework would impact the business's ability to serve its customers.

This holds for businesses in the e-commerce arena as well. The ability to architect applications that scale easily to accommodate growth is key to achieving the company's goals. To scale effectively, systems require mechanisms to ensure efficient management of system resources and services such as database connections and transactions. They need access to features such as automatic load balancing without any effort on the part of the application developer. Applications should be able to run on any server appropriate to anticipate client volumes and to switch server configurations easily when the need arises. J2EE-compliant application servers such as WebLogic and WebSphere provide these features in the form of database pooling, server clustering, and fail-over functionality.

The Architect Must Be Able to Integrate J2EE and Legacy Systems

In many enterprises, the data of value to organizations, also called "books and records," has been collected over the years by existing information systems. The investment resides in applications on those same systems. The business rules, the procedures, and Y2K code all work, perform the business functionality properly, and cost a great deal of time and money to produce. The challenge for developers of enterprise applications is how to reuse and capitalize on this value by betting on middleware, which can converse with the legacy systems.

Architects need to use the J2EE standard to help application developers by providing standard ways to access middle-tier and back-end services such as database management systems and transaction monitors.

The J2EE Standard Promotes Competition and Choices

RAD environments advance programmer productivity by obviating and facilitating the assembly of software components. As J2EE is maturing, integrated development environments (IDEs) are starting to resemble their client-server counterparts. The remaining challenge will be deployment. Architects must possess the ability to mix and match solutions to come up with the optimum configuration to accommodate the task at hand. As the vendor application server shakeout continues, freedom of choice in enterprise application development should soon extend from servers to tools to components.

As vendors adhere to the J2EE standard, choices among server products will give an organization the ability to select configurations tailored to its application requirements. Much like SQL, the J2EE standard provides the organization the ability to move quickly and easily from one configuration to another (for example, SQL: Sybase DB converted to Oracle), as internal and external demand requires.

Access to the proper development tools for the job is another important choice. Development teams should be able to use new tools as needs arise, including tools from server vendors and third-party tool developers. What's more, each member of a development team should have access to the tools most appropriate to his or her skill set and contribution.

Finally, developers should be able to choose from a market of off-the-shelf application components to take advantage of external expertise and to enhance development productivity. J2EE standardization over the coming years will advance systems development just as SQL advanced database development.

Design Goals of J2EE Architecture

The web architecture required for J2EE is somewhat analogous to the architecture required to run vendor-based SQL database servers. The same qualities of performance, reliability, and security must be present for web application servers to provide a host for an application. Speed is key, and the good architect must find a way to provide it. The competition will win out every time if it is able to provide faster response to the client. The user can click away to a competitor if a response is too slow on your site.

Mastering this requirement is a difficult task for the architect, because the user base can change rapidly. Not only should the architect be concerned with domestic customers and business hours, but he or she must consider the effects of globalization. J2EE application servers need to be efficient and scalable. These qualities will pare down the field to those few venders who can provide the speed to handle a local customer base with thousands of simultaneous hits.

J2EE Architects Should Strive for Service Availability

Users want the application to be available 24×7. This is the attraction of doing business on the web, as users don't have to worry about the doors being closed after hours. Additionally, users want to be able to speak to customer service representatives without having to wait until Monday. In addition to general availability, the reliability of the application server and the application software it runs is critical. Interruption of the business cycle—downtime—is unacceptable. The business depends on the application being up and ready to serve.

J2EE architects must provide reliable server configurations (clustering) as well as safe and clear fail-over procedures. J2EE application server architects also must consider privacy issues. They must be able to maintain passwords and logins and to hide sensitive data. The data must be tamper proof, and architects must be able to allow for encrypted communication for sensitive portions of the business transactions.

J2EE Architecture and Connectivity to Existing Data

Having been part of the development of mainframe systems that still maintain the "books and records" of large enterprises such as Merrill Lynch, Goldman Sachs, Phillip Morris, and most of the banks located in New York, it is easy for this author to understand why most of these systems are still in operation 25 years later. They simply work, and replacing them would be deleteriously expensive.

Specialized access to enterprise resource planning and mainframe systems such as IBM's CICS and IMS is or will be provided in J2EE through the *connector* architecture. Because each of these systems is highly complex and specialized, each requires unique tools and support to ensure utmost simplicity to application developers. As J2EE evolves, enterprise beans will be able to combine the use of connector access objects and service APIs with middle-tier business logic to accomplish their business functions, as demonstrated in Figure 1-3.

Expanded User Definition: Customers, Employees, and Partners

In the past, a desktop was the sole means of interfacing with an enterprise system, but those days are gone. Users today want to connect from virtually anywhere. The

FIGURE 1-3 J2EE combines presentation, business processes, and enterprise connectivity.

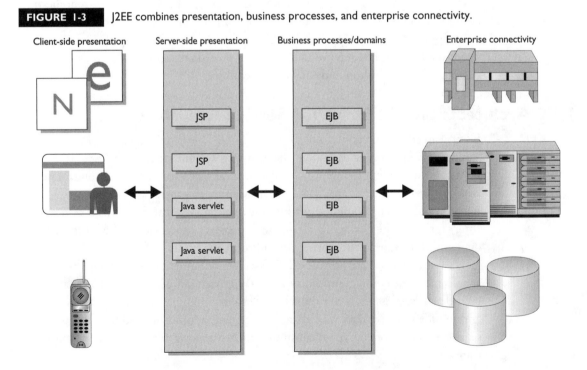

Client-side presentation Server-side presentation Business processes/domains Enterprise connectivity

JSP — EJB

JSP — EJB

Java servlet — EJB

Java servlet — EJB

access begins during their commute and might continue through the workday and while traveling to remote business sites.

Flexible User Interaction

J2EE provides choices for graphical user interfaces (GUIs) across an enterprise intranet or on the World Wide Web. Clients can use desktops, laptops, PDAs (personal digital assistants), cell phones, and other devices. Pure client-side user interfaces can use standard HTML and Java applets. Support for HTML facilitates prototypes and support for a broader range of clients. In addition, J2EE supports automatic download of the Java plug-in to add applet support. J2EE also supports stand-alone Java application clients.

For server-side deployment of dynamic content, J2EE supports both the Java Servlets API and JavaServer Pages (JSP) technology. The Java Servlets API enables developers to easily implement server-side behaviors that take full advantage of the power of the rich Java API. JSP technology combines the ubiquity of HTML with the power of server-side scripting in the Java programming language. The JSP specification supports static templates, dynamic HTML generation, and custom tags.

Flexible Business Component Model

Since its introduction, the EJB technology has developed significant momentum in the middleware marketplace. It enables a simplified approach to multi-tier application development, concealing application complexity, and enabling the component developer to focus on business logic. J2EE is the natural evolution of EJB technology.

EJB technology allows the developer to model the full spectrum of objects useful in the enterprise by defining three distinct types of EJB components: session beans, entity beans, and message-driven beans. Session beans represent behaviors associated with client sessions, such as a user purchase transaction on an e-commerce site. Entity beans represent collections of data, such as rows in a relational database and encapsulate operations on the data they represent. Entity beans are intended to be persistent, surviving as long as the data with which they are associated remains viable. The message-driven bean is the coupling of Java Message Service (JMS) with EJB to create an EJB type designed to handle asynchronous JMS messages.

J2EE extends the power and portability of EJB components by defining a complete infrastructure that includes standard clients and service APIs for their use.

Sun Certified Enterprise Architect Distinguishes the JAVA Professional

Because of the complexities involved, it is becoming increasingly important for IT architects to become a Sun Certified Enterprise Architect (SCEA) for the J2EE technology. This is the highest certification in Sun Microsystems Java technology. With certification, you prove that you are qualified to architect J2EE applications. This will obviously mean opportunities for professional advancement, such as salary increases, job role modifications, or promotions.

The SCEA for J2EE exam is the ultimate test in the Sun series. The series presently includes the following certifications:

- Sun Certified Java Programmer (SCJP)
- Sun Certified Web Component Developer (SCWCD)
- Sun Certified Java Developer (SCJD)
- Sun Certified Enterprise Architect (SCEA)

The SCEA for J2EE exam tests the concepts you've gained as a professional architect. These concepts are typically gained in a career that spans 10 or more years. It includes diverse languages and technology beyond Java. The exam tests your ability to produce an enterprise architecture using J2EE. The SCEA certification covers the topics discussed in the following sections. The objectives tested follow each topic as bullet items. All of these objectives are covered in the chapters that follow.

Common Architectures

- Given an architecture described in terms of network layout, list benefits and potential weaknesses associated with it.

Legacy Connectivity

- Distinguish appropriate from inappropriate techniques for providing access to a legacy system from Java technology code, given an outline description of that legacy system.

Enterprise JavaBeans

- List the required classes/interfaces that must be provided for an EJB component.

- Distinguish between stateful and stateless session beans.

- Distinguish between session and entity beans.

- Recognize appropriate uses for entity, stateful session, and stateless session beans.

- State the benefits and costs of container-managed persistence.

- State the transactional behavior in a given scenario for an enterprise bean method with a specified transactional attribute as defined in the deployment descriptor.

- Given a requirement specification detailing security and flexibility needs, identify architectures that would fulfill those requirements.

- Identify costs and benefits of using an intermediate data-access object between an entity bean and the data resource.

Enterprise JavaBeans Container Model

- State the benefits of bean pooling in an EJB container.

- Explain how the EJB container does lifecycle management and has the ability to increase scalability.

Protocols

- Given a list of some of its features, identify a protocol that is one of the following: HTTP (Hypertext Transfer Protocol), HTTPS, IIOP, or JRMP.

- Given a scenario description, distinguish appropriate from inappropriate protocols to implement that scenario.

- Select common firewall features that might interfere with the normal operation of a given protocol.

Applicability of J2EE Technology

- Identify application aspects that are suited to implementation using J2EE technology.

- Identify application aspects that are suited to implementation using EJB technology.

- Identify suitable J2EE technologies for the implementation of specific application aspects.

Design Patterns

- Identify the most appropriate design pattern for a given scenario.

- Identify the benefits of using design patterns.

- State the name of a Gamma et al. design pattern given the UML diagram and/or a brief description of the pattern's functionality.

- Identify benefits of a specified Gamma et al. design pattern.

- Identify the Gamma et al. design pattern associated with a specified J2EE technology feature.

Messaging

- Identify scenarios that are appropriate to implementation using messaging, EJB technology, or both.

- List benefits of synchronous and asynchronous messaging.

- Identify scenarios that are appropriate to implementation using messaging.

- Identify scenarios that are more appropriate to implementation using asynchronous messaging, rather than synchronous.

- Identify scenarios that are more appropriate to implementation using synchronous messaging, rather than asynchronous.

Internationalization

- State three aspects of any application that might need to be varied or customized in different deployment locales.

- List three features of the Java programming language that can be used to create an internationalizable/localizable application.

Security

- Identify security restrictions that Java 2 technology environments normally impose on applets running in a browser.

- Given an architectural system specification, identify appropriate locations for implementation of specified security features, and select suitable technologies for implementation of those features.

The SCEA exam comprises three parts: a multiple-choice exam, an architecture and design project, and an essay exam. The exam is administrated by Prometric, a leading worldwide provider of comprehensive technology-based testing and assessment services (see *www.prometric.com*).

After you have successfully completed all three of the exam components, you will have earned the title of Sun Certified Enterprise Architect (SCEA) for the Java 2 Platform.

The exam components and summary details are as follows:

- **SCEA Part 1**   Exam # (CX 310-051) is currently available at Prometric for $150 U.S. dollars. There are no prerequisites. The exam includes 48 multiple-choice, short answer, and drag-and-drop questions. Candidates have 75 minutes to take the exam, and the pass score is 68 percent.

- **SCEA Part 2**   The architecture and design project must be completed via Sun's certification database. You must complete exam # (CX 310-051) before completing the project. There is no time limit, and the passing score is 70 percent, subject to the evaluation of the essay exam and validation of the authenticity of the assignment. The current cost is $250 U.S. dollars.

- **SCEA Part 3**   Exam # (CX 310-061), an essay exam, can be completed at Prometric testing centers for a current cost of $150 U.S. dollars. To take this exam, you must have passed Parts 2 and 3. You have 90 minutes to complete four essay questions.

exam
ⓦatch   *For detailed information on these exams, refer to the Certification Success Guide at www.suned.sun.com/US/images/certification_archj2ee_07_01.pdf.*

In addition to reading this book, you can prepare for the SCEA exam in other ways. Because of the complexity of the examination (especially Parts 2 and 3) and based upon your individual background, we recommend studying the information in a combination of books that provide detailed information covering the entire list of objectives:

- *Sun Certified Enterprise Architect for J2EE Technology Study Guide*, by Mark Cade and Simon Roberts (Prentice Hall PTR, 2002)

- *J2EE Unleashed*, by Joseph J Bambara and Paul Allen, et al (SAMS, 2002)

- *Mastering Enterprise JavaBeans*, by Ed Roman (John Wiley & Sons, 2001)

- *Design Patterns*, by Erich Gamma, et al (Addison-Wesley, 1995)

- *UML Distilled*, by Martin Fowler (Addison-Wesley, 1999)

exam

ⓦatch

The current version of the SCEA exam tests your knowledge of J2EE 1.3 API. See www.java.sun.com/apis.html for complete J2EE API specs and related documentation.

Becoming familiar with an application server is an integral part of the preparation for the SCEA. You can use any application server, providing it is compliant with the J2EE 1.3 specification. Here are the links to the downloadable versions of BEA WebLogic and IBM WebSphere application servers:

- **WebLogic** *www.commerce.bea.com/downloads/products.jsp*
- **WebSphere** *www.14.software.ibm.com/webapp/download/product.jsp?id= MCOS-5FUSYK*

Many quality tutorials and articles on various J2EE technologies are also available. Following are a couple of them that cover the objectives of the SCEA exam:

- **J2EE Tutorial** *www.java.sun.com/j2ee/tutorial/index.html*
- **TheServerSide, Your J2EE Community** *www.theserverside.com*

There is nothing like learning from the experience of successful people who have been through the process of obtaining SCEA certification. You should seek out colleagues who have taken the exam and can provide insight. In addition, you can engage in discussions with members of the following use groups and at web sites:

- **SCEA_J2EE** *www.groups.yahoo.com/group/scea_j2ee*
- **SCEA_PREP** *www.groups.yahoo.com/group/scea_prep*
- **JavaRanch** *www.saloon.javaranch.com/cgi-bin/ubb/ultimatebb.cgi?ubb= forum&f=26*

In addition, courses are offered by Sun certified trainers, which can be helpful in preparing for the exam:

- **SUN's Course SL-425, from the creators of SCEA exam** *www.suned.sun.com/US/catalog/courses/SL-425.html*
- **SUN's Course Object-Oriented Analysis (OO-226)** *www.suned.sun.com/US/catalog/courses/OO-226.html*
- **Middleware Company, a premier J2EE training company** *www.middleware-company.com*

This book comes with multiple choice and essay practice questions, plus an example case study that you need to consider to prepare for the exam. The CD contains code and additional exam questions. Even after accessing various resources, though, you may still require preparation for different reasons—clearing your doubts about a topic, understanding the latest exam pattern, and so on.

General SCEA Test Preparation Tips

To prepare for Part 1, you must understand each of the exam objectives mentioned at the beginning of this chapter and within the chapters that follow. Those with comprehensive experience need only concentrate on their weaknesses. Others with less experience can take anywhere from weeks to months to learn what needs to be known.

- As a whole, Part 1 may require that you spend a few hours (for an experienced architect) to six months or more of dedicated preparation (for a beginner).

- Part 2 is project work, which requires a lot of focused and concentrated effort. On average, it may require 100 hours of study, typically spread over a period of a few months.

- Part 3 is an essay exam on your work in Part 2. Your success depends on your efforts during Part 2. If you did your homework, no special preparation is required at this stage.

Let's review some test-taking tips:

- *Prepare summary notes for Part 1.* Even though you may have read everything for the exam, having a few summary pages is a good idea. You can do a quick revision of all topics before the exam.

- *Cramming doesn't work.* If you have followed a study plan, the night before Part 1 you should do a quick review and get to sleep early. Remember that your brain and body need rest to function well.

- *Approach the exam as you would approach any large task.* It might be daunting, but you can do it! A positive attitude goes a long way toward success.

- *Those tricky problems can knock you off balance.* Don't get frustrated. Reread the question to make sure you understand it, and then try to solve it. If you're still clueless, mark it and move on. You can come back to it later. What if you have no idea about the answer? Review your options and take your best shot.

- *The process of elimination can help you choose the correct answer in a multiple-choice question.* Start by crossing off the answers that are obviously incorrect. Then spend your time focusing on the potentially correct choices before selecting your answer.

- *Prepare for scenario-based questions.* The test is geared toward testing your architectural skills. Hence, many lengthy scenarios are described, followed by questions that test your knowledge on what technology may be most appropriate in the given situation and why.

- *Read each scenario question twice.* Often the real issues will be imbedded within a descriptive situation, and the real question will be hidden. Concentrate on the architecture issues and try to put the scenario to the back of your mind.

- *They say a picture is worth a thousand words, so when attempting to answer scenario questions, try to diagram what is being described.* If, for example, the question is describing a legacy system communicating with an application server, it helps to draw a diagram.

- *Use scrap paper.* Before you start the test, create a grid to represent the questions and your comfort level with the answer. Even when you mark off questions for review, having this in front of you will help you estimate the time required for revision.

- *This exam tests your architectural abilities, not necessarily your coding ability, so you should focus on the concepts, not on the code.* While the test wants you to know what code performance is, it will not give you a code snippet and ask you to optimize it.

- *Although it's not in the requirements, a sound understanding of the J2EE patterns is useful in Part 1 and essential in Parts 2 and 3.*

- *Try to build up a broad knowledge of other technologies, not just J2EE.* Learn about messaging, mainframe technology, and perhaps some file and database terminology, because Sun assumes you have overview of all of the technologies.

CERTIFICATION SUMMARY

The most important issue with regard to SCEA certification is how it promotes your career goals and helps you to earn a better job (and, hence, more money). With the current economy, it is somewhat difficult to compare the service rates, quantity, and quality of development opportunities. However, your opportunities will increase.

What you learn while preparing for the certification is what matters the most. The objectives for the architect certification are the best self-study curriculum for a Java architect and developer. They are practical and cover most of the issues not only with respect to Java technologies, but also with respect to computing architecture and software development. The test preparation is a forced technique for mastering the material. It pumps up your confidence as well. It helps you to organize what you know and to find the voids. It also prepares you for interviews. Many recruiting companies are using their own tests to determine the programmer's qualification. Someone with a SCEA certification is, generally speaking,

- Knowledgeable in Enterprise JavaBeans
- Knowledgeable in Uniform Modeling Language
- Knowledgeable in design patterns
- Knowledgeable in the architecture and protocols of distributed applications
- A potential project leader

The following chapters will put you in a position to take and pass all three parts of the SCEA and will provide you with a quick review for any interview or Java architect skills test. Good luck.

2

Common Architectures and Protocols

The role of the architect, especially when it revolves around J2EE, is on the increase as the need to build web-enabled systems increases. The architect must consider not only the functional requirements of the system but also the nonfunctional requirements as well. Is the system capable, scalable, secure, extensible? The architect must consider these issues and utilize J2EE, especially its security, speed, reliability, and cross-platform capabilities, to address them. To that end, this chapter will cover the topics that follow:

- Role of an architect
- Architecture defined
- Architectural terms
- Architecture versus design
- Fundamentals of architecture
- Capabilities of an architecture
- Design goals of architecture
- Architecture tiers and layers
- Benefits and weaknesses of architecture
- Protocols: HTTP, HTTPS, IIOP

Anyone who has seen the movie *My Big Fat Greek Wedding* knows how the main character, Toula's father, thinks every English word is derived from the Greek language. In the case of the word *architect,* he is correct. *Arkhitekton* is the Greek term meaning "head builder," from which the word *architect* is derived. Originally it described the leading stonemason of the ancient Greek temples of 500 B.C. It goes like so: *Arkhi* means head, chief, or master; *Tekton* means worker or builder. The word is related to *Tekhne,* the Greek term meaning art or skill.

The architect's goal is always to rearrange the environment—to shape, construct, and devise, whether it be buildings, institutions, enterprises, or theories. Architects look upon the world as little more than raw material to be reshaped according to their design. Author Ayn Rand describes this characteristic in the architect Howard Roark, her protagonist in *The Fountainhead:*

"He looked at the granite…. These rocks, he thought, are here for me; waiting for the drill, the dynamite and my voice; waiting to be split, ripped, pounded, reborn, waiting for the shape my hands will give to them." [*The Fountainhead,* pp 15–16]

What purpose does an architect serve in today's world? Architects visualize the behavior of a system. They create the blueprint for the system, and they define the way in which the elements of the system work together. Architects distinguish between functional and nonfunctional system requirements, and they are responsible for integrating nonfunctional requirements into the system.

This chapter describes architecture and the role of an architect from a conceptual viewpoint and introduces and explores some of the nomenclature and terminology associated with architecture. It also explores Java 2 Enterprise Edition (J2EE) and its architecture.

Types of Architecture

Webster's dictionary provides the following definitions for the term *architecture:*

- The art or practice of designing and building structures and especially habitable ones
- Formation or construction as the result of a conscious act
- Architectural product or work
- A method or style of building

Architecture refers to an abstract representation of a system's components and behaviors. Ideally, architecture does not contain details about implementation (that's left for the developers, or engineers). The architect gathers information about the problem and designs a solution, which satisfies the functional and nonfunctional requirements of the client and is flexible enough to evolve when the requirements change.

Needless to say, defining architecture is a creative process. An architect's challenge is to balance creativity and pragmatism using the available technology in the form of models, frameworks, and patterns. Architecture may refer to a *product*, such as the architecture of a building, or it may refer to a *method* or *style*, such as the knowledge and styles used to design buildings. In addition, architecture needs to be reconfigurable to respond to changing environments and demands.

System Architecture

System architecture corresponds to the concept of "architecture as a *product*." It is the result of a design process for a specific system and must consider the functions of components, their interfaces, their interactions, and constraints. This specification is the basis for application design and implementation steps.

Defining architecture for a system serves many objectives. It abstracts the description of dynamic systems by providing simple models. In this way, architecture helps the designer define and control the interfaces and the integration of the system components. During a redesign process, the architecture strives to reduce the impact of changes to as few modules as possible. The architectural system model allows the architect to focus on the areas requiring the most change.

The architecture indicates the vital system components and constructs that should be adhered to when adapting the system to new uses. Violating the architecture decreases the system's ability to adapt gracefully to changing constraints and requirements. The architecture is a means of communication during the design process. It provides several abstract views on the system, which serve as a discussion basis to crystallize each party's perception of the problem area. Architectures are best represented graphically using a tool such as UML (Unified Modeling Language). An architect communicates the design of the system to other members of the team using UML.

Drawing the analogy with the architecture of buildings provides good insight in understanding the characteristics of a system architecture, because it shows how architectures provide multiple views and abstractions, different styles, and the critical influence of both engineering principles and materials. A building architect works with a number of different views in which some particular aspect of the building is emphasized. For example, elevations and floor plans give exterior views and top views, respectively. Scale models can be added to give the impression of the building's size. For the builder, the architect provides the same floor plans plus additional structural views that provide an immense amount of detail about various design considerations, such as electrical wiring, heating, and other elements. For the customer of a computer-based information system, the most important views on architecture are those that focus on system performance, user interface, maintainability, and extendibility. The architect of the system will be interested in detailed views on resource allocation, process planning, maintenance, monitoring, statistics, and other similar types of information.

System architecture can be formulated in a *descriptive* or *prescriptive* style. Descriptive style defines a particular codification of design elements and formal arrangements. The descriptive style is used during discussions between the client and the architect. Prescriptive style limits the design elements and their formal arrangements. This style is applied in plans used during the construction of a building. The builder, or development team, shall build according to plan.

The relationship between engineering principles and architectural style is fundamental. It is not just a matter of aesthetics, because engineering principles are also essential to the project. In a similar way, a reconfigurable computer-based information system cannot be built without a notion of such object-oriented concepts as metadata.

In addition, the influence of materials is of major importance in enabling certain architectural styles. Materials have certain properties that can be exploited in providing a particular style. For example, one cannot build a modern, stable skyscraper with wood and rope; concrete and iron are indispensable materials in realizing this construction. Like high-tech building architecture, Internet/intranet-enabled information system architectures currently under development rely on recent technologies (such as fast networks and distributed processing); such systems could not have been developed in the past.

Reference Architecture

Reference architecture corresponds to "architecture as a *style* or *method*." It refers to a coherent design principle used in a specific domain. Examples of such architectures are the Gothic style for building and the Java 2 Enterprise Edition (J2EE) model for computer-based information systems. This architecture describes the kinds of system components and their responsibilities, dependencies, possible interactions, and constraints.

The reference architecture is the basis for designing the system architecture for a particular system. When designing a system according to an architectural style, the architect can select from a set of well-known elements (standard parts) and use them in ways appropriate to the desired system architecture. The J2EE architecture is a component-based service architecture. The architect designs the system to utilize the appropriate components for each task. For example, as we will see later in the book, Java ServerPages (JSP) can be used to provide a user view of the system response to a user gesture.

This architecture gathers the principles and rules concerning system development in a specific domain to achieve the following:

- A unified, unambiguous, and widely understood terminology

- System architecture design simplicity, possibly allowing less expensive and more efficient design

- High-quality systems that rely on proven concepts of the reference architecture

- Interfacing and possible reusability of modules among different projects or system generations

- Implementation tasks that can be partitioned among different teams, ideally allowing each team to bring in its best expertise and available equipment

- Traceability between solution-independent requirements and final realizations

The architecture shall clearly indicate and justify how and at what stage in the development process external constraints and engineering design decisions are introduced. Successful achievement of these goals relies on the adoption of a clear and systematic methodology. Again, an analogy can be made with building architecture with regard to the science, methods, and styles of building. Since the architectural methods are a generalization and abstraction of the architecture as a product, the remarks concerning multiple views and abstractions, different architectural styles, and the important influence of both engineering principles and materials are equally valid. In this case, however, architecture describes system domain elements and their functions and interactions; it does not describe how they actually function and interact in a specific system. For example, building architecture describes load-sharing component pools as elements serving the goal of performance; it does not specify how the pools should be implemented by each certified J2EE vendor.

Flexible Reference Architecture

Reference architecture refers to engineering and design principles used in a specific domain. A reference architecture aims at structuring the design of a system architecture by defining a unified terminology, describing the responsibilities of components, providing standard (template) components, giving example system architectures, and defining a development methodology.

A reconfigurable and flexible system is able to evolve according to changing needs; it enables easy redesign, and its functions can be extended. In other words, the system allows you to add, remove, and modify system components during system operation. In addition, flexible systems minimize the need to adapt by maximizing their range of normal situations. To this end, reference architecture for reconfigurable/flexible systems shall specify the following:

- Special elements to enable and support reconfiguration and adaptation. In a J2EE system, this could be a Java Naming and Directory Interface (JNDI) agent who knows what system elements are present, where they are, and what services they offer.

- Common characteristics of ordinary system elements to support reconfiguration and adaptation. In other words, using JNDI, we can make objects available via their names, and new components can be constructed to leverage them without knowing the specifics regarding their implementation.

■ Design rules to safeguard system flexibility. For instance, when designing a system element, the developer shall not build on system constraints induced by other system elements with lower expected lifetime; otherwise, the system will lock into (arbitrary) design choices, which may need (nonarbitrary) revisions.

Moreover, the system architecture for reconfigurable/flexible systems has specific characteristics. Using the analogy of building architectures, the load-sharing elements are moved out of the way of the functional space. Note that flexible system architecture gives little indication on how the system is used or even what customer service the system provides. It is no surprise that a flexible architecture leaves many questions unanswered; when all questions have been addressed and anticipated, the result is often an inflexible system.

Reconfiguration and adaptation often require the capacity to provide maneuvering space. For instance, some buffer space is needed for a workstation that is temporarily unavailable during reconfiguration so as not to halt the entire production line. System architecture is an abstract description of a specific system. Indicating the functions of the system components, their interactions, and constraints helps to (re)develop the system. The architecture depends on engineering principles and available technology.

The design of reconfigurable systems puts additional demands on the reference architecture, because the architecture shall allow adding, updating, and deleting system components during operation.

Architectural Design and Principles

Architecture is the overall structure of a system, and it can contain subsystems that interface with other subsystems. Architecture considers the scalability, security, and portability of the system. The implementation normally follows the architecture. At the architectural level, all implementation details are hidden.

The software architecture is the high-level structure of a software system. The important properties of software architecture must consider whether it is at a high enough level of abstraction that the system can be viewed as a whole. Also, the structure must support the functionality required of the system. Thus, the dynamic behavior of the system must be taken into account when the architecture is designed.

The structure or architecture must also conform to the system capabilities (also known as nonfunctional requirements). These likely include performance, security and reliability requirements associated with current functionality, as well as flexibility or extensibility requirements associated with accommodating future functionality at a reasonable cost of change.

These requirements may conflict, and tradeoffs among alternatives are an essential part of the design of architecture.

Where Architecture Fits in Analysis, Design, and Development

In most project alignments, the architects are members of the development team. On a large project, they work with the system designers, team leads, enterprise modelers, developers, testers, QA staff, configuration experts, and business domain experts. On a small team, architects may be playing one or more of these roles. Architects are responsible for interacting with customers, beta testers, and end users to make sure that user requirements are satisfied.

Architecture vs. Design

An architect is *not* a designer. An application architecture's scope is the system's major structure, its architectural design patterns, and the frameworks upon which you can add components. The architecture's concern realizes nonfunctionality, whereas design is concerned with the business use cases to convert the domain object model into a technical object model. Application architecture is the project's structure.

The key difference between the terms *architecture* and *design* is in the level of details. Architecture operates at a high level of abstraction with less detail. Design operates at a low level of abstraction, obviously with more of an eye to details of implementation. Together they produce a solution that meets the functional and nonfunctional constraints of the requirements. The solution describes how to perform the task.

The architecture addresses structural issues, organizes subsystems, and assigns functionality to components. It defines the protocols for communication, synchronization, and data access; it physically allocates components to processors. Most important, it delivers the architectural design of the component interface specifications.

At this point, the designers step in and provide internal details of each component in the architecture, including an interface for each component class, the details for input/output, and the data structures and algorithms used.

The reality of most situations can cause this separation to break down for the following reasons:

■ **Time** There may not be enough time to consider the long-term architectural implications of the architectural design and implementation decisions.

- **Cost**   Architecture is expensive, especially when a new domain such as J2EE is being explored.

- **Experience**   Even when we have the time as well as the inclination to take architectural concerns into account, an architect's experience with a domain can limit the degree of architectural sophistication that can be brought to the system.

- **Skill**   Developers differ in their levels of skill, as well as in experience.

- **Visibility**   Only people who build a Java class see how it looks inside. Architecture is invisible.

- **Complexity**   Software often reflects the inherent complexity of the application domain.

- **Change**   Architecture is a hypothesis of the future.

- **Scale**   The architecture required for a large project is typically very different from that of smaller ones, making the architect's challenge all the more difficult.

Today's architect must comport theory and best practices with the reality of the target system requirement and available resources. For a hierarchical picture of the balancing that is the challenge, see Figure 2-1.

As J2EE architecture is relatively new, the deliverables for a J2EE architect are not well defined. It is sometimes difficult to draw a line where architecture stops and design begins. The assignment part of Sun's J2EE Enterprise Architect certification requires deliverables to be in UML, which is important but sometimes insufficient for real-world J2EE applications.

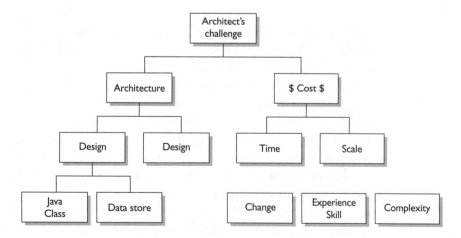

FIGURE 2-1

Balancing architecture, design, and reality

To get started, the architecture specification and process require at least the following:

- A system architecture document to describe your existing hardware, software, network topology, and other components.

- An application architecture document to describe the application's major structure, including a logical view of all architecturally significant components, use case components, and legacy components.

- A components design guideline to describe all design guidelines and architectural decisions, explain all those decisions, and describe possible consequences if an alternative option is used. These guidelines should capture all-important base determinants that the new component design must respect to maintain the system's architectural integrity.

- An architectural prototype to evaluate new technologies, gain experience developing and deploying J2EE applications, build architectural frameworks, and address risks by measuring performance and scalability, as well as proof of concept for the project stakeholders.

Steps in Software Development

Knowing we must make many architectural decisions, we establish a process for architecture development. The typical steps in software development include requirement analysis or the problem statement, object-oriented analysis and architectural analysis, object-oriented design and architectural design, and ultimately the object creation.

Requirement Analysis/Problem Statement   This phase involves the domain specification of the software in need. Suppose, for example, that we want to create a bookstore application that is accessible from the web. An example outcome of this phase would be the domain—in other words, what types of functionality do we need and whether or not the system being specified is feasible. The software's functionality would include interface features that users would like to see: interfaces to retrieve information regarding the books available in the company and those that would allow users to purchase books online using a credit card.

The requirement analysis describes what the system should do so that developers and customers can create a business contract. Analysts generate domain models: classes, objects, and interactions. The requirement analysis should theoretically be free from any technical or implementation details and should contain an ideal model.

The result of requirement and object analyses is the entry point for J2EE architecture development. You can apply experience to domain objects, and let that knowledge serve as a design guideline for the object design stage. Enterprise-wide system architecture covers hardware and software infrastructure, network topology, development, testing, production environment, and other factors. Before development, you want to evaluate existing software and hardware infrastructure and perhaps add components and upgrade your existing system if it cannot fully support J2EE. You need to evaluate hardware, including computers, routers, network switches, and network topology, as they all impact system performance and reliability.

Object-Oriented/Architectural Analysis   This phase involves the analysis of the domain. The requirement analysis sets the boundary for this phase. A modeling tool using UML might be used (more on this in Chapter 3).

The analysts would do the following:

- Develop use case diagrams for all the business processes. Use case diagrams are high-level descriptions of the system actors and the system functionality.

- Develop sequence diagrams. These diagrams show the sequence of operation as a function of time.

- Develop class diagrams. Class diagrams show the system functionality as classes and their methods.

- Develop collaboration diagrams. Collaboration diagrams depict how the classes interact.

Architectural Design   This phase involves creating the architectural design for the software. The development of the architecture is based on the output of the object-oriented analysis. This phase tries to give a framework within which all the components will work to satisfy all the customer requirements. In this phase, implementation details are not documented. The outcome would be to decide upon and document the architecture. For example, the architect must decide which framework to use—J2EE, CORBA (Common Object Request Broker), RMI (Remote Method Invocation), or DCOM (Distributed Component Object Model), for example. (These frameworks are discussed later in the chapter.) Any new hardware and software requirements are defined, along with how security will be handled. The architect would also define how performance is achieved. Pragmatically, the architect would work out a solution with security, performance, cost, and consideration of reusing existing technology and business logic in the legacy system.

In a typical enterprise, many application projects are underway in a partial state of development—some of which could span years, resulting in system evolution of many cycles. As a result, common frameworks, reusable software architectures that provide the generic structure and behavior, are needed for a family of software applications.

From the object-oriented design perspective, the architect would do the following:

- Develop package dependency diagrams.
- Decide how the classes in different packages interact.
- Develop deployment diagrams.
- Decide where the software components will reside in deployment.

Guided by architectural specifications, the design technically adapts the analysis result. While domain object modeling at the analysis phase should be free from technical details, the object design fully accounts for technical factors, including what kind of platform, language, and vendors are selected in the architecture development stage. Guided by architectural decisions, a detailed design effort should address specification of all classes, including the necessary implementation attributes, their detailed interfaces, and code or plain text descriptions of the operation. With a good architecture and detailed design, implementation should be clear.

In many organizations, developers often arrive at the implementation stage too early. This problem is compounded when managers pressure the developer to ensure they're writing code since, to them, anything else is a waste of time.

Object-Oriented Design and Creation   In this phase, the design for the implementation is complete, and the decision is made as to whether the client tier is an applet or HTML. All the classes are defined with their intended directory hierarchies identified. Design patterns are used, and object reuse is considered. Any architectural considerations arising out of the implementation design are discussed. If the client uses HTML, the server-side servlet can be communicated via HTTP without any modification in the existing systems. If the client uses an applet instead of HTML, HTTP tunneling is considered on the server side. The objects and code are implemented and some standard notation is used—for example, UML is the standard notation for architecture and may be used freely in all of the phases of architecting and designing a system.

In addition, during the implementation stage, the application is in the hands of its users, for whom you must provide documentation and training. Users will find issues and request modifications to functionality. These must be handled through proper change management procedures.

Architectural Terminology

As mentioned, *architecture* refers to an abstract representation of a system's components and behaviors. A good system architecture leads to reusable components, because each component is broken into parts that may be repeated and can therefore be reused. Abstraction naturally forms layers representing different levels of complexity. Each layer describes a solution. These layers are then integrated with each other in such a way that high-level abstractions are affected by low-level abstractions.

The following architectural terms are important for the certification exam and as a group they seem to be unique to Sun's view of system architecture. Synonymous terminology will be applied where appropriate.

Abstraction

The term *abstraction* implies the use of a symbol for something used repeatedly in a design; it's a component that hides details and is a clear representation. We use abstractions every day when we discuss computer models using boxes with lines connecting them to represent the components we are trying to glue together. Abstraction is the first step of the design process, when we break down the intended system into an extended hierarchy and examine each level of the hierarchy in terms of the functions and intentions of the design. This breakdown is described from the point of view of the architect, as he or she is the central actor of the system. Clients, who have certain requirements for the structure to be built, transfer their goals and constraints to the architect, who employs the materials and directs the people involved in the system to produce a structure design that the client is happy with.

In addition to identifying the goals of the system, the abstraction hierarchy also shows us that the system involves a large amount of communication. The client communicates with the architect to provide initial design requirements and feedback on working designs. The architect communicates with developers to determine the constraints of the design in terms of physical limitations, limitations imposed by availability, and limitations inherent in architecture.

Figure 2-2 shows some examples of how we all use abstraction in our day-to-day communications.

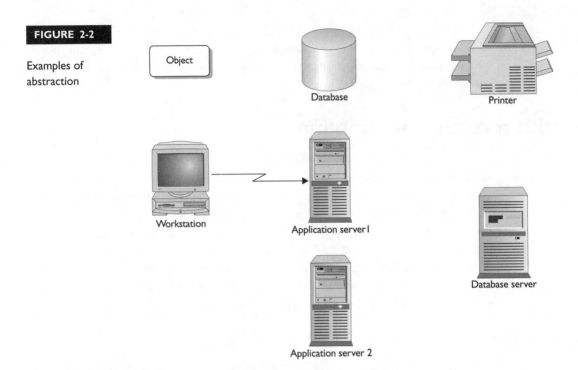

FIGURE 2-2

Examples of abstraction

Surface Area

Surface area is a term used to describe the way in which components interact with one another in a defined way. It's important to note that the greater the surface area, the more ways a change in one component can affect another. Figure 2-3 shows two simple examples of surface area.

In Figure 2-3, the class *Employee* has the methods +GetName(), +GetCurrentAge(), +GetSalary(), +GetAddress(), and +GetSkill(). This is a large surface area that can be difficult to maintain and is not reusable. The revised classes comprise all of the methods contained in the original *Employee* class. *EmployeeDemographics,* the smaller surface area, includes only methods pertaining to the employee's demographics: +GetName(), GetCurrentAge(), and +GetAddress(). The other new class, *EmployeeJob,* includes only methods pertaining to the employee's job: +GetSalary() and +GetSkill.

Boundaries

Boundaries are the areas where two components interact. For example, the line drawn between two boxes in a computer model diagram represents boundaries.

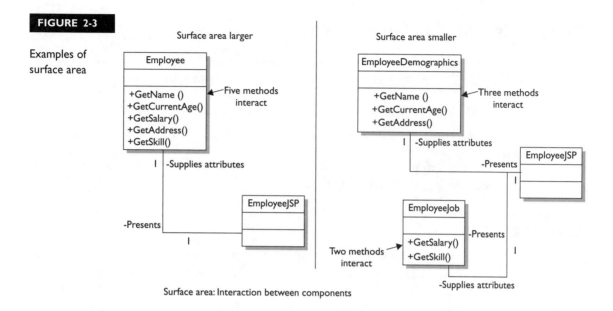

FIGURE 2-3

Examples of
surface area

Surface area: Interaction between components

Brittleness

Brittleness is the degree to which small changes will impact large portions of the system. Software tends to be unwieldy for many reasons, but a primary reason is brittleness. Software breaks before it bends; it demands perfection in a universe that prefers statistics. This in turn leads to "legacy lock-in" and other perversions. The distance between the ideal computers architects imagine and the real-world computer systems we know and work on is unfortunate and due in large part to brittleness.

Capabilities, Friction, and Layering

Capabilities are the non-functional, observable system qualities including scalability, manageability, performance, availability, reliability, and security, which are defined in terms of context. Capabilities are discussed later in the chapter in the section "Capabilities of an Architecture."

Friction refers to how much interaction occurs between two components. Friction is measured based on how a change in one component affects both components.

Layering is a hierarchy of separation.

Principles of Architecture

For system architects, all techniques for *decomposing* (breaking a large object into smaller component parts) software systems address two main concerns:

- Most systems are too complex to comprehend in their entirety.
- Different audiences require different perspectives of a system.

The next few paragraphs describe techniques for decomposing an architecture using concepts known as layers and tiers.

Layering

The *layers* of architecture are systems in themselves, and they do what all systems do: they obtain input from their environment and provide output to their environment. Figure 2-4 shows a depiction of the architectural layers in an application system.

Bi-directional-layered systems provide *and* procure major services at their upper and lower sides. Unidirectional-layered systems procure major services in one direction while providing major services in the opposite direction.

Most engineering disciplines, especially software, strive to construct "unidirectional" layered systems, or *strict* layering. The services a layer provides at its upper side make it possible for a higher layer to operate, while the services it procures through its lower side are those the layer requires for its own operation.

In strict layering, classes or objects in a layer should depend, for compilation and linking purposes (physical dependency purposes), on classes or objects within the same or lower layers. Constructing a layer and its objects in such a manner makes it possible to construct lower layers before higher ones. At the same time, classes or objects in one single-layer package should not have a cyclic dependency on objects in other packages—either within or outside the layer. This eliminates "spaghetti-like" physical dependencies, which cause small changes to ripple through a larger number of code units than they should. It also helps to lessen compilation and interpretation times.

FIGURE 2-4

Architectural layers

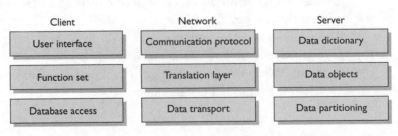

What makes it possible to swap one layer for another is a well-known layer interface protocol—Internet Interoperability protocol (IIOP)—that lies between the layer and both its upper and lower adjacent layers.

Tiers

In a multi-tier environment, the client implements the presentation logic (thin client). The business logic is implemented on an application server(s), and the data resides on a database server(s). The following three component layers thus define a multi-tier architecture:

- A front-end component, which is responsible for providing portable presentation logic, such as an web server

- A back-end component, which provides access to dedicated services, such as a database server

- A middle-tier component(s), which allows users to share and control business logic by isolating it from the actual application, such as an application server

Figure 2-5 shows a three-tiered architecture.

FIGURE 2-5   Architectural tiers

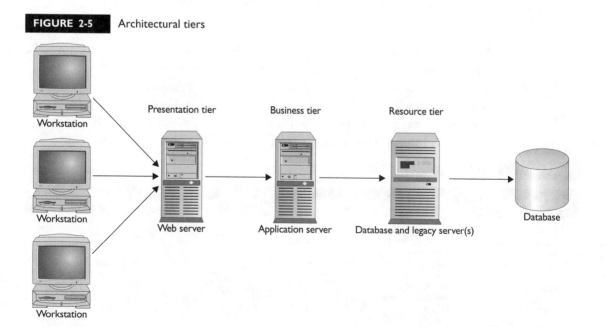

Advantages of multi-tier client-server architectures include the following:

- Changes to the user interface or to the application logic are largely independent from one another, allowing the application to evolve easily to meet new requirements.

- Network bottlenecks are minimized because the application layer does not transmit extra data to the client; instead, it transmits only what is needed to handle a task.

- When business logic changes are required, only the server has to be updated. In two-tier architectures, each client must be modified when logic changes.

- The client is insulated from database and network operations. The client can access data easily without having to know where data is or how many servers are on the system.

- Database connections can be "pooled," and are thus shared by several users, which greatly reduces the cost associated with per-user licensing.

- The organization has database independence because the data layer is written using standard SQL, which is platform independent. The enterprise is not tied to vendor-specific stored procedures.

- The application layer can be written in standard third- or fourth-generation languages, such as Java or C, with which the organization's in-house programmers are experienced.

Basic Three-Tier Java Technology Architecture

The three-tier Java architecture is achieved by using interactive components—HTML, applets, the Java application that resides on the client, and the servlets and JSPs that reside on the middle tier. JDBC communication is used on the middle tier to create the *persistence* data that resides or the third or back-end tier—which is the database layer.

Table 2-1 shows these technologies and where they reside in the architecture.

TABLE 2-1	Basic Three-Tier Java Technology Architecture

Client	Client-Middle	Middle	Middle-Persistence	Persistence
HTML HTML with applet	HTTP	Servlet JSP	JDBC	RDBMS Legacy File
Java application	JRMP	RMI Server	JDBC	RDBMS, Legacy File
Java application	RMI- IIOP	EJB	JDBC	RDBMS, Legacy File
Java application (not a Java 3 tier)	IIOP	CORBA	JDBC	RDBMS, Legacy File

The Architecture of Tiered Software

The three-tier software architecture emerged in the 1990s to overcome the limitations of the two-tier client-server architecture. The third tier (a middle-tier server) resides between the user interface (client) and the data management (server) components. This middle tier provides process management where business logic and rules are executed and can accommodate thousands of users (as compared to only hundreds of users with the two-tier architecture) by providing functions such as message queuing, application execution similar to session EJBs, and database connection pooling. The client-server architecture put a heavy burden on the database server tier because each client needed a database connection.

Three-tier architecture is used when an effective distributed design is needed to provide (when compared to client-server) increased performance, flexibility, maintainability, reusability, and scalability, while masking the complexity of distributed processing from the user.

The *N-tier* architecture is the same as the three-tier architecture, except it has multiple (*N*) application and database servers. The N-tier architecture also overcomes the shortcomings of the two-tier client-server architecture. It can distribute components across servers and access data in multiple databases. A pool of database connections can be acquired at server startup and then shared among clients as needed. The architecture contains a client workstation, a component or application server, and a database server(s). The user interface is on the client side, while business logic and data management reside on the dedicated tiers. Business logic resides on an application server, where it can be easily managed. An N-tier environment requires careful planning of component interfaces to enable reuse and sharing.

Capabilities of an Architecture

As mentioned, *capabilities* are the nonfunctional, observable system qualities including scalability, manageability, performance, availability, reliability, and security, which are defined in terms of context. Measures of system quality typically focus on performance characteristics of the system under study. Some research has examined resource utilization and investment utilization, hardware utilization efficiency, reliability, response time, ease of terminal use, content of the database, aggregation of details, human factors, and system accuracy.

Table 2-2 lists some well-known system quality measures.

TABLE 2-2	Capabilities and System Quality

System Quality	Definition
Availability	The degree to which a system is accessible. The term *24×7* describes total availability. This aspect of a system is often coupled with performance.
Reliability	The ability to ensure the integrity and consistency of an application and its transactions.
Manageability	The ability to administer and thereby manage the system resources to ensure the availability and performance of a system with respect to the other capabilities.
Flexibility	The ability to address architectural and hardware configuration changes without a great deal of impact to the underlying system.
Performance	The ability to carry out functionality in a timeframe that meets specified goals.
Capacity	The ability of a system to run multiple tasks per unit of time.
Scalability	The ability to support the required availability and performance as transactional load increases.
Extensibility	The ability to extend functionality.
Validity	The ability to predict and confirm results based on a specified input or user gesture.
Reusability	The ability to use a component in more than one context without changing its internals.
Security	The ability to ensure that information is not accessed and modified unless done so in accordance with the enterprise policy.

Availability

This aspect of a system is often coupled with performance. Availability is the degree to which a system, subsystem, or equipment is operable and in a committable state at the start of a session, when the session is called for at an unknown, or *random*, time. The conditions determining operability must be specified. Expressed mathematically, availability is 1 minus the unavailability. Availability is the ratio of (a) the total time a functional unit is capable of being used during a given interval to (b) the length of the interval. An example of availability is 100/168, if the unit is capable of being used for 100 hours in a week. Typical availability objectives are specified in decimal fractions, such as 0.9998.

Reliability

Reliability is the ability of an item to perform a required function under stated conditions for a specified period of time. Reliability is the probability that a functional unit will perform its required function for a specified interval under stated conditions. For example, it is the continuous availability of communication services to the general public, and emergency response activities in particular, during normal operating conditions and under emergency circumstances with minimal disruption.

The proper functioning of a company's computer systems has always been key to the operation of the company. An outage of an airline's computer systems, for example, can effectively shut down the airline. Many computer failures may be invisible to customers—a temporary hiccup during the catalog order process, for example ("I can't check the availability of that item right now, but I'll take your order and call you back if there's a problem"), or cashiers having to use hand calculators to ring up sales. However, on the Internet, a company's computing infrastructure is on display in the store window—in fact, the company's infrastructure *is* the store window, so a computer problem at Amazon.com would be tantamount to every Barnes and Noble branch in the world locking its doors.

In the arena of Internet appliances and ubiquitous computing, the consumer cannot be placed in the position of troubleshooting the computer system. Reliability is critical because, eventually, people will expect their computers to work just as well as any other appliance in their home. After all, who has heard of a TV program that is "incompatible with the release level of your television"?

What does *reliability* mean from the standpoint of computer architecture? It is instructive to examine a system that is designed to have high fault tolerance and to allow repair without shutting down the system. For example, the IBM G5 series of S/390 mainframes have shown mean time to failure of 45 years, with 84 percent of all repairs performed while the system continues to run. To achieve this level of fault tolerance, the G5 includes duplicate instruction decode and execution pipeline stages. If an error is seen, the system retries the failing instruction. Repeated failures result in the last good state of the CPU being moved to another CPU, the failed CPU being stopped, and a spare CPU being activated (if one is available). At the other end of the design spectrum, most PC systems do not have parity checking of their memory, even though many of these systems can now hold gigabytes of memory. Clearly, there is much room for computer architects to move high-end reliability and serviceability down into low-end servers, personal computers, and ubiquitous computing devices.

Manageability and Flexibility

Manageability refers to the set of services that ensures the continued integrity, or correctness, of the component application. It includes security, concurrency control, and server management. A metric example of manageability would be the number of staff hours per month required to perform normal upgrades. *Server management* refers to the set of system facilities used for starting and stopping the server, installing new components, managing security permissions, and performing other tasks. These services can be implemented through a "best of breed" third-party product approach, integrated in a middle-tier server product, or implemented through operating system facilities.

Flexibility is the key to an available, reliable, and scalable application. Flexibility can be improved through location independence of application code. An example of flexibility would be a J2EE system that uses internationalization code and property files to allow changes in the presentation language (for example, English to German). Regarding metrics, there is no standard way of measuring flexibility. The business measure is the cost of change in time and money, but this depends on what types of change can be anticipated.

As flexibility, reliability, and availability are increased, manageability can suffer. Flexibility is also essential for keeping pace with rapid change. It's enhanced when the middle-tier technology is a component-based solution that easily accommodates the integration of multiple technologies. Independence from hardware, operating system, and language creates the most adaptable and portable solutions. The connectivity mechanisms to multiple data sources also increase adaptability. Fortunately, this area is one in which several solutions are available, including the database connection standards (ODBC and JDBC), native database drivers, messaging, remote procedure calls (to database stored procedures), object request brokers, and database gateways.

Performance

Response time and response ratio are important to an application. The most important task resulting in good performance is to identify and control expensive calls. The architect should state target performance criteria before implementing within a production environment. For example, the first visible response in any application browser view when the application is under maximum specified load must occur in less than 3 seconds, 95 percent of the time. Measurement is made at the enterprise's external firewall.

Today, when measuring performance, the architect must consider and attempt to quantify the cost of an operation (data or computational)—which can involve a myriad of servers across a sea of network connections—before finally returning a response view to the user requestor.

Today, performance is the ability to execute functions fast enough to meet goals. Response time and response ratio (the time it takes to respond/time it takes to perform the function) are important to an application. Both figures should be as low as possible, but a ratio of 1 is the target. For example, suppose a user requests functionality requiring a great deal of processing or database searching and it takes a minute to process. The user will not see a result for a minute—seemingly a long time to wait, but if the result can be viewed in 1 minute plus 20 seconds (a response ratio of 1.3333), that is still good performance. Alternatively, suppose that the processing takes only 1 second but the user does not see the result for 20 seconds (response ratio of 20); that is not good performance.

Capacity

No benchmark can predict the performance of every application. It is easy to find two applications and two computers with opposite rankings, depending on the application; therefore, any benchmark that produces a performance ranking must be wrong on at least one of the applications. However, memory references dominate most applications.

For example, there is considerable difference between a kernel-like information retrieval product and one that performs complex business rules of a heuristic trading system that does a matrix multiply. Most "kernels" are code *excerpts*. The work measure is typically something like the number of iterations in the loop structure, or an operation count (ignoring precision or differing weights for differing operations). It accomplishes a petty but useful calculation and defines its work measure strictly in terms of the quality of the answer instead of what was done to get there. Although each iteration is simple, it still involves more than 100 instructions on a typical serial computer and includes decisions and variety that make it unlikely to be improved by a hardware engineer.

Scalability

Vertical scalability comes from adding capacity (memory and CPUs) to existing servers. Horizontal scalability comes from adding servers. In terms of scalability, a system can scale to accommodate more users and higher transaction volumes in several different ways:

- *Upgrade the hardware platform.* Solutions that offer platform independence enable rapid deployment and easier integration of new technology.

- *Improve the efficiency of communications.* In a distributed environment, the communications overhead is often a performance bottleneck. Session management will improve communication among clients and servers through session pooling.

- *Provide transparent access to multiple servers to increase throughput during peak loads.* Load balancing is especially necessary to support the unpredictable and uncontrollable demands of Internet applications. Some application server products offer load balancing.

- *Improve communication between the application component server and various data sources through connection pooling management.*

It used to be easier to predict a system load. The Internet has certainly changed that, and it can create scaling problems. During the 1999 *Super Bowl*, for example, an advertisement by sexy underwear merchant Victoria's Secret resulted in 1.5 million people simultaneously attempting to access a live web event, overwhelming the pool of 1000 servers that had been prepared. This phenomenon, called the "Slashdot Effect," was named for a popular technology news and discussion site: *ssadler.phy.bnl.gov/adler/SDE/SlashDotEffect.html*. It can create huge amounts of traffic for sites. Stock-trading sites used to be (and hopefully will again be) vulnerable to huge (and unpredictable) peaks in traffic caused by events in the market.

Even on longer time scales, it is difficult at best to predict the growth or popularity of an Internet business. What is required is for Internet infrastructures to scale evenly (without discontinuities in performance), simply, quickly, and inexpensively. It should not be necessary to re-architect a system repeatedly as it grows.

Scalability is more a system problem than a CPU architecture problem. The attributes that a system needs include the following:

- Graceful degradation all the way up to 100 percent system load

- The ability to add capacity incrementally (CPUs, memory, I/O, and/or disk storage) without disrupting system operation

- The ability to prioritize the workload so that unneeded work can be suspended at times of peak activity

Some web sites, such as *www.CNN.com*, revert to lower overhead pages (smaller pages with less graphics) during traffic peaks. One possibility for the future would be to provide peak offload facilities for web merchants. If groups of sites used relatively similar architectures, a site with spare capacity could be kept ready for whoever needs it. If an unexpected peak occurred—or an expected peak that didn't justify buying more hardware—the contents of the site could be shadowed to the offload facility and traffic divided between the two sites.

Techniques such as logical partitioning can also be used to shift system resources. Logical partitioning is available in mainframe systems and allows one large CPU complex to contain multiple logical system images, which are kept completely separate by the hardware and operating system. Portions of the system resources can be assigned to the partitions, with the assignments enforced by the hardware. This allows resources to be shifted from development to production, or between different systems involved in production by simply shifting the percentages assigned to the partitions. Capacity is affected by scalability—for example, one machine handles 500 transactions or five machines handle 100 transactions each.

Extensibility, Validity, and Reusability

Extensibility requires careful modeling of the business domain to add new features based on a model.

Validity or testability is the ability to determine what the expected results should be. Multi-tier architecture provides for many connection points and hence many points of failure for intermediate testing and debugging.

Reusability of software components can be achieved by employing the interfaces provided by frameworks. This is accomplished by defining generic components that can be reapplied to create new applications. Framework reusability leverages the domain knowledge and prior effort of experienced developers to avoid re-creating and revalidating common solutions to recurring application requirements and software design challenges. Reuse of framework components can yield substantial improvements in programmer productivity, as well as enhance other system qualities such as performance, reliability, and interoperability.

Security

Security is essential for ensuring access to component services and for ensuring that data is appropriately managed; these issues are particularly important in Internet applications. Integrated network, Internet, server, and application security is the most manageable solution. This approach can be described by "single login," which requires a rich infrastructure of network and system services. Firewalls and authentication mechanisms must also be supported for Internet security. With concurrency control, multi-user access can be managed without requiring explicit application code.

A goal of information security is to protect resources and assets from loss. Resources may include information, services, and equipment such as servers and networking components. Each resource has several assets that require protection:

- **Privacy**   Preventing information disclosure to unauthorized persons

- **Integrity**   Preventing corruption or modification of resources

- **Authenticity**   Proof that a person has been correctly identified or that a message is received as transmitted

- **Availability**   Assurance that information, services, and equipment are working and available for use

The classes of threats includes accidental threats, intentional threats, passive threats (those that do not change the state of the system but may include loss of confidentiality but not of integrity or availability), and active threats (those that change the state of the system, including changes to data and to software).

A *security policy* is an enterprise's statement defining the rules that regulate how it will provide security, handle intrusions, and recover from damage caused by security breaches. Based on a risk analysis and cost considerations, such policies are most effective when users understand them and agree to abide by them.

Security services are provided by a system for implementing the security policy of an organization. A standard set of such services includes the following:

- **Identification and authentication**   Unique identification and verification of users via certification servers and global authentication services (single sign-on services)

- **Access control and authorization**   Rights and permissions that control how users can access resources

- **Accountability and auditing**   Services for logging activities on network systems and linking them to specific user accounts or sources of attacks

- **Data confidentiality**   Services to prevent unauthorized data disclosure

- **Data integrity and recovery**   Methods for protecting resources against corruption and unauthorized modification—for example, mechanisms using checksums and encryption technologies

- **Data exchange**   Services that secure data transmissions over communication channels

- **Object reuse**   Services that provide multiple users secure access to individual resources

- **Non-repudiation of origin and delivery**   Services to protect against attempts by the sender to falsely deny sending the data, or subsequent attempts by the recipient to falsely deny receiving the data

- **Reliability**   Methods for ensuring that systems and resources are available and protected against failure

Creating an Architecture Using Distributed Services and J2EE

Often in the world of corporate information technology, a new implementation paradigm arises, and the architects must apply their acquired skills to the emerging set of tools and building materials to create systems that make the best use of the available resources. Here are some examples of that situation.

In the '60s, IBM released a multitasking operating system called OS MVT/MFT. For the first time, an enterprise could run multiple batch jobs on the same machine. This heralded the beginning of what we affectionately called the "batch night cycle." All transactions for an entire firm, whatever the business happened to be, would be collected daily and then keyed into punch cards. This information was then fed to one or more of these batch COBOL jobs, which would record the information to create the firm's "books and records." This was fine, but the information was always out of date by a day.

In the '70s, IBM brought us online data entry. This functionality was made possible by software called Customer Information Control System (CICS) and Virtual Storage Access Method (VSAM). CICS provided for terminal access and entry of data. VSAM provided a way to store the data with indexes and keys to facilitate access. This was better, and now the information was fairly up to date, even intraday.

In the '80s, Microsoft improved on the IBM "greenscreen" and released the personal computer equipped with a mouse and a personal drive space for storing information locally. Additionally, a host of other vendors (including IBM) brought us SQL. Because it was done by committee, SQL became the de facto standard for working with data and databases.

In the '90s, Microsoft popularized the client-server platform. This seemed like a good idea, and it certainly provided an example for so-called "user-friendly" ways of combining business transactions and computers. The problem was distribution. If an organization had 1000 workstations, it would be difficult if not impossible to maintain each of these workstations at the same level of software.

In the 2000s, Sun Microsystems and other vendors brought us J2EE. Once again, a committee has created a standard way to architect business processes that run on almost any platform. This is powerful, because these computer classes are portable and interoperable.

From a development perspective, these major revolutions involved only SQL and J2EE, because these are standards to which almost everyone has adhered.

Just as SQL defines the standard for querying multi-user relational databases, J2EE defines the standard for developing multi-tier enterprise applications. J2EE, much like the SQL paradigm, simplifies enterprise applications by basing them on standardized, modular components; by providing a complete set of services to those components; and by handling many details of application behavior automatically, without the need for complex programming.

J2EE takes advantage of many features of standard Java 2, such as "write once, run anywhere" portability, the JDBC API for database access, RMI, CORBA technology for interaction with existing enterprise resources, and a security model.

Building on this base, J2EE adds support for EJB components, the Java Servlets API, JSP, and Extensible Markup Language (XML) technology. The J2EE standard includes complete specifications and compliance tests to ensure portability of applications across the wide range of existing enterprise systems capable of supporting J2EE. This portability was also a key factor in the success of SQL.

Standards such as SQL and J2EE help enterprises gain competitive advantage by facilitating quick development and deployment of custom applications. Whether they are internal applications for staff use or Internet applications for customer or vendor services, this timely development and deployment of an application is key to success.

Portability and scalability are also essential for long-term viability. For example, our company has ported a single SQL application database using five different vendors: Oracle, Sybase, Informix, Microsoft SQL Server, and IBM DB/2. Enterprise applications must scale from small working prototypes and test cases to complete 24×7, enterprise-wide services that are accessible by tens, hundreds, or even thousands of clients simultaneously. In the global finance market, 24×7 is especially important.

Multi-tier applications are difficult to architect. They require merging a variety of skill sets and resources, perhaps also including legacy data and legacy code. In today's heterogeneous environment, enterprise applications must integrate services from a variety of vendors with a diverse set of application models and other standards. Existing daily cycle applications at Merrill Lynch, for example, use all of the database vendors in addition to legacy databases such as IDMS, ADABAS, IMS, and a host of others. Industry experience shows that integrating these resources can take up to 50 percent of application development time.

J2EE will hopefully break the barriers inherent to current enterprise systems. The unified J2EE standard permits an API set that in full maturity will wrap and embrace existing resources required by multi-tier applications with a unified, component-based application model. This will initiate the next generation of components, tools, systems, and applications for solving the strategic requirements of the enterprise.

Figure 2-6 provides a glimpse of how a J2EE server fits into the frame of a net-enabled enterprise application. The good news is that it can salvage and extend life to legacy systems that have been in production and are sensitive to change.

Although Sun Microsystems invented the Java programming language, the J2EE standard represents collaboration between leaders from throughout the enterprise software arena. Partners include OS and database management system providers IBM and Microsoft, middleware and tool vendors BEA WebLogic and IBM WebSphere, and vertical market applications and component developers. Sun has defined a robust, flexible platform that can be implemented on the wide variety of existing enterprise systems currently available. This platform supports the range of applications that IT organizations need to keep their enterprises competitive.

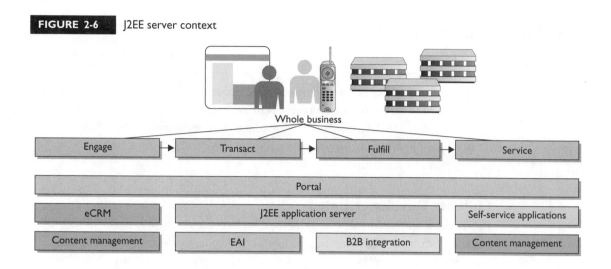

FIGURE 2-6   J2EE server context

If your enterprise architecture only partially supports an early release of J2EE, you might first upgrade your system. If you cannot upgrade due to budget or timing concerns, then you may have to work within the technical constraints associated with older versions.

Enterprise JavaBeans

A major part of the J2EE architecture is EJBs. That is because the EJB server-side component model facilitates development of middleware components that are transactional, scalable, and portable.

Consider transaction management. In the past, developers have had to write and maintain transaction management code or rely on third-party transaction management systems, generally provided through proprietary, vendor-specific APIs. This second-generation web development helped to promote Java and highlighted the need for a standard. In contrast, EJB technology enables components to participate in transactions, including distributed transactions. The EJB server itself handles the underlying transaction management details, while developers focus specifically on the business purpose of the objects and methods. EJB components can be deployed on any platform and operating system that supports the EJB standard. The list of these J2EE-compliant application servers is numerous and can be viewed at the Sun web site (*http://java.sun.com/j2ee/*).

Distributed Application Lifecycle

One of the strengths of the J2EE platform is that the implementation process is divided naturally into roles that can be performed by team members with specific skills. Because of this role-based development, staff can be used efficiently. Developers can do what they do best—code business applications—without worrying about the details of the user interface. The designers can do what they do best—design attractive, easy-to-use interfaces—without having to be involved in the application's coding.

Multiple Developer Roles

Before the emergence of SQL as a standard for data access, the role of the developer included writing and maintaining the application code, maintaining the files, and facilitating data access. SQL-facilitated distributed application data and the added requirements of database, design, creation, and maintenance required new development administration roles. Therefore, with a set of features designed specifically to expedite the process of distributed application development, the J2EE platform offers several benefits but requires additional developer roles (see Figure 2-7).

The J2EE standard describes the following roles for developers who must perform the different types of tasks necessary to create and deploy a J2EE/EJB application.

Entity Enterprise Bean Developer   The entity enterprise bean developer defines both the home and remote interfaces representing the client view of the bean. They also create classes that implement the entity bean enterprise interface, as well as methods corresponding to those classes in the bean's home and remote interfaces.

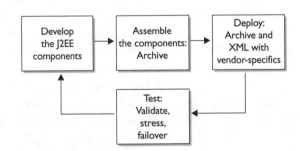

FIGURE 2-7

The J2EE application lifecycle: iterative process with multiple development roles

The Bean Developer   The bean developer, sometimes known as the bean provider, has the following responsibilities:

- To write Java code reflecting business logic.

- To provide interfaces and implementations.

- To make course references to data and security access. There is no need to code for security when controlling access at the method level. The bean developer can also use generic security references, such as accounting.

- To integrate code with third-party objects.

- To set transaction attributes.

- To control access programmatically within a method.

- To do nothing, allowing the application assembler to add roles and associate these roles with methods.

- To create a home interface that is used to create and find beans.

- To create a remote interface for business logic methods.

- To create an implementation of the bean class itself and utility classes if needed.

- To create a deployment descriptor giving security and transaction descriptions for the EJB's methods.

The Application Assembler   The application assembler combines components and modules into deployable application units. An application assembler may be a high-level business analyst who designs overall applications on the component level. The responsibilities include the following:

- Building applications using EJBs. This usually includes the presentation layer.

- Specifying transaction management requirements.

- Setting transaction attributes for either all of the bean's methods or none of them.

- Defining security roles.

- Associating roles with methods by adding permissions.

- Specifying which roles belong to particular methods or using a wildcard (*) to apply to all methods.

The Bean Deployer   The bean deployer adapts applications for a specific server's environment as well as making final customizations. The skills required would be those of a database administrator (DBA) and an application administrator. Responsibilities include the following:

- Managing persistence by mapping fields to actual database columns
- Managing security by defining roles, users, and user/groups
- Using deployment tools to create wrapper classes
- Making sure that all methods of the deployed bean have been assigned a transaction attribute
- Mapping roles of users and user groups for specific environments

Third-party software companies can play several roles in the EJB framework, such as component provider, application server provider, and EJB container provider.

The Component Provider   The responsibilities of the component provider lie in the business domain such as business process, software object modeling, Java programming, EJB architecture, and XML. They implement business functions with portable components such as EJBs or web components.

Application Server Provider   The application server provider provides the platform on which distributed applications can be developed and provides runtime environment. The application server provider will usually contain an EJB container such as IBM WebSphere or BEA WebLogic.

EJB Container Provider   The EJB container provider provides the runtime environment for EJB and binds it to the server. It may also generate standard code to transact with data resources. The application server provider is often the container provider as well.

Iterative Development/MVC

The authors of this book have been developing enterprise systems for an average of 15 years, and we are all too familiar with the application lifecycle. In Chapter 5, we discuss patterns of developing application architectures. The Model View Controller (MVC) application architecture is one of those patterns and will be used in the book to analyze features of distributed applications. This abstraction helps in the process of dividing an application into logical components that can be built more easily. This section explores the general features of MVC.

The MVC provides an application development breakout for developing with J2EE.

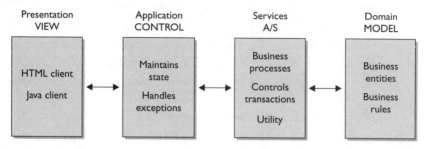

The MVC architecture provides a way to divide the functionality involved in maintaining and presenting data (see Figure 2-8). The MVC architecture is not new, as it appears in IBM CICS implementations as well as in client-server with PowerBuilder. It was originally developed to map the traditional input, processing, and output tasks to the user-interaction model. However, it is straightforward to map these concepts into the domain of multi-tier web-based enterprise applications.

In the MVC architecture, the *model* represents application data and the business rules that govern access and modification of this data. The model maintains the persistent state of the business and provides the controller with the ability to access application functionality encapsulated by the model.

A *view* component renders the contents of a particular part of the model. It accesses data from the model and specifies how that data should be presented. When the model changes, it is the view's responsibility to maintain consistency in its presentation. The view forwards user actions to the controller.

A *controller* defines application behavior; it interprets user actions, and maps them into processing to be performed by the model. In a web application client, these user actions could be button clicks or menu selections. The actions performed by the model include activating business processes or changing the state of the model. Based on the user action and the outcome of the model processing, the controller selects a view to be rendered as part of the response to this user request. There is usually one controller for each set of related functionality.

Simplified Architecture and Development

The J2EE platform supports a simplified, component-based development model. Because it is based on the Java programming language and the Java 2 Platform, Standard Edition (J2SE), this model offers "write once, run anywhere" portability, supported by any server product that conforms to the J2EE standard.

J2EE applications have a standardized, component-based architecture that consist of components (including JSPs, EJBs, and servlets) that are bundled into modules. Because J2EE applications are component based, you can easily reuse components in multiple applications, saving time and effort, and enabling you to deliver applications quickly. Also, this modular development model supports clear division of labor across development, assembly, and deployment of applications so you can best leverage the skills of individuals at your site.

J2EE applications are for the most part distributed and multi-tiered. J2EE provides server-side and client-side support for enterprise applications. J2EE applications present the user interface on the client (typically, a web browser), perform their business logic and other services on the application server in the middle tier, and are connected to enterprise information systems on the back end. With this architecture, functionality exists on the most appropriate platform.

J2EE applications are standards-based and portable. J2EE defines standard APIs that all J2EE-compatible vendors must support. This ensures that your J2EE development is not tied to a particular vendor's tools or server, and you have your choice of tools, components, and servers. Because J2EE components use standard APIs, you can develop them in any J2EE development tool, develop components or purchase them from a component provider, and deploy them on any J2EE-compatible server. You choose the tools, components, and server that make the most sense for you.

J2EE applications are scalable. J2EE applications run in containers, which are part of a J2EE server. The containers themselves can be designed to be scalable, so that the J2EE server provider can handle scalability without any effort from the application developer.

J2EE applications can be easily integrated with back-end information systems. The J2EE platform provides standard APIs for accessing a wide variety of enterprise information systems, including relational database management systems, e-mail systems, and CORBA systems.

Component-Based Application Models

Component-based application models map easily and with flexibility to the functionality desired from an application. As the examples presented throughout this book illustrate, the J2EE platform provides a variety of ways to configure the architecture of an application, depending on factors such as client types required, level of access required to data sources, and other considerations. Component-based design also simplifies application maintenance. Because components can be updated and replaced independently, new functionality can be shimmed into existing applications simply by updating selected components.

on the
⑥ o b *Component assembly and solution deployment are especially important in J2EE development. The development and production environment could be quite different. In an extensible architecture, the system structure should be stable but should also support incremental deployment of components without affecting the whole system.*

Components can expect the availability of standard services in the runtime environment, and they can be connected dynamically to other components providing well-defined interfaces. As a result, many application behaviors can be configured at the time of application assembly or deployment, without modification. Component developers can communicate their requirements to application deployers through specific settings stored in XML files. Tools can automate this process to expedite development.

Components help divide the labor of application development among specific skill sets, enabling each member of a development team to focus on his or her ability. For example, JSP templates can be created by graphic designers, their behavior can be coded by Java programming language coders, the business logic can be coded by domain experts, and application assembly and deployment can be effected by the appropriate team members. This division of labor also helps expedite application maintenance. For example, the user interface is the most dynamic part of many applications, particularly on the web. With the J2EE platform, graphic designers can modify the look and feel of JSP-based user interface components without the need for programmer intervention.

Containers

Central to the J2EE component-based development model is the notion of *containers*, standardized runtime environments that provide specific component services. Components can expect these services to be available on any J2EE platform from any vendor. For example, all J2EE web containers provide runtime support for responding to client requests, performing request-time processing (such as invoking JSP or servlet behavior), and returning results to the client. All EJB containers provide automated support for transaction and lifecycle management of EJB components, as well as bean lookup and other services. Containers also provide standardized access to enterprise information systems—for example, providing RDBMS access through the JDBC API (see Figure 2-9).

In addition, containers provide a mechanism for selecting application behaviors at assembly or deployment time. Through the use of *deployment descriptors* (text files that specify component behavior in terms of well-defined XML tags), components can be configured to a specific container's environment when deployed, rather than in component code. Features that can be configured at deployment time include security checks, transaction control, and other management responsibilities.

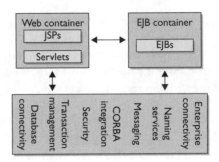

FIGURE 2-9

J2EE components
for web and EJB
are run from
containers.

Although the J2EE specification defines the component containers that must be supported, it doesn't specify or restrict the configuration of these containers. Thus, both container types can run on a single platform, web containers can live on one platform and EJB containers on another, or a J2EE platform can be made up of multiple containers on multiple platforms.

Support for Client Components

The J2EE client tier provides support for a variety of client types, both within the enterprise firewall and outside. Clients can be offered through web browsers by using plain HTML pages, dynamic HTML generated with JSP technology, or Java applets. Clients can also be offered as stand-alone Java language applications. J2EE clients are assumed to access the middle tier primarily using Web standards, namely HTTP, HTML, and XML.

Although use of the J2EE client tier has been difficult to perfect and it is therefore rarely used, it can be necessary to provide functionality directly in the client tier. Client-tier JavaBeans components would typically be provided by the service as an applet that is downloaded automatically into a user's browser. To eliminate problems caused by old or nonstandard versions of the JVM in a user's browser, the J2EE application model provides special support via tags used in JSPs for automatically downloading and installing the Java plug-in.

Client-tier beans can also be contained in a stand-alone application client written in the Java programming language. In this case, the enterprise would typically make operating system–specific installation programs for the client available for users to download through their browsers. Users execute the installation file and are then ready to access the service. Because Java technology programs are portable across all environments, the service need only maintain a single version of the client program. Although the client program itself is portable, installation of the Java technology client typically requires code specific to the operating system. Several commercial tools automate the generation of these OS-specific installation programs.

Support for Business Logic Components

In the J2EE platform, business logic is implemented in the middle tier as EJB components. Enterprise beans enable the component or application developer to concentrate on the business logic while the complexities of delivering a reliable, scalable service are handled by the EJB server.

The J2EE platform and EJB architecture have complementary goals. The EJB component model is the backbone of the J2EE programming model. The J2EE platform complements the EJB specification by fully specifying the APIs that an enterprise bean developer can use to implement enterprise beans.

This defines the larger, distributed programming environment in which enterprise beans are used as business logic components. Application servers such as SilverStream, WebLogic, and WebSphere provide the environment, which must be scalable, secure, and reliable.

The J2EE application is packaged in an archive or "Zip" file known as an Enterprise Archive (EAR). The EAR contains the web, EJB, and client components (see Figure 2-10).

The web, EJB, and client components are encased in their own archive files (web archive, or WAR; Java archive, or JAR; and client archive, or CAR) as shown in Figure 2-11.

The archives are accompanied by XML files that describe the deployment specifics of the EAR, WAR, JAR, and CAR archives.

FIGURE 2-10	

The J2EE enterprise application equals the enterprise archive plus the deployment XML file.

Enterprise Application = EAR + application.xml
Archived components plus XML to describe deployment

Enterprise Archive (.ear)
application.xml

| Web archive (.war) web.xml | EJB archive (.jar) ejb-jar.xml | Client archive (.car) application-client.xml |

FIGURE 2-11 The enterprise archive file encapsulates the web archive, client archive, and EJB archive.

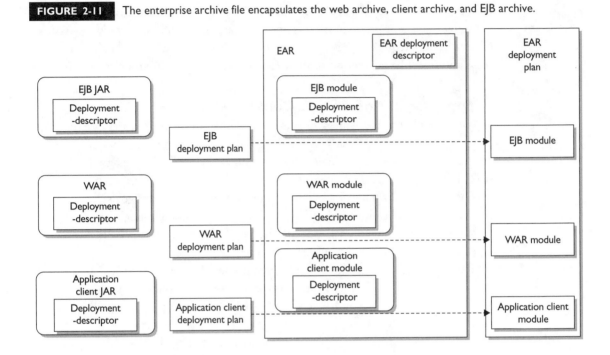

J2EE APIs and Certification

The J2EE platform, together with the J2SE platform, includes a number of industry-standard APIs for access to existing enterprise information systems. The following APIs provides basic access to these systems:

- JDBC, the API for accessing relational data from Java
- The Java Transaction API (JTA), the API for managing and coordinating transactions across heterogeneous enterprise information systems
- The Java Naming and Directory Interface (JNDI), the API for accessing information in enterprise name and directory services
- The Java Message Service (JMS), the API for sending and receiving messages through enterprise-messaging systems such as IBM MQ Series and TIBCO Rendezvous
- JavaMail, the API for sending and receiving e-mail
- Java IDL, the API for calling CORBA services

The J2EE standard is defined through a set of related specifications; key among these are the EJB specification, the Servlet specification, and the JSP specification. Together, these specifications define the architecture described in this book. In addition to the specifications, several other offerings are available to support the J2EE standard, including the J2EE Compatibility Test Suite (CTS) and the J2EE SDK.

The J2EE CTS helps maximize the portability of applications by validating the specification compliance of a J2EE platform product. This test suite begins where the basic Java Conformance Kit (JCK) ends. The CTS tests conformance to the Java standard extension APIs not covered by the JCK. In addition, it tests a J2EE platform's ability to run standard end-to-end applications.

The J2EE SDK is intended to achieve several goals. First, it provides an operational definition of the J2EE platform, used by vendors as the "gold standard" to determine what their product must do under a particular set of application circumstances. To verify the portability of an application, developers can use it, and it is used as the standard platform for running the J2EE CTS.

The J2EE SDK exists to provide the developer community with a free implementation of the J2EE platform. This is Sun's way of expediting adoption of the J2EE standard.

The J2EE specifications have, by design, set the bar for platform compatibility. Owing to the collaborative way in which the platform specifications have been developed thus far, Sun gave platform vendors the opportunity to supply implementations of the J2EE platform. Obvious and unreasonable implementation hurdles were avoided. For example, no restrictions exist on vendors adding value to J2EE products by supporting services not defined in the specifications.

J2EE-component portability is primarily a function of the dependency a component has on the underlying container. The rule is (as it was with SQL), where possible, follow the standard to ensure portability or else mark the divergent parts of the application. Components using a vendor-specific feature that falls outside of the J2EE requirements can have limitations in the area of portability. J2EE specifications, however, spell out a base set of capabilities that a component can count on; hence, an application should be able to achieve a minimum cross-container portability. An application developer expecting to deploy on a specific vendor implementation of the J2EE platform should carefully engineer the design to implement the application across a wide range of operating systems and hardware architectures.

Sun Microsystems set a new standard for client-side computing with the J2SE. That experience, coupled with input from enterprise software vendors and developers, has led to a full support program for the J2EE standard. This program includes four specific deliverables: the CTS to validate the J2EE brand, the J2EE specification, a complete J2EE reference implementation, and the J2EE Sun BluePrint.

J2EE Specification

Based on input and feedback from a variety of enterprise technology leaders and the industry at large, the J2EE specification is the beginning of a definition for a consistent yet flexible approach to implementing the platform. The J2EE specification enumerates the APIs to be provided with all J2EE platforms and includes full descriptions of the support levels expected for containers, clients, and components. It defines a standard that can be built on either a single system or deployed across several servers, each providing a specific set of J2EE support services. Hopefully, this will mean that a wide range of existing enterprise systems in use throughout industry will be able to support J2EE.

J2EE Reference Implementation

The J2EE Reference Implementation provides all the specified technologies, plus a range of sample applications, tools, and documentation. This basic implementation of the J2EE standard is provided for two purposes: it provides system vendors with a standard by which to compare their implementations, and it provides application developers with a way to become familiar with J2EE technology as they explore commercial products for full-scale deployment of J2EE applications.

Sun BluePrint Design Guidelines for J2EE

Provided as both documentation and complete examples, the Sun BluePrint Design Guidelines for J2EE will describe and illustrate "best practices" for developing and deploying component-based enterprise applications in J2EE. Topics explored will include component design and optimization, division of development labor, and allocation of technology resources.

XML and J2EE

Prior to 1998, the exchange of data and documents was limited to proprietary or loosely defined document formats. The advent of HTML offered the enterprise a standard format for exchange with a focus on interactive visual content. Adversely, HTML is rigidly defined and cannot support all enterprise datatypes; therefore, those shortcomings provided the impetus to create the XML. The XML standard enables the enterprise to define its own markup languages with emphasis on specific tasks, such as electronic commerce, supply-chain integration, data management, and publishing.

For these reasons, XML has become the strategic instrument for defining corporate data across a number of application domains. The properties of XML make it suitable for representing data, concepts, and contexts in an open, platform-, vendor-, and language-neutral manner. It uses *tags*, identifiers that signal the start and end of a related block of data, to create a hierarchy of related data components called *elements*. In turn, this hierarchy of elements provides *encapsulation* and *context*. As a result, there is a greater opportunity to reuse this data outside of the application and data sources from which it was derived.

XML technology has already been used successfully to furnish solutions for mission-critical data exchange, publishing, and software development. Additionally, XML has become the incentive for groups of companies within a specific industry to work together to define industry-specific markup languages (sometimes referred to as *vocabularies*). These initiatives create a foundation for information sharing and exchange across an entire domain rather than on a one-to-one basis.

Sun Microsystems, IBM, Novell, Oracle, and even Microsoft support the XML standard. Sun Microsystems coordinated and underwrote the World Wide Web Consortium (W3C) working group that delivered the XML specification. Sun also created the Java platform, a family of specifications that form a ubiquitous application development and runtime environment.

XML and Java technologies have many complementary features, and when used in combination they enable a powerful platform for sharing and processing data and documents. Although XML can clearly define data and documents in an open and neutral manner, there is still a need to develop applications that can process it. By extending the Java platform standards to include XML technology, companies will obtain a long-term secure solution for including support for XML technologies in their applications written in the Java programming language.

Because XML is a recommendation of the W3C, it reflects a true industry accord that provides the first real opportunity to liberate the business intelligence that is trapped within disparate data sources found in the enterprise. XML does this by providing a format that can represent structured and unstructured data, along with rich descriptive delimiters, in a single atomic unit. In other words, XML can represent data found in common data sources, such as databases and applications, but also in nontraditional data sources, such as word processing documents and spreadsheets. Previously, nontraditional data sources were constrained by proprietary data formats and hardware and operating system platform differences.

Why Use XML?

XML technology enables companies to develop application-specific languages that better describe their business data. By applying XML technology, one is essentially creating a new markup language. For example, an application of XML would produce the likes of an Invoice Markup Language or a Book Layout Markup Language. Each markup language should be specific to the individual needs and goals of its creator.

Part of creating a markup language includes defining the elements, attributes, and rules for their use. In XML, this information is stored inside a document type definition (DTD). J2EE 1.4 uses XML Schemas instead of a DTD. Also, some J2EE products are XML Schema based—such as WebLogic Integration. A DTD can be included within an XML document or it can be external. If the DTD is stored externally, the XML document must provide a reference to the DTD. If a document does provide a DTD and the document adheres to the rules specified in the DTD, it is considered valid.

SAX (Simple API for XML) is a Java technology interface that enables applications to integrate with any XML parser to receive notification of parsing events. Every major Java technology-based parser available now supports this interface.

Here are some other ways that the Java platform supports the XML standard:

- The Java platform intrinsically supports the Unicode standard, simplifying the processing of an international XML document. For platforms without native Unicode support, the application must implement its own handling of Unicode characters, which adds complexity to the overall solution.

- The Java technology binding to the W3C Document Object Model (DOM) provides developers with a highly productive environment for processing and querying XML documents. The Java platform can become a ubiquitous runtime environment for processing XML documents.

- The Java platform's intrinsic support of the object-oriented programming means that developers can build applications by creating hierarchies of Java objects. Similarly, the XML specification offers a hierarchical representation of data. Because the Java platform and XML content share this common underlying feature, they are extremely compatible for representing each other's structures.

- Applications written in the Java programming language that process XML can be reused on any tier in a multi-tiered client-server environment, offering an added level of reuse for XML documents. The same cannot be said of scripting environments or platform-specific binary executables.

Electronic Data Exchange and E-Commerce

Given the industry's vast knowledge of communications, networking, and data processing, validating and processing data from other departments and/or enterprises should be a simple task. Unfortunately, that's not the case. Validating data formats and ensuring content correctness are still major hurdles to achieving simple, automated exchanges of data.

Using XML technology as the format for data exchange can quickly remedy most of these problems for the following reasons:

- Electronic data exchange of nonstandard data formats requires developers to build proprietary parsers for each data format. XML technology eliminates this requirement by using a standard XML parser.

- An XML parser can immediately provide some content validation by ensuring that all the required fields are provided and are in the correct order. This function, however, requires the availability of a DTD. Additional content validation is possible by developing applications using the W3C DOM.

In addition, content and format validation can be completed outside of the processing application and perhaps even on a different machine. The effect of this approach is twofold: It reduces the resources used on the processing machine and speeds up the processing application's overall throughput because it does not need to first validate the data. In addition, the approach offers companies the opportunity to accept or deny the data at time of receipt instead of requiring them to handle exceptions during processing.

Electronic Data Interchange (EDI)

EDI is a special category of data exchange that nearly always uses a VAN (value-added network) as the transmission medium. It relies on either the X12 or EDIFACT standards to describe the documents that are being exchanged. Currently, EDI is a very expensive environment to install and possibly requires customization depending on the terms established by the exchanging parties. For this reason, a number of enterprises and independent groups are examining XML as a possible format for X12 and EDIFACT documents, although no decisions have been reached as of this writing.

Enterprise Application Integration (EAI)

EAI is best described as making one or more disparate applications act as a single application. This is a complex task that requires that data be replicated and distributed to the correct systems at the correct time. For example, when integrating accounting and sales systems, it can be necessary for the sales system to send sales orders to the accounting system to generate invoices. Furthermore, the accounting system must send invoice data into the sales system to update data for the sales representatives. If done correctly, a single sales transaction will generate the sales order and the invoice automatically, thus eliminating the potentially erroneous manual re-entry of data.

Software Development and XML

XML has impacted three key areas of software development: the sharing of application architectures, the building of declarative environments, and scripting facilities.

In February 1999, the OMG (Object Management Group, a consortium of 11 companies, founded in April 1989) publicly stated its intention to adopt the XMI (XML Metadata Interchange) specification. XMI is an XML-based vocabulary that describes application architectures designed using the UML.

With the adoption of XMI, it is possible to share a single UML model across a large-scale development team that is using a diverse set of application development tools. This level of communication over a single design makes large-scale development teams much more productive. Also, because the model is represented in XML, it can easily be centralized in a repository, which makes it easier to maintain and change the model as well as provide overall version control. See the object Management Group site at *www.omg.org* for detailed specifications on UML.

XMI illustrates how XML simplifies the software development process, but it also can simplify design of overall systems. Because XML content exists within a document that must be parsed to provide value, it is a given that an XML technology-based application will be a declarative application. A *declarative* application decides what a document means for itself. A declarative environment would first parse the file, examine it, and make a decision about what type of document it is. Then, based on this information, the declarative application would take a course of action. In contrast, an *imperative* application will make assumptions about the document it is processing based on predefined logic. The Java compiler is imperative because it expects any file it reads to be a Java class file.

The concept of declarative environments is extremely popular right now, especially when it comes to business rules processing. These applications enable developers to declare a set of rules that are then submitted to a rules engine, which will match behavior (actions) to rules for each piece of data they examine. XML technology can also provide developers with the ability to develop and process their own action (scripting) languages.

XML is a meta-language; it can be used to create any other language, including a scripting language. This is a powerful use of XML technology that the industry is just starting to explore.

XML Technology and the Java Platform

Since 1998, early adopters of the XML specification have been using Java technology to parse XML and build XML applications for a variety of reasons. Java technology's portability provides developers with an open and accessible market for sharing their work, and XML data portability provides the means to build declarative, reusable application components.

Development efforts within the XML community clearly illustrate this benefit. In contrast to many other technology communities, those building on XML technology have always been driven by the need to remain open and facilitate sharing. Java technology has enabled these communities to share markup languages as well as code to process markup languages across most major hardware and operating system platforms.

Java Platform Standard Extension for XML Technology

The Java Platform Standard Extension for XML technology proposes to provide basic XML functionality to read, manipulate, and generate text. This functionality will conform to the XML 1.0 specification and will leverage existing efforts around Java technology APIs for XML technology, including the W3C DOM Level 1 Core Recommendation and the SAX programming interface version 1.0.

The intent in supporting an XML technology standard extension is to

- Ensure that it easy for developers to use XML and XML developers to use Java technologies

- Provide a base from which to add XML features in the future

- Provide a standard for the Java platform to ensure compatible and consistent implementations

- Ensure a high-quality integration with the Java platform

The Java community process gives Java technology users the opportunity to participate in the active growth of the Java platform. The extensions created by the process will eventually become supported standards within the Java platform, thus providing consistency for applications written in the Java programming language going forward. The Java Platform Standard Extension for XML technology will offer companies a standard way to create and process XML documents within the Java platform.

XML provides a data-centric method of moving data between Java and non-Java technology platforms. Although CORBA represents the method of obtaining interoperability in a process-centric manner, it is not always possible to use CORBA connectivity.

XML defines deployment descriptors for the EJB architecture. Deployment descriptors describe for EJB implementations the rules for packaging and deploying an EJB component. XML is an industry-wide recognized language for building representations of semi-structured data that can be shared intra- and inter-enterprise. However, XML enables companies to describe only the data and its structure. Additional processing logic must be applied to ensure document validity, transportation of the documents to interested parties, and for transforming the data into a form more useful to everyday business systems.

Distributed Programming Services

The EJB container and application server are also responsible for maintaining the distributed object environment. This means that they must manage the logistics of the distributed objects as well as the communications between them.

Naming and Registration

For each class installed in a container, the container automatically registers an EJBHome interface in a directory using the JNDI API. Using JNDI, any client can locate the EJBHome interface to create a new bean instance or to find an existing entity bean instance. When a client creates or finds a bean, the container returns its EJBObject interface.

Remote Method Invocation (RMI)

RMI is a high-level programming interface that makes the location of the server transparent to the client. The RMI compiler creates a stub object for each remote interface. The stub object is either installed on the client system or it can be downloaded at runtime, providing a local proxy object for the client. The stub implements all the remote interfaces and transparently delegates all method calls across the network to the remote object.

The EJB framework uses the Java RMI API to define and provide access to EJBs. The EJBHome and EJBObject interfaces, which are both required when creating EJBs, are extended from the java.rmi.Remote interface.

When a client object invokes methods on either a session bean or an entity bean, the client is using RMI in a synchronous fashion. This is different from a message-driven bean, which has its methods invoked by messages in an asynchronous fashion.

Protocols

The EJB specification asserts no requirements for a specific distributed object protocol. RMI is able to support multiple communication protocols. The Java RMI is the native protocol, supporting all functions within RMI. The next release of RMI plans to add support for communications using the CORBA standard communications protocol, IIOP, which supports almost all functions within RMI. EJBs that rely only on the RMI/IIOP subset of RMI are portable across both protocols. Third-party implementations of RMI support additional protocols, such as Secure Sockets Layer (SSL).

Using Protocols to Communicate Across Tiers

Table 2-3 shows some protocol suggestions for communication across tiers.

A comparison of various protocols is presented in Table 2-4.

TABLE 2-3   Tier-to-Tier Communication

Tiers Communicating	Possible Protocols
Communication between the user interface and business tiers	HTTP, RMI, CORBA, DCOM, JMS
Communication between the business and persistence tiers	JDBC, IDL to COM bridge, JMS, plain socket, native APIs via JNI embedded in resource adapters

TABLE 2-4	Distributed Object Communication

Protocol	Advantages	Disadvantages
HTTP	Well established protocol that is firewall-friendly and stateless, so that if servers fail between requests, the failure may be undetected by clients. The stateless nature makes it easy to scale and load balance HTTP servers.	Limited to communication with a servlet and JSP. Because it is stateless (session tracking requires cookies and/or URL rewriting), it's difficult to secure or maintain session state.
RMI	Object is passed by value. The client or server can reconstitute the objects easily. The data type can be any Java object. Any Java objects can be passed as arguments. Arguments must implement the Serializable interface or java.rmi.Remote object.	Heterogeneous objects are not supported.
CORBA	Heterogeneous objects are supported. Basically the opposite of RMI. Well established in the industry, with 800+ members in the OMG supporting the standard. IIOP wire protocol guarantees interoperability between vendor products. Bundled with well-known and well-documented services such as COSNaming and CORBASec to extend the capabilities of the ORB.	Objects are not passed by value; only the argument data is passed. The server/client has to reconstitute the objects with the data. Only commonly accepted datatypes can be passed as arguments unless CORBA 2.3/Objects By Value specification used.
DCOM	Fits well with the Windows OS deployment platform.	Works best in the Windows environment.

Distributed Object Frameworks

The current distributed object frameworks are CORBA, RMI, DCOM, and EJB. The EJB specification is intended to support compliance with the range of CORBA standards, current and proposed. The two technologies can function in a complementary manner. CORBA provides a great standards-based infrastructure on which to build EJB containers. The EJB framework makes it easier to build an application on top of a CORBA infrastructure. Additionally, the recently released CORBA components specification refers to EJB as the architecture when building CORBA components in Java.

CORBA

CORBA is a language independent, distributed object model specified by the OMG. This architecture was created to support the development of object-oriented applications across heterogeneous computing environments that might contain different hardware platforms and operating systems.

CORBA relies on IIOP for communications between objects. The center of the CORBA architecture lies in the Object Request Broker (ORB). The ORB is a distributed programming service that enables CORBA objects to locate and communicate with one another. CORBA objects have interfaces that expose sets of methods to clients. To request access to an objects method, a CORBA client acquires an object reference to a CORBA server object. Then the client makes method calls on the object reference as if the CORBA object were local to the client. The ORB finds the CORBA object and prepares it to receive requests, to communicate requests to it, and then to communicate replies back to the client. A CORBA object interacts with ORBs either through an ORB interface or through an Object Adapter.

Native Language Integration   By using IIOP, EJBs can interoperate with native language clients and servers. IIOP facilitates integration between CORBA and EJB systems. EJBs can access CORBA servers, and CORBA clients can access EJBs. Also, if a COM/CORBA internetworking service is used, ActiveX clients can access EJBs, and EJBs can access COM servers. Eventually there may also be a DCOM implementation of the EJB framework.

Java/RMI

Since a Bean's remote and home interfaces are RMI compliant, they can interact with CORBA objects via RMI/IIOP, Sun, and IBM's adaptation of RMI that conforms to the CORBA-standard IIOP protocol. The Java Transaction API (JTA), which is the transaction API prescribed by the EJB specification for bean-managed transactions, was designed to be well integrated with the OMG Object Transaction Service (OTS) standard.

Java/RMI relies on a protocol called the Java Remote Method Protocol (JRMP). Java relies heavily on Java Object Serialization, which allows objects to be marshaled (or transmitted) as a stream. Since Java Object Serialization is specific to Java, both the Java/RMI server object and the client object have to be written in Java. Each Java/RMI server object defines an interface, which can be used to access the server object outside of the current JVM and on another machine's JVM. The interface exposes a set of methods, which are indicative of the services offered by the server object.

For a client to locate a server object for the first time, RMI depends on a naming mechanism called an *RMIRegistry* that runs on the server machine and holds information about available server objects. A Java/RMI client acquires an object reference to a Java/RMI server object by performing a lookup for a server object reference and invokes methods on the server object as if the Java/RMI server object resided in the client's address space. Java/RMI server objects are named using URLs, and for a client to acquire a server object reference, it should specify the URL of the server object as you would with the URL to a HTML page. Since Java/RMI relies on Java, it also can be used on diverse operating system platforms from IBM mainframes to UNIX boxes to Windows machines to hand-held devices, as long as a JVM implementation exists for that platform.

Distributed Component Object Model DCOM

DCOM supports remote objects by running on a protocol called the Object Remote Procedure Call (ORPC). This ORPC layer is built on top of Distributed Computing Environment's (DCE) Remote Procedure Call (RPC) and interacts with Component Object Model's (COM) runtime services. A DCOM server is a body of code that is capable of serving up objects of a particular type at runtime. Each DCOM server object can support multiple interfaces, each representing a different behavior of the object. A DCOM client calls into the exposed methods of a DCOM server by acquiring a pointer to one of the server object's interfaces. The client object then starts calling the server object's exposed methods through the acquired interface pointer as if the server object resided in the client's address space. As specified by COM, a server object's memory layout conforms to the C++ vtable layout. Since the COM specification is at the binary level, it allows DCOM server components to be written in diverse programming languages such as C++, Java, Object Pascal (Delphi), Visual Basic, and even COBOL. As long as a platform supports COM services, DCOM can be used on that platform. DCOM is now heavily used on the Windows platform.

CERTIFICATION OBJECTIVE 2.01

Given an Architecture Described in Terms of Network Layout, List Benefits and Potential Weaknesses Associated with It

The following five exercises are in the form of practice essay questions:

1. Read the question.

2. Develop an essay style answer.

3. Review the draft and finalize your response.

4. Review the answer in the book.

EXERCISE 2-1

Role of Architect

Question   Define the role of an architect.

Answer   An Architect visualizes the behavior of the system. Architects create the blueprint for the system. They define the way in which the elements of the system work together and distinguish between functional and nonfunctional system requirements. Architects are responsible for integrating non-functional requirements into the system.

EXERCISE 2-2

Architecture Terminology

Question   Define the term architecture and its variations for system software.

Answer   Architecture refers to the art or practice of designing and building structures. It refers to a method or style for the formation or construction of a product or work. System architecture refers to the architecture of a specific construction or system. System architecture corresponds to "architecture as a product." It is the result of a design process for a specific system and specifies the functions of components, their interfaces, their interactions, and constraints. This specification is the basis for detailed design and implementation steps. The architecture is a means of communication during the design or re-design process. It may provide several abstract views on the system that serve as a discussion basis to clarify each party's perception of the problem area. Reference architecture corresponds to "architecture as a style or method." It refers to a coherent design principle used in a specific domain. An example of such architecture is the J2EE model for a computer-based information system. The architecture describes the kinds of system components, their responsibilities, dependencies, possible interactions, and constraints. The reference architecture is the basis for designing the system architecture for a particular system. When designing a system according to an architectural style, the architect can select from a set of well-known elements (standard parts) and use them in ways appropriate to the desired system architecture. In summary, architecture refers to an abstract representation of a system's components and behaviors. Architecture does not contain details about implementation. Architectures are best represented graphically. An architect communicates the design of the system to other members of the team. Defining architecture is a creative process. The creative process can have positive and negative aspects. Architects try to balance creativity with science in the form of models, frameworks, and patterns.

EXERCISE 2-3

Abstraction, Boundaries, Brittleness, and Capabilities

Question   Explain architectural terms such as abstraction, boundaries, brittleness, and capabilities.

Answer   An abstraction is a symbol for something used repeatedly in a design that hides details and is a clear representation. Boundaries are the area where two components interact. Brittleness is the degree to which small changes will break large portions of the system. Capabilities are the non-functional, observable system qualities including scalability, manageability, performance, availability, reliability, and security that are defined in terms of context. Friction is how much interaction occurs between two components. Friction is measured based on how a change in one affects both components. Layering is a hierarchy of separation. Surface Area is a list of methods that are exposed to the client. The key difference between architecture and design is in the level of detail.

EXERCISE 2-4

Fundamentals of System Architecture

Question   Identify the fundamentals of system architecture.

Answer   System architecture refers to the architecture of a specific construction or system. System architecture corresponds to "architecture as a product." It is the result of a design process for a specific system and specifies the functions of components, their interfaces, their interactions, and constraints. This specification is the basis for detailed design and implementation steps. Designs may include implementation details not present at the architectural level.

EXERCISE 2-5

Abstraction

Question   Explain the concept of abstraction and how it is implemented in system architecture.

Answer   Defining architecture for a system serves multiple objectives. It uses abstraction to provide help in representing complex dynamic systems by providing simple models. This way architecture helps the designer in defining and controlling the interfaces and the integration of the system components. During a re-design process, the architecture enables the designer to reduce the impact of changes to as few modules as possible. The architectural model of a system allows focusing on the areas requiring major change.

CERTIFICATION SUMMARY

This chapter described architecture as the practice of designing and building structures. It described the role played by the architect in the development of computer applications, especially those developed using the J2EE standard. It contrasted architecture and design. It covered the fundamentals, capabilities, and design goals of architecture using tables which will be useful in preparing for the exam. The rest of the book's chapters will embellish upon the tasks performed by the architect.

TWO-MINUTE DRILL

Given an Architecture Described in Terms of Network Layout, List Benefits and Potential Weaknesses Associated with It

❑ *Architecture* refers to an abstract representation of a system's components and behaviors. A good system architecture leads to reusable components because each component is broken into parts that may be repeated and can therefore be reused. Abstraction naturally forms layers representing different levels of complexity.

❑ *System* architecture corresponds to the concept of architecture as a *product*. It is the result of a design process for a specific system and must consider the functions of components, their interfaces, their interactions, and constraints. This specification is the basis for application design and implementation steps.

❑ *Reference* architecture corresponds to architecture as a *style* or *method*. It refers to a coherent design principle used in a specific domain.

❑ The key difference between the terms *architecture* and *design* is in the level of details. Architecture operates at a high level of abstraction with less detail. Design operates at a low level of abstraction, obviously with more of an eye to the details of implementation.

❑ The *layers* of architecture are systems in themselves. They obtain input from their environment and provide output to their environment.

❑ The capabilities of architecture include the following:

    ❑ **Availability** The degree to which a system is accessible. The term *24×7* describes total availability. This aspect of a system is often coupled with performance.

    ❑ **Reliability** The ability to ensure the integrity and consistency of an application and its transactions.

    ❑ **Manageability** The ability to administer and thereby manage the system resources to ensure the availability and performance of a system with respect to the other capabilities.

    ❑ **Flexibility** The ability to address architectural and hardware configuration changes without a great deal of impact to the underlying system.

❑ **Performance**   The ability to carry out functionality in a timeframe that meets specified goals.

❑ **Capacity**   The ability of a system to run multiple tasks per unit of time.

❑ **Scalability**   The ability to support the required availability and performance as transactional load increases.

❑ **Extensibility**   The ability to extend functionality.

❑ **Validity**   The ability to predict and confirm results based on a specified input or user gesture.

❑ **Reusability**   The ability to use a component in more than one context without changing its internals.

❑ **Security**   The ability to ensure that information is not accessed and modified unless done so in accordance with the enterprise policy.

SELF TEST

The following questions will help you measure your understanding of the material presented in this chapter. Read all the choices carefully because there might be more than one correct answer. Choose all correct answers for each question.

Given an Architecture Described in Terms of Network Layout, List Benefits and Potential Weaknesses Associated with It

1. Which of the following is true about the requirements of a banking system?

    A. The need for security is a classic example of a functional service level requirement, and a checking account rule is an example of a non-functional requirement.

    B. Security and the mandatory checking account both illustrate functional service level requirements.

    C. Neither security nor the mandatory checking account is an example of any kind of requirement, theoretically speaking.

    D. Security is an architectural non-functional requirement and the mandatory checking account a functional design requirement.

    E. They are both examples of business use cases.

2. Which of the following are non-functional requirements?

    A. Scalability, availability, extensibility, manageability, and security

    B. Performance, reliability, elaboration, transition, documentation, and security

    C. Specification, elaboration, construction, transition, use cases, and security

    D. Performance, availability, scalability, and security

    E. Reliability, availability, scalability, manageability, and security

3. Which of the following is the most important item that should be considered when designing an application?

    A. Scalability

    B. Maintainability

    C. Reliability

    D. Meeting the needs of the customer

    E. Performance

    F. Ensuring the application is produced on time and within budget

4. Your have been contracted by a company to help them improve the performance of their e-commerce application. You have suggested that the hardware on which the application is currently deployed (two web servers and a database server) be migrated to three web servers, an application server, and a database server (all on different machines). You assure them that all the required software rewrites will be worth it in the long run. What are the characteristics of your suggested architecture?

A. Fat clients

B. Thin clients

C. Good separation of business logic

D. Good scalability

E. Poor separation of business logic

F. Poor scalability

G. There is no difference in the separation of business logic.

SELF TEST ANSWERS

Given an Architecture Described in Terms of Network Layout, List Benefits and Potential Weaknesses Associated with It

1. ☑ **D** is correct. Successful software architecture deals with addressing the non-functional service level requirements of a system. The design process takes all functional business requirements into account. Security is considered a non-functional requirement and specific business rules, such as the one described for the checking account, are considered functional requirements. Choice **D** is the only choice that accurately describes this.

   ☒ **A, B, C,** and **E** are not true. Choice **A** is incorrect because the functional and non-functional requirements are switched. Choice **B** is incorrect because only one of them is a functional requirement. Choice **C** is incorrect because, as described above, one of them is a functional requirement and the other, a non-functional requirement. Finally, Choice **E** is incorrect because business analysis may start with use cases.

2. ☑ **D** is correct. The non-functional service level requirements discussed are performance (I: The system needs to respond within five seconds); availability (II: The system needs to have a 99.9 percent uptime); scalability (III: An additional two hundred thousand subscribers will be added); and security (IV: HTTPS is to be used). Hence, choice **D** is correct.

   ☒ **A, B, C,** and **E** are incorrect. There is no mention of extensibility (ability to easily add or extend functionality) and manageability (ability to monitor the health of the system). Hence, choice **A** is incorrect. Specification, elaboration, construction, transition, documentation, and use cases are not non-functional service level requirements. Hence, choices **B** and **C** are incorrect. While scalability and reliability may be related (Will the system perform as reliably when more users operate on it?), there is no mention of reliability in the question. Hence, choice **E** is incorrect.

3. ☑ **D** is correct. The most important consideration when designing an application is that it meets the needs of the customer.

   ☒ **A, B, C, E,** and **F** are incorrect. Ensuring the application is produced on time and within budget is something that should be done but it is not the number one concern. The application does not have to be the best possible solution under the circumstances. As long as it meets the customer's needs, it is considered adequate. All of the other considerations are secondary to meeting the customer's needs.

4. ☑ **B, C,** and **D** are correct. The system you have suggested they migrate to is a three-tier system. The characteristics of a three-tier system are thin clients, good separation of business logic, and good scalability. This is due to the fact that each tier is separate from the other (for example, it would be possible to change the data store without affecting the business logic).

   ☒ **A, E, F,** and **G** are incorrect. Choice **A** is incorrect; the suggested system has thin clients, the business logic residing on the application server, in the middle tier. Because there is a good separation of business logic, choices **E** and **G** are incorrect. Choice **F** is incorrect as the three-tier nature of the system makes it very scalable.

J2EE

SUN® CERTIFIED ENTERPRISE ARCHITECT

3

Object-Oriented Analysis and Design

CERTIFICATION OBJECTIVES

✓ Two-Minute Drill

Q&A Self Test

One of the fundamental challenges facing software architects is change. The need to develop maintainable software systems has driven interest in approaches to software development and design. Object-oriented technology has proven over time to be one of the most promising paradigms for design and implementation of large scale systems. The distinctive features of object-oriented technology include classes and instances and abstraction. We assume that most readers have some grounding in these concepts so we will concentrate on the information that will prove valuable for the certification exam.

Analysis and Design of Object-Oriented Architecture

Modeling is a visual process used for creating in a preserved form the design and structure of an application. Before, during, and after development, it is typical and prudent to outline an application, depicting dependencies and relationships among the components and subsystems. Like any good development tool, today's modeling tools facilitate this process by tracking changes made in the model to reflect the cascading effects of changes. Use of modeling tools gives developers a high-level and accurate view of the system.

Modeling can be used at any point in a project. Most modeling tools can reengineer and use code as input to create a visual model. The standard for modeling tools is the Unified Modeling Language (UML). This standard unifies the many proprietary and incompatible modeling languages to create one modeling specification. Use of modeling tools for development projects is increasing. With the increasing complexity of enterprise Java applications and components, modeling is a virtual necessity. It can reduce development time while ensuring that code is well formed.

Modeling is useful whether the objective is to understand and modify an existing computer-based business system or to create an entirely new one. An obstacle to engineering successfully is the inability to analyze and communicate the numerous interactive activities that make up a business process. Conversational languages, such as English, are ambiguous and therefore ineffective for communicating such objectives and activities. Formal languages are unintelligible to most functional (business) experts. What is needed instead is a technique that structures conversational language to eliminate ambiguity, facilitating effective communication and understanding.

In a process model, extraneous detail is eliminated, thus reducing the apparent complexity of the system under study. The remaining detail is structured to eliminate any ambiguity, while highlighting important information. Graphics (pictures, lines, arrows, and other graphic standards) are used to provide much of the structure, so most people consider process models to be pictorial representations. However, well-written definitions of the objects, as well as supporting text, are also critical to a successful model.

In engineering disciplines, the model is typically constructed before an actual working system is built. In most cases, modeling the target business process is a necessary first step in developing an application. The model becomes the road map that will establish the route to the final destination. Deciding the functionality of the target destination is essential. To be effective, it must be captured and depicted in detail.

In today's software development environment, we speak of *objects* as things that encapsulate *attributes* and *operations*. Before we proceed to the modeling standards being used today by software architects, let's begin with some basic definitions of object programming and its intending analysis, design, and lifecycle.

Key Features of OOP: Objects and Classes

Object-oriented programming (OOP) is the methodology used for programming classes based on defined and cooperating objects. OOP is based on objects rather than procedural actions, data rather than logic. In days past, a program had been viewed as a logical procedure that used input data to process and produce output data. Object-oriented programming focuses on the objects we want to manipulate rather than the logic required to manipulate them. Object examples range from human beings (described by name, address, and so forth) to inanimate objects whose properties can be described and managed, such as the controls on your computer desktop—buttons, scroll bars, and so on.

Step one in OOP is to identify the objects to be manipulated and their relationships to each other—that is, *modeling*. Once you've identified an object, you generalize it as a class of objects and define the kind of data it contains and logic that can manipulate it. The logic is known as *methods*. A real instance of a class is called an *object* or an *instance of a class*. The object or class instance is executed on the computer. Its methods provide computer instructions, and the class object characteristics provide relevant data. You communicate with objects and they communicate with each other with defined interfaces called *messages*.

The concepts and rules used in OOP provide these important benefits:

■ The concept of a data class makes it possible to define subclasses of data objects that share some or all of the main class characteristics. This is known as *inheritance*, and it is a property of OOP that facilitates thorough data analysis, reduces development time, and ensures more accurate coding.

- Since a class defines only the data it needs, when an instance of that class is run, the code will not be able to access other program data improperly. This characteristic of data hiding provides greater system security and avoids unintended data corruption.

- The definition of a class is reusable not only by the program for which it is initially created but also by other object-oriented programs. This facilitates distribution for use in other domains.

- The concept of data classes allows a programmer to create new datatypes that are not defined in the language itself.

Defining Object-Oriented Analysis and Design

In terms of computing software, *analysis* is the development activity consisting of the discovery, modeling, specification, and evaluation of requirements. Object-Oriented analysis (OOA) is the discovery, analysis, and specification of requirements in terms of objects with identities that encapsulate properties and operations, message passing, classes, inheritance, polymorphism, and dynamic binding. Object-oriented design (OOD) is the design of an application in terms of objects, classes, clusters, frameworks, and their interactions.

In comparing the definition of traditional analysis with that of object-oriented analysis and design (OOAD), the only aspect that is new is thinking of the world or the problem in terms of *objects* and *object classes*. A *class* is any uniquely identified abstraction—that is, a model—of a set of logically related instances that share the same or similar characteristics. An *object* is any abstraction that models a single element, and the term *object* as mentioned is synonymous with *instance*. Classes have attributes and *methods,* as they are more commonly known.

Project Lifecycle

The project lifecycle is a pivotal concept in terms of understanding what a projects is; the lifecycle is a mapping of the progress of the project from start to finish. Projects, by definition, have a start and finish, like any good game. At the simplest level, projects have two phases: planning and executing. Planning and executing are okay for a simple, short-term project. Larger, long-term endeavors require another layer to be added to the lifecycle of the projects. This can be achieved by subdividing each phase: plan and execute into two further phases, leading to a lifecycle of analysis, design, development, and implementation.

Table 3-1 summarizes the classic project lifecycle phases and mentions activities to be planned and executed for each phase. UML deliverables mentioned in this table are discussed in the sections that follow.

For the sake of completeness, we should also mention the Unified Process—or RUP (Rational Unified Process), as it has been trademarked by Rational (*www.rational.com*). The RUP is an incremental process used by development managers to manage a

TABLE 3-1   Project Lifecycle Phases

Primary Phase	Subphase	Activities
Analysis	Requirements analysis	Take a concept statement and define detailed requirements and the externally visible characteristics of the system. Write a validation plan that maps to the requirements specification. Short form: Is it possible to resolve the requirements?
	System-context analysis	Define the context of the system via use cases and scenarios. External messages, events, and actions are defined. The system is treated as a black box. Use care and scenario models are the deliverables. For real-time systems, characterize the sequence and synchronization details of the messages/responses. Short form: What would the big picture solution look like?
	Model analysis	Identify the classes, objects, and associations that solve the problem, using class and object diagrams. Response behavior is modeled using state charts. Interaction among objects is shown with sequence or collaboration diagrams. Short form: A further refinement of the big picture solution arrived at by decomposing subsystems into high-level classes.
Design	Architectural design	Define the important architectural decisions. Physical architecture of the system is modeled using deployment diagrams, software component architecture is modeled using component diagrams, and concurrency models are captured using class diagrams identifying the active objects. Design patterns are used here as well. Note: One key element of design is that "hard" dependencies on specific hardware, software, and other infrastructure is fleshed out as we move closer to implementation. For example, an architect may decide to use BEA WebLogic as the J2EE server. A designer may find that, while trying to build some XML parsing components, a decision needs to be made about whether to use BEA-specific APIs or perhaps use JAXP APIs.

TABLE 3-1	Project Lifecycle Phases *(continued)*

Primary Phase	Subphase	Activities
	Mechanistic design	Define the collaborative behavior of classes and objects. This information is captured on class and object diagrams. Sequence and collaboration diagrams capture specific instances of collaborations and state charts are enhanced to define the full behavior.
	Detailed Design	Define the detailed behavior and structure of individual classes using activity diagrams and notations.
Development		Develop class code, database definition, and message structures in the target language, DBMS, and messaging system.
Implementation	Unit testing	Test the internal structure and behavior of each class.
	Integration testing	Test the integration of various components. This take place recursively at multiple levels of decomposition based on the scale of the system.
	Validation testing	Test the delivered system against the requirements as defined in the validation test plan.
	System delivered	Pass the delivered system and user guide and other operational documentation to the user and technical support staff.

software project. Using the RUP, the project is broken down into phases and iterations. The iterations are oriented toward decreasing risk. Each phase should deliver a product, usually software, that can be demonstrated and validated against the project's requirements and use cases. The development manager uses iteration plans to manage the project. An iteration plan provides a detailed description of the upcoming phase of work. It defines the roles involved as well as activities and artifacts to be delivered in that iteration. The RUP outlines a set of criteria by which productivity and progress can be measured during the iteration. As with all planning tools, it defines specific start and end dates for product delivery.

The RUP identifies four phases for projects. Each phase focuses the team on an aspect of the project and has associated milestones.

1. **Inception**   The focus of this phase is the project scope.

2. **Elaboration**   The architecture as well as the requirements of the product being built must be defined by the end of this phase.

3. **Construction**   The software must be developed or constructed in this phase.

4. **Transition**   The software must be rolled out to users during this phase.

The RUP phases in some respects parallel the classic lifecycle phases—analysis, design, development, and implementation. They are, however, targeted at managing risks in project development. They consider that today's development is iterative. They are a framework geared for project leaders as opposed to architects and developers. The RUP management discipline provides a process that software development managers use to produce an overall project plan. The plan must be focused on deliverables, and it must be measurable, flexible, and aligned to real progress. The plan also must define the responsibilities and dependencies of the development team.

Unified Modeling Language

The Unified Modeling Language (UML) is a language used for specifying, constructing, visualizing, and documenting the components of a software system. The UML combines the concepts of Booch, Object Modeling Technique ("OMT"), and Object-Oriented Software Engineering ("OOSE"). The result is a standard modeling language. The UML authors targeted the modeling of concurrent and distributed systems; therefore, UML contains the elements required to address these domains. UML concentrates on a common model that brings together the syntax and semantics using a common notation.

This nonexhaustive treatment of UML is arranged in parts. First we describe the basic elements used in UML. Then we discuss relationships among elements. The follow-up is the resultant UML diagrams. Within each UML diagram type, the model elements that are found on that diagram are listed. It is important to note that most model elements are usable in more than one diagram.

author's note   *UML is an evolving language. This chapter was written when OMG UML version 1.4 was current and 2.0 was in draft specification.*

Elements Used in UML

In UML, an *element* is an atomic constituent of a model. A *model* element is an element that represents an abstraction drawn from the system being modeled. Elements are used in UML diagrams, which will be covered in the following sections. UML defines the following elements:

Class

As mentioned, a class is any uniquely identified abstraction that models a single thing, and the term *object* is synonymous with *instance*. Classes have attributes and methods. The class is represented in UML by a rectangle with three parts. The name part is required and contains the class name and other documentation-related information. For example, the name could be *data_access_object <<javabean>>*. The attributes part is optional and contains characteristics of the class. The operations part is also optional and contains method definitions. For example: `method (argument(s)) return type: get_order ( order_id ) hashmap.`

Interface

An *interface* is a collection of operations that represent a class or that specify a set of methods that must be implemented by the derived class. An interface typically contains nothing but virtual methods and their signatures. Java supports interfaces directly. The interface is represented in UML by a rectangle with three parts. The name part, which is required, contains the class name and other documentation-related information. For example, the name could be *data_access_object <<javabean>>*. The attributes part (optional) contains characteristics of the class. The operations part (optional) contains method definitions. For example: `method (argument(s)) return type: get_order ( order_id ) hashmap.`

Package

A *package* is used to organize groups of like elements. The package is the only group type element, and its function is to represent a collection of functionally similar classes. Packages can nest. Outer packages are sometimes called *domains*. Some outer packages are depicted by an "upside-down tuning fork" symbol, denoting them as *subsystems*. The package name is part of the class name—for example, given the class *accessdata* in the *ucny.trading.com* package, the fully qualified class name is *ucny.trading.com.accessdata.*

Collaboration

Collaboration defines the interaction of one or more roles along with their contents, associations, relationships, and classes. To use collaboration, the roles must be bound to a class that supports the operations required of the role. A use of collaboration is shown as a dashed ellipse containing the name of the collaboration. A dashed line is drawn from the collaboration symbol to each of the objects, depending on whether it appears within an object diagram that participates in the collaboration. Each line is labeled by the role of the participant.

Use Case

A *use case* is a description that represents a complete unit of functionality provided by something as large as a system or as small as a class. The result of this functionality is manifested by a sequence of messages exchanged among the system (or class) and one or more outside actors combined with actions performed by another system (or class).

There are two types of use cases: *essential* and *real*. Essential use cases are expressed in an ideal form that remains free of technology and implementation detail. The design decisions are abstracted, especially those related to the user interface. A real use case describes the process in terms of its real design and implementation. Essential use cases are important early in the project. Their purpose is to illustrate and document the business process. Real use cases become important after implementation, as they document how the user interface supports the business processes documented in the essential use case. In either type, a use case is represented as a solid line ellipse containing the name of the use case. A stereotype keyword may be placed above the name, and a list of properties is included below the name.

Component

The *component* represents a modular and deployable system part. It encapsulates an implementation and exposes a set of interfaces. The interfaces represent services provided by elements that reside on the component. A component is typically deployed on a node. A component is shown as a rectangle with two smaller rectangles extending from its left side. A component type has a type name: *component-type*. A component instance has a name and a type. The name of the component and its type may be shown as an underlined string, either within the component symbol or above or below it, with the syntax *component-name ':' component-type*. Either or both elements are optional.

Node

The *node* is a physical element object that represents a processing resource, generally having memory and processing capability—such as a server. Obviously, nodes include computers and other devices, but they can also be human resources or any processing resources. Nodes may be represented as types and instances. Runtime computational instances, both objects and component instances, may reside on node instances. A node is typically depicted as a cube. A node type has a type name: *node-type*. A node instance has a name and a type name. The node may have an underlined name within the cube or below it. The name string has the syntax *name ':' node-type*. The name is the name of the individual node, and the node-type says what kind of a node it is.

State

The *state* is a condition that can occur during the life of an object. It can also be an interaction that satisfies some condition, performs some action, or waits for some event. A *composite* state has a graphical decomposition. An object remains in a particular state for an interval of time. A state may be used to model the status of in-flight activity. Such an activity can be depicted as a state machine. A state is graphically shown as a rectangle with rounded corners. Optionally, it may have an attached name tab. The name tab is a rectangle and it contains the name of that state.

Relationships Used in UML

The object is the center of an object-oriented (OO) system. The OO model defines the system structure by describing objects (such as classes) and the relationships that exist among them. Class diagrams, as you will see, comprise classes, objects, and their relationships. The classes appear as rectangles that contain the class name. This rectangle is divided into sections, with the class name appearing in the first section, class attributes in the second section, class operations in the third, class exceptions in the fourth, and so on. The object names are underlined and have a colon as a suffix. As in any system, objects are connected by relationships.

UML defines and includes the types of relationships detailed in Table 3-2.

TABLE 3-2   UML Relationships

Relationship	Description	Notation
Generalization (aka Inheritance)	A specialized version of another class	Solid line with a closed arrowhead pointing to the more general class
Association	Uses the services of another class	Solid line connecting the associated classes, with an optional open arrowhead showing direction of navigation
Aggregation	A class "owns" another class	A form of association with an unfilled diamond at the "owner" end of the association
Composition	A class is composed of another class; refers to an aggregation within which the component parts and the larger encompassing whole share a lifetime	A form of aggregation, shown with either a filled diamond at the "composite" end, or with the composite graphically containing the "component"
Refinement	A refined version of another class; refinement within a given model can be shown as a dependency with the stereotype <<refines>> or one of its more specific forms, such as <<implements>>	Dashed line with a closed hollow arrowhead pointing to the more refined class
Dependency	A class dependent on another class.	Dashed line with an open arrowhead pointing to the dependency

Diagrams Used in UML

The following sections detail the graphical diagrams defined within UML.

Use Case Diagram

The use case diagram shows actors, a set of use cases enclosed by a system boundary, communication or participation associations among the actors and the use cases, and generalizations among the use cases. See Figure 3-1.

Class Diagram

The class diagram shows modeling elements. It may also contain types, packages, relationships, and even instances such as objects and links. A class is the descriptor for a set of objects that have a similar structure, behavior, and relationships. UML provides notation for declaring, specifying, and using classes. Some modeling elements that are similar to classes (such as types, signals, or utilities) are notated as stereotypes of classes. Classes are declared in class diagrams and used in most of the other diagrams. See Figure 3-2.

Package Diagram

The package diagram is a mechanism used for dividing and grouping model elements such as classes. In UML, a folder represents a package. The package provides a name space so that two elements with the same name can exist by placing them in two separate packages. Packages can also be nested within other packages. Dependencies between two packages indicate dependencies between any two classes in the packages. See Figure 3-3.

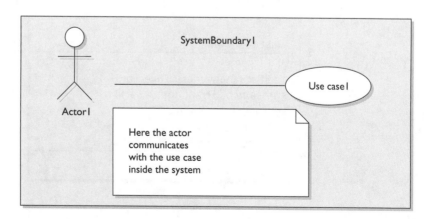

FIGURE 3-2 Class diagram

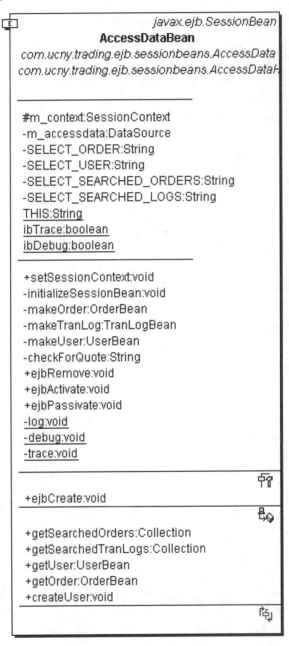

FIGURE 3-3

Package diagram

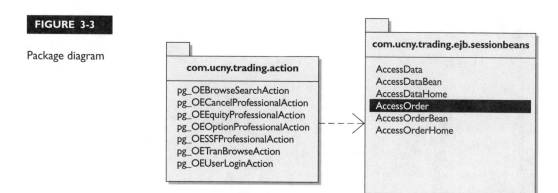

State Diagram

The state diagram is a two-part diagram showing states and transitions. It shows states connected by physical containment and tiling. The entire state diagram is attached through the model to a class or a method—that is, an operation implementation. See Figure 3-4.

Activity Diagram

An activity diagram is a special case of a state diagram in which all or most of the states are action states and in which all or most of the transitions are triggered by completion of the actions in the source states. The entire activity diagram is attached via the model to a class or to the implementation of an operation or a use case. This diagram concentrates on activity driven by internal processing as opposed to external forces. Activity diagrams are used for situations in which all or most of the events represent the completion of internal actions. Alternatively, ordinary state diagrams are used for situations in which *asynchronous* events occur. See Figure 3-5.

FIGURE 3-4   State diagram

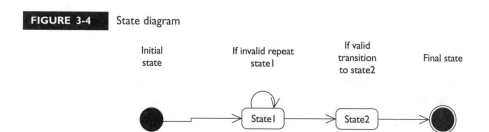

FIGURE 3-5 Activity diagram

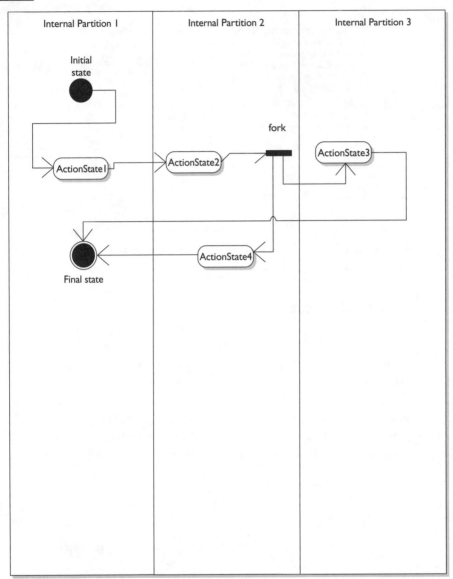

Sequence Diagram

A sequence diagram describes how groups of objects collaborate in some behavior over time. It records the behavior of a single use case. It displays objects and the messages passed among these objects in the use case. A design can have lots of methods in different classes. This makes it difficult to determine the overall sequence of behavior. This diagram is simple and logical, so as to make the sequence and flow of control obvious. See Figure 3-6.

Collaboration Diagram

A collaboration diagram models interactions among objects; objects interact by invoking messages on each other. A collaboration diagram groups together the interactions among different objects. The interactions are listed as numbered interactions that help to trace the sequence of the interactions. The collaboration diagram helps to identify all the possible interactions that each object has with other objects. See Figure 3-7.

Component Diagram

The component diagram represents the high-level parts that make up the modeled application. This diagram is a high-level depiction of the components and their relationships. A component diagram depicts the components refined post development or construction phase. See Figure 3-8.

FIGURE 3-6   Sequence diagram

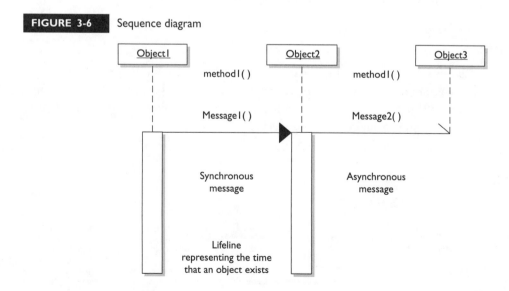

FIGURE 3-7 Collaboration diagram

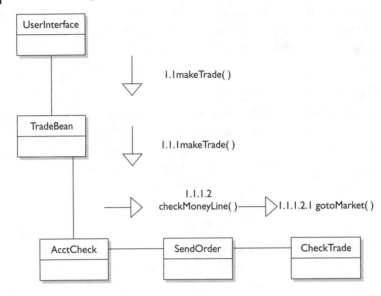

Deployment Diagram

A deployment diagram captures the configuration of the runtime elements of the application. This diagram is obviously most useful when a application is complete and ready to be deployed. See Figure 3-9.

Stereotypes

A *stereotype* is a new class of modeling element that is introduced during modeling time. Certain restrictions are in place: stereotypes must be based on certain existing classes in the meta model, and they may extend those classes only in certain predefined ways. They provide an extensibility mechanism for UML.

FIGURE 3-8 Component diagram

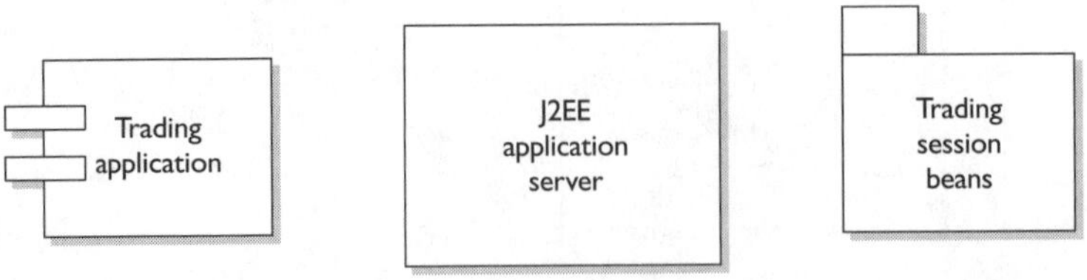

| Trading application | J2EE application server | Trading session beans |

 Deployment diagram

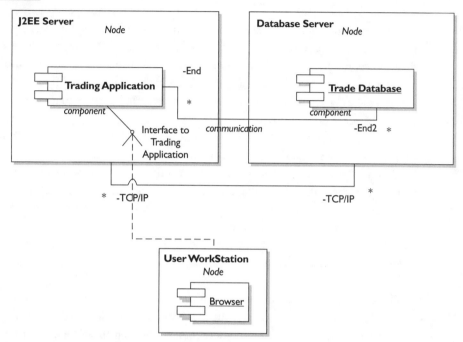

Practical Use of UML Diagrams

The scope of a typical software system is one of the barriers preventing the thorough understanding necessary for effective maintenance of systems. Even standard visualization approaches such as graphs and flow charts are overwhelming when attempting to depict a system. As you start to analyze such a system, you often want to begin with a high-level understanding of the overall structure and design of the system. You then delve into lower-level details once you have bounded the problem at hand. And at other times, the scope of the problem requires that you continue to work from the higher-level view.

UML provides a number of abstraction mechanisms to help you study the high-level architecture of your software. Within the Unified Modeling Language notation, diagrams are the primary representation of a system. UML will help you understand the objects, interactions, and relationships of your system software and hardware.

Use Case Diagram

The use case lends itself to a problem-centric approach to analysis and design, providing an understanding and a model of your system from a high-level business perspective—that is, how a system or business works or how you wish it to work. The use case diagram represents the functionality of a system as displayed to external interactions as *actors* of the system. A use case view represents the interface or interfaces that a system makes visible to the outside world, the external entities that interact with it, and their interrelationships.

Each use case step is either automated or manual. The objective of each step is to make a business decision or carry out a action. We typically assign responsibility for each business decision and action either to the system in the case of an automated action or to the actor in the manual case. This responsibility impacts the system delivered because the automated steps manifest themselves as system operations to make these decisions or execute these actions.

The diagram represents the processes within the system, which are visible to the outside world—that is, the actors of the system being modeled and the relationships among them.

Use cases are the functions or services of the system—those that are visible to its actors. They constitute a complete unit of functionality provided by a system as manifested by sequences of messages exchanged among the system and one or more actors together with actions performed by the system.

Actors are representative of the role of an object outside of a system that interacts directly with it as part of a complete work unit. An actor element characterizes the role played by an outside object, where one physical object may play multiple positions. For example, one entity may actually play different positions and assume different identities.

You can think of use case as a model that describes the processes of a business—order processing, for example—and its interactions with external parties such as clients and vendors. It is helpful in identifying the fundamental components of a system, namely the following:

- The business processes of the system
- External entities of the system
- The relationships among them

Use case diagrams are closely connected to *scenarios*. A scenario is an example of what happens when someone interacts with the system. For example, here is a scenario for a security trade: a trader accesses an Internet-based system and chooses the type of security he or she wants to trade. See Figure 3-10.

Annotated use case diagram

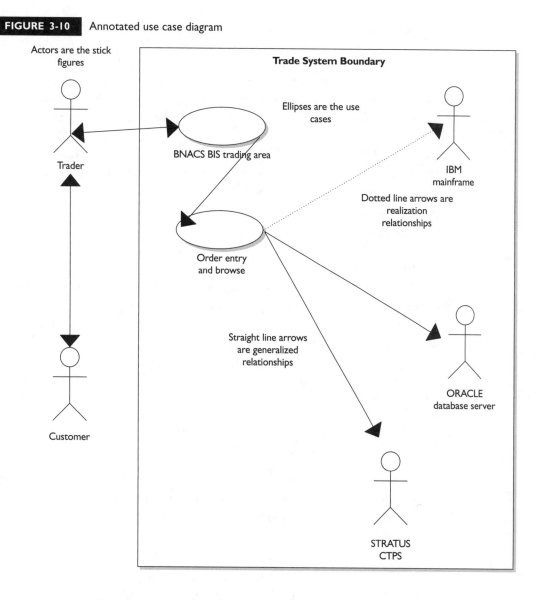

Figure 3-10 shows a trade use case for the online trading site. The actor is a trader. The connection between actor and use case is a communication association. Actors are represented by stick figures. Use cases are represented by ovals. A common issue regarding drawing use cases is having two "actions" tied to each other, essentially showing a "flowchart." In Figure 3-10, the trading system menu is invoked before the "order browse" functionality and subsequent calls to the Stratus CTPS and Oracle database. Communications are represented by lines that link actors to use cases.

A use case diagram is a collection of actors, use cases, and their communications. A single use case can have multiple actors. A system boundary rectangle separates the system from the external actors. A use case generalization shows that one use case is a special kind of another use case. Use case diagrams are important to use when you are

- Determining new requirements

- Communicating with clients—their simplicity makes use case diagrams a good way to communicate the system to users

- Validating the system—the different scenarios for a use case make a good set of test cases

Class Diagram

A class diagram provides an overview of a system by showing its classes and the relationships among them. Class diagrams are static; they display what interacts but not what happens when they do interact. The class diagram shown in Figure 3-11 models an EJB session bean used to order equities from a securities market. The central method is makeOrder that creates and returns an orderBean. Associated with it is the makeUser that creates and returns an userBean. UML class notation is a rectangle divided into three parts: class name, attributes, and operations. Names of abstract classes, such as *com.ucny.trading.ejb.sessionbeans.AccessData,* are in italics. Relationships among classes are the connecting links.

A class diagram can have three kinds of relationships:

- *Association* is a relationship between instances of the two classes. An association exists between two classes if an instance of one class must know about the other to perform its work. In a diagram, an association is a link connecting two classes.

- *Aggregation* is an association in which one class belongs to a collection. An aggregation shows a diamond end pointing to the part containing the whole.

- *Generalization* is an inheritance link indicating one class is a superclass of another. A generalization shows a triangle pointing to the superclass.

An association has two ends. An end may include a role name to clarify the nature of the association. For example, an *OrderDetail* is a line item of each *Order.*

FIGURE 3-11   Annotated class diagram

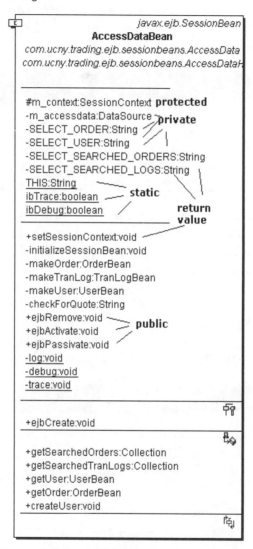

A navigability arrow on an association shows which direction the association can be traversed or queried. An *OrderDetail* can be queried about its *Item*, but not the other way around. The arrow also lets you know who "owns" the association's implementation; in this case, *OrderDetail* has an *Item*. Associations with no navigability arrows are bidirectional.

The multiplicity of an association end is the number of possible instances of the class associated with a single instance of the other end. Multiplicities, shown in the following table, are single numbers or ranges of numbers. In our example, there can be only one *User* for each *Order*, but a *User* can have any number of *Order*s.

Multiplicities	Meaning
0..1	Zero or one instance; the notation $n .. m$ indicates n to m instances
0..* *or* *	No limit on the number of instances (including none)
1	Exactly one instance
1..*	At least one instance

Every class diagram has classes, associations, and multiplicities. Navigability and roles are optional items placed in a diagram to provide clarity. The class notation is a three-piece rectangle with the class name, attributes, and operations. Attributes and operations can be labeled according to access and scope.

It is preferable that you name classes as singular nouns, such as *User* instead of *Users*. Static members are underlined, and Instance members are not. The operations follow this form: *<access specifier> <name> (<parameter list>) : <return type>*. The parameter list shows each parameter type preceded by a colon. Access specifiers, shown in the following, appear in front of each member.

Symbol	Access
+	Public
–	Private
#	Protected

Package Diagram

To simplify complex class diagrams, you can group classes into *packages*. A package is a collection of logically related UML elements. The diagram shown in Figure 3-12 is a business model in which the classes are grouped into packages. Packages appear as rectangles with small tabs at the top. The package name is on the tab or inside the rectangle. The dotted arrows show dependencies. One package depends on another if changes in the other could possibly force changes in the first. Object diagrams show instances instead of classes. They are useful for explaining small pieces with complicated relationships, especially recursive relationships.

FIGURE 3-12   Annotated package diagram

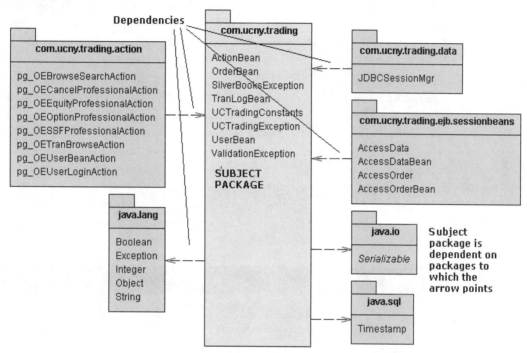

Sequence Diagrams

The sequence diagram shows the explicit series of interactions as they flow through the system to cause the desired objective or result. The sequence view is especially useful in systems with time-dependent functionality (such as real-time applications) and for complex scenarios where time dependencies are critical. It has two dimensions:

- One that represents time
- Another that represents the various objects participating in a sequence of events required for a purpose

Usually, only the sequence of events to which the objects of the system are subject is important; in real-time applications, the time axis is an important measurement. This view identifies the roles of the objects in your system through the sequence of states they traverse to accomplish the goal. This view is an event-driven perspective of the system. The relationships among the roles is not shown.

Class and object diagrams present static views. Interaction diagrams are dynamic. They describe how objects collaborate or interact. A sequence diagram is an interaction diagram that details the functionality and messages (requests and responses) and their timing. The time progresses as you move down the page. The objects involved in the operation are listed from left to right according to when they take part in the message sequence. Figure 3-13 shows a sequence diagram that illustrates the software calls and hardware used to service the calls in a sequence of time, with synchronous messages between each object in the diagram.

Each vertical dotted line in Figure 3-13 is a lifeline, representing the time that an object exists. Each arrow is a message call. An arrow goes from the sender to the top of the activation bar of the message on the receiver's lifeline. The activation bar represents the duration of execution of the message. The sequence diagram can have a clarifying note, text inside a dog-eared rectangle. Notes can be put into any kind of UML diagram. The UML uses the following message conventions for sequence diagrams:

Symbol	Meaning
⟶	Simple message that may be synchronous or asynchronous
⟵ - - - -	Simple message return (optional)
⟶	A synchronous message
⟶ or ⟶ or ⟶	An asynchronous message

Collaboration

Collaboration diagrams are also interaction diagrams. They convey the same information as sequence diagrams, but they focus on object roles instead of the times that messages are sent. In a sequence diagram, object roles are the vertices and messages are the connecting links. The object-role rectangles are labeled with either class or object names (or both). Class names are preceded by colons (:). Each message in a collaboration diagram has a sequence number. The top-level message is number 1. Messages at the same level (sent during the same call) have the same decimal prefix but suffixes of 1, 2, 3, and so on, according to when they occur.

The collaboration diagram is similar to the sequence diagram in terms of the information displayed, but it's different in its depiction. A collaboration diagram shows the relationships among objects. It is intended to assist in the understanding

FIGURE 3-13 Annotated sequence diagram

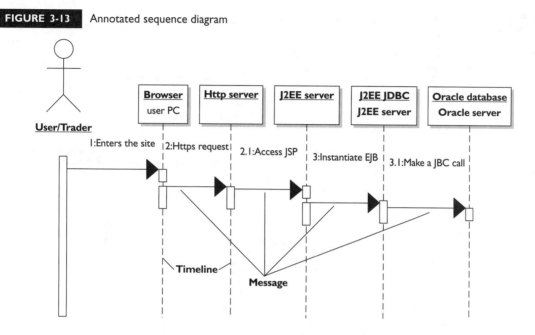

the effects on a given object. It provides a procedural perspective rather than a chronological view. A collaboration diagram shows interactions organized around the objects in a particular interaction, especially their links to one another. A collaboration diagram shows the relationships among the object roles.

The collaboration diagram shown in Figure 3-14 shows you a model of the behavior of the objects in the trading system and the messages involved in accomplishing a purpose—in this case, making a trade (checking the trader account for sufficient funds and sending the order to the market place), projected from the larger trading system of which this collaboration is just a part. It is a representation of a set of participants and relationships that are meaningful for a given set of functionality.

The description of behavior itself involves two characteristics:

■ The structural description of its participants

■ The behavioral description of its execution

These two characteristics are combined, but they can be separated, because at times it is useful to describe the structure and behavior separately.

Collaboration diagrams can be enhanced by the inclusion of the dynamic behavior of the message sequences exchanged among objects to accomplish a specific purpose.

FIGURE 3-14   Annotated collaboration diagram

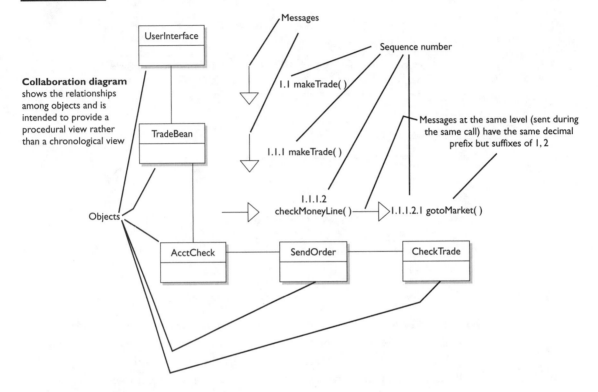

This is called an *interaction,* and it helps in understanding the dynamics of the system and its participating objects.

State

Objects have *state* or *status.* The state of an object depends on the current activity or condition. A state diagram illustrates the states of the object and the input and transitions that cause changes in the state. The state diagram shows the sequences of states that an object passes through during its lifetime. They correspond to prompts for input coupled with the responses and actions.

A *state machine* is a diagram of states and transitions that describe the response of an object of a given class to the receipt of external stimuli, and it is generally attached to a class or a method. A state diagram represents a state machine: a state being a condition during the life of an object or an interaction during which it satisfies some condition, performs some action, or waits for some event. A state may correspond to ongoing activity. Such activity is expressed as a nested state machine. For example, you may reprompt the user to enter missing form items that are required to process a transaction, such as user login. Alternatively, ongoing activity may be represented by a pair of actions—one that starts the activity on entry to the state and one that terminates the activity on exit from the state.

The example state diagram shown in Figure 3-15 models the login part of an online trading system. Logging in consists of entering a valid user ID and password, and then submitting the information for validation against a security database of

FIGURE 3-15 Annotated state diagram

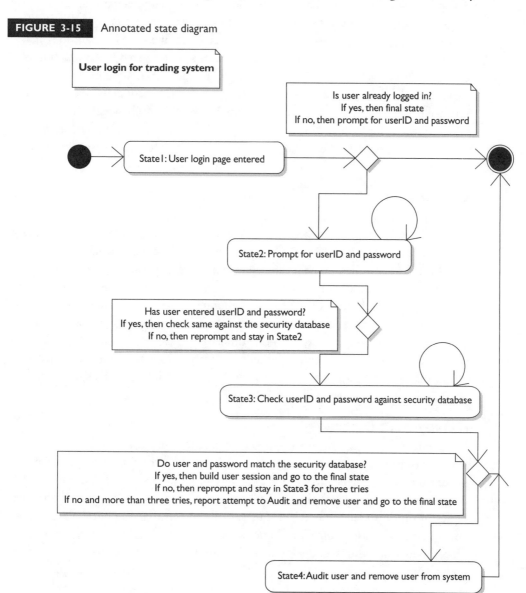

valid users and their passwords. Logging in can be factored into four nonoverlapping states: checking whether user ID is logged in, getting user ID and password, validating same, and rejecting/accepting the user. From each state comes a complete set of transitions that determine the subsequent state.

Activity Diagram

An activity diagram is essentially a fancy flowchart. Activity diagrams and state diagrams are related. An activity diagram—in a similar manner to the relationship between an object and class diagram—is a special case of a state diagram in which all the states are action states and all the transitions are triggered by completion of the actions in the source states. The entire activity diagram is attached to a class or a use case. The purpose of this diagram is to focus on the functionality that flows from internal processing. Activity diagrams are used in situations for which the events represent the completion of internally generated actions—that is, procedure flow. State diagrams, on the other hand, are used in situations for which asynchronous events predominate. Figure 3-16 shows the process for making a trade.

Component

Component diagrams are physical versions of class diagrams. A component diagram shows the relationships and dependencies between software components, including Java source code components, Java class components, and Java deployable components— JAR (Java Archive) files. Within the deployment diagram, a software component may be represented as a component type.

With respect to Java and J2EE, some components exist at compile time (such as *makeTrade.java*), some exist at archive time (*makeTrade.class*), and some exist at runtime (*Trade.ear*); some exist at more than one time. So you can say that a compile-only component is one that is meaningful only at compile time; the runtime component in this case would be an executable program. You can think of this diagram as a kind of compile, JAR, and deploy description.

Deployment Diagram

Deployment diagrams show the physical configurations of software and hardware. The deployment diagram complements the component diagram. It shows the configuration of runtime processing elements such as servers and other hardware and the software components, processes, and objects that they comprise. Software component instances represent runtime manifestations of classes. Components that do not exist as runtime entities (such as *makeTrade.java*) do not appear on these diagrams; they are shown on component diagrams. A deployment diagram is a graphical representation of nodes connected by communication links or associations. Nodes may contain

FIGURE 3-16   Annotated activity diagram

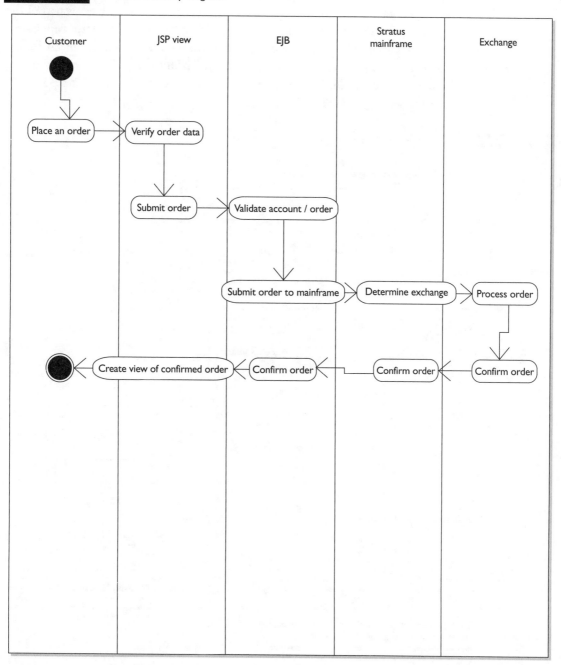

component instances, which indicate that the component resides and runs on the node. Components may contain objects, which indicate that the object is part of the component. The deployment diagram can be used to show which components run on which nodes. The migration of components from node to node or objects from component to component may also be represented. The deployment diagram shown in Figure 3-17 depicts the relationships among software and hardware components involved in security trading transactions.

FIGURE 3-17   Annotated deployment diagram

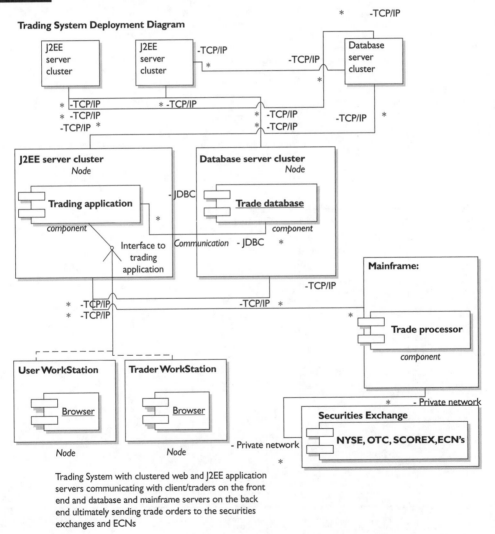

Trading System with clustered web and J2EE application servers communicating with client/traders on the front end and database and mainframe servers on the back end ultimately sending trade orders to the securities exchanges and ECNs

CERTIFICATION SUMMARY

The UML is a language used for specifying, constructing, visualizing, and documenting the components of a software system. The primary design goals of the UML areas follow:

■ Provide users with a visual modeling language to develop and exchange comprehensive models.

■ Provide mechanisms for extensibility and specialization that extend the core concepts.

■ Create a standard specification that is independent of particular computing languages.

■ Provide a formal base for a modeling language.

■ Support high-level development concepts such as components, collaborations, frameworks, and patterns.

■ Integrate best practices.

TWO-MINUTE DRILL

UML defines the following elements:

- ❑ **Class** Any uniquely identified abstraction that models a single thing, where the term *object* is synonymous with *instance*. Classes have *attributes* and *methods*.

- ❑ **Interface** A collection of operations that represents a class or specifies a set of methods that must be implemented by the derived class. An interface typically contains nothing but virtual methods and their signatures.

- ❑ **Package** Used to organize groups of like kind elements. The package is the only group type element and its function is to represent a collection of functionally similar classes.

- ❑ **Collaboration** Defines the interaction of one or more roles along with their contents, associations, relationships, and classes.

- ❑ **Use Case** A description that represents a complete unit of functionality provided by something as large as a system or as small as a class.

- ❑ **Component** Represents a modular and deployable system part. It encapsulates an implementation and exposes a set of interfaces.

- ❑ **Node** A physical element object that represents a processing resource, generally having memory and processing capability, such as a server.

- ❑ **State** A condition that can occur during the life of an object. It can also be an interaction that satisfies some condition, performs some action, or waits for some event.

UML defines the following relationships:

- ❑ **Generalization** A specialized version of another class.

- ❑ **Association** Uses the services of another class.

- ❑ **Aggregation** A class "owns" another class.

- ❑ **Composition:** A class is composed of another class. Refers to an aggregation within which the component parts and the larger encompassing whole share a lifetime.

- ❑ **Refinement** A refined version of another class.

- ❑ **Dependency** A class dependent on another class.

UML defines the following diagrams:

❑ **Use case diagram**   Used to identify the primary elements and processes that form the system. The primary elements are termed as *actors* and the processes are called *use cases*. The use case diagram shows which actors interact with each use case.

❑ **Class diagram**   Used to define a detailed design of the system. Each class in the class diagram may be capable of providing certain functionalities. The functionalities provided by the class are termed *methods* of the class.

❑ **Package diagram**   Groups objects or classes.

❑ **State diagram**   Represents the different states that objects in the system undergo during their lifecycle. Objects in the system change states in response to events.

❑ **Activity diagram**   Captures the process flow of the system. An activity diagram also consists of activities, actions, transitions, and initial and final states.

❑ **Sequence diagram**   Represents the interaction between different objects in the system. The important aspect of a sequence diagram is that it is time ordered. Objects in the sequence diagram interact by passing messages.

❑ **Collaboration diagram**   Groups together the interactions between different objects. The interactions are listed as numbered interactions that help to trace the sequence of the interactions. The collaboration diagram helps to identify all the possible interactions that each object has with other objects.

❑ **Component diagram**   Represents the high-level parts that make up the system. This diagram depicts what components form part of the system and how they are interrelated. It depicts the components culled after the system has undergone the development or construction phase.

❑ **Deployment diagram**   Captures the configuration of the runtime elements of the application. This diagram is useful when a system is complete and ready for deployment.

UML can be used to view a system from various perspectives:

❑ **Design view**   Structural view of the system; class diagrams and package diagrams form this view of the system.

❑ **Process view**   Dynamic behavior of a system; state diagram, activity diagram, sequence diagram, and collaboration diagram form this view.

❑ **Component view**   Software and hardware modules of the system modeled using the component diagram.

❑ **Deployment view**   The deployment diagram of UML is used to combine component diagrams to depict the implementation and deployment of a system.

❑ **Use Case view**   View a system from this perspective as a set of activities or transactions; use case diagrams.

SELF TEST

The following questions will help you measure your understanding of the material presented in this chapter. Read all the choices carefully because there may be more than one correct answer. Choose all correct answers for each question.

1. Which one of the following items is *not* one of the phases of the Unified Process?

   A. Inception

   B. Design

   C. Construction

   D. Transition

2. What *is* true about a use case?

   A. It is a complete end-to-end business process that satisfies the needs of a user.

   B. It is a description that represents a complete unit of functionality provided by something as large as a system or as small as a class.

   C. It defines the interaction of one or more roles along with their contents, associations, relationships, and classes.

   D. It is a collection of operations that represents a class or specifies a set of methods that must be implemented by the derived class.

3. Which item is *not* true when speaking of a class?

   A. A class is a nonunique structure.

   B. An *instance* is one computer executable copy of a class, also referred to as an *object*.

   C. Multiple instances of a particular class can exist in a computer's main memory at any given time.

   D. A class is a structure that defines the attribute data and the methods or functions that operate on that data.

4. What is *not* true about use cases?

   A. There are three types of use cases: essential, real, and virtual.

   B. A virtual use case describes the user's virtual view of the problem and is technology independent.

   C. A real use case describes the process in terms of its real design and implementation.

   D. Essential use cases are of importance early in the project. Their purpose is to illustrate and document the business process.

5. What is *not* true about a sequence diagram?

   A. It has two dimensions.

   B. One sequence diagram dimension represents time.

   C. One sequence diagram dimension represents the different objects participating in a sequence of events required for a purpose.

   D. Sequence diagrams are static model views.

6. Which item is *not* an example of things that a state diagram could effectively model?

   A. Life could be modeled: birth, puberty, adulthood, death.

   B. A computer system infrastructure.

   C. A banking transaction.

   D. A soccer match could be modeled: start, half time, injury time, end.

7. What is *not* true about a collaboration diagram?

   A. A collaboration diagram models interactions among objects, and objects interact by invoking messages on each other.

   B. A collaboration diagram groups together the interactions among different objects.

   C. The interactions in a collaboration diagram are listed as alphabetically collated letters that help to trace the sequence of the interactions.

   D. The collaboration diagram helps to identify all the possible interactions that each object has with other objects.

8. What item is *not* true about a component?

   A. A component represents a modular and deployable system part. It encapsulates an implementation and exposes a set of interfaces.

   B. The component interfaces represent services provided by elements that reside on the component.

   C. A node may be deployed on a component.

   D. A component is shown as a rectangle with two smaller rectangles extending from its left side. A component type has a type name *component-type*.

9. Which item(s) is *not* part of a class in a UML class diagram?

   A. Name

   B. Attributes

   C. Method

   D. Comments

10. Which item is *not* one of the three kinds of relationships a class diagram can have?

A. Association

B. Aggregation

C. Generalization

D. Specialization

11. In a class diagram, what does a line with an arrow from one class to another denote?

A. Attribute visibility

B. Class visibility

C. Method visibility

D. Global visibility

12. What is *not* a type of visibility between objects?

A. Local

B. Method

C. Attribute

D. Global

13. Which statement is *not* true about state machine and state diagrams?

A. A state machine is basically a diagram of states and transitions that describes the response of an object of a given class to the receipt of external stimuli, and it is generally attached to a class or a method.

B. The state diagram shows the sequences of states that an object passes through during its lifetime.

C. A state diagram represents a state machine: a state being a condition during the life of an object or an interaction during which it satisfies some condition, performs some action, or waits for some event.

D. State diagrams are used in situations for which all or most of the events represent the completion of internally generated actions (that is, procedural flow of control).

14. Which of the following UML diagrams may be best suited for a business analyst?

A. Deployment

B. Class

C. Use case

D. Activity

E. Collaboration

F. Sequence

15. In a UML class diagram, Private, Protected, and Public attributes are shown by which one of the following sets of symbols?

    A. -, +, #

    B. +, -, hash

    C. #, -, +

    D. -, #, +

    E. +, #, -

    F. #, +, -

SELF TEST ANSWERS

1. ☑ **B** is correct because design is not a phase in the unified process.
   ☒ **A, C,** and **D** are incorrect because the phases of the unified process include inception, whose focus is the scope of the project; elaboration, in which the architecture and the requirements of the product being built must be defined by the end of this phase; construction, during which the software must be developed or constructed; and transition, during which the software must be rolled out to users.

2. ☑ **A** and **B** are correct because a use case is a complete end-to-end business process that satisfies the needs of a user. It is also a description that represents a complete unit of functionality provided by something as large as a system or as small as a class.
   ☒ **C** and **D** are incorrect because a collaboration defines the interaction of one or more roles along with their contents, associations, relationships, and classes. A class diagram is a collection of operations that represents a class or specifies a set of methods that must be implemented by the derived class.

3. ☑ **A** is correct because a class is unique.
   ☒ **B, C,** and **D** are incorrect because they are true. A class is a unique structure that defines the attribute data and the methods or functions that operate on that data. An instance is one computer executable copy of a class, also referred to as an object. Multiple instances of a particular class can exist in a computer's main memory at any given time.

4. ☑ **A** and **B** are correct because they are false. There are two types of use cases: essential and real.
   ☒ **C** and **D** are incorrect because they are true. Essential use cases are expressed in an ideal form that remains free of technology and implementation detail. The design decisions are abstracted, especially those related to the user interface. A real use case describes the process in terms of its real design and implementation. Essential use cases are of importance early in the project. Their purpose is to illustrate and document the business process. Real use cases become important after implementation, as they document how the user interface supports the business process documented in the essential use case.

5. ☑ **D** is correct because it is false. Class and object diagrams are static model views; sequence diagrams are dynamic.
   ☒ **A, B,** and **C** are incorrect because they are true. The sequence diagram shows the explicit sequence of interactions as they flow through the system to affect a desired operation or result. It has two dimensions; one dimension represents time, and another dimension represents the different objects participating in a sequence of events required for a purpose. Class and object diagrams are static model views.

6. ☑ B is correct because it is false. A computer system infrastructure does not have dynamic states; it is more or less static and the modeler would use a deployment diagram to depict the infrastructure.

   ☒ A, C, and D are incorrect because they are true. Life could be modeled. A banking transaction and a soccer match could also be modeled.

7. ☑ C is correct because it is false. The interactions in a collaboration diagram are listed as numbered interactions that help to trace the sequence of the interactions.

   ☒ A, B, and D are incorrect because they are true. A collaboration diagram models interactions among objects, and objects interact by invoking messages on each other. A collaboration diagram groups together the interactions among different objects. The interactions in a collaboration diagram are listed as numbered interactions that help to trace the sequence of the interactions.

8. ☑ C is correct because it is false. A component may be deployed on a node.

   ☒ A, B, and D are incorrect because they are true. A component represents a modular and deployable system part. It encapsulates an implementation and exposes a set of interfaces. The interfaces represent services provided by elements that reside on the component. A component is shown as a rectangle with two smaller rectangles extending from its left side.

9. ☑ D is correct because it is false. A comment is not part of a UML class diagram.

   ☒ A, B, and C are incorrect because they are true. UML class notation is a rectangle divided into three parts that include class name, attributes, and operations.

10. ☑ D is correct because it is false. Specialization is not a relationship type.

    ☒ A, B, and C are incorrect because they are true. Association is a relationship between instances of the two classes. An association exists between two classes if an instance of one class must know about the other to perform its work. In a diagram, an association is a link connecting two classes. Aggregation is an association in which one class belongs to a collection. An aggregation has a diamond end pointing to the part containing the whole. Generalization is an inheritance link indicating one class is a superclass of the other. A generalization has a triangle pointing to the superclass.

11. ☑ A is correct.

    ☒ B, C, and D are incorrect.

12. ☑ B is correct.

    ☒ A, C, and D are incorrect.

13. ☑   **D** is correct because it is false. Activity diagrams are used in situations for which all or most of the events represent the completion of internally generated actions (that is, procedural flow of control). State diagrams, on the other hand, are used in situations for which asynchronous events predominate.

☒   **A, B,** and **C** are incorrect because they are true. The state diagram shows the sequences of states through which an object passes during its lifetime. They correspond to prompts for input couples with the responses and actions. A state machine is basically a diagram of states and transitions that describe the response of an object of a given class to the receipt of external stimuli, and it is generally attached to a class or a method. A state diagram represents a state machine: a state being a condition during the life of an object or an interaction during which it satisfies some condition, performs some action, or waits for some event.

14. ☑   **C** is correct because use case diagrams show a set of use cases and actors and their relationships. Use case diagrams show the static view of a system. These diagrams are especially important in organizing and modeling the behaviors of a system. Use case diagrams are frequently used by business analysts to capture business requirements of a system.

☒   **A, B, D, E,** and **F** are incorrect. Deployment diagrams show the configuration of runtime processing nodes and the components that live within these nodes. Deployment diagrams address the static view of the architecture. Architects frequently use deployment diagrams. A class diagram shows a set of classes, interfaces, and collaborations and their relationships. Class diagrams address the static design view of a system. Software designers frequently use class diagrams. Activity diagrams are a special kind of state chart diagram that shows the flow from activity to activity within the system. This type of diagram is important in modeling the function of a system and emphasizing the flow of control among objects. Designers and developers frequently use activity diagrams. A collaboration diagram is an interaction diagram that emphasizes the structural organization of objects that send and receive messages. Designers and developers frequently use interaction diagrams.

15. ☑   **D** is correct because in UML notation, access modifiers are shown by the -, #, and + symbols to represent private, protected, and public, respectively.

☒   **A, B, C, E,** and **F** are incorrect because they do not have the right combination.

4

Applicability of J2EE Technology

T hin client multi-tiered applications are hard to write because they involve many lines of intricate code to handle transaction and state management, multithreading, resource pooling, and other complex low-level details. The component-based and platform-independent J2EE architecture facilitates application development because business logic is organized into reusable components and the J2EE server provides underlying services in the form of a container for every component type. In this chapter, we will explore this architecture in more detail.

CERTIFICATION OBJECTIVE 4.01

Explain the J2EE Architecture and System Requirements

The Java 2 Enterprise Edition (J2EE) platform uses a multi-tiered distributed application model, in which application logic is divided into components according to function. The various components that a J2EE application comprises are installed on different machines. A component's location depends on which tier or layer that component belongs to in the multi-tiered J2EE environment. Figure 4-1 shows two multi-tiered J2EE applications divided into the tiers described here:

- Client tier components run on the client machine.
- Web tier components run on the J2EE server.
- Business tier components run on the J2EE server.
- Enterprise Information System (EIS) tier software runs on the EIS server.

FIGURE 4-1

Multi-tiered J2EE applications

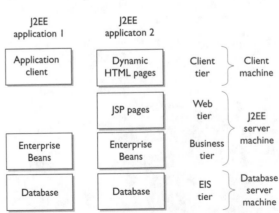

J2EE Technology Layers Applied

While a J2EE application can consist of three or more tiers, J2EE multi-tiered applications are generally considered to be three-tiered applications, because they are distributed across three different locations: client machines, the J2EE server machine, and the database or legacy machines at the back end. Three-tiered applications that run in this way extend the standard two-tiered client-server model by placing a multithreaded application server between the client application and back-end storage.

The Client Layer

The client layer or tier of a web application is typically implemented as Hypertext Markup Language (HTML) displayed in a web browser running on the user's machine. It may also be implemented using Java. Its function is to display data, providing the user with a place to enter and update data. Generally, one of two common approaches is used for building the client layer:

- **A pure HTML-only client**   In this scenario, virtually all of the intelligence is placed in the middle tier. When the user submits the web pages, all the validation is done on the J2EE server (the middle tier). Errors are then posted back to the client.

- **A hybrid HTML/Dynamic HTML (DHTML)/JavaScript client**   In this scenario, some intelligence is included in the web pages, which run on the client. The client will do some basic validations (for example, ensuring that mandatory columns are completed before allowing users to submit information). The client may also include some DHTML for functions such as hiding fields when they are no longer applicable due to earlier selections.

The pure HTML approach is less efficient for end users because all operations require the server for even the most basic functions. On the other hand, as long as the browser understands HTML, it will generally work with this basic approach, making it possible to work on basic wireless or text-only browsers. The second argument in favor of this approach is that it provides a better separation of business logic and presentation. The hybrid client approach is more user-friendly, requiring fewer trips to the server. Typically, DHTML and JavaScript are written to work with more recent versions of mainstream browsers.

As mentioned, the J2EE application client may also provide client layer functionality, providing the user with a place to maintain data. A J2EE application client is a thick (RMI-IIOP [Remote Method Invocation–Internet Inter-ORB Protocol]) Java application; it differs from a stand-alone Java application client because it is a J2EE component. Like other J2EE components, a J2EE application client is created with the application deployment tool and added to a J2EE application.

Because it is part of a J2EE application, a J2EE application client has two advantages over a stand-alone Java application client: First, a J2EE application client is bundled in an Enterprise Archive (EAR) file with all the required software making it easily portable—that is, it will run on any J2EE-compliant server. Second, because it is bundled with the required libraries, it has access to the full array of J2EE services. Its weight sometimes makes it a poor choice, and the emergence of the JavaServer Page (JSP) has curbed its popularity.

The Presentation Layer

The presentation layer generates web pages and any dynamic content in the web pages. The dynamic content is typically obtained from a database; for example, content may consist of a list of transactions conducted during the last month. The other major job of the presentation layer is to package requests contained on the web pages coming back from the client.

The presentation layer can be built with a number of different tools. The presentation layers for the first web sites were built as Common Gateway Interface (CGI) programs. Netscape servers also offered server-side JavaScript for web sites. Contemporary web sites generally have presentation layers built using the Microsoft solution, Active Server Pages (ASP), which may be generated by Visual InterDev, or they us the Java solution, which utilizes some combination of servlets and JSP. Tools provide methods to facilitate embedding dynamic content inside other static HTML in the web page. They also provide tools for simple parsing of the web pages coming back from the client to extract the user-entered information.

The presentation layer is generally implemented inside a web server (such as Microsoft IIS, BEA WebLogic, or IBM WebSphere). The web server typically handles requests for several applications in addition to requests for the site's static web pages. Based on the initial configuration, the web server knows to which application to forward the client-based request (or which static web page to serve up).

The Business Logic Layer

The bulk of the application logic is written in the business logic layer. The challenge here is to allocate adequate time and resources to identify and implement this logic. Business logic includes the following:

- Performance of all required calculations and validations
- Workflow management (including keeping track of session data)
- Management of all data access for the presentation layer

In modern web applications, business logic is frequently built using the Java solution, with Enterprise JavaBeans (EJBs) that are built to carry out the business operations. Language-independent Common Object Request Broker Architecture (CORBA) objects can also be built and accessed with a Java presentation tier. The main component of CORBA is the Object Request Broker (ORB). It encapsulates the communication infrastructure necessary to locate objects, manage connections, and deliver data. The ORB core is responsible for the communication of requests. The basic functionality provided by the ORB consists of passing the requests from clients to the object implementations on which they are invoked. The ORB then transfers the request to the object implementation, which receives the request, processes it, and returns an object result.

Much like the presentation layer, the business logic layer is generally implemented inside the application server. The application server automates many services, such as transactions, security, persistence/connection pooling, messaging, and name services. Isolating the business logic from the need to manage resources allows the developer to focus on building application logic. In the application server marketplace, vendors differentiate their products based on manageability, security, reliability, scalability, and tools support.

The Data Layer

The data layer is responsible for data management. A data layer may be as simple as a modern relational database; on the other hand, it may include data access procedures to other data sources such as nonrelational databases, legacy files, or message-oriented middleware. The data layer provides the business logic layer with required data when needed and stores data when requested.

To avoid making an application less interoperable, the architect should strive to keep validation and business logic out of the data layer; that logic belongs in the business logic layer. Sometimes basic database design rules can overlap with business logic. There is usually some basic business logic in the data tier. For example, both *not null* constraints and *foreign key* constraints, which designate that certain columns must have a value and that the value must match an existing foreign row's corresponding key value, could be considered "business rules" that should be known only to the business logic layer. Most product designers would agree that it is necessary to include such simple constraints in the database to maintain data integrity, changing them as the business rules evolve.

J2EE Application Components

J2EE applications are made up of *components*: self-contained functional software units assembled into J2EE applications with their related classes and files. These components communicate with other components. The J2EE specification defines the following components:

- **Client components**   Application clients and applets
- **Web components**   Java Servlet and JSP technology
- **Business components**   EJB components

These components are written in the Java programming language and compiled in the same manner as any other program written in Java. When working with the J2EE platform, the difference is that J2EE components are assembled into a J2EE application, where it is verified that they are well formed and compliant with the J2EE specification. They are then deployed to production, where they are run and managed by the J2EE server.

Client Components

A J2EE application can either be web-based or non-web-based. Non-web-based components are an extension of the heretofore common client server applications. In a non-web-based J2EE application, an application client executes on the client machine. For a web-based J2EE application, the web browser downloads web pages and applets to the client machine.

Application Clients   Application clients run on a client machine, providing a way for users to handle tasks such as J2EE system or application administration. Usually, a graphical user interface (GUI) is created using Swing or Abstract Windowing Toolkit (AWT) APIs; however, a command-line interface is also possible. Application clients directly access enterprise beans that run in the business tier. On the other hand, an application client can open an HTTP connection establishing communication with a servlet running in the web tier if warranted by the J2EE application.

Web Browsers   The user's web browser downloads static or dynamic HTML, Wireless Markup Language (WML), eXtensible Markup Language (XML), or pages in other formats from the web tier. Servlets and JSPs running in the web tier provide the ability to generate dynamic web pages.

Applets   Web pages downloaded from the web tier can include embedded applets. These are small client applications, written in the Java programming language, which execute in the Java Virtual Machine (JVM) installed in the web browser. Client systems often need an additional Java plug-in and perhaps even a security policy file so the applet can successfully execute in the web browser.

JSPs are the preferred API for the creation of web-based client programs, where plug-ins and security policy files are not necessary on the client system. In addition, JSPs enable cleaner, more modular application designs because they provide a way to separate application programming from web-page design. This means web-page designers do not need to know Java to do their jobs.

Applets running in other network-based systems such as handheld devices and cell phones are able to render WML pages generated by a JSP or servlets running on the J2EE server. The WML page is delivered using the Wireless Application Protocol (WAP). The network configuration requires a gateway to translate WAP to HTTP and back again. This gateway translates the WAP request from the handheld device to an HTTP request for the J2EE server, translating the HTTP server response and WML page to a WAP server response and WML page for display on the device.

JavaBeans Component Architecture   The client tier sometimes includes a component based on the JavaBeans component architecture for managing data flow between the application client or applet and components running on the J2EE server. The J2EE specification does not regard JavaBeans components as components. As will be explained later in this book, JavaBeans are not the same as EJBs. JavaBeans components have instance variables as well as get and set methods for accessing the data in those instance variables. When used in this manner—that is, as a place to persist user entered data—JavaBeans components tend to be simple in design and implementation. They should, however, conform to the naming and design conventions specified in the JavaBeans component architecture.

J2EE Server Communications   Figure 4-2 shows the various elements that make up the client tier. The client communicates with the business tier running on the J2EE server either directly (as in the case of a client running in a browser) or by going through JSPs or servlets running in the web tier.

FIGURE 4-2

Elements of the
client tier

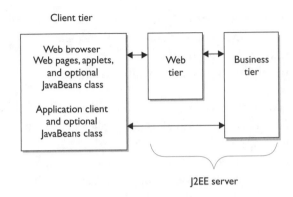

Thin Clients J2EE applications use a lightweight interface to the application, known as a *thin client*, which does not perform functions such as querying databases, executing complex business rules, or connecting to legacy applications. Instead, these operations are off-loaded to web or enterprise beans that execute on the J2EE server. Here, the security, speed, services, and reliability of J2EE server-side technologies are maximized.

Web Components

J2EE web components are either JSP pages or servlets. Servlets are Java classes that dynamically process requests and construct responses. JSP pages are text-based documents containing static content along with snippets of Java code used to generate dynamic content. When a JSP page loads, a background servlet executes the code snippets, returning a response.

Although static HTML pages and applets are bundled with web components during application assembly, they are not considered web components by the J2EE specification. In the same manner, server-side utility classes are often bundled with web components yet are not themselves considered web components.

The web tier, shown in Figure 4-3, might include JavaBeans objects for managing user input, sending that input to enterprise beans running in the business tier to be processed. JavaBeans that encapsulate UI controls or other dynamic functionality can be used to emulate the client-server user interface on a web-based page.

Business Components

Business code is logic that solves the functional requirements of a particular business domain such as banking, retail, or finance. This code is handled by enterprise beans that run in the business tier. Figure 4-4 demonstrates how an enterprise bean receives

FIGURE 4-3

Elements of the
web tier

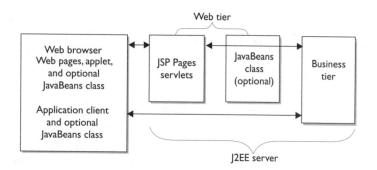

data from client programs, processes it, and then sends it to the enterprise information system tier to be stored. In addition, an enterprise bean retrieves data from storage, processes it, and then sends it back to the client program.

There are three kinds of enterprise beans: session beans, entity beans, and message-driven beans. Session beans represent transient conversations with a client. When the client completes execution, the session bean and its accompanying data are gone. On the other hand, entity beans represent persistent data, which typically is stored in one row of a database table. Entity beans can map to more than one row/record of a relational database table or legacy data store. If the client quits or the server shuts down, underlying services ensure that the entity bean data is saved. Message-driven beans feature a session bean and a Java Message Service (JMS) message listener. They allow business components to receive asynchronous JMS messages.

Enterprise Information System Tier   The EIS tier is a giant "catch-all" for handling EIS software. It includes enterprise infrastructure systems such as Enterprise Resource Planning (ERP), mainframe transaction processing, database systems, and other legacy information systems. J2EE application components access EISs for functions such as database connectivity. The reality is that most enterprise computing

FIGURE 4-4

Business and EIS
tiers

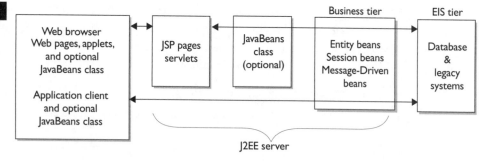

environments typically have a legacy system to maintain the so-called "books and records" of the firm. Moreover, new applications based on J2EE will have to be able to interface and communicate request and response processing with the legacy systems. Architects must be able to build and use EIS to handle this important requirement.

To this end, the J2EE Connector Architecture is a standard architecture for connecting to EIS from the J2EE platform. The architecture defines a set of scalable, secure, and transactional mechanisms that describe the integration of EISs to an application server and enterprise applications. This architecture enables an EIS vendor to provide a resource adapter for its EIS that can be plugged into any application server that supports the J2EE Connector Architecture. IBM in particular has embraced this standard to open access to mainframe-based online transaction processing (OLTP) systems such as Customer Information Control Systems (CICS).

J2EE Architecture

Typically, thin-client, multi-tiered applications are difficult to write because they involve complex programming for handling transaction management, multithreading, database connection pooling, and other low-level details. The component-based and platform-independent J2EE architecture makes J2EE applications desirable and easier to develop because business logic is organized into reusable components, and the J2EE server provides underlying services in the form of a container for every component type.

Containers and Services

Components are installed in their containers during deployment. Containers are the interface between a component and the platform-specific functionality supporting that component. Before a web component can be executed, it must first be assembled into a J2EE application and then deployed into its container.

The process of assembly involves specifying container settings for each component within the J2EE application as well as for the application itself. These settings customize the underlying support provided by the J2EE server, including services such as security, transaction management, Java Naming and Directory Interface (JNDI) lookups, and remote connectivity. Following are some examples:

- The J2EE security model allows configuration of a web component or enterprise bean so that only authorized users can access system resources.

- The J2EE transaction model provides for relationships among methods that make up a single transaction; therefore, all methods in one transaction are treated as a single unit of work.

- JNDI lookup services provide an interface to multiple naming and directory services in the enterprise, allowing application components to access naming and directory services.

The J2EE remote connectivity model manages the communication between clients and enterprise beans. After an enterprise bean is created, methods are invoked on it by the client as if it were in the same virtual machine.

Because the J2EE architecture provides configurable services, application components within the same J2EE application can behave differently based on where they are deployed. For instance, an enterprise bean can have security settings, allowing it a certain level of access to database data in one production environment and a different level of database access in another production environment.

Containers also manage services such as enterprise bean and servlet lifecycles, database connection resource pooling, data persistence, and access to the J2EE platform APIs. Although data persistence is a nonconfigurable service, the J2EE architecture allows you to include code in your enterprise bean implementation to override container-managed persistence (CMP) when more control is desired than the default provided by CMP. For example, bean-managed persistence (BMP) may be used to implement your own finder methods or to create a customized database cache.

Container Types

The deployment process installs J2EE application components in the J2EE containers, as shown in Figure 4-5. An EJB container manages the execution of all enterprise beans for a single J2EE application. Enterprise beans and their accompanying containers run on the J2EE server. A web container manages the execution of all JSP and servlet components for a single J2EE application. Web components and their accompanying containers run on the J2EE server. An application client container manages the execution of all application client components for a single J2EE application. Application clients and their accompanying containers run on the client machine. An applet container is the web browser and Java plug-in combination that runs on the client machine.

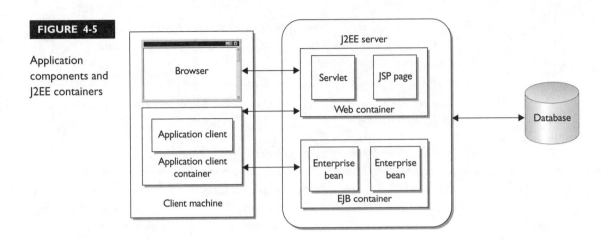

FIGURE 4-5

Application components and J2EE containers

EXERCISE 4-1

J2EE Architecture and the Nonfunctional Requirements of a System

Question   Describe how J2EE architecture affects the nonfunctional requirements of a system.

Answer   The success of a software development project is dependent on many factors in addition to software functionality. It is important that you differentiate between functional and nonfunctional requirements. Nonfunctional requirements include the environment, platforms, tools, and networking components within which an application is implemented; they include quality-related issues such as scalability, speed of execution and response time, ease of installation, maintainability, and reliability. These nonfunctional requirements affect the capabilities of the functional requirements.

The J2EE architect actively needs to account for all requirements, functional and nonfunctional, and needs to include all aspects of the project, including the packaging, installation, deployment, and maintenance of a software solution. Architects are often tasked with providing infrastructure design and layout for applications based on J2EE technology. The J2EE infrastructure provided by compliant and certified application servers typically offers techniques that meet nonfunctional requirements such as scalability, compatibility, and so on.

Nonfunctional requirements are specific. The ability to support a specified number of concurrent users, expected transaction throughput, maximum allowable response time, supported data growth rate, and acceptable end-to-end latency are important nonfunctional requirements that must be satisfied if the application is to be successful.

These J2EE application server solutions have evolved to a point wherein nonfunctional requirements are addressed by built-in feature sets from these application infrastructure services. This allows application developers to focus their efforts on building functionality or business services. These applications use basic J2EE services that are already built into servers sold by multiple vendors. For example, multithreading, concurrency handling, connection pooling, state/session synchronization, container-managed transactions, and persistence are feature sets of the application servers that address the nonfunctional requirements.

The nonfunctional requirements supported by J2EE are divided into six categories:

- **Scalability**   Concurrent connections, data growth rates, user-population growth rates, storage capacity, compute capacity, performance characteristics, and response-time requirements can be solved by connection pooling and application server clustering.

- **Security**   Application-level security is handled by J2EE via deployment descriptors, protection domains as well as network security, OS security, and database security.

- **Adaptability**   Extensibility of the application; flexibility of the configuration; adaptive nature of the compute, storage, and network resources to changing demands from the application and application infrastructure are supported by J2EE.

- **Compatibility**   J2EE provides multi-platform support (all UNIX, Win NT, Win XP), cross-certification of application infrastructure solutions, multiple client devices, and back-end connectivity to legacy resources.

- **Manageability**   Change management, problem management, asset management, and network/systems management.

- **Availability**   Platform reliability, application infrastructure stability, and uptime requirements.

Development Methodology and Process

A J2EE application is usually assembled from two different types of modules: enterprise beans and web components. Both of these modules are reusable; therefore, new applications can be built from preexisting enterprise beans and components. The modules are also portable, so the application that comprises them will be able to run on any J2EE server conforming to the specifications. To build these modules, you will first need to consider designing the application using a modeling tool before using a development tool to implement code. The remainder of this section will take a look at each of these areas before moving into a discussion of what makes up a J2EE application and the development phases of a J2EE project.

Modeling Tools

Modeling is the visual process used for constructing and documenting the design and structure of an application. The model is an outline of the application, showing the interdependencies and relationships among the components and subsystems. Tools are available to facilitate this process, allowing you to show a high-level view of many objects. The Unified Modeling Language (UML) was created to unify the many proprietary and incompatible modeling languages that existed.

The use of modeling tools makes sense with the increasing complexity of Enterprise Java applications and components. However, learning to model comes from experience and from sharing knowledge about best practices and bad practices. Today, modeling involves the use and reuse of patterns. A *pattern* is commonly defined as a three-part rule that expresses a relationship between a certain context, a problem, and a solution. In other words, a pattern can represent a solution to a recurring problem or issue.

Development Tools

To be productive with technology such as J2EE, analysts and programmers will inevitably need visual development tools for building J2EE applications and components. When constructing a J2EE application, a developer must not only create Java code, but also build an archive file to house the classes and other supporting files, including XML deployment descriptors and reference resolutions. This archive must then be deployed to a server and tested. These sets of tasks will be repeated several times over before the application is finally ready to be deployed to a production environment. All of these tasks typically need to be coordinated among multiple developers. The tools available at this time are still maturing, and tool vendors frequently release newer versions of tools to ease the development process.

In addition to the tools themselves, application *frameworks* provide components and services based on the best patterns, practices, and standards available. The ideal framework would implement extendable design patterns on the presentation, business, and data/services layers. These implementations should work for any J2EE-certified server.

The use of a framework or "best practice" may be helpful in preparing for and completing Part 2 of the SCEA exam. The following frameworks and guidelines are a nonexhaustive sample of what is available:

- **realMethods framework**   Supports all of the major J2EE technologies, on all tiers (web, EJB, and data access). See *http://www.realmethods.com/* for more information.

- **Struts framework**   An implementation of the Model View Controller (MVC) pattern. This framework can be used when developing web components consisting of JSPs and servlets. See *http://jakarta.apache.org* for more information.

- **Sun's J2EE BluePrints (Pet Store)**   A set of "best practice" guidelines for developing J2EE applications. Along with the guidelines is a practical implementation of them, known as the Pet Store application. This application is the classic web shopping cart for buying a pet. This application is a good one to study and know before taking Part 2 of the exam, as it can provide some good working J2EE code examples.

Contents of a J2EE Application

The hierarchy of a J2EE application is shown in Figure 4-6. A J2EE application may contain any number of enterprise beans, web components, and J2EE application clients. The deployment descriptor in Figure 4-6 refers to a file that defines structural information such as class names, location, and other attributes to facilitate the deployment of the web or enterprise application.

Enterprise beans comprise three class files: the EJB class, the remote interface, and the home interface. Web components may contain files such as servlet classes, JSPs, HTML files, and GIFs. A J2EE application client is a Java application, typically Java classes that providing a user interface that runs in a container, and is allowed access to J2EE services.

Each J2EE application, web component, and enterprise bean includes an XML file called a deployment descriptor (DD) that describes the component. An EJB DD has functions to declare transaction attributes and security authorizations for an enterprise bean. This information is declarative; it can be changed without subsequent modification

FIGURE 4-6

Contents of a
J2EE application

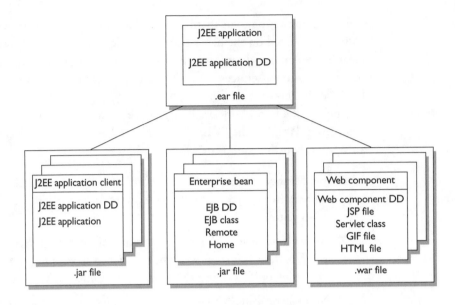

to the bean's source code. The J2EE server reads this information at runtime, acting upon the bean accordingly. Each module is bundled into a file with a particular format, as seen in Table 4-1.

As the EISs repaired before the year 2000 refuse to go away, implementations that utilize user developed or vendor-based APIs to access these systems with J2EE are growing in popularity. To facilitate these APIs, a resource adapter is a J2EE component that implements the J2EE connector architecture for a specific EIS. It is through the resource adapter that a J2EE application communicates with an EIS. Stored in a Resource Adapter Archive (RAR) file, a resource adapter may be deployed on any J2EE server, much like the EAR file of a J2EE application.

Development Phases of J2EE Applications

J2EE applications pass through the following developmental phases:

- Enterprise bean creation
- Web component creation
- Application assembly
- Application deployment

In larger organizations, separate individuals or teams may perform each of these phases. This division of labor is made more feasible by the creation of a portable file

TABLE 4-1   Files Used in J2EE Applications

File Content	File Extension
J2EE Enterprise Application	.ear
J2EE application deployment descriptor	.xml
Enterprise JavaBeans	.jar
EJB deployment descriptor	.xml
EJB class	.class
Remote interface	.class
Home interface	.class
Web application component	.war
Web component deployment descriptor	.xml
JSP file	.jsp
Resource Adapter Archive file	.rar
Servlet class	.class
Image files	.gif and .jpg
HTML file	.html
J2EE application client	.jar
J2EE application client deployment descriptor	.xml
Java class	.class

output by each phase. This file contains the input for the subsequent phase. In the optional enterprise bean creation phase, for example, a developer delivers EJB JAR files. In the web component creation phase, for example, a developer delivers web components in a WAR file. These phases are not sequential, but the assembly and deployment phases are sequential and required. During the application assembly phase, another developer combines these files into a J2EE application, saving it in an EAR file. Ultimately, a system administrator uses that EAR file to install the J2EE application into an application server at deployment time. These final stages are illustrated in Figure 4-7.

Java and XML are a natural match for the creation of applications that exploit the web of information, where different classes of clients consume and generate

FIGURE 4-7 Development phases of a J2EE application

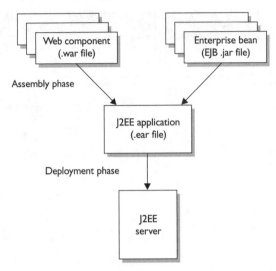

information that is exchanged between servers that run on various system platforms. The portability and extensibility of both XML and Java make them the ideal choices for the flexibility and wide availability requirements of the web. The following

How Does XML Fit into the J2EE Environment?

XML is the preferred technology in many information-transfer scenarios because of its ability to encode information in a way that is easy to read, process, and generate. Java is an ideal companion to XML: both languages share a similar historical background (C++, SGML); both have goals of simplicity, portability, and flexibility; and both continue to be developed in groups that involve industry, development community, and academia (W3C, JCP). Not surprisingly, Java is the overwhelmingly preferred language for server and client-side XML application development.

The Java software platform has a comprehensive collection of core APIs specifically targeted at building XML-based applications:

- Java API for XML Processing (JAXP)

- Java Architecture for XML Binding (JAXB)

- Java API for XML Messaging (JAXM)

- Java API for XML RPC (JAX RPC)

- Java API for XML Registry (JAXR)

sections summarize the development phases for J2EE applications. Because a J2EE application does not necessarily need both enterprise beans and web components, one of the first two phases is often skipped; all other phases are required.

Enterprise Bean Creation   Enterprise bean creation is performed by software developers, who are responsible for coding and compiling the Java source code needed by the enterprise bean, specifying the deployment descriptor for the enterprise bean, and bundling the .class files and deployment descriptor into an EJB JAR file. That EJB JAR file is subsequently delivered to facilitate the next step. See Chapter 7 for more information.

Web Component Creation   Web component creation can be performed by web designers, who create the JSP components, along with software developers, who are responsible for the servlets. Java source code for the servlet is coded and compiled, JSP and HTML files are written, the deployment descriptor for the web component is specified, and the .class, JSP, HTML, and deployment descriptor files are bundled into the WAR file. That WAR file is delivered to facilitate the next step.

J2EE Application Assembly   The application assembler is the person who takes an EJB archive file (EJB JAR) and a web components archive file (WAR) and assembles them into a J2EE Enterprise Archive, or EAR, file. The next step is to resolve any references, which include the following:

- Database connection pools
- Mail sessions
- URL connections
- JMS queues and topics
- EJB references

This process is handled by defining elements in one or more additional XML documents, also known as deployment descriptors or deployment plans. The assemblers or deployers can edit the deployment properties directly or use tools that add these XML tags. These additional files map internal references along with server-specific properties to JNDI or other names that exist in the destination J2EE application server. The application assemblers perform the following tasks to deliver an EAR file containing the J2EE application.

- Assemble EJB JAR and web components (WAR) files created in the previous phases into a J2EE application (EAR) file.
- Specify the deployment descriptor for the J2EE application.
- Verify that the contents of the EAR file are well formed and comply with the J2EE specification.
- The final deliverable for this stage is the completed EAR file containing the J2EE enterprise application.

J2EE Application Deployment The deployer is the person who configures and deploys the J2EE application, administers the computing and networking infrastructure where J2EE applications run, and oversees the runtime environment. Duties include setting security attributes, setting transaction controls, and specifying database connection pools. During configuration, the deployer follows instructions supplied by the application component provider to resolve external dependencies, specify security settings, and assign transaction attributes. During installation, the deployer is responsible for moving the components to the server and generating the classes and interfaces specific to the destination container.

The deployer performs the following tasks to install and configure a J2EE application:

- Stage the initial J2EE application (EAR) file created in the preceding phase to the J2EE server.
- Configure the J2EE application for the operational environment by modifying the DD of the J2EE application.
- Verify that the contents of the EAR file are well formed and comply with the J2EE specification.
- Deploy (install) the J2EE application EAR file into the J2EE server.

CERTIFICATION OBJECTIVE 4.02

Explain the Use of Patterns in the J2EE Framework

In the context of computer architecture, design patterns are proven solutions to recurring business problems. They consider the particular context of the problem and the consequences of the solution. A good designer will use a pattern because it is proven—that is, the designer has used it before successfully or has built and validated a proof of concept. Good architects use the experience, knowledge, and insights of developers who have used these patterns successfully in their own work. When a problem is common, a good designer doesn't have to devise a new solution; instead, he or she follows the pattern and adapts it to the current environment.

Use of Patterns in the J2EE Framework

The J2EE framework employs patterns to support these capabilities. J2EE uses the following core patterns to enable flexible association of EJB classes with other components. The Proxy pattern provides a separate implementation of interface and working code for location transparency. The Decorator provides a similar contract for a class but with added functionality. The Factory Method provides ability to define a contract for creating an object but defers instantiation to subclasses. The Abstract Factory provides a contract for creating families of related or dependent objects without specifying concrete classes. Table 4-2 details the patterns used with the J2EE framework.

TABLE 4-2   Patterns Used with the J2EE Framework

Pattern	Use	J2EE Implementation
Proxy	Provides method calls to a principal object to occur indirectly through a proxy object that acts as an agent for the principal object, delegating method calls to that object	EJB remote interface
Decorator	Extends the functionality of a class such that it is transparent to its clients	EJBObject
Factory Method	Provides a reusable class independent of the classes it instantiates because it delegates the choice of which class to instantiate to another object; refers to the newly created object via a common interface	EJB home interface
Abstract Factory	Provides a way to create instances of those abstract classes from a corresponding set of concrete subclasses	EJB home interface

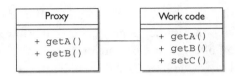

The Proxy Pattern

The Proxy pattern (as shown in Figure 4-8) decouples interface and implementation by providing two objects. If the implementation class changes, the proxy remains the same. This is because the proxy interface includes only the method invocations and their signatures. So it is lightweight in comparison to the implementation class (the working code). As architects, we typically examine what types of operations are expensive. For example, object creation and initialization is usually expensive. To improve application performance, it is a sound approach to defer object creation and object initialization to the time when you need the object. The Proxy pattern reduces the cost of accessing objects. It accomplishes this cost reduction because it uses another object (the proxy) to act as a stand-in for the real object. The proxy creates the implementation object only if the user requests it. An example of the proxy pattern implemented in J2EE is the EJB remote interface.

Decorator Pattern

The Decorator pattern provides the same contract for a class but with extended functionality. The pattern is used when functionality needs to be added to objects dynamically. The solution involves encapsulating the original object inside an abstract wrapper interface. Both the decorator objects and the base object inherit from this abstract interface. The interface is generic such that it allows a theoretically unlimited number of decorative layers to be added to each base object. Decorators would seem to be especially useful when you wish to add functionality when you do not have the actual code source of the class. If you know enough about the object—that is, the interface—when you want to decorate you can provide a decoration for it.

It is important to note that the decorator is a subclass of the component class that it decorates. This is counterintuitive because the instance is a parent of the component it decorates. Decorators share the "wrapper" approach. The difference, however, is intent. The decorator has value only if it changes the behavior of the "wrapee." The EJBObject is a decorator for the bean because the bean's functionality is expanded to include remote behavior.

FIGURE 4-9   Factory Method

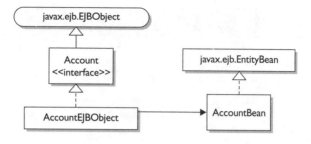

Factory Method Pattern

The Factory Method pattern (as shown in Figure 4-9) provides the ability to define an interface for creating an object but defers instantiation to subclasses. J2EE technology uses this pattern for the EJB home interface, which creates new EJB objects. (For information, consult the book *Design Patterns: Elements of Reusable Object-Oriented Software* by Erich Gamma, Richard Helm, Ralph Johnson, and John Vlissides.)

Abstract Factory Pattern

The Abstract Factory pattern provides an interface for creating families of related or dependent objects without specifying concrete classes. J2EE technology uses this pattern for the EJB home interface, which creates new EJB objects.

EXERCISE 4-2

Patterns in the J2EE Framework and Development

Question   Describe the use of patterns in the J2EE framework and development.

Answer   A pattern is a recurring solution to a problem in a context. A *context* is the environment, surroundings, situation, or interrelated conditions within which something exists. A *problem* is an unsettled question, something that needs to be investigated and solved. A problem can be specified by a set of causes and effects. Typically, the problem is constrained by the context in which it occurs. Finally, the *solution* refers to the answer to the problem in a context that helps resolve the issues.

TABLE 4-3	Framework Patterns	

Pattern Name	Description	J2EE Implementation
Proxy	Provides method calls to a principal object to occur indirectly through a proxy object that acts as a agent for the principal object, delegating method calls to that object	EJB remote interface
Decorator	Extends the functionality of a class such that it's transparent to its clients	EJBObject
Factory Method	Provides a reusable class independent of the classes it instantiates, because it delegates the choice of which class to instantiate to another object; refers to the newly created object via common interface	EJB home interface
Abstract Factory	Provides a way to create instances of those abstract classes from a corresponding set of concrete subclasses	EJB home interface

In addition to the framework patterns used by J2EE, patterns are used in development and they are typically listed according to functionality. The presentation tier patterns contain the patterns related to servlets and JSP technology. The business tier patterns contain the patterns related to the enterprise beans technology. The integration tier patterns contain the patterns related to JMS and JDBC. Tables 4-3, 4-4, 4-5, and 4-6 contain partial lists of applicable patterns along with descriptions to provide a high-level overview of the patterns. The presentation tier patterns, business tier patterns, and integration tier patterns will all be discussed in detail in later chapters.

TABLE 4-4	Presentation Tier Patterns

Pattern Name	Description
Decorating Filter	Facilitates pre- and post-processing of a request
Front Controller	Provides a centralized controller for managing the handling of a request
View Helper	Encapsulates logic that is not related to presentation formatting into Helper components
Composite View	Creates an aggregate View from atomic subcomponents
Service To Worker	Combines a Dispatcher component in coordination with the Front Controller and View Helper Patterns
Dispatcher View	Combines a Dispatcher component in coordination with the Front Controller and View Helper Patterns, deferring many activities to View processing

TABLE 4-5   Business Tier Patterns

Pattern Name	Description
Business Delegate	Decouples presentation and service tiers and provides a facade and proxy interface to the services
Value Object	Exchanges data between tiers
Session Facade	Hides business object complexity, and centralizes workflow handling
Aggregate Entity	Represents a best practice for designing coarse-grained entity beans
Value Object Assembler	Builds composite value object from multiple data sources
Value List Handler	Manages query execution, results caching, and result processing
Service Locator	Hides complexity of business service lookup and creation; locates business service factories

TABLE 4-6   Integration Tier Patterns

Pattern Name	Description
Data Access Object	Abstracts data sources; provides transparent access to data
Service Activator	Facilitates asynchronous processing for EJB components

CERTIFICATION OBJECTIVE 4.03

Describe the Concepts of "Best Practices" and "Guidelines"

Successful companies establish the use of refactoring, best practices, patterns, and tools; they spread the awareness of these among their J2EE programmers and architects. Successful developers share their knowledge and pass on their proven techniques to others. The net result is productivity. The ultimate product is the implementation of solid applications.

The challenges we face in software development today as always are twofold:

- Obtaining and maintaining the architectural and developmental skills to build effective enterprise systems
- Meeting market-driven timelines for developing new applications while maintaining quality in our implementations

Experienced architects often make tradeoffs to meet deadlines. These tradeoffs include the use of refactoring and other techniques to optimize development time and address the inherent performance considerations. We tend to hold onto our software designs for too long. Even after they become unwieldy, we continue to use and reuse code that is no longer maintainable—because it works, we are afraid to modify it. But this is typically not cost effective. When we refactor, we remove redundancy, eliminate unused functionality, and reengineer designs. Refactoring throughout the entire project lifecycle saves time and increases quality. Refactoring keeps the design simple, and avoids needless complexity, keeps code clean and concise, and makes it easier to understand, modify, and extend the code. Moreover, application behavior is known to change throughout the application lifecycle—that is, from development to production. As performance and stability issues are discovered, the application should be amended and improved.

Experience yields blueprints for solving recurring problems: therefore, the term *best practice*. A best practice is a technique used to drive design at the component level. For example, a best practice might be to use session beans as facades to entity beans. On the other hand, a *guideline* is a rule applied horizontally to the design. For example, to minimize network traffic, the architect attempts to maximize the content of data requests—that is, we try to get as much as we can out of each request.

As mentioned, the J2EE architecture typically consists of three basic tiers in the platform, as shown in Figure 4-10. With respect to each tier, we will introduce and review some the best practices.

Identifying the Need for Best Practices

In development, the question should not be "Is there a best practice?" Instead, it should be "Will this best practice improve our application?" For example, caching of frequently used data and references will benefit any J2EE application; however, determining what is *frequently used* can be difficult in development. By testing early releases of an application, developers can locate and correct inappropriate design decisions.

FIGURE 4-10   J2EE tiers

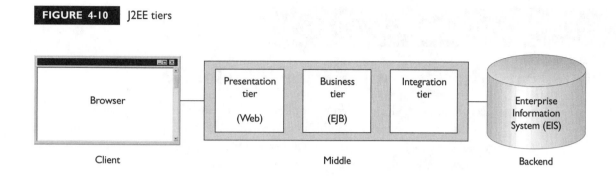

In the quality assurance (QA) stage of an application lifecycle, it is often assumed that best practices and appropriate patterns have already been applied. The typical QA team is unlikely to have the expertise needed to identify the need for best practices. If the application is deemed to perform poorly or fail, it will have to be amended by the development team at a great expense. It is therefore extremely important to determine the application hotspots and suggest the primary candidates for reworking.

In the enterprise production environment, applying new design patterns and best practices to a production system is more than difficult—both technically and politically. It can, however, be essential to creating a mature and ultimately successful application. Interrupting service to clients to redeploy a production application will commonly happen if the application fails or is unusable. What the good architect has is the uncommon ability to identify when performance is under par and justify expending additional resources to refactor by specifying the nature of the problem.

You can apply best practices and guidelines in each tier, including the client tier, web tier (presentation), EJB tier (business logic), and database or EIS integration tier (integration). You can also apply refactoring and guidelines to orthogonal services that span tiers including security and transaction processing.

Best Practice—Client Tier

The Client tier serves as an interface with any number of other systems. A transaction enters the workflow, for example, as an HTML request from a standard web browser or as an XML-formatted electronic message from another system. You should decouple the client type from the enterprise application by using HTML browser, applet, a Java application, and, last and but certainly not least, a non-Java application.

CERTIFICATION OBJECTIVE 4.04

Illustrate the Use of J2EE for Workflow

A common method for designing applications is to organize them around an event-driven user interface. In this design pattern, the developer creates the interface and subsequently writes code that will execute the desired application actions in response to user gestures. This structure can be successful for small, single-user systems that will require little alteration to the functionality over time. However, it is not suitable for larger, distributed projects for the following reasons:

- More sophisticated applications may require data to be viewed and manipulated in several different ways. When business logic is implemented in the display code, display inconsistencies can result because the logic can be copied and modified in one object and not another. In addition, any change to the data display requires updates in several places.

- When data manipulation logic, format and display code, and user event handling are entangled, application maintenance can be very difficult, especially over a long span of time.

- User interfaces cannot be reused if the application logic has been combined with the code for an existing interface.

- Added functionality may require several changes to existent code, which may be difficult to locate.

- Business logic code may access a vendor-specific product (a database, for example), thus making the application much less portable.

- Changes to a single piece of code may have far-reaching side effects.

- Development cannot occur on a modular basis, as everything is dependent on everything else. This problem is amplified on large-scale development projects because it is difficult for a large team of developers to split tasks.

- Code is less reusable, because components are dependent on one another; therefore, they are less usable in other contexts.

To overcome these shortcomings, utilizing the MVC design pattern best practice results in a separation of the application data from the ways that the data can be accessed or viewed as well as from the mapping between system events (such as user interface events) and application behaviors.

Best Practice—MVC Pattern

The MVC pattern consists of three component types:

- **Model** Represents the application data along with methods that operate on that data.
- **View** Displays that data to the user.
- **Controller** Translates user actions such as mouse movement and keyboard input and dispatches operations on the Model.

As a result, the Model will update the View to reflect changes to the data. Figure 4-11 illustrates the functions of each of these component types as well as the relationships among them.

When this best practice is used properly, the Model should have no involvement in translating the format of input data. This translation should be performed by the Controller. In addition, the Model should not carry any responsibility for determining how the results should be displayed.

Table 4-7 displays the participants and collaborations involved with the three components.

The MVC model should be used as follows:

- For distributed applications
- For larger applications
- For applications with a long lifetime
- Where interface and back-end portability are important
- Where data must be viewed and manipulated in multiple ways

FIGURE 4-11

Relationships among components

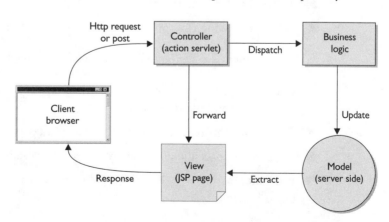

TABLE 4-7	MVC Participants and Collaborations

Component	Participants	Collaborations
Model	Extrapolates the business logic of the application Maintains the application state Provides access to functions of the application Manages persistence Extracts data for the View component Informs interested parties of changes to data	Informs the View when it makes changes to the application data Can be queried by the View Gives the Controller access to application functionality
View	Extrapolates data presentation Responds to users with data Maintains consistency with Model data	Provides Model data for the user Refreshes display when informed of data changes by the Model Transfers user input to the Controller
Controller	Extrapolates user interaction/application semantic map Transforms user actions into application actions Determines the appropriate data display based on user input and context	Transforms user inputs and dispatches class logic or application actions on the Model Selects the View to present based on user input and Model action outcomes

- To facilitate maintenance

- To support simultaneous, modular development by multiple developers

- To allow division of labor by skill set

- To facilitate unit testing

- When employing enterprise beans that are reusable across applications

MVC offers the following benefits:

- Clarifies application design through separation of data modeling issues from data display and user interaction

- Allows the same data to be viewed in many ways and by many users

- Simplifies impact analysis, thereby improving extensibility

- Facilitates maintenance by encapsulating application functions behind trusted APIs

■ Enhances reusability by separating application functionality from presentation

■ Facilitates distribution of the application, as MVC boundaries are natural distribution interface points

■ Can be used to divide deployment as well as make incremental updates possible

■ Forces clear designation of responsibilities and functional consistency, thereby facilitating testability

■ Increases flexibility, because data model, user interaction, and data display can be made "pluggable"

MVC designs may encounter the following problems:

■ *Components aren't able to take advantage of knowledge of other components' implementation details.* This may have a negative effect on application performance. Skillful API design that optimizes the length of the code path (number of machine cycles) for each API function can assist in avoiding this problem to some extent.

■ *Communication volume and other latency issues must be carefully addressed; otherwise, MVC may not scale well in distributed systems.* Latency comes from several sources. Web application servers may take some time to process a request, especially if they are overloaded and model components are not local. Web clients can add delay if they do not efficiently handle the retrieved data and display it for the user. Latency caused by client or sluggish servers, however, can in principle be solved simply by providing a faster server or clustering.

■ *Maintenance of an MVC application may be difficult if the Model API is unstable, because the Controller is written in terms of the Model API.* There should be a decoupling between the sender and the receiver. A sender is an object that invokes an operation, and a receiver is an object that receives the request to execute a certain operation. The term *request* here refers to the command that is to be executed. This also allows us to vary when and how a request is fulfilled. This decoupling provides us with flexibility as well as extensibility. The command pattern turns the request into an object that can be stored and passed around in the same way as other objects. This provides a hook for Controller extensions to handle new Model functions. In addition, an adapter can often provide backward API compatibility.

MVC and the Struts Framework

The Struts framework has been developed by the Jakarta Project, which is sponsored by the Apache Software Foundation, to provide an open-source framework for building web applications with Java Servlet and JavaServer Pages (JSP) technology. Struts supports application architectures based on the MVC design paradigm. The official Struts home page can be found at *http://jakarta.apache.org/struts.*

The primary areas of functionality included in Struts are

- **A controller servlet**   Dispatches requests to appropriate Action classes provided by the application developer
- **JSP custom tag libraries**   Facilitate creation of interactive, form-based applications
- **Utility classes**   Provide support for XML parsing, automatic population of JavaBeans properties, and internationalizing prompts and messages

Struts applications adhere to the MVC design pattern. The three major components are the servlet Controller, JavaServer Pages (the View), and the application's business logic (the Model), as shown in Figure 4-12.

The following text describes the process illustrated in Figure 4-12.

First, the user request goes to a Controller that initializes the context/session for the overall transaction and alerts Page A's Model. The Controller then forwards execution to Page A's View (JSP).

Page A posts back to the Controller, which calls Model A to validate the posted form data. If the input is invalid, Model A returns a result that the Controller uses to forward/redisplay Page A. The entire *HttpServletRequest* might be made available to the Model A bean, or the Controller might be clever enough to call setters for each posted form field via introspection.

The Controller determines who is next in the chain through use of a multitude of options: straight if-else (or switch-case) code, an XML document, database records, or a rules engine.

The Controller is the centralized "traffic cop" that knows when all required steps in a transaction are complete. The Model preserves the "state" (posted form fields) and holds validation logic. If the user action is invalid, the Controller is alerted to redisplay the same View/JSP.

The Controller bundles and directs HTTP requests to other objects in the framework, including JSP. After it has been initialized, the Controller parses a

FIGURE 4-12 Simple MVC/Struts example flow

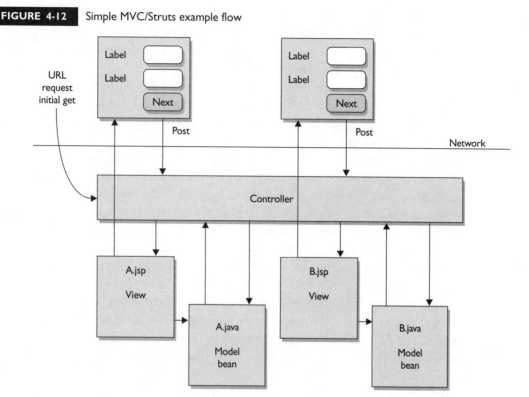

configuration resource file. This resource file defines the action mappings for the application. These mappings are used by the Controller, turning HTTP requests into application actions.

At the very least, a mapping must specify a request path as well as what object type is to act upon the request. The action object either handles the request and responds to the client (usually a web browser) or indicates that control should be forwarded to another action.

Because action objects are linked to the application's Controller, they have access to that servlet's methods. When an object is forwarding control, it can indirectly forward one or more shared objects, such as JavaBeans, by putting them in a standard collection shared by Java Servlets.

Most of the business logic in a Struts application can be represented using JavaBeans. In addition, JavaBeans can be used to manage input forms, eliminating the common problem with retaining and validating user input between requests. Using Struts, data can be stored in a form bean. The bean can then be saved in a shared context collection, making it accessible to other objects, especially action objects. It could be used by a JSP to collect data, by an action object to validate user input, and then by the JSP again to repopulate the form fields.

In the case of validation errors, Struts has a shared mechanism for raising and displaying error messages. Struts form beans are defined in the configuration resource and then linked to an action mapping via a common property name. When a request calls for an action that utilizes a form bean, the controller servlet will either retrieve the form bean or create one. That form bean is passed to the action object. The action object checks the contents of the form bean before its input form is displayed, queuing messages that are to be handled by the form. When the action object is ready, it can return control by forwarding to its input form, which is usually a JSP. The controller is then able to respond to the HTTP request, directing the client to the JSP.

Custom tags are included within the Struts framework. They have the ability to automatically populate fields from a form bean. Most JSPs must know only the proper field names and where to submit the form. Components such as messages set by the action object can be output using a single custom tag. Application-specific tags can be defined to hide implementation details from the JSP pages.

These custom tags are designed to use the Java platform internationalization features. All field labels and messages can be retrieved from a message resource, with Java automatically providing correct resources for the client's country and language. Providing messages for another language requires only the addition of another resource file.

Other benefits of custom tags are consistent labeling between forms and the ability to review all labels and messages from a central location.

In most applications, action objects should pass requests to other objects, primarily JavaBeans. To enable reuse on other platforms, business logic JavaBeans should not refer to any web application objects. Action objects should translate required details from the HTTP request, passing those along to business-logic beans as regular Java variables.

In database applications, business-logic beans may connect to and query the database, returning the result set to the action's servlet, where it is stored in a form bean and then displayed by the JSP.

The Model

The Model in an MVC-based application can be divided two parts: the internal state of the system and the actions that can be taken to alter that state.

A web application using the Struts framework typically represents the internal state of the system as a set of one or more JavaBeans with properties that represent the details of that state. These beans may be self-contained and able to save their state information persistently. Additionally, they may be facades that know how to retrieve information from external sources such as databases when that information is requested. Entity EJBs (Enterprise JavaBeans) can also be used to represent internal state.

Larger applications often represent possible business logic actions for a system as methods. Other systems may represent possible actions separately, often as Session EJBs. Smaller scale applications may embed the available actions within the Action classes that are part of the Controller role. This is effective only when the logic is simple and reuse is not an issue. It is a good idea always to separate the business logic from the roles of the Action classes.

The View

Struts-based applications generally utilize JSPs to construct the View component. The JSP environment includes a set of standard action tags such as `<jsp:useBean>` as well as the ability to define custom tags and organized custom tag libraries. In addition, it is sometimes necessary for business objects to render themselves in HTML or XML, based on their state at request time. It is easy to include the output from these objects in a resulting JSP page by using the `<jsp:include>` standard action tag.

The Controller

The Controller portion of the application focuses on receiving requests from the client (most often a user running a web browser), deciding what business logic function is to be performed, and delegating responsibility for producing the next phase of the user interface to an appropriate View component. Struts utilizes a servlet of class *ActionServlet* as the main component of the Controller. This servlet is configured through definition of a set of mappings that are described by a Java class *ActionMapping*. Each mapping defines a path, matched against the request URI of the incoming request as well as the fully qualified class name of an Action class. The Action class is responsible for performing the desired business logic and subsequently dispatching control to the appropriate View component to create the response.

In addition, Struts supports the ability to use *ActionMapping* classes with additional properties beyond the standard ones needed to operate the framework. This enables storage of additional application-specific information while utilizing the remaining features of the framework. Furthermore, Struts allows definition of logical names for the forwarding of the control. The method can ask for the logical name of the page without knowing the actual name of the corresponding JSP page.

EXERCISE 4-3

Structuring Development

Question   When building a J2EE application within an enterprise where valuable legacy systems exist and Java with J2EE is growing in use but not the strong suite in the skill set of the current majority of the enterprise developers, how can you structure the development to maximize productivity?

Answer   Productivity with a new technology can generally be achieved by striving for the following goals:

- **Code and design reuse**   Maximize code reuse so as to decrease the cost for development, provide incremental quality improvements, and establish design best practices that everyone in the organization understands.

- **Rational functional decomposition**   Every class in the design should play a clearly defined role in the application. The resulting design clarity will facilitate maintenance, impact analysis and system extension, and flatten the learning curve for new developers.

- **Development tasks isolated by skill sets**   The design should partition the application into chunks that reflect the skill sets of subteams in the development group. For example, the design specifies using JSP tag libraries, instead of JSP pages with embedded code, and then web page designers with no knowledge of programming can operate in parallel with programmers, and programmers can focus on solving coding problems.

- **Decouple classes with differing rates of change**   Design such that parts of the application that change quickly will require both ease of change and looser coupling to the rest of the system. Subsystems that change more slowly can be more tightly coupled, providing efficiency opportunities.

- **Extensibility**   The application functionality must be able to keep up with organizational growth and technological change.

- **Modularity**   We should break the design into modules that interact through well-defined interfaces, thereby allowing the developer to work independently, enhance maintainability and testability, and provide opportunities for using purchased components and outsourcing some development.

■ **Security** Data security enforcement is crucial, especially if the application is performing financial transactions, for the privacy and security of customers.

■ **Common look-and-feel** The application GUI should be designed such that the user can always intuitively know where to look for desired information.

■ **Minimize network traffic** The application should avoid transmitting data needlessly or redundantly.

■ **Allow for multiple user interfaces** The data should be represented in a way most appropriate for the task at hand. New types of user interfaces should be easy to add.

■ **Persistent data must always be consistent** The design should fulfill the goal by using the MVC design pattern to separate form, function, and data; by dividing the application into functional modules and multiple tiers; and by applying several design patterns, which are common problem solutions that have been found to work well in the past. The existing legacy systems can be accessed via the J2EE components by using the Proxy, Adapter, or Facade patterns to "wrap" legacy systems with Java-based APIs such as JNI (Java Native Interface) so that legacy developers can continue their work and J2EE developers can interface with the technology, obviating the need to rebuild the legacy functionality in J2EE. The legacy systems are given a new life as they are now J2EE-enabled.

EXERCISE 4-4

Defining Best Practice and Guideline

Question Define the concepts of *best practice* and *guideline*.

Answer A best practice is a technique used to drive design at the component level. A best practice is an optimal process that is recognized by peers in similar situations. It is applicable to a cross-section of scenarios with varying resources and sizes. It takes design requirements into consideration. For example, a best practice might be to use session beans as facades to entity beans.

On the other hand, a guideline is a rule applied horizontally to the design. Guidelines reflect agreements on practices or operations by recognized professional associations. This includes formal, approved standards, as contrasted to de facto standards and proprietary standards that are exceptions to this concept. For example, to minimize network traffic, the architect attempts to maximize the content of a data requests—that is, we try to get as much as we can out of each request.

Review Best Practices Applicable for All Tiers

The MVC best practice is a design pattern that can be applied across all tiers. The MVC architecture is a way to divide functionality among objects involved in maintaining and presenting data so as to minimize the degree of coupling between the objects. The MVC architecture was originally developed to map the traditional input, processing, and output tasks to the graphical user interaction model. However, it is straightforward to map these concepts into the domain of multi-tier web-based enterprise applications.

In the MVC architecture, the Model represents application data and the business rules that govern access and modification of this data. The Model can be represented in many ways, including but not limited to EJB's and JavaBeans. The Model notifies views when it changes and provides the ability for the View to query the Model about its state. It also provides the ability for the Controller to access application functionality encapsulated by the Model. View renders the contents of a Model. It is usually implemented as a JSP. It accesses data from the Model and specifies how that data should be presented. When the Model changes, it is the View's responsibility to maintain consistency in its presentation. The View forwards user gestures to the controller.

A Controller defines application behavior; it interprets user gestures and maps them into actions to be performed by the model. The servlet best fits this task. In a stand-alone GUI client, these user gestures could be button clicks or menu selections. In a web application, they appear as GET and POST HTTP requests to the web tier. The actions performed by the Model include activating business processes or changing the state of the Model. Based on the user gesture and the outcome of the Model commands, the Controller selects a View to be rendered as part of the response to this user request. Usually, one Controller exists for each set of related functionality.

The implementation of MVC pattern offers the following benefits:

- Clarifies application design through separation of data modeling (Model) issues from data display (View) and user interaction (Controller)

- Facilitates distribution of the application, as MVC boundaries are natural distribution interface points

CERTIFICATION OBJECTIVE 4.06

Review Best Practices for the Client Tier

Thin-client solutions (HTML on a browser) are important to Internet-based applications. The browser acts as your client for rendering the presentation as encoded in HTML.

In addition to that which can be rendered with static HTML, the following items can be used to create web content: JSPs, servlets, applets, and JavaScript can be used to enhance the browser interface.

CERTIFICATION OBJECTIVE 4.07

Enumerate the Components and Categories of the Web Tier

The web tier produces responses that can be handled by the use of *web component*, a software entity that provides a response to a request. A web component typically generates the user interface for a web-based application. The J2EE platform specifies two types of web components: servlets and JSP pages.

Web components are hosted by servlet containers, JSP containers, and web containers. In addition to standard container services, a *servlet container* provides network services by which requests and responses are sent, decodes requests, and formats responses. All servlet containers must support HTTP as a protocol for requests and responses, but they may also support additional request-response protocols such as HTTPS. A *JSP container* provides the same services as a servlet container and an engine that interprets and processes a JSP page into a servlet. A *web container* provides the same services as a JSP container and provides access to the J2EE service and communication APIs.

CERTIFICATION OBJECTIVE 4.08

Explain How to Apply MVC to the Web Tier

The MVC design pattern can be applied to the web tier because it results in a separation of the application data from the ways that the data can be accessed or viewed as well as from the mapping between system events (such as user-interface events) and application behaviors.

As mentioned, the MVC pattern consists of three component types. The Model represents the application data along with methods that operate on that data. The View component displays that data to the user. The Controller translates user actions such as mouse movement and keyboard input and dispatches operations on the Model. As a result, the Model will update the View to reflect changes to the data. The View consists of JSP amended with JavaScript and embedded tags that can provide the full function user interface. The Controller is usually a servlet and the Model can be a JavaBean or an EJB.

CERTIFICATION OBJECTIVE 4.09

Review the Best Practices for the Presentation Layer

To avoid needlessly complex presentation components in the web tier, follow these practices:

■ Separate HTML from Java.

- Try to place business logic in JavaBeans.

- Factor general behavior out of custom tag handler classes.

- Favor HTML in Java handler classes over Java in JSPs.

- Use an appropriate inclusion mechanism.

- Use a JSP template mechanism.

- Use stylesheets.

- Use the MVC pattern.

- Use available custom tag libraries.

- Determine the appropriate level of XML compliance.

- Use JSP comments in most cases.

- Follow HTML best practices.

- Utilize the JSP exception mechanism.

EXERCISE 4-5

Illustrate the Use of J2EE for Workflow

Question   In a web application, what type of component is usually used for the View and Controller elements of the MVC pattern? What type of component is usually used for the Model element?

Answer   Most applications implementing the MVC generally utilize JSPs to construct the View component. Most applications generally utilize a servlet as the main component of the Controller. An application typically represents the Model, which is the internal state of the system, as a set of one or more JavaBeans with properties that represent the details of that state. These beans may be self-contained, and they are able to save their state information persistently. Additionally, they may be facades that know how to retrieve information from external sources such as databases when that information is requested. Entity EJBs can also be used to represent internal state.

CERTIFICATION OBJECTIVE 4.10

Review the Internationalization and Localization

To operate in a global economy, J2EE information systems must address a number of additional requirements, including the following:

- **Language requirements** Users of a globally available application may speak different languages. The relationship between geographic region and language spoken is not simple. Representation of such quantities as numbers, dates, times, and currency vary by region.

- **Legal differences** Countries vary in customs law and information privacy requirements. Some governments place limitations on ideas, images, or speech.

- **Financial considerations** Currencies are not necessarily freely convertible. Forms of payment may differ; for example, not all customers can be assumed to have a credit card or purchase order number. Governments have different requirements for customs restrictions, tariffs, and taxes.

Internationalization terminology is commonly used inconsistently, even within the internationalization field. This section presents definitions of common internationalization terms as they are used in the rest of the chapter.

Internationalization, Localization, and Locale

The set of location-specific elements represented in an application is called a locale. To be effective, applications should customize data presentation to each user's locale. Internationalization is the process of separating locale dependencies from an application's source code. Interestingly, internationalization is also known as "I18n" because the first character is I, and between the first and last character there are 18 characters with a last character of *n*. Examples of locale dependencies include messages and user interface labels, character sets, encoding, and currency and time formats. Localization (also called "L10n") is the process of adapting an internationalized application to a specific locale. An application must first be internationalized before it can be localized. Internationalization and localization make a J2EE application available to a global audience.

An internationalized J2EE application does not assume the locale. If requests from clients arrive with an associated locale, then the response should be tailored for the locale. Internationalizing an existing application requires refactoring. Internationalization is fundamentally an architectural issue. Internationalization is facilitated if it is integrated into the application design. A project's design phase should identify and separate locale dependencies if the application might ever need to support multiple locales.

EXERCISE 4-6

Localization and Internalization

Question: Describe the use of *localization* and *internalization*.

Answer Internationalization, also known as *I18n*, is the process of separating locale dependencies from an application's source code. Examples of locale dependencies include messages and user interface labels, character sets, encoding, and currency and time formats. Localization, also called *L10n*, is the process of adapting an internationalized application to a specific locale. An application must first be internationalized before it can be localized. Internationalization and localization make a J2EE application available to a global audience.

The EJB Tier

The EJB tier hosts the application-specific business objects and the system-level services (such as transaction management, concurrency control, and security). The EJB tier is a critical link between the web tier and the EIS integration tier. It typically hosts the entity beans and session beans, data access objects and value objects, and perhaps master-detail modeling using enterprise beans.

J2EE Best Practices—Data Access Objects

Unfortunately, most systems in use today rely on specific features of the enterprise's standard system resources, such as a vendor DBMS; they merge business logic and data access mechanisms. The result is lack of portability. As these standard resources become obsolete, the application systems tied to a resource become a real chore to upgrade. A good architect wants to avoid tying an application's business logic components to a resource, so the architect upgrades to a system with the least amount of resistance.

The data-access object (DAO) pattern separates the interface to a system resource from the code used to access that resource by encapsulating the access to the data. Each enterprise bean that accesses a back-end resource in the application may have an associated DAO class, which defines an abstract API of operations on the resource. This allows a clean separation of bean and database access code. This also ensures easier migration to and from bean to container-managed persistence for entity beans and allows for cross-database and cross-schema capability. This abstract API makes no reference to how the resource is implemented. The DAO simply has to know how to operate from the persistent store based on some identity information such as a filename. For example, an enterprise bean uses data it obtains from the DAO, not directly from the database. In this way, the enterprise bean defers its persistence mechanism to the DAO, allowing it to concentrate entirely on implementing business methods.

J2EE Best Practices—Value Objects

Some enterprise information objects have values that are used together. For example, in a shopping cart application, the fields of the Address object are always used together. Using a complete remote interface for such entity beans is overkill and results in unacceptably high server communication.

The data for an Address object can be retrieved once, sent to the client from the server in serialized form, and instantiated on the client. From then on, the local copy of the Address information can serve as a proxy for the Address property of the remote Order object. Subsequent accesses to the Address object's state are local, require no server communication, and use fewer resources. If the Address object is updated and sent to the server to update the server-side object, the entire object is sent. Furthermore, local accesses obviously have lower latency than accesses deferred through a remote interface.

Such a client-side object is called a *Value Object*, because it represents a composite value from the server, not a reference to an object on the server. Value Objects tend to be more-or-less ad hoc groupings of data values to support a use case (or group of use cases).

Use Value Objects for business objects that represent structure with accessor get and set behavior only.

You should use a Value Object when the business entity being modeled has:

- Only methods that get values from the object's internal state (that is, immutable state)
- A lifecycle that is completely controlled by another object
- A relatively small size

Whenever you update a bean by passing it a Value Object, the code should inspect all attributes of the Value Object and update the corresponding model bean attributes with their values. It should also check whether the version number of the Value Object is different from the model bean's version number. If this is the case, it should throw an exception, which indicates that the bean has been updated by another client.

J2EE Best Practices—Session Bean Facade

The session bean facade (SBF), shown in Figure 4-13, provides a simple, single point of entry to shared entity beans. It shields the client from complex entity bean relationships. The most obvious rationale for using session beans to abstract entity beans is that the approach also abstracts the structure of your data stores. The presumption is that you do not want to expose the inner workings of your application's data store (such as the database tables and columns), or even the specifics of how that data is stored. In other words, letting users (potential hackers) know your database schema is a not a good idea. Problems can arise when you allow direct access to the entity bean layer.

The methods in entity beans typically map directly to underlying fields in the data schema. This will become more important as service-based computing increases. Instead of providing complete applications, the J2EE specification (or Web Services: UDDI, SOAP) indicates that organizations are focusing more on components than on complete applications. Interchanging data components from enterprise A's application with presentation components from enterprise B's application is becoming the standard. As a result, it is unsafe to assume that only your enterprise will be accessing your business layer and EJBs. For these reasons, a sound design of the business layer can save trouble when beans you worked on must be accessible by a new business partner.

By interjecting a layer of indirection in the form of a session bean, these problems were easily solved (as shown in Figure 4-13). The session beans become responsible for determining user permissions, providing greater flexibility and reuse. Session beans perform collections of calls to the entity beans on behalf of the remote clients,

FIGURE 4-13 Session bean facade

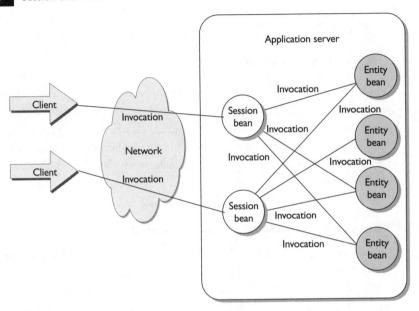

reducing network traffic. The transactional scope can be applied to methods that call groupings of entity beans, thus reducing the transactional overhead. Client tier code requirements are simplified as more business logic is executed on the server.

J2EE Best Practices—Master Detail

In a master-detail relationship, one object serves as a parent node to another. A master-detail relationship is a one-to-many type relationship. For example, if you receive an order and a set of items placed for each order, a master-detail relationship is created by having the order number as a common field between the two. An application can use this master-detail relationship to enable users to navigate through the order data and see the detailed item data for orders placed.

When modeling a master-detail relationship as enterprise beans, the guidelines for using entity or session beans still hold. The choice is not affected by the master-detail relationship. However, the relationship is relevant when designing the behavior of the master. For example, suppose the master object should be modeled as a session bean and the details object should be an entity bean. In analyzing various possible combinations of session beans, entity beans, or value objects to represent master and detail objects, these questions are relevant only when the details are entity beans. For this case, two scenarios are possible:

- If the client modifies the detail entity object, the master object needs to expose the underlying entity object to the clients.

- If the client does not modify the detail entity object, the master object can have the necessary business logic to know which detail bean to access to construct the logical master-detail object. The client should not be exposed to the logic associated with accessing and aggregating the entity beans representing the details.

EXERCISE 4-7

Data Access Objects

Question   Define data access objects and describe their purpose.

Answer   The DAO pattern separates the interface to a system resource from the code used to access that resource. The DAO class defines an abstract API of operations on the resource. The DAO knows how to operate from a persistent store, based on some identity information such as a filename. The enterprise bean defers its persistence mechanism to the DAO, allowing the EJB to concentrate entirely on implementing business methods. Use the DAO to encapsulate access to data, maintain clean separation of bean and database access code, ensure easier migration to container-managed persistence for entity beans, and allow for cross-database and cross-schema capability.

EXERCISE 4-8

Value Objects

Question   Define Value Objects and describe their purpose.

Answer   A Value Object represents a composite value from the server, not a reference to an object on the server. Value Objects are ad hoc groupings of data values to support a use case (or group of use cases). Value Objects can be used for fine-grained business objects that represent structure with get/set behavior only. Use a Value Object when the business entity being modeled has

- Only methods that get values from the object's internal state (that is, immutable state)
- A lifecycle that is completely controlled by another object
- A relatively small size

EXERCISE 4-9

Facades

Question   Describe the use of session bean facades and their purpose.

Answer   The SBF provides a simple, single point of entry to shared entity beans. It shields the client from complex entity bean relationships. SBF manages workflow on the client's behalf, and it reduces remote calls to the server. Architects using EJB technologies discovered almost immediately that providing access to entity beans from the client layer presents multiple problems, such as an overabundance of network traffic and latency, awkward security management, inefficient transactional behavior, and limits in reusability.

J2EE Best Practices—EIS Integration Tier

The EIS Integration tier provides the information infrastructure for an enterprise. Accessing EIS can be complex, requiring vendor-specific knowledge of the following:

- Application programming model
- Transactions
- Security

J2EE reduces the complexity of accessing an enterprise information system by relying on the web and EJB containers to handle transactions, security, and scalability. JDBC accesses relational data. JNDI accesses enterprise name and directory services. JMS sends and receives messages using enterprise messaging systems. JavaMail sends and receives mail. JavaIDL calls CORBA services. JNI calls services written in other languages—JNI can interact with native languages.

As more businesses move toward an e-business strategy, integration with existing EISs becomes the key to success. Enterprises with successful e-businesses need to integrate their existing EISs with new web-based applications, possibly using the J2EE APIs that match the existing EIS functionality. J2EE APIs extend the reach of the EISs to support business-to-business (B2B) transactions.

Before the J2EE Connector architecture was defined, no specification for the Java platform addressed the problem of providing a standard architecture for integrating heterogeneous EISs. Most EIS vendors and application server vendors use nonstandard vendor-specific architectures to provide connectivity between application servers and EISs. Figure 4-14 illustrates the complexity of a heterogeneous environment.

The J2EE Connector architecture provides a Java solution to the problem of connectivity among the many application servers and EISs already in existence. By using the J2EE Connector architecture, EIS vendors no longer need to customize

FIGURE 4-14   The heterogeneous enterprise architecture

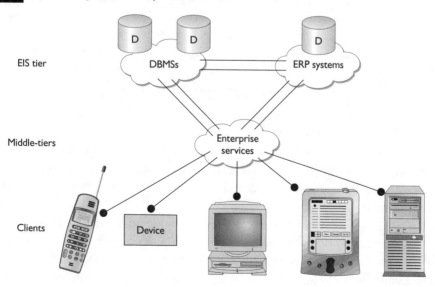

their products for each application server. Application server vendors who conform to the J2EE Connector architecture do not need to add custom code whenever they want to add connectivity to a new EIS.

The J2EE Connector architecture is based on the technologies that are defined and standardized as part of the J2EE.

J2EE Connector Overview

The J2EE Connector architecture defines a standard architecture for connecting the J2EE platform to heterogeneous EISs. Examples of EISs exist in almost any enterprise computing environment. A nonexhaustive list includes ERP, mainframe transaction processing, database systems, and legacy applications not written in the Java programming language. By defining a set of scalable, secure, and transactional mechanisms, the J2EE Connector architecture enables the integration of EISs with application servers and enterprise applications.

The J2EE Connector architecture enables an EIS vendor to provide a standard resource adapter for its EIS. The resource adapter plugs into an application server, providing connectivity among the EIS, the application server, and the enterprise application. If an application server vendor has extended its system to support the J2EE Connector architecture, it has connectivity to multiple EISs. An EIS vendor needs to provide just one standard resource adapter that has the capability to plug into any application server that supports the J2EE Connector architecture.

Multiple resource adapters (that is, one resource adapter per type of EIS) are pluggable into an application server. This capability enables application components deployed on the application server to access the underlying EISs.

Figure 4-15 illustrates the J2EE Connector architecture.

Resource Adapter

To achieve standard, system-level plugability between application servers and EISs, the J2EE Connector architecture defines a standard set of system-level contracts between an application server and EIS. The resource adapter implements the EIS-side of these system-level contracts.

A resource adapter is a system-level software driver used by an application server or an application client to connect to an EIS. By plugging into an application server, the resource adapter collaborates with the server to provide the underlying mechanisms, the transactions, security, and connection pooling mechanisms. A resource adapter is used within the address space of the application server.

The J2EE Connector architecture

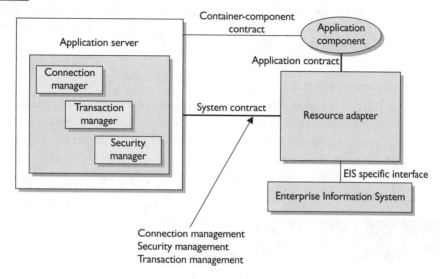

System Contract

An application server and an EIS collaborate to keep all system-level mechanisms, such as transactions, security, and connection management, transparent from the application components. As a result, an application component provider focuses on the development of business and presentation logic for its application components and need not get involved in the system-level issues related to EIS integration. This promotes easier and faster development of scalable, secure, and transactional enterprise applications that require connectivity with multiple EISs.

The J2EE Connector architecture defines the following set of system-level contracts between an application server and EIS:

- A Connection Management contract that lets an application server pool connect to an underlying EIS and lets application components connect to an EIS. This leads to a scalable application environment that can support a large number of clients requiring access to EISs.

- A Transaction Management contract between the transaction manager and an EIS that supports transactional access to EIS resource managers. This contract lets an application server use a transaction manager to manage transactions across multiple resource managers. This contract also supports transactions that are managed internal to an EIS resource manager without the necessity of involving an external transaction manager.

■ A Security Contract that enables a secure access to an EIS. This contract provides support for a secure application environment, which reduces security threats to the EIS and protects valuable information resources managed by the EIS.

Common Client Interface (CCI)

The J2EE Connector architecture also defines a common client interface (CCI) for EIS access. The CCI defines a standard client API for application components. The CCI enables application components and enterprise application integration (EAI) frameworks to drive interactions across heterogeneous EISs using a common client API. The CCI is intended for use by the EAI and enterprise tools vendors.

CERTIFICATION OBJECTIVE 4.11

Illustrate When to Use J2EE Technology for Given Situations

This scenario illustrates the use of the J2EE Connector architecture in a B2B e-commerce scenario. Morris Phillips Corp. is a manufacturing firm that aims to adopt an e-business strategy. Morris Phillips has huge existing investments in its EIS systems, which include an ERP system and a mainframe transaction processing system. Morris Phillips needs to drive B2B interactions with its multiple supplier vendors and it wants to leverage its existing EIS investment while adopting the new e-business architecture.

With these goals in mind, Morris Phillips buys a J2EE-based server (called the B2B server) from B2B, Inc. The B2B server can drive B2B interactions with multiple buyers and suppliers. The B2B interactions are driven using XML over HTTP (or HTTPS). The J2EE Connector architecture enables Morris Phillips to integrate its existing EISs with the B2B server. Morris Phillips buys off-the-shelf resource adapters for its existing set of EISs. It then integrates its B2B server and applications (deployed on the B2B server) with its EISs using these connectors.

The applications deployed on the B2B server extract data from the underlying EISs. The extracted data may be in XML or converted into XML by the applications. The loosely coupled B2B interactions with suppliers are then driven by exchanging XML data over the HTTP (or HTTPS) protocol.

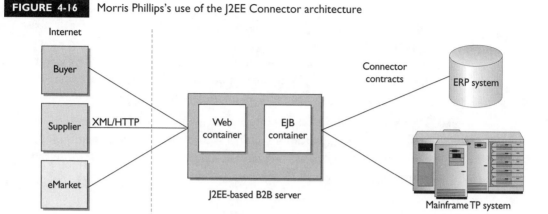

FIGURE 4-16   Morris Phillips's use of the J2EE Connector architecture

Figure 4-16 illustrates Morris Phillips's use of the J2EE Connector architecture to run its business.

EISs provide the information infrastructure critical to the business processes of an enterprise. Examples of EISs include relational databases, ERP systems, mainframe transaction processing systems, and legacy database systems.

The EIS integration problem has assumed great importance because enterprises are striving to leverage their existing systems and resources while adopting and developing new technologies and architectures. Today, enterprise application development is more about integration rather than developing an enterprise application from scratch. Enterprises cannot afford to discard their investments in existing applications and EISs. The emergence of web-based architectures and Web services has made it more imperative for enterprises to integrate their EISs and applications and expose them to the web.

The EIS integration problem is one part of the broader scope of EAI. EAI entails integrating applications and enterprise data sources so that they can easily share business processes and data. We will focus on the following aspects of EAI, including discussions of recommended guidelines:

- **Application integration**   Existing enterprise applications may be off-the-shelf bundled applications or they may be developed in-house. Two examples are supply chain management (SCM) and customer relationship management (CRM) applications. While such applications expose business-level functionality used directly by end users or integrated with other enterprise applications, they usually do not expose the underlying data on which the business functionality is built.

- **Data integration**   An enterprise environment often contains more than one database system upon which its business processes run. These database systems may be relational, object-based, hierarchical, file-based, or legacy stores. Data integration focuses on integrating existing data with enterprise applications. For example, an integration might entail integrating a web-based order management system with an existing order and customer database.

- **Legacy integration**   Legacy integration involves integrating new enterprise applications with applications and EISs that have been in operation for some time, often referred to as an enterprise's *legacy* systems. An enterprise cannot afford any disruption in these legacy systems.

EIS Guidelines—Data Access

Here the architect must rely on vendor tools for EIS integration, such as data and function mining tools, object-oriented analysis and design tools, application code generation tools, application composition tools, and of course deployment tools. In-house deployers who are knowledgeable in the enterprise organization should be charged to set transaction, security, and deployment requirements.

EIS Access Objects

Access objects abstract complex, low-level details of EIS system access into access objects; provide a common, consistent access to various types of EISs; and separate access objects from business objects. Access objects can be made into well-known JavaBeans for use in development tools.

When implementing access objects, do not make assumptions about environments outside access objects. Architects should strive to design for reusability across tiers and components. Access objects should not define declarative transactions or security requirements. It is important to maintain consistency in programming restrictions between business objects and access objects.

Guidelines—Connections

Components should acquire and release connections within a single method. They should account for differences across component types in connection management such as JSP and servlets, stateful and stateless session beans, and entity beans. Components should avoid opening multiple concurrent connections to a single database, because this is not supported by some JDBC drivers.

Performance-Related Best Practices Data Caching

Much of the interesting data in a system can remain unchanged for minutes, hours, or even longer. When accessing interesting information of such a static nature, or in noncrucial use cases wherein a client does not require real-time data, network traffic and database usage can be greatly reduced through the use of data caching. Here are some tips:

- If clients have slow back-end connections, consider compressing data for network communication.

- Minimize the number of network round trips required by the application.

- For applications to scale to many users, minimize the amount of shared memory that requires updating.

- Cache data to minimize lookup time, although this can reduce scalability if locks are required to access the cache.

- If there are more accesses than updates to a cache, share the access lock among all the accessors, but be aware that this reduces the window for updaters to lock the cache.

- Eliminate memory leaks before tuning execution speed.

- Ensure that the development environment approximates/simulates the production deployment environment.

- Consider metrics: maximum response ration and CPU utilization under various activity loads. How well does the application scale when additional users are added?

- Spend your time wisely: For example, improving the performance of a method that is called 1000 times is better than improving the performance of a method that is called only 10 times.

- Don't cache data unless you know how and when to invalidate the cached entries.

J2EE Best Practices Services

The Service-locator is used when accessing common services within J2EE, such as JMS factories, data sources, *EJBHome* objects, and so on. The application will use the JNDI API. This will require the creation of an initial context object (the root of the naming service), followed by a lookup or search for the desired resource or service. This lookup (if successful) results in the transferring of that resource's serializable representative to the interested party.

Some major design problems become evident when the clients are co-located and not local to the EJB or other accessed service:

- Entire seconds can go by each time these operations are carried out.

- Each interested client must be complicated by the inclusion of JNDI-API-specific code.

- Unnecessary network traffic is added to the system.

Avoid some of this overhead by caching references to the service object (for example, *EJBHome* references) to avoid JNDI lookup overhead. An EJB call is expensive, owing to the requirements for an EJB. For example, a method call from the client could cover all the following: get Home reference from the NamingService (one network round trip); get EJB reference (one or two network round trips plus remote creation and initialization of Home and EJB objects); call method and return value on EJB object (two or more network round trips: client-server and [multiple] server-DB; several costly services used such as transactions, persistence, security, and so on; multiple serializations and deserializations).

To prevent performance problems, do the following:

- If an EJB service for an object is overkill (for example, if the object will only be accessed locally), use a plain Java object and not an EJB object.

- You can use local interfaces (from EJB2.0) if EJB calls another EJB (or a servlet calling an EJB) from the same container and the same virtual machine.

- Wrap entity beans in a session bean to change multiple EJB remote calls into one session bean remote call and several local calls. (This is the pattern discussed earlier in the chapter known as the *session bean facade*.)

- Change multiple remote method calls into one remote method call with all the data combined into a parameter object.

- Control serialization by modifying unnecessary data variables with a transient key word to avoid unnecessary data transfer over network.

- Cache *EJBHome* references to avoid JNDI lookup overhead (as we just discussed the pattern called *ServiceLocator*).

- Declare nontransactional methods of session beans with *NotSupported* or *Never* transaction attributes (in the *ejb-jar.xml* deployment descriptor file). If the code calling a method in this bean has a transaction running, suspend that transaction until the method called in this bean completes. No transaction context is created for this bean.

- Transactions should span the minimum time possible as transactions lock database rows. This depends on transaction isolation that is defined in terms of isolation levels called dirty reads, repeatable reads, and phantom reads. A repeatable read is when the data read is guaranteed to look the same if read again during the same transaction. Repeatable reads typically means that the data read is locked against changes. If the data is locked, it cannot be changed by any other transaction until this transaction ends. A dirty read occurs when the first transaction reads uncommitted changes made by a second transaction. If the second transaction is rolled back, the data read by the first transaction becomes invalid because the rollback undoes the changes. The first transaction won't be aware that the data it has read has become invalid.

Security

Threats to enterprise-critical assets can include such events as disclosure of confidential information, the modification or destruction of information, the misappropriation of protected resources, the compromise of accountability, and misappropriation that compromises availability. Exposure to threats can be mitigated using software that provides authentication, authorization, and auditing.

A good security guideline is to support consistent end-to-end security architecture. This is accomplished by integrating with existing security environments. This is known as *identity management.* Large firms have provisioning systems that manage user accounts across different application domains and operating systems. The proper security guidelines should support authentication and authorization. Another objective of good security is to be transparent to application components and enable applications to be portable across security environments. A good technique is to have the user identity passed from the calling application.

Security Terminology

An *entity* is something that can have access rights applied to it. A *principal* is an entity to which privileges can be assigned. A *role* is a collection of privileges. *Authentication* is a mechanism by which callers and service providers prove that they are acting on behalf of specific users or systems. Web-tier authentication consists of HTTP basic authentication, form-based authentication, and HTTPS mutual authentication.

Authentication in the EJB and EIS Integration Tiers

The EJB tier authentication can be accomplished using protection domains, by placing a protected web resource in front of a protected EJB resource, or by linking protected web resources on every web resource that calls EJB resources. On the EIS integration tier, authentication can be accomplished using container-managed resource manager sign-on or an application-managed resource manager sign-on.

Protection Domains

In a J2EE application, *protection domain* refers to a set of entities that are *assumed*, or known to trust each other. When a component interacts with components in the same protection domain, no constraint is placed on the identity that it associates with its call. The caller may *propagate* the caller's identity, or choose an identity based on knowledge of authorization constraints imposed by the called component, since the caller's ability to claim an identity is based on trust. If the concept of protection domains is employed to avoid the need for authentication, there must be a means to establish the boundaries of protection domains, so that trust in unproven identities does not cross these boundaries.

In J2EE, a container provides an authentication boundary between external callers and the components it hosts. Containers enforce the boundaries, and implementations are likely to support protection domains that span containers. A container is not required to host components from different protection domains, although an implementation may choose to do so.

Authorization

Authorization entails applying security policies to regulate what specific users, or groups of users, can access in the system. An access control limits the resources a user has access to based on their permissions. Access control can also be used to limit the type of access a user has to a resource, such as read or write access. Two approaches can be used to define access control rules: the capabilities are examined to focus on what a caller can do, and permissions focus on who can do what. The J2EE application programming model focuses on permissions.

With declarative authorization, the container-enforced access control rules associated with a J2EE application are established by the deployer. The deployer uses a deployment tool to map an application permission model to policy specific to the operational environment. The application permission model is contained in a deployment descriptor.

The deployment descriptor defines logical privileges, called *security roles,* and associates them with components to define the privileges required to be granted permission to access components. The deployer assigns these logical privileges to specific callers to establish the capabilities of users in the runtime environment. Callers are assigned logical privileges based on the values of their security attributes.

The EJB container grants permission to access a method to callers that have at least one of the privileges associated with the method. Security roles also protect web resource collections—that is, a URL pattern and an associated HTTP method, such as GET. The web container enforces authorization requirements similar to those for an EJB container. Note that when a resource has no associated security role, permission to access the resource will be granted to all.

In both tiers, access control policy is defined at deployment time, rather than application development. The deployer can modify the policy provided by the application assembler. The deployer refines the privileges required to access the components and defines the correspondence between the security attributes presented by callers and the container privileges. In any container, the mapping from security attributes to privileges is scoped to the application, so that the mapping applied to the components of one application may be different from that of another application.

With programmatic authorization, a J2EE container makes access control decisions before dispatching method calls to a component. As a result, the state of a component doesn't affect the access decisions. A component can use two methods, EJBContext .isCallerInRole for enterprise bean code and HttpServletRequest .isUserInRole for web components. A component uses these methods to determine whether a caller has been granted a privilege selected by the component based on the parameters, the state of the component, or factors such as the time of the call.

The application component provider of a component that calls one of these functions must declare the complete set of distinct *roleName* values used in all of its calls. These declarations appear in the deployment descriptor as *security-role-ref* elements. Each *security-role-ref* element links a privilege name embedded in the application as a *roleName* to a security role. It is ultimately the deployer that establishes the link between the privilege names embedded in the application and the security roles defined in the deployment descriptor. The link between privilege names and security roles may differ for components in the same application.

Use declarative authorization where possible and programmatic authorization when more functionality is required. When using declarative authorization, ensure that access control is not bypassed. Apply the same access control rules to all the methods in a component. There is a trade-off between the external access control policy configured by the deployer and the internal policy embedded in the application code. The former is flexible after the application has been written. The latter provides more options in terms of functionality. The former is transparent and completely comprehensible. The latter is hidden in the application code and may be understood only by the application developers. These trade-offs should be considered in choosing the authorization model.

Controlling Access to Resources

To control access to web resources, specify the constraint in the deployment descriptor. To control access to EJB resources, specify the roles in the deployment descriptor. You can also specify the methods of the remote and home interface that each security role is allowed to invoke. The proper assignment of users to roles determines whether a resource is protected.

To ensure message integrity, the following measures can be used:

- **Message signature**   A cryptographically enciphered message digest of the message contents
- **Message confounder**   Ensures message authentication is useful only once

Message signatures might be required for component-to-component invocations that traverse unprotected networks. Specify message protection only for critical messages and components in the deployment descriptor.

Transactions

A *transaction* is a bracket of processing that represents a logical unit of work; it is an "all-or-nothing" contract, and all of the processing must be completed or else the transaction management should restore the application to the status quo ante—as it was before the transaction. Transactions are basically a specific sequence of operations on resources, typically the data actions *select*, *insert*, and *update*, which transform the system from one consistent state to another. To reflect the correct state of the system, a transaction should have the following properties:

■ **Atomicity** This is the all-or-nothing property. Either the entire sequence of operations is successful or the sequence is entirely unsuccessful. Completed transactions are committed. Partially executed transactions are rolled back.

■ **Consistency** A transaction maps one consistent state of the resources to another. Consistency is concerned with correctly reflecting the reality of the state of the resources.

■ **Isolation** A transaction should not reveal its results to other concurrent transactions before it commits. Certain isolation levels (serialization) assure that transactions do not access data that is being concurrently updated.

■ **Durability** The results of the committed transactions are permanent. Resource managers ensure that the results of a transaction are not altered due to system failures.

Transactions ensure data integrity by controlling access to data. This frees an application programmer from the complex issues of failure recovery and multiple-user programming. Transactions are a mechanism used for simplifying the development of distributed multi-user enterprise applications. Two types of transaction demarcation can be used: bean-managed and container-managed. In container-managed transaction demarcation, six different transaction attributes—*Required*, *RequiresNew*, *NotSupported*, *Supports*, *Mandatory*, and *Never*—can be associated with an enterprise bean's method.

Transaction Guidelines in the Web Tier
A servlet or JSP can use JNDI to look up a *UserTransaction* and use the Java Transaction API (JTA) to demarcate transactions. A servlet should start a transaction only in its service method. A transaction should not span multiple web requests. It is typically bracketed by a *begin* and a *commit* or *rollback*, as the following code snippet illustrates.

```
Context ic = new InitialContext();
UserTransaction t =(UserTransaction)ic.lookup("java:comp/UserTransaction");
t.begin();
// perform processing
if (everything_worked)
{t.commit();}
else
{t.rollback();}
```

In a multi-tier environment, when using EJB, the use of JTA in the web tier is not recommended. In bean-managed transaction demarcation, the EJB bean uses *UserTransaction*. Only session beans can choose to use bean-managed transactions. In container-managed transaction demarcation, the EJB container is responsible for transaction demarcation. Moreover, you should use container-managed transaction demarcation because it is less prone to error and you let the container handle transaction demarcation automatically. It frees the component provider from writing transaction demarcation code in the component. It is easier to group enterprise beans to perform a certain task with specific transaction behavior. The bottom line is that the application assembler can customize the transaction attributes in the deployment descriptor without modifying the code.

EJB Tier—Container-Managed

Transaction *demarcation* is the vehicle by which transaction behavior of EJB is specified declaratively; it frees the developer from writing code. It is less error-prone because the container handles all the transaction servicing. It is easier to compose multiple enterprise beans to perform a certain task with transaction behavior. It can result in improved performance. A transaction attribute supports declarative transaction demarcation and conveys to the container the intended transactional behavior of the associated EJB component's method.

Six transactional attributes are possible for container-managed transaction demarcation:

- **NotSupported** The bean runs outside the context of a transaction. Existing transactions are suspended during method calls. The bean cannot be invoked within a transaction. An existing transaction is suspended until the method called in this bean completes.

- **Required** Method calls require a transaction context. If one already exists, it will be used; if one does not exist, it will be created. The container starts a new transaction if no transaction exists. If a transaction exists, the bean uses that transaction.

- **Supports** Method calls use the current transaction context if one exists but don't create one if none exists. The container will not start a new transaction. If a transaction already exists, the bean will be included in that transaction. Note that with this attribute, the bean can run without a transaction.

- **RequiresNew** Containers create new transactions before each method call on the bean and commit transactions before returning. A new transaction is always started when the bean method is called. If a transaction already exists, that transaction is suspended until the new transaction completes.

- **Mandatory** Method calls require a transaction context. If one does not exist, an exception is thrown. An active transaction must already exist. If no transaction exists, the *javax.ejb.TransactionRequired* exception is thrown.

- **Never** Method calls require that no transaction context be present. If one exists, an exception is thrown. The bean must never run with a transaction. If a transaction exists, the *java.rmi.RemoteException* exception is thrown.

With respect to transaction attributes, you should use *Required* for the default transaction attribute. The *RequiresNew* attribute is useful when the bean methods need to commit unconditionally. The *NotSupported* attribute can be used when the resource manager is not supported by the J2EE product. The blueprint recommends not using the attribute *Supports*. *Mandatory* and *Never* can be used when it is necessary to verify the transaction is associated with the client.

Transaction Guidelines in EIS

For proper handling of transactions within the EIS integration tier, it is recommended that a component use JTA whenever possible when accessing EIS systems. Using JTA transaction allows multiple components accessing EIS to be grouped in a single transaction. If a component marks the transaction as rollback only, all enterprise information system work will be rolled back automatically. With local transactions, each EIS accessed will have to be committed or rolled back explicitly. In addition, components need extra logic to deal with individual EIS rollbacks or failures.

To handle a group of EIS operations to work as a transaction, you might need compensating transactions. For example, in an "identity management system," let's say that when a new user starts his job, EJBs are used to create a Windows NT ID, a UNIX ID, and a mainframe ID. We want this group of provisioned applications to be a transaction. Suppose the NT and UNIX IDs are created but the mainframe fails; we need to compensate or undo the transactions for the NT and UNIX IDs.

A compensating transaction is a *transaction*, or group of operations, used to undo the effect of a previously committed transaction. They are useful if a component needs to access an EIS that does not support JTA.

A number of problems can arise when using compensating transactions: It is not always possible to undo the effect of a committed transaction, and the required atomicity could be broken if the server crashes when a compensating transaction is used. In addition, database "locks" notwithstanding, inconsistent data might be seen by concurrent EIS access.

EXERCISE 4-10

Security Guidelines

Question   Describe security guidelines, terminology, and forms of authentication.

Answer   A good security guideline is to provide a consistent end-to-end security architecture. This is accomplished by seamlessly integrating with existing security environments such as EIS support authentication and authorization. Another objective of good security is to be transparent to application components and enable applications to be portable across security environments.

With respect to security terminology, an *entity* is something that can have access rights applied to it. A *principal* is an entity to which privileges can be assigned. A *role* is a collection of privileges. An *authentication mechanism* is one by which callers and service providers prove that they are acting on behalf of specific users or systems. Good web-tier authentication can consist of HTTP basic authentication, form-based authentication, and HTTPS mutual authentication for transactions that need added security for sensitive data.

EXERCISE 4-11

The Role of Transactions

Question   Describe the role of transactions.

Answer   Transactions ensure data integrity by controlling access to data. Transactions free an application programmer from the complex issues of failure recovery and multiple-user programming. Transactions are a mechanism for simplifying the development of distributed multi-user enterprise applications. Transactions span across all tiers.

CERTIFICATION SUMMARY

As you have seen, the J2EE platform is a multi-tiered distributed application model, where application logic is divided into components according to their function. The various components of a J2EE application are installed on different machines. A component's location depends on which tier or layer in the multi-tiered J2EE environment that component belongs to. These components will already exist (legacy, client-server databases, messaging) and must be integrated with the J2EE components. The enterprise architect must be aware of the way in which the J2EE application framework can be used to integrate seamlessly with the existing myriad of business components that make up the enterprise environment.

As you have seen in the chapter, these components reside at various tiers in the framework. The architect must understand the client tier components, web tier components, and business tier components that run on the J2EE server, and, probably most important for the enterprise, the EIS tier.

TWO-MINUTE DRILL

Explain the J2EE Architecture and System Requirements

❑ While a J2EE application can consist of three or more tiers or layers, J2EE multi-tiered applications are generally considered to be three-tiered applications because they are distributed across three different locations: client machines, J2EE server machine, and the database or legacy machines at the back end. J2EE applications consist of client components, web components, and business components.

❑ J2EE applications are made up of components: self-contained functional software units assembled into J2EE applications with their related classes and files. These components communicate with other components.

❑ The component-based and platform-independent J2EE architecture facilitates development, because business logic is organized into reusable components, and the J2EE server provides underlying services in the form of a container for every component type.

❑ A J2EE application is usually assembled from two different types of modules: enterprise beans and web components. Both of these modules are reusable; therefore, new applications can be built from preexisting enterprise beans and components. The modules are also portable, so the application that comprises them will be able to run on any J2EE server conforming to the specifications.

Explain the Use of Patterns in the J2EE Framework

❑ The J2EE framework employs design patterns to support these capabilities. J2EE uses the following core patterns to enable flexible association of EJB classes with other components. The Proxy Pattern provides a separate implementation of interface and working code for location transparency. The Decorator provides a similar contract for a class but with added functionality. The Factory Method provides ability to define a contract for creating an object but defers instantiation to subclasses. The Abstract Factory provides a contract for creating families of related or dependent objects without specifying concrete classes.

❑ The use of best practices, design patterns, and guidelines is important for J2EE architects. Successful architects and developers share their knowledge and pass on their proven techniques to others. The net result is productivity. The ultimate product is the implementation of solid applications.

Describe the Concepts of "Best Practices" and "Guidelines"

❑ A best practice is an optimal process that is recognized and approved by peers in similar situations. It is applicable to a cross-section of scenarios with varying resources and sizes. It takes design requirements into consideration.

❑ A guideline is a rule applied horizontally to the design. Guidelines reflect agreements on practices or operations by recognized professional associations. This includes formal, approved standards, as contrasted to de facto standards and proprietary standards that are exceptions to this concept.

Illustrate the Use of J2EE for Workflow

❑ A common method for designing applications is to organize them around an event-driven user interface. Utilizing the MVC design pattern best practice results in a separation of the application data from the ways that the data can be accessed or viewed as well as from the mapping between system events (such as user interface events) and application behaviors.

Review Best Practices Applicable for All Tiers

❑ The Enterprise JavaBeans (EJB) tier hosts the application-specific business objects and the system-level services (such as transaction management, concurrency control, and security). The EJB tier is a critical link between the web tier and the EIS integration tier. It typically hosts the entity beans and session beans, data access objects and value objects, and perhaps master-detail modeling using enterprise beans.

Review Best Practices for the Client Tier

❑ Thin-client solutions (HTML on a browser) are important to Internet-based applications. The browser acts as your client for rendering the presentation as encoded in HTML.

❏ In addition to that which can be rendered with static HTML, the following items can be used to create web content: JSPs, servlets, applets, and JavaScript can be used to enhance the browser interface.

Enumerate the Components and Categories of the Web Tier

❏ The two types of components currently specified for the web tier are servlets and JSP pages.

❏ Web components are hosted by servlet containers, JSP containers, and web containers.

❏ In addition to standard container services, a servlet container provides network services by which requests and responses are sent and that decode requests and format responses. All servlet containers must support HTTP as a protocol for requests and responses, but they may also support additional request-response protocols such as HTTPS.

❏ A JSP container provides the same services as a servlet container and an engine that interprets and processes a JSP page into a servlet.

❏ A web container provides the same services as a JSP container and provides access to the J2EE service and communication APIs.

Explain How to Apply MVC to the Web Tier

❏ MVC is applied to the Web Tier by separating the application data from the ways that the data is accessed or viewed. The MVC pattern consists of three component types:

❏ The Model, usually a JavaBean or an EJB, represents the application data along with methods that operate on that data.

❏ The View component, usually a JSP, displays the data to the user.

❏ The Controller, which is usually a servlet, translates user actions such as mouse movement and keyboard input and dispatches operations on the Model.

Review the Best Practices for the Presentation Layer

❏ Separate HTML from Java.

❏ Try to place business logic in JavaBeans.

❑ Factor general behavior out of custom tag handler classes.

❑ Favor HTML in Java handler classes over Java in JSPs.

❑ Use an appropriate inclusion mechanism.

❑ Use a JSP template mechanism.

❑ Use stylesheets.

❑ Use the MVC pattern.

❑ Use available custom tag libraries.

❑ Determine the appropriate level of XML compliance.

❑ Use JSP comments in most cases.

❑ Follow HTML best practices.

❑ Utilize the JSP exception mechanism.

Review the Internationalization and Localization

❑ The set of political, cultural, and region-specific elements represented in an application is called a *locale*. Applications should customize data presentation to each user's locale. Internationalization, also known as *I18n*, is the process of separating locale dependencies from an application's source code. Examples of locale dependencies include messages and user interface labels, character sets, encoding, and currency and time formats. Localization (also called *L10n*) is the process of adapting an internationalized application to a specific locale. An application must first be internationalized before it can be localized. Internationalization and localization make a J2EE application available to a global audience.

Illustrate When to Use J2EE Technology for Given Situations

❑ With respect to security, an entity is something that can have access rights applied to it. A principal is an entity to which privileges can be assigned. A role is a collection of privileges.

❑ Authentication is a mechanism by which callers and service providers prove that they are acting on behalf of specific users or systems. Web-tier authentication consists of HTTP basic authentication, form-based authentication, and HTTPS mutual authentication.

❑ Authorization entails applying security policies to regulate what specific users, or groups of users, can access in the system. An access control limits the resources a user can access based on permissions. Access control can also be used to limit the type of access a user has to a resource, such as read or write access. There are two approaches to defining access control rules: capabilities are examined to focus on what a caller can do, and permissions focus on who can do what.

❑ For proper handling of transactions within the EIS integration tier, it is recommended that a component use JTA whenever possible when accessing EIS systems. Using JTA transaction allows multiple components accessing EIS to be grouped in a single transaction. If a component marks the transaction as rollback only, all EIS work will be rolled back automatically.

SELF TEST

The following questions will help you measure your understanding of the material presented in this chapter. Read all the choices carefully because there might be more than one correct answer. Choose all correct answers for each question.

Explain the J2EE Architecture and System Requirements

1. Which of the following is not true about J2EE containers?

   A. An EJB container manages the execution of all enterprise beans for a single J2EE application. Enterprise beans and their accompanying containers run on the J2EE server.

   B. A web container manages the execution of all JSP and servlet components for a single J2EE application. Web components and their accompanying container run on the J2EE server.

   C. An application client container manages the execution of all application client components for a single J2EE application. Application clients and their accompanying containers run on the J2EE server.

   D. An applet container is the web browser and Java plug-in combination that runs on the client machine.

2. Which statement is *not* true when discussing the EJB tier?

   A. The Enterprise JavaBeans (EJB) tier hosts the application-specific business objects.

   B. The Enterprise JavaBeans (EJB) tier does not host system-level services (such as transaction management, concurrency control, and security); they are hosted on the EIS tier.

   C. The EJB tier is a link between the web tier and the EIS integration tier.

   D. The EJB tier hosts the entity beans and session beans, data access objects and value objects, and perhaps master-detail modeling using enterprise beans.

3. Which of the following is *not* true when put in the context of J2EE transaction processing?

   A. A compensating transaction is a transaction, or group of operations, used to undo the effect of a previously committed transaction.

   B. When choosing a transaction attribute, use *Required* for the default transaction attribute.

   C. When choosing a transaction attribute, use *RequiresNew* when the bean methods need to commit unconditionally.

   D. When using a compensating transaction, it is always possible to undo the effect of a committed transaction.

Explain the Use of Patterns in the J2EE Framework

4. J2EE uses the core patterns to enable flexible association of EJB classes with other components. Which of the following is *not* used by J2EE?

    A. Proxy

    B. Decorator

    C. Designer

    D. Factory

Describe the Concepts of "Best Practices" and "Guidelines"

5. Which statement is *not* true when discussing best practices?

    A. Data access objects are a useful best practice, as they encapsulate access to data and maintain a clean separation of bean and database access code.

    B. Session bean facade provides a simple, single point of entry to shared entity beans.

    C. Session bean facade does not shield the client from complex entity bean relationships and manages workflow on a client's behalf.

    D. Session bean facade avoids the problems associated with access to entity beans from the client layer—namely overabundance of network traffic and latency and awkward security management.

Review Best Practices Applicable for All Tiers

6. In which of the following cases would an application not necessarily benefit from the use of Enterprise Java Beans?

    A. Small Scale deployment

    B. Large scale deployment

    C. Transactional in nature

    D. No Transactional requirements

7. The J2EE platform uses a multi-tiered distributed application model; which of the following is not considered a tier in this architecture?

    A. Client tier

    B. Web tier

    C. Enterprise information system (EIS) tier

    D. Security tier

8. Which of the following are "best practices" for large distributed systems?

A. Avoid business logic implementation in the display code; display inconsistencies can result because the logic can be copied and modified in one object and not another.

B. Coding data manipulation logic, format and display code, and user event handling together can make application maintenance simple.

C. Facilitate reuse of user interfaces by segregating application logic from the code for an existing interface.

D. Utilizing the MVC design pattern results in a separation of the application data from the ways that the data can be accessed or viewed as well as from the mapping between system events (such as user interface events) and application behaviors.

9. Which of the following are *not* benefits of using the MVC best practice?

A. Clarifies application design through separation of data modeling issues from data display and user interaction

B. Enhances reusability by separating application functionality from presentation

C. Facilitates maintenance by encapsulating application functions behind trusted APIs

D. Simplifies database design because only the View components access the database

10. Which of the following is *not* true of using the MVC best practice?

A. The Model in an MVC-based application can be divided into two parts: the internal state of the system and the actions that can be taken to alter that state.

B. The Controller portion of the application focuses on receiving requests from the client (most often a user running a web browser), deciding what business logic function is to be performed, and delegating responsibility for producing the next phase of the user interface to an appropriate View component.

C. The Model determines how the results should be displayed.

D. The View transfers user input to the Controller.

Explain How to Apply MVC to the Web Tier

11. Which of the following are not components of the MVC ?

A. Model

B. Calculator

C. View

D. Controller

12. Which of the following is *not true* of the MVC?

    A. View extrapolates data presentation and responds to users with data.

    B. The Controller extrapolates user interaction/application semantic map and transforms user actions into application actions.

    C. The Model manages persistence.

    D. The Controller maintains the application state.

Review the Best Practices for the Presentation Layer

13. Which of the following is *not* typically considered a threat to enterprise-critical assets?

    A. The disclosure of confidential information

    B. The modification or destruction of information

    C. The misappropriation of protected resources

    D. A misappropriation that does not compromise availability

Illustrate When to Use J2EE Technology for Given Situations

14. Which of the following are not true about screen scrapers?

    A. Screen scrapers function as terminal emulators on one end and as object interfaces on the other.

    B. Screen scraping may be a useful tool when used in conjunction with the off-board servers.

    C. Changes to legacy UI have little or no impact on the new GUI.

    D. Screen Scraping is best used when the legacy clients have loose coupling with other tiers.

15. If the telephone company were to rewrite its existing legacy code using newer J2EE technology, what technology would you choose to accommodate both the block purchase and the individual query?

    A. Java Applet technology for the CORBA call and custom socket programming for vanity number requests

    B. Java Servlet API for the CORBA call and JSP for the custom socket programming

    C. Entity EJBs for both

    D. Session EJBs for both

    E. JNDI for both

    F. MQ Series with a JMS based solution for both

16. Your company's web-site offers the customers price comparisons on a variety of different products. You are in charge of converting the web-based solution over to the appropriate J2EE technology. Which of the following should you use?

   A. JSP, Servlets

   B. JSP, Servlets, EJBs

   C. Applets, EJBs

   D. No need to change it

   E. PERL/CGI scripts is the best solution

17. Regarding the J2EE EIS integration, which of the following statements is *not* true?

   A. Before the J2EE Connector architecture was defined, no specification for the Java platform addressed the problem of providing a standard architecture for integrating heterogeneous EISs.

   B. The J2EE Connector architecture provides a Java solution to the problem of connectivity between the many application servers and only new EISs, not those already in existence.

   C. Application server vendors who conform to the J2EE Connector architecture do not need to add custom code whenever they want to add connectivity to a new EIS.

18. Regarding the J2EE EIS integration Contracts, which of the following statements is *not* true?

   A. A Connection Management contract allows an application server to pool connections to an underlying EIS.

   B. A Transaction Management contract lets an application server use a transaction manager to manage transactions across multiple resource managers.

   C. A Security Contract provides support for a secure application environment, which reduces security threats to the EIS and protects valuable information resources managed by the EIS.

   D. A Transaction Management contract does not support transactions that are managed internal to an EIS resource manager without the necessity of involving an external transaction manager.

19. Which is the following is *not* true about enterprise applications and integration?

   A. Data integration focuses on integrating existing data with enterprise applications. For example, an integration might entail integrating a web-based order management system with an existing order and customer database.

   B. Legacy integration involves integrating new enterprise applications with applications and EISs that have been in operation for some time, often referred to as an enterprise's *legacy* systems.

C. Application integration—existing enterprise applications may be off-the-shelf bundled applications or they may be developed in-house.

D. Enterprise application development is about building an enterprise application from scratch.

SELF TEST ANSWERS

Explain the J2EE Architecture and System Requirements

1. ☑ **C** is correct. An application client container manages the execution of all application client components for a single J2EE application. Application clients and their accompanying container run on the client's machine and not the J2EE server.
   ☒ **A, B,** and **D** are incorrect because they are true.

2. ☑ **B** is correct. The Enterprise JavaBeans (EJB) tier does host system-level services such as transaction management, concurrency control, and security.
   ☒ **A, C,** and **D** are incorrect because they are true.

3. ☑ **D** is correct. When using a compensating transaction, it is not always possible to undo the effect of a committed transaction, even if the server crashes.
   ☒ **A, B,** and **C** are incorrect because they are true.

Explain the Use of Patterns in the J2EE Framework

4. ☑ **C** is correct. J2EE uses the core patterns to enable flexible association of EJB classes with other components. The Designer pattern is not one of them.
   ☒ **A, B,** and **D** are incorrect because they are true. Decorator, factory, and proxy are core patterns to enable flexible association of EJB classes with other components.

Describe the Concepts of "Best Practices" and "Guidelines

5. ☑ **C** is correct. Session bean facade *does* shield the client from complex entity bean relationships and manages workflow on the client's behalf.
   ☒ **A, B,** and **D** are incorrect because they are true.

Review Best Practices Applicable for All Tiers

6. ☑ **A** and **D** are correct. Enterprise Java Beans are best used with large and complex enterprise applications with high deployment and transactional requirements.
   ☒ **B** and **C** are incorrect.

7. ☑ **D** is correct. The security tier is not considered a J2EE tier.
   ☒ **A, B,** and **C** are incorrect because they are true because client, web, and EIS are J2EE tiers.

8. ☑ B is correct. Coding data manipulation logic, format and display code, and user event handling together can complicate and make application maintenance problematic and costly.
   ☒ A, C, and D are incorrect because they are true.

9. ☑ D is correct. Does not necessarily simplify database design and typically, the model and not the view component accesses the database.
   ☒ A, B, and C are incorrect because they are true.

10. ☑ C is correct. The View and not the Model determines how the results should be displayed.
    ☒ A, B, and D are incorrect because they are true.

Explain How to Apply MVC to the Web Tier

11. ☑ B is correct. The Calculator is not a component of the MVC pattern.
    ☒ A, C, and D are incorrect because they are true as Model, View, and Controller are the components of the MVC pattern.

12. ☑ D is correct. The Model, not the Controller, maintains the application state.
    ☒ A, B, and C are incorrect because they are true.

Review the Best Practices for the Presentation Layer

13. ☑ D is correct. A misappropriation that does not compromise availability is not typically considered a threat to enterprise-critical assets.
    ☒ A, B, and C are incorrect because they are true. The disclosure of confidential information, the modification or destruction of information, and the misappropriation of protected resources are typically considered threats to enterprise-critical assets.

Illustrate When to Use J2EE Technology for Given Situations

14. ☑ C and D are correct. When using screen scrapers, any changes to the legacy user interface will also affect the new GUI. In addition, screen scraping is the best alternative only if the existing UI is tightly coupled with the business tier of the legacy application. Therefore, choices C and D are false and, therefore, the correct choices.
    ☒ A and B are true about screen scrapers and, therefore, the incorrect choices.

15. ☑ D is correct. Session beans can be used for making both the CORBA call for block purchase of telephone numbers and the custom synchronous call to request a special vanity number.

☒ A, B, C, E, and F are incorrect. Both operations represent business processes involving partner OSS integration. Applets are not used for modeling the business workflow of a system. Therefore, choice **A** is incorrect. JSP represents the view construction process in an MVC application. It should not be used for processing business logic. Therefore, **B** is incorrect. Entity beans represent the business model of an application and provide a representation of enterprise data. They are not to be used for workflow processing, which is better accomplished by using session beans. Therefore, **C** is incorrect. JNDI provides Naming and Directory interfaces, not workflow processing. Therefore, choice **E** is incorrect. The question specifically says that a synchronous mechanism is to be used for the vanity number request. The CORBA RPC call for TN reservation is also synchronous. MQ Series is a MOM used for messaging. Messaging is an inherently asynchronous communication mechanism. Therefore, choice **F** is incorrect.

16. ☑ **A** is correct as using JSP and servlets is the best option.
    ☒ **B, C,** and **D** are incorrect. The important element to this question is that the revenue is generated by click-through sales. This implies that there are no transactions invol`ved and you do not need to use EJBs. Therefore, choices **B** and **C** are not the best options. PERL/CGI scripts are harder to maintain than Java code. Therefore, choice **D** is not the best option.

17. ☑ **B** is correct. The J2EE Connector architecture provides a Java solution to the problem of connectivity between the many application servers and most EISs, not just those already in existence.
    ☒ **A, C,** and **D** are incorrect because they are true.

18. ☑ **D** is correct. A Transaction Management contract *does* support transactions that are managed internal to an EIS resource manager without the necessity of involving an external transaction manager.
    ☒ **A, B,** and **C** are incorrect because they are true.

19. ☑ **D** is correct. Enterprise application development is about building an enterprise application from scratch or integrating new enterprise applications with applications and EISs that have been in operation for some time; they are often referred to as an enterprise's *legacy* systems.
    ☒ **A, B,** and **C** are incorrect because they are true.

SUN® CERTIFIED ENTERPRISE ARCHITECT

5

Design Patterns

Design *patterns*, or patterns, are solutions to recurring problems in a given context amid competing concerns. They try to bring together and document the core solution to a given problem. They are identified and documented in a form that's easy to share, discuss, and understand. They are useful problem-solving documentation for software designers and are used repeatedly to help solve common problems that arise in the course of software engineering. Documentation for the design pattern should provide a discussion on the difficulties and interests surrounding the problem and arguments as to why the given solution balances these competing interests or constraints that are inherent in the issue being solved.

The value of the pattern is not just the solution to the problem; value can also be found in the documentation that explains the underlying motivation, the essential workings of the solution, and why the design pattern is advantageous. The pattern student will be able to experience all or at least some of the experience and insight that went into providing the solution. This will undoubtedly help the designer to use the pattern and possibly adapt it or adjust it further to address needs accordingly.

Patterns can be combined and used in concert to solve larger problems than cannot be solved with just one pattern. Once the pattern student has become more familiar with these patterns, their combined applicability to a new set of problems will become much easier to identify.

The Origin of the Term "Pattern" in Design

It is human nature to follow a pattern to try to achieve success in some endeavor. Although perhaps not *formally* identified as such, patterns have clearly existed throughout the history of human civilization. For example, we have learned to farm the land essentially by using a *pattern* of *success* that was adopted and gradually communicated around the world.

The most commonly cited origin of the use of the term *pattern* in regard to design is attributed to an architect by the name of Christopher Alexander. He used the term *pattern* to refer to recurring solution-structures in his two books: *A Pattern Language: Towns, Buildings, Construction* (Oxford University Press, 1977) and *The Timeless Way of Building* (Oxford University Press, 1979).

By the early 1990s, using patterns for object-oriented software design was becoming more popular. Patterns became even more useful and widespread soon after the publication of the book *Design Patterns: Elements of Reusable Object-Oriented Software*, by Erich Gamma, Richard Helm, Ralph Johnson, and John Vlissides (Addison-Wesley, 1995). This book received widespread acceptance and praise—so much so, in fact, that the authors are also identified as the "Gang of Four," or GoF.

Fast forwarding to today, we can see that Sun has also joined the pattern business with its Core J2EE Patterns. Sun describes the Core J2EE Patterns as a method for describing and then solving the typical problems encountered by enterprise application developers. However, as with all pattern creators, the goal is always to capture the core issues of a problem and offer a solution that works in practical as well as theoretical terms.

CERTIFICATION OBJECTIVE 5.01

Identify the Benefits of Using Design Patterns

Design patterns are beneficial because they describe a problem that occurs repeatedly, and then they explain the solution to the problem in a way that can be used many times over. Design patterns are helpful for the following reasons:

- They help designers quickly focus on solutions if the designers can recognize patterns that have been successful in the past.
- The study of patterns can inspire designers to come up with new and unique ideas.
- They provide a common language for design discussions.
- They provide solutions to real-world problems.
- Their format captures knowledge and documents best practices for a domain.
- They document decisions and the rationale that lead to the solution.
- They reuse the experience of predecessors.
- They communicate the insight already gained previously.
- They describe the circumstances (when and where), the influences (who and what), and the resolution (how and why it balances the influences) of a solution.

Nevertheless, patterns are not the be-all and end-all, they are by no means a "silver bullet" or panacea, and they cannot be universally applied to all situations.

You can't always find the solution to every problem by consulting the pattern playbook. Patterns have been excessively hyped and have been used by designers to make them appear knowledgeable.

The Gang of Four's Design Patterns

The GoF described patterns as "a solution to a problem in a context." These three elements—problem, solution, and context—are the essence of a pattern. As with all pattern creators, the GoF used a template to document patterns. Before we review the 23 patterns documented by the GoF, let's take a look at the format for these patterns.

Format for the GoF Design Patterns

Table 5-1 shows the elements and sections for the GoF Design Patterns format.

TABLE 5-1   GoF Design Patterns Elements, Sections, Descriptions

Element/Section	Description
Name	Used to help convey the essence of the pattern.
Classification	Categories are **Creational** Patterns concerned with creation **Structural** Patterns concerned with composition **Behavioral** Patterns concerned with interaction and responsibility
Intent	What problem does the pattern address? What does it do?
Also Known As	Other common names for the pattern.
Motivation	Scenario that illustrates the problem.
Applicability	Situations in which the pattern can be used.
Structure	Diagram representing the structure of classes and objects in the pattern. The GoF uses Object Modeling Technique (OMT) or Booch notation. Today Unified Modeling Language (UML), a unification of OMT, Booch, and others, is commonly used.
Participants	Classes and/or objects participating in the design pattern along with their responsibilities.
Collaborations	How the participants work together to carry out their responsibilities.
Consequences	What objectives does the pattern achieve? What are the trade-offs and results?
Implementation	Implementation details (pitfalls, hints, or techniques) to consider. Are there language-specific issues?

TABLE 5-1   GoF Design Patterns Elements, Sections, Descriptions *(continued)*

Element/Section	Description
Sample Code	Sample code in C++ or Smalltalk.
Known Uses	Examples from the real world.
Related Patterns	Comparison and discussion of related patterns; scenarios where this pattern can be used in conjunction with another.

If you are new to patterns, Table 5-2 will be useful. It is a suggestion for the sequence in which you can easily study the GoF Design Patterns.

TABLE 5-2   Study Sequence for GoF Design Patterns

Sequence	Design Pattern	Comment
1	Factory Method	Frequently used and also well utilized by other patterns.
2	Strategy	Frequently used, so early familiarity helps.
3	Decorator	Considered the "skin" to the "guts" of Strategy.
4	Composite	Often used along with Chain of Responsibility, Interpreter, Iterator, and Visitor.
5	Iterator	Looping through anything is widespread in computing, so why not through objects, too?
6	Template Method	Helps to reinforce your understanding of Strategy and Factory Method.
7	Abstract Factory	Create more than one type of a group of objects.
8	Builder	Another way to create, similar to Factory Method and Abstract Factory.
9	Singleton	You want only one of something.
10	Proxy	Controlled access to a service is needed.
11	Adapter	Gain access to a service with an incompatible interface.
12	Bridge	Decouples the function from the implementation.
13	Mediator	Yet another middleman.
14	Facade	Single interface simplifying multiple interfaces in a subsystem.
15	Observer	A form of the publish/subscribe model.

TABLE 5-2	Study Sequence for GoF Design Patterns *(continued)*

Sequence	Design Pattern	Comment
16	Chain of Responsibility	Passes the message along until it's dealt with.
17	Memento	Backs up and restores an object's state.
18	Command	Separates invoker from performer.
19	Prototype	Similar to cloning.
20	State	Object appears to change class and alter its behavior.
21	Visitor	Object that represents an operation that operates on elements of an object structure.
22	Flyweight	Allows you to utilize sharing to support large numbers of objects efficiently.
23	Interpreter	Defines a grammar and an interpreter that uses the grammar to interpret sentences.

CERTIFICATION OBJECTIVE 5.02

Identify the Most Appropriate Design Pattern for a Given Scenario

We will now review each of the Gamma et al. design patterns, starting first with those that are used to create objects (Creational), and then moving on to those that are concerned with composition of classes and objects (Structural), and finally covering those that are concerned with the interaction and responsibility of objects (Behavioral).

GoF Creational Design Patterns

Creational design patterns are concerned with the way objects are created. These patterns are used when a decision must be made at the time a class is instantiated. Typically, the details of the concrete class that is to be instantiated are hidden from (and unknown to) the calling class by an abstract class that knows only about the abstract class or the interface it implements. The following creational patterns are described by the GoF:

- Abstract Factory
- Builder
- Factory Method
- Prototype
- Singleton

Abstract Factory

The Abstract Factory pattern's intent is to provide an interface to use for creating families of related or dependent objects without actually specifying their concrete classes. For a given set of related abstract classes, this pattern supplies a technique for creating instances of those abstract classes from an equivalent set of concrete subclasses. On some occasions, you may need to create an object without having to know which concrete subclass of object to create.

The Abstract Factory pattern is also known as Kit. The UML representation is shown in Figure 5-1.

Benefits   Following is a list of benefits of using the Abstract Factory pattern:

- It isolates client from concrete (implementation) classes.
- It eases the exchanging of object families.
- It promotes consistency among objects.

Applicable Scenarios   The following scenarios are most appropriate for the Abstract Factory pattern:

- The system needs to be independent of how its objects are created, composed, and represented.
- The system needs to be configured with one of a multiple family of objects.
- The family of related objects is intended to be used together and this constraint needs to be enforced.
- You want to provide a library of objects that does not show implementations and only reveals interfaces.

FIGURE 5-1

UML for the
Abstract Factory
pattern

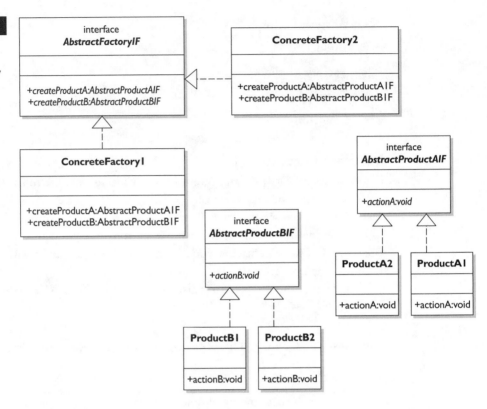

J2EE Technology Features and J2SE API Association   The J2EE

technology features associated with the Abstract Factory pattern are

- Data Access Object (Sun)
- Value Object Assembler (Sun)

The Java 2 Platform, Standard Edition (J2SE) API associated with the Abstract
Factory pattern is *java.awt.Toolkit*.

Example Code   Following is example Java code that demonstrates the Abstract

Factory pattern:

```
package j2ee.architect.AbstractFactory;
public class AbstractFactoryPattern {
  public static void main(String[] args) {
```

```
      System.out.println("Abstract Factory Pattern Demonstration.");
      System.out.println("--------------------------------------");
      // Create abstract factories
      System.out.println("Constructing abstract factories.");
      AbstractFactoryIF factoryOne = new FordFactory();
      AbstractFactoryIF factoryTwo = new GMFactory();
      // Create cars via abstract factories
      System.out.println("Constructing cars.");
      AbstractSportsCarIF  car1 = factoryOne.createSportsCar();
      AbstractEconomyCarIF car2 = factoryOne.createEconomyCar();
      AbstractSportsCarIF  car3 = factoryTwo.createSportsCar();
      AbstractEconomyCarIF car4 = factoryTwo.createEconomyCar();
      // Execute drive on the cars
      System.out.println("Calling drive on the cars.");
      car1.driveFast();
      car2.driveSlow();
      car3.driveFast();
      car4.driveSlow();
      System.out.println();
  }
}

package j2ee.architect.AbstractFactory;
public interface AbstractFactoryIF {
  public AbstractSportsCarIF createSportsCar();
  public AbstractEconomyCarIF createEconomyCar();
}

package j2ee.architect.AbstractFactory;
public interface AbstractSportsCarIF {
  public void driveFast();
}

package j2ee.architect.AbstractFactory;
public interface AbstractEconomyCarIF {
  public void driveSlow();
}

package j2ee.architect.AbstractFactory;
public class FordFactory implements AbstractFactoryIF {
  public AbstractSportsCarIF createSportsCar() {
    return new Mustang();
  }
  public AbstractEconomyCarIF createEconomyCar() {
    return new Focus();
  }
}

package j2ee.architect.AbstractFactory;
```

```
public class GMFactory implements AbstractFactoryIF {
  public AbstractSportsCarIF createSportsCar() {
    return new Corvette();
  }
  public AbstractEconomyCarIF createEconomyCar() {
    return new Cavalier();
  }
}

package j2ee.architect.AbstractFactory;
public class Mustang implements AbstractSportsCarIF {
  public void driveFast() {
    System.out.println("Mustang.driveFast() called.");
  }
}

package j2ee.architect.AbstractFactory;
public class Focus implements AbstractEconomyCarIF {
  public void driveSlow() {
    System.out.println("Focus.driveSlow() called.");
  }
}

package j2ee.architect.AbstractFactory;
public class Corvette implements AbstractSportsCarIF {
  public void driveFast() {
    System.out.println("Corvette.driveFast() called.");
  }
}

package j2ee.architect.AbstractFactory;
public class Cavalier implements AbstractEconomyCarIF {
  public void driveSlow() {
    System.out.println("Cavalier.driveSlow() called.");
  }
}
```

Builder

The Builder pattern's intent is to separate the construction of a complex object from its representation so that the same construction process can create different objects. The Builder pattern is useful when several kinds of complex objects with similar rules for assembly need to be joined at runtime but result in different object types. It achieves this by separating the process of building the object from the object itself.

The Builder pattern creates complex objects in multiple steps instead of in a single step, as in other patterns. The UML is shown in Figure 5-2.

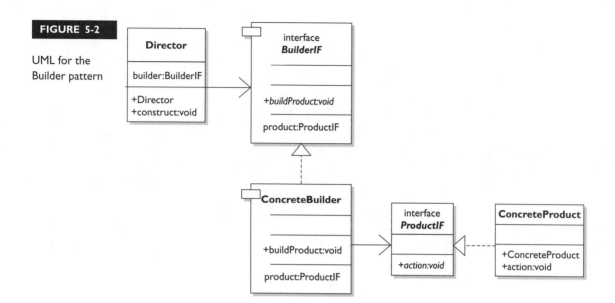

FIGURE 5-2

UML for the
Builder pattern

Benefits   The following benefits are achieved when using the Builder pattern:

- It permits you to vary an object's internal representation.
- It isolates the code for construction and representation.
- It provides finer control over the construction process.

Applicable Scenarios   The following scenarios are most appropriate for the Builder pattern:

- The algorithm for creating a complex object needs to be independent of the components that compose the object and how they are assembled.
- The construction process is to allow different representations of the constructed object.

Example Code   Following is some example Java code that demonstrates the Builder pattern:

```
package j2ee.architect.Builder;
public class BuilderPattern {
  public static void main(String[] args) {
```

```
        System.out.println("Builder Pattern Demonstration.");
        System.out.println("----------------------------");
        // Create builder
        System.out.println("Constructing builder.");
        BuilderIF builder = new ConcreteBuilder();
        // Create director
        System.out.println("Constructing director.");
        Director director = new Director(builder);
        // Construct customer via director
        System.out.println("Constructing customer.");
        director.construct();
        // Get customer via builder
        CustomerIF customer = builder.getCustomer();
        // Use customer method
        System.out.println("Calling action on the customer.");
        customer.action();
        System.out.println();
    }
}

package j2ee.architect.Builder;
public interface BuilderIF {
    public void buildCustomer();
    public CustomerIF getCustomer();
}


package j2ee.architect.Builder;
public class ConcreteBuilder implements BuilderIF {
    CustomerIF customer;
    public void buildCustomer() {
        customer = new ConcreteCustomer();
        // You could add more customer processing here...
    }
    public CustomerIF getCustomer() {
        return customer;
    }
}


package j2ee.architect.Builder;
public class ConcreteCustomer implements CustomerIF {
    public ConcreteCustomer() {
        System.out.println("ConcreteCustomer constructed.");
    }
    public void action() {
        System.out.println("ConcreteCustomer.action() called.");
    }
}


package j2ee.architect.Builder;
```

```
public interface CustomerIF {
  public void action();
}

package j2ee.architect.Builder;
public class Director {
  BuilderIF builder;
  public Director(BuilderIF parm) {
    this.builder = parm;
  }
  public void construct() {
    builder.buildCustomer();
  }
}
```

Factory Method

The Factory Method pattern's intent is to define an interface for creating an object but letting the subclass decide which class to instantiate. In other words, the class defers instantiation to subclasses. The client of the Factory Method never needs to know the concrete class that has been instantiated and returned. Its client needs to know only about the published abstract interface.

The Factory Method pattern is also known as Virtual Constructor. Figure 5-3 shows the UML.

Benefits   Following is a list of benefits of using the Factory Method pattern:

- It removes the need to bind application-specific classes into the code. The code interacts solely with the resultant interface, so it will work with any classes that implement that interface.

- Because creating objects inside a class is more flexible than creating an object directly, it enables the subclass to provide an extended version of an object.

Applicable Scenarios   The following scenarios are most appropriate for the Factory Method pattern:

- A class is not able to anticipate the class of objects it needs to create.

- A class wants its subclasses to specify the objects it instantiates.

- Classes assign responsibility to one of several helper subclasses, and you want to localize the knowledge of which helper subclass is the delegate.

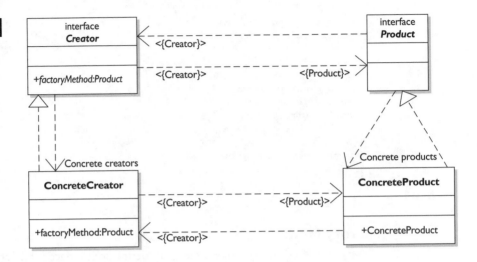

FIGURE 5-3

UML for the
Factory Method
pattern

J2EE Technology Features and J2SE API Associations   The J2EE

technology features associated with the Factory Method pattern are listed here:

- *javax.ejb.EJBHome*
- *javax.ejb.EJBLocalHome*
- *javax.jms.QueueConnectionFactory*
- *javax.jms.TopicConnectionFactory*

The J2SE APIs have many classes and interfaces that are associated with the
Factory Method pattern. Here are some examples:

- *java.text.Collator*
- *java.net.ContentHandlerFactory*
- *javax.naming.spi.InitialContextFactory*
- *javax.net.SocketFactory*

Example Code   Following is some example Java code that demonstrates the

Factory Method pattern:

```
package j2ee.architect.FactoryMethod;
public class FactoryMethodPattern {
```

```
    public static void main(String[] args) {
      System.out.println("FactoryMethod Pattern Demonstration.");
      System.out.println("----------------------------------");
      // Create creator, which uses the FactoryMethod
      CreatorIF creator = new ConcreteCreator();
      // Create trade via factory method
      TradeIF trade = creator.factoryMethod();
      // Call trade action method
      trade.action();
      System.out.println();
    }
}

package j2ee.architect.FactoryMethod;
public class ConcreteCreator implements Creator {
  public TradeIF factoryMethod() {
    return new ConcreteTrade();
  }
}

package j2ee.architect.FactoryMethod;
public class ConcreteTrade implements TradeIF {
  public void action() {
    System.out.println("ConcreteTrade.action() called.");
  }
}

package j2ee.architect.FactoryMethod;
public interface CreatorIF {
  public abstract TradeIF factoryMethod();
}

package j2ee.architect.FactoryMethod;
public interface TradeIF {
  public void action();
}
```

Prototype

The Prototype pattern's intent is to specify the kinds of objects that need to be created using a prototypical instance, and to then be able to create new objects by copying this prototype. This is similar to the clone() method of *java.lang.Object*. The UML is shown in Figure 5-4.

UML for the
Prototype
pattern

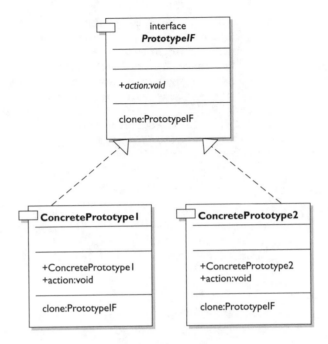

Benefits   Following are the benefits of using the Prototype pattern:

- It lets you add or remove objects at runtime.
- It lets you specify new objects by varying its values or structure.
- It reduces the need for subclassing.
- It lets you dynamically configure an application with classes.

Applicable Scenarios   The following scenarios are most appropriate for the Prototype pattern:

- The classes to instantiate are specified at runtime.
- You need to avoid building a class hierarchy of factories that parallels the hierarchy of objects.
- Instances of the class have one of only a few different combinations of state.

J2SE API Association   The J2SE API associated with the Prototype pattern is *java.lang.Object.*

Example Code The following is example Java code for demonstrating the Prototype pattern. There are two viewpoints on the Prototype pattern. The first is that it is there to simplify creating new instances of objects without knowing their concrete class. The second is it is there to simplify creating exact copies (or clones) of an original object.

The following example does not contain any state information in the objects prior to the call to getClone(). It demonstrates the first form of Prototype.

```java
package j2ee.architect.Prototype;
public class PrototypePattern {
  public static void main(String[] args) {
    System.out.println("Prototype Pattern Demonstration.");
    System.out.println("-------------------------------");
    // Create prototypes
    System.out.println("Constructing prototypes.");
    PrototypeIF prototype1 = new ConcretePrototype1();
    PrototypeIF prototype2 = new ConcretePrototype2();
    // Get clones from prototypes
    System.out.println("Constructing clones from prototypes.");
    PrototypeIF clone1 = prototype1.getClone();
    PrototypeIF clone2 = prototype2.getClone();
    // Call actions on the clones
    System.out.println("Calling actions on the clones.");
    clone1.action();
    clone2.action();
    System.out.println();
  }
}


package j2ee.architect.Prototype;
public class ConcretePrototype1 implements PrototypeIF {
  public ConcretePrototype1() {
    System.out.println("ConcretePrototype1 constructed.");
  }
  public PrototypeIF getClone() {
    // if required, put deep copy code here
    return new ConcretePrototype1();
  }
  public void action() {
    System.out.println("ConcretePrototype1.action() called");
  }
}
```

```
package j2ee.architect.Prototype;
public class ConcretePrototype2 implements PrototypeIF {
  public ConcretePrototype2() {
    System.out.println("ConcretePrototype2 constructed.");
  }
  public PrototypeIF getClone() {
    // if required, put deep copy code here
    return new ConcretePrototype1();
  }
  public void action() {
    System.out.println("ConcretePrototype2.action() called.");
  }
}

package j2ee.architect.Prototype;
public interface PrototypeIF {
  public PrototypeIF getClone(); // as opposed to Object.clone()
  public void action();
}
```

Singleton

The Singleton pattern's intent is to ensure that a class has only one instance and provides a global point of access to it. It ensures that all objects that use an instance of this class are using the same instance. Figure 5-5 shows the UML.

Benefits   Following are the benefits of using the Singleton pattern:

- It controls access to a single instance of the class.

- It reduces name space usage.

- It permits refinement of operations and representation.

- It can also permit a variable number of instances.

- It is more flexible than class methods (operations).

Applicable Scenario   The scenario most appropriate for the Singleton pattern is when a single instance of a class is needed and must be accessible to clients from a well-known access point.

J2SE API Association   The J2SE API associated with the Singleton pattern is *java.lang.Runtime.*

FIGURE 5-5

UML for the
Singleton pattern

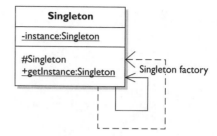

Example Code

The following example Java code demonstrates the Singleton
pattern:

```
package j2ee.architect.Singleton;
public class SingletonPattern {
  public static void main(String[] args) {
    System.out.println("Singleton Pattern Demonstration.");
    System.out.println("-------------------------------");
    System.out.println("Getting Singleton instance (s1)");
    Singleton s1 = Singleton.getInstance();
    System.out.println("s1.getInfo()="+s1.getInfo());
    System.out.println("Getting Singleton instance (s2)");
    Singleton s2 = Singleton.getInstance();
    System.out.println("s2.getInfo()="+s2.getInfo());
    System.out.println("s1.setValue(42)");
    s1.setValue(42);
    System.out.println("s1.getValue()="+s1.getValue());
    System.out.println("s2.getValue()="+s2.getValue());
    System.out.println("s1.equals(s2)="+s1.equals(s2)
       + ", s2.equals(s1)="+s2.equals(s1));
    // The following will not compile
    // Singleton s3 = (Singleton) s1.clone();
    System.out.println();
  }
}


package j2ee.architect.Singleton;
/*
 * Singletons really are "per classloader" and
 * in a J2EE application, many developers make
 * the mistake of assuming that a singleton really
 * is a singleton in a cluster of application servers.
 * This is not true!
 */
public final class Singleton {
  private static Singleton instance;
  private int value;
  private Singleton() {System.out.println("Singleton constructed.");}
  public static synchronized Singleton getInstance() {
```

```
// if it has not been instantiated yet
if (instance == null)
  // instantiate it here
  instance = new Singleton();
return instance;
}
// remaining methods are for demo purposes
// your singleton would have it's business
// methods here...
public String getInfo() {
  return getClass().getName() +
    // Uncomment line below to also see the loader
    //+", loaded by " + getClass().getClassLoader();
    ", id#" + System.identityHashCode(this);
}
public int getValue() {return value;}
public void setValue(int parm) {value = parm;}
public boolean equals(Singleton parm) {
  return (System.identityHashCode(this)
    == System.identityHashCode(parm));
}
}
```

GoF Structural Design Patterns

Structural patterns are concerned with composition or the organization of classes and objects, how classes inherit from each other, and how they are composed from other classes.

Common Structural patterns include Adapter, Proxy, and Decorator patterns. These patterns are similar in that they introduce a level of indirection between a client class and a class it wants to use. Their intents are different, however. Adapter uses indirection to modify the interface of a class to make it easier for a client class to use it. Decorator uses indirection to add behavior to a class, without unduly affecting the client class. Proxy uses indirection transparently to provide a stand-in for another class.

The following Structural patterns are described by GoF:

- Adapter
- Bridge
- Composite
- Decorator
- Facade

- Flyweight
- Proxy

Adapter

The Adapter pattern converts the interface of a class into an interface that a client requires. It acts as an intermediary and lets classes work together that couldn't otherwise because of an incompatible interface.

The Adapter pattern is also known as Wrapper. The UML is shown in Figure 5-6.

Benefits   Following are the benefits of using the Adapter pattern:

- It allows two or more previously incompatible objects to interact.
- It allows reusability of existing functionality.

Applicable Scenarios   The following scenarios are most appropriate for the Adapter pattern:

- An object needs to utilize an existing class with an incompatible interface.
- You want to create a reusable class that cooperates with classes that don't necessarily have compatible interfaces.

FIGURE 5-6

UML for the
Adapter pattern

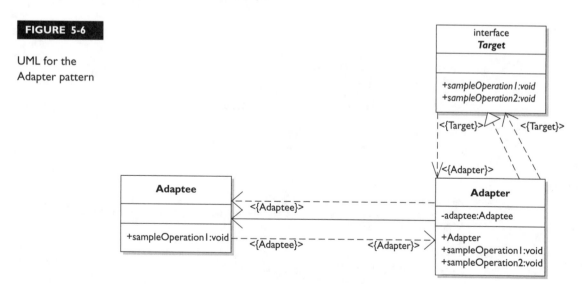

■ You need to use several existing subclasses but do not want to adapt their interfaces by subclassing each one.

J2EE Technology Feature and J2SE API Association   The J2EE technology feature associated with the Adapter pattern is Java Connector Architecture (JCA), from an architectural viewpoint.

The J2SE API associated with the Adapter pattern is *java.awt.event .ComponentAdapter*.

Example Code   The following example Java code demonstrates the Adapter pattern:

```
package j2ee.architect.Adapter;
public class AdapterPattern {
  public static void main(String[] args) {
    System.out.println("Adapter Pattern Demonstration.");
    System.out.println("----------------------------");
    // Create targets.
    System.out.println("Creating targets.");
    TargetIF target1 = new AdapterByClass();
    TargetIF target2 = new AdapterByObject();
    // Call target requests
    System.out.println("Calling targets.");
    System.out.println("target1.newRequest()->"+target1.newRequest());
    System.out.println("target2.newRequest()->"+target2.newRequest());
    System.out.println();
  }
}

package j2ee.architect.Adapter;
public class Adaptee {
  public Adaptee() {
    System.out.println("Adaptee constructed.");
  }
  public String oldRequest() {
    return "Adaptee.oldRequest() called.";
  }
}

package j2ee.architect.Adapter;
public class AdapterByClass extends Adaptee implements TargetIF {
  public AdapterByClass() {
    System.out.println("AdapterByClass constructed.");
  }
  public String newRequest() {
    return oldRequest();
```

```
    }
  }

  package j2ee.architect.Adapter;
  public class AdapterByObject implements TargetIF {
    private Adaptee adaptee;
    public AdapterByObject() {
      System.out.println("AdapterByObject constructed.");
    }
    public String newRequest() {
      // Create an Adaptee object if it doesn't exist yet
      if (adaptee == null) { adaptee = new Adaptee(); }
      return adaptee.oldRequest();
    }
  }

  package j2ee.architect.Adapter;
  public interface TargetIF {
    public String newRequest();
  }
```

Bridge

The Bridge pattern's intent is to decouple the functional abstraction from the implementation so that the two can be changed and can vary independently.

The Bridge pattern is also known as Handle/Body. The UML is shown in Figure 5-7.

Benefits   Following is a list of benefits of using the Bridge pattern:

- It enables the separation of implementation from the interface.
- It improves extensibility.
- It allows the hiding of implementation details from the client.

Applicable Scenarios   The following scenarios are most appropriate for the Bridge pattern:

- You want to avoid a permanent binding between the functional abstraction and its implementation.
- Both the functional abstraction and its implementation need to be extended using subclasses.
- Changes to the implementation should not impact the client (not even a recompile).

UML for the
Bridge pattern

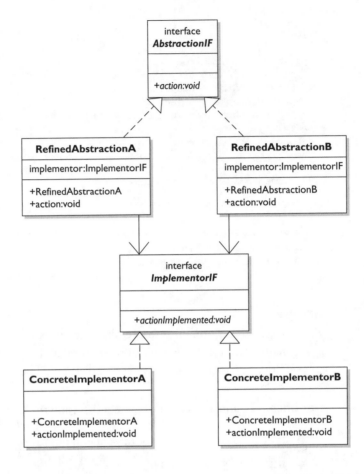

Example Code   The following example Java code demonstrates the Bridge pattern:

```
package j2ee.architect.Bridge;
public class BridgePattern {
  public static void main(String[] args) {
    System.out.println("Bridge Pattern Demonstration.");
    System.out.println("----------------------------");
    System.out.println("Constructing SportsCar and EconomyCar.");
    AbstractionIF car1 = new SportsCar ();
    AbstractionIF car2 = new EconomyCar();
    System.out.println(
      "Calling action() on SportsCar and EconomyCar.");
    car1.action();
    car2.action();
```

```
      System.out.println();
  }
}

package j2ee.architect.Bridge;
public interface AbstractionIF {
  public void action();
}

package j2ee.architect.Bridge;
public class SportsCarImplementor implements ImplementorIF {
  public SportsCarImplementor() {
    System.out.println("SportsCarImplementor constructed.");
  }
  public void actionImplemented() {
    System.out.println("SportsCarImplementor.actionImplemented() called.");
  }
}

package j2ee.architect.Bridge;
public class EconomyCarImplementor implements ImplementorIF {
  public EconomyCarImplementor() {
    System.out.println("EconomyCarImplementor constructed.");
  }
  public void actionImplemented() {
    System.out.println("EconomyCarImplementor.actionImplemented() called.");
  }
}

package j2ee.architect.Bridge;
public interface ImplementorIF {
  public void actionImplemented();
}

package j2ee.architect.Bridge;
public class SportsCar implements AbstractionIF {
  ImplementorIF implementor = new SportsCarImplementor();
  public SportsCar() {
    System.out.println("SportsCar constructed.");
  }
  public void action() {
    implementor.actionImplemented();
  }
}

package j2ee.architect.Bridge;
```

```
public class EconomyCar implements AbstractionIF {
  ImplementorIF implementor = new EconomyCarImplementor();
  public EconomyCar() {
    System.out.println("EconomyCar constructed.");
  }
  public void action() {
    implementor.actionImplemented();
  }
}
```

Composite

The Composite pattern's intent is to allow clients to operate in a generic manner on objects that may or may not represent a hierarchy of objects.

The UML is shown in Figure 5-8.

Benefits Following are benefits of using the Composite pattern:

- It defines class hierarchies consisting of primitive and complex objects.

- It makes it easier for you to add new kinds of components.

- It provides the flexibility of structure with a manageable interface.

FIGURE 5-8

UML for the
Composite
pattern

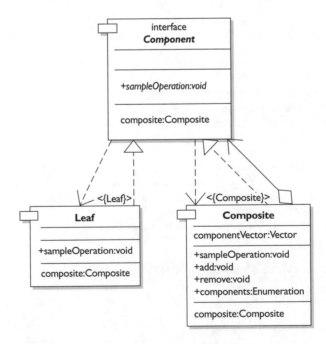

Applicable Scenarios   The following scenarios are most appropriate for the Composite pattern:

- You want to represent a full or partial hierarchy of objects.

- You want clients to be able to ignore the differences between the varying objects in the hierarchy.

- The structure is dynamic and can have any level of complexity: for example, using the Composite view from the J2EE Patterns Catalog, which is useful for portal applications.

Example Code   The following example Java code demonstrates the Composite pattern:

```
package j2ee.architect.Composite;
public class CompositePattern {
  public static void main(String[] args) {
    System.out.println("Composite Pattern Demonstration.");
    System.out.println("-------------------------------");
    System.out.println("Creating leaves, branches and trunk");
    // Create leaves
    Component leaf1 = new Leaf("    leaf#1");
    Component leaf2 = new Leaf("    leaf#2");
    Component leaf3 = new Leaf("    leaf#3");
    // Create branches
    Component branch1 = new Composite("  branch1");
    Component branch2 = new Composite("  branch2");
    // Create trunk
    Component trunk = new Composite("trunk");
    // Add leaf1 and leaf2 to branch1
    branch1.add(leaf1);
    branch1.add(leaf2);
    // Add branch1 to trunk
    trunk.add(branch1);
    // Add leaf3 to branch2
    branch2.add(leaf3);
    // Add branch2 to trunk
    trunk.add(branch2);
    // Show trunk composition
    System.out.println("Displaying trunk composition:");
    trunk.display();
    // Remove branch1 and branch2 from trunk
    trunk.remove(branch1);
```

```
    trunk.remove(branch2);
    // Show trunk composition now
    System.out.println("Displaying trunk composition now:");
    trunk.display();
    System.out.println();
  }
}

package j2ee.architect.Composite;
public abstract class Component {
  public abstract void display();
  public void add(Component c) { // override in concrete class; }
  public void remove(Component c) { // override in concrete class; }
  public Component getChild(int index) { return null; }
  public String getName() { return null; }
}

package j2ee.architect.Composite;
import java.util.*;
public class Composite extends Component {
  String name = null;
  List children = new ArrayList();
  public Composite(String parm) {
    this.name = parm;
    System.out.println(parm.trim()+" constructed.");
  }
  public String getName() { return name; }
  public Component getChild(int parm) {
    Component child;
    try {child = (Component) children.get(parm);}
    catch (IndexOutOfBoundsException ioobe) {child = null;}
    return child;
  }
  public void add(Component parm) {
    try {
      System.out.println("Adding "+parm.getName().trim()
        +" to "+this.getName().trim());
      children.add(parm);
    }
    catch (Exception e) {System.out.println(e.getMessage());}
  }
  public void remove(Component parm) {
    try {
      System.out.println("Removing "+parm.getName().trim()
        +" from "+this.getName().trim());
      children.remove(parm);}
```

```
    catch (Exception e) {System.out.println(e.getMessage());}
  }
  public void display() {
    Iterator iterator = children.iterator();
    System.out.println(this.getName()
      +(iterator.hasNext()?" with the following: ":" that is bare."));
    while (iterator.hasNext()) {((Component) iterator.next()).display();}
  }
}

package j2ee.architect.Composite;
public class Leaf extends Component {
  private String name;
  public Leaf(String parm) {
    this.name = parm;
    System.out.println(parm.trim()+" constructed.");
  }
  public void display() {
    System.out.println(this.getName());
  }
  public String getName() {
    return name;
  }
}
```

Decorator

An alternative to subclassing to extend functionality, the Decorator pattern's intent is to attach flexible additional responsibilities to an object dynamically. The Decorator pattern uses composition instead of inheritance to extend the functionality of an object at runtime.

The Decorator pattern is also known as Wrapper. The UML is shown in Figure 5-9.

Benefits   Following is a list of benefits of using the Decorator pattern:

- It provides greater flexibility than static inheritance.

- It avoids the need to place feature-laden classes higher up the hierarchy.

- It simplifies coding by allowing you to develop a series of functionality-targeted classes, instead of coding all of the behavior into the object.

- It enhances the extensibility of the object, because changes are made by coding new classes.

FIGURE 5-9

UML for the
Decorator
pattern

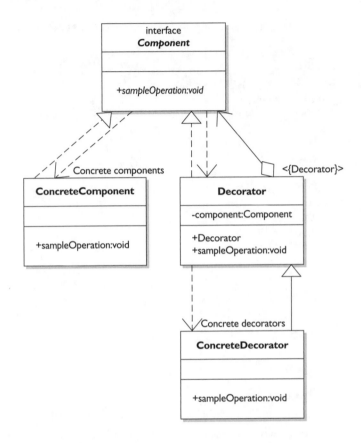

Applicable Scenarios   The following scenarios are most appropriate for the Decorator pattern:

- You want to transparently and dynamically add responsibilities to objects without affecting other objects.

- You want to add responsibilities to an object that you may want to change in the future.

- Extending functionality by subclassing is no longer practical.

J2EE Technology Feature and J2SE API Association   The J2EE technology feature associated with the Decorator pattern is *javax.ejb.EJBObject*. The J2SE API associated with the Decorator pattern is *java.io.BufferedReader*.

Example Code   The following example Java code demonstrates the Decorator pattern:

```java
package j2ee.architect.Decorator;
public class DecoratorPattern {
  public static void main(String[] args) {
    System.out.println("Decorator Pattern Demonstration.");
    System.out.println("-------------------------------");
    // Create object decorated with A
    System.out.println("Creating component decorated with A.");
    ComponentIF decorated1 = new ConcreteDecoratorA();
    // Call action on object decorated with A
    System.out.println("Calling action() on component decorated with A.");
    decorated1.action();
    // Create object decorated with B
    System.out.println("Creating component decorated with B.");
    ComponentIF decorated2 = new ConcreteDecoratorB();
    // Call action on object decorated with B
    System.out.println("Calling action() on component decorated with B.");
    decorated2.action();
    System.out.println();
  }
}


package j2ee.architect.Decorator;
public interface ComponentIF {
  public void action();
}


package j2ee.architect.Decorator;
public class ConcreteComponent implements ComponentIF {
  public void action() {
    System.out.println("ConcreteComponent.action() called.");
  }
}


package j2ee.architect.Decorator;
public class ConcreteDecoratorA extends Decorator {
  String addedVariable;
  public void action() {
    super.action();
    System.out.println("ConcreteDecoratorA.action() called.");
    addedVariable = "extra";
    System.out.println("ConcreteDecoratorA.addedVariable="+addedVariable);
  }
```

```
}

package j2ee.architect.Decorator;
public class ConcreteDecoratorB extends Decorator {
  public void action() {
    super.action();
    System.out.println("ConcreteDecoratorB.action() called.");
    addedMethod();
  }
  private void addedMethod() {
    System.out.println("ConcreteDecoratorB.addedMethod() called.");
  }
}

package j2ee.architect.Decorator;
public class Decorator implements ComponentIF {
  ComponentIF component = new ConcreteComponent();
  public void action() {
    component.action();
  }
}
```

Facade

The Facade pattern's intent is to provide a unified and simplified interface to a set of interfaces in a subsystem. The Facade pattern describes a higher level interface that makes the subsystem(s) easier to use. Practically every Abstract Factory is a type of Facade.

Figure 5-10 shows the UML.

Benefits   Following is a list of benefits of using the Facade pattern:

■ It provides a simpler interface to a complex subsystem without reducing the options provided by the subsystem.

■ It shields clients from the complexity of the subsystem components.

■ It promotes looser coupling between the subsystem and its clients.

■ It reduces the coupling between subsystems provided that every subsystem uses its own Facade pattern and other parts of the system use the Facade pattern to communicate with the subsystem.

FIGURE 5-10

UML for the
Facade pattern

Facade
+action:void

SubSystem1
+function1A:void
+function1B:void
+function1C:void

SubSystemN
+functionN1:void
+functionN2:void

Applicable Scenarios   The following scenarios are most appropriate for the Facade pattern:

- You need to provide a simple interface to a complex subsystem.

- Several dependencies exist between clients and the implementation classes of an abstraction.

- When layering the subsystems is necessary or desired.

J2SE API Association   The J2SE API associated with the Facade pattern is *java.net.URL.*

Example Code   The following example Java code demonstrates the Facade pattern:

```
package j2ee.architect.Facade;
public class FacadePattern {
  public static void main(String[] args) {
    System.out.println("Facade Pattern Demonstration.");
    System.out.println("---------------------------");
    // Construct and call Façade
    System.out.println("Constructing facade.");
    Façade façade = new Façade();
    System.out.println("Calling facade.processOrder().");
    façade.processOrder();
    System.out.println();
  }
}

package j2ee.architect.Facade;
public class Façade {
```

```
    public void processOrder() {
        // Call methods on sub-systems to complete the process
        SubSystem1 subsys1 = new SubSystem1();
        subsys1.getCustomer();
        subsys1.getSecurity();
        subsys1.priceTransaction();
        SubSystemN subsysN = new SubSystemN();
        subsysN.checkBalances();
        subsysN.completeOrder();
    }
}

package j2ee.architect.Facade;
public class SubSystem1 {
  public void getCustomer() {
      // Place functionality here...
      System.out.println("SubSystem1.getCustomer() called.");}
  public void getSecurity() {
      // Place functionality here...
      System.out.println("SubSystem1.getSecurity() called.");}
  public void priceTransaction() {
      // Place functionality here...
      System.out.println("SubSystem1.priceTransaction() called.");}
}

package j2ee.architect.Facade;
public class SubSystemN {
  public void checkBalances() {
      // Place functionality here...
      System.out.println("SubSystemN.checkBalances() called.");}
  public void completeOrder() {
      // Place functionality here...
      System.out.println("SubSystemN.completeOrder() called.");}
}
```

Flyweight

The Flyweight pattern's intent is to utilize sharing to support large numbers of fine-grained objects in an efficient manner.

Figure 5-11 shows the UML.

Benefits   Following are benefits of using the Flyweight pattern:

■ It reduces the number of objects to deal with.

■ It reduces the amount of memory and storage devices required if the objects are persisted.

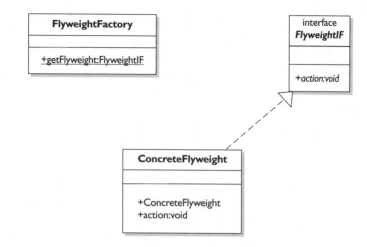

FIGURE 5-11

UML for the
Flyweight pattern

Applicable Scenarios
The following scenarios are most appropriate for the Flyweight pattern:

- An application uses a considerable number of objects.
- The storage costs are high because of the quantity of objects.
- The application does not depend on object identity.

J2SE API Association
The J2SE API associated with the Flyweight pattern is *java.lang.String*.

Example Code
The following example Java code demonstrates the Flyweight pattern:

```
package j2ee.architect.Flyweight;
public class FlyweightPattern {
  public static void main(String[] args) {
    System.out.println("Flyweight Pattern Demonstration.");
    System.out.println("-------------------------------");
    // Create states
    State stateF = new State(false);
    State stateT = new State(true);
    // Get reference to (and in doing so create) flyweight
    FlyweightIF myfwkey1 = FlyweightFactory.getFlyweight("myfwkey");
    // Get new reference to the same flyweight
```

```
      FlyweightIF myfwkey2 = FlyweightFactory.getFlyweight("myfwkey");
      // Call action on both references
      System.out.println("Call flyweight action with state=false");
      myfwkey1.action(stateF);
      System.out.println("Call flyweight action with state=true");
      myfwkey2.action(stateT);
      System.out.println();
  }
}

package j2ee.architect.Flyweight;
public class ConcreteFlyweight implements FlyweightIF {
  // Add state to the concrete flyweight.
  private boolean state;
  public ConcreteFlyweight(State parm) {
    this.state = parm.getState();
  }
  public void action(State parm) {
    // Display internal state and state passed by client.
    System.out.println("ConcreteFlyweight.action("
      +parm.getState()+") called.");
    this.state = parm.getState();
    System.out.println("ConcreteFlyweight.state = "
      + this.state);
  }
}

package j2ee.architect.Flyweight;
import java.util.*;
public class FlyweightFactory {
  private static Map map = new HashMap();
  public static FlyweightIF getFlyweight(String parm) {
    // Return the Flyweight if it exists,
    // or create it if it doesn't.
    FlyweightIF flyweight = null;
    try {
      if (map.containsKey(parm)) {
        // Return existing flyweight
        flyweight = (FlyweightIF) map.get(parm);
      } else {
        // Create flyweight with a 'true' state
        flyweight = new ConcreteFlyweight(new State(true));
        map.put(parm, flyweight);
        System.out.println("Created flyweight "+parm+" with state=true");
        System.out.println("");
```

```
      }
    } catch (ClassCastException cce) {
      System.out.println(cce.getMessage());
    }
    return flyweight;
  }
}

package j2ee.architect.Flyweight;
public interface FlyweightIF {
      // method to receive and act on extrinsic state.
  public void action(State parm);
}

package j2ee.architect.Flyweight;
public class State {
  private boolean state;
  public State(boolean parm) {this.state = parm;}
  public boolean getState() {return state;}
}
```

Proxy

The Proxy pattern's intent is to provide a surrogate or placeholder for another object to control access to it. The most common implementations are remote and virtual proxy.

The Proxy pattern is also known as Surrogate. Figure 5-12 shows the UML.

Benefits   Following is a list of benefits of using the Proxy pattern:

- The remote proxy can shield the fact that the implementation resides in another address space.

- The virtual proxy can perform optimizations—for example, by creating objects on demand.

Applicable Scenario   The Proxy pattern is appropriate when a more versatile or sophisticated reference to an object, rather than a simple pointer, is needed.

J2EE Technology Feature   The J2EE technology feature associated with the Proxy pattern is *javax.ejb.EJBObject* (EJB remote reference) in a structural sense. Actually the "stub" object in the client's address space provides the proxy.

FIGURE 5-12

UML for the
Proxy pattern

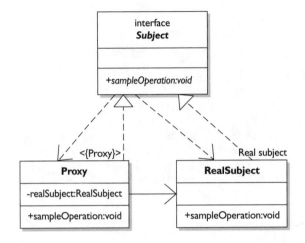

Example Code   The following Java code demonstrates the Proxy pattern:

```
package j2ee.architect.Proxy;
public class ProxyPattern {
  public static void main(String[] args) {
    System.out.println("Proxy Pattern Demonstration.");
    System.out.println("--------------------------");
    // Create service proxy (instantiates service too)
    System.out.println("Creating proxy to service.");
    ServiceIF proxy = new Proxy();
    // Call action method on service via proxy
    System.out.println("Calling action method on proxy.");
    proxy.action();
    System.out.println();
  }
}

package j2ee.architect.Proxy;
public class Proxy implements ServiceIF {
  // Proxy to be the service
  private Service service = new Service();
  public void action() {
    service.action();
  }
}

package j2ee.architect.Proxy;
public class Service implements ServiceIF {
```

```
  // Service to be proxied
  public Service() {
    System.out.println("Service constructed.");
  }
  public void action() {
    System.out.println("Service.action() called.");
  }
}

package j2ee.architect.Proxy;
public interface ServiceIF {
  // Interface for Service and Proxy
  public void action();
}
```

GoF Behavioral Design Patterns

Behavioral patterns are concerned with the interaction and responsibility of objects. They help make complex behavior manageable by specifying the responsibilities of objects and the ways they communicate with each other.

The following Behavioral patterns are described by GoF:

- Chain of Responsibility

- Command

- Interpreter

- Iterator

- Mediator

- Memento

- Observer

- State

- Strategy

- Template Method

- Visitor

Chain of Responsibility

The Chain of Responsibility pattern's intent is to avoid coupling the sender of a request to its receiver by giving multiple objects a chance to handle the request. The request is passed along the chain of receiving objects until an object processes it. Figure 5-13 shows the UML.

Benefits   Following are the benefits of using the Chain of Responsibility pattern:

■ It reduces coupling.

■ It adds flexibility when assigning responsibilities to objects.

■ It allows a set of classes to act as one; events produced in one class can be sent to other handler classes within the composition.

Applicable Scenarios   The following scenarios are most appropriate for the Chain of Responsibility pattern:

■ More than one object can handle a request and the handler is unknown.

■ A request is to be issued to one of several objects and the receiver is not specified explicitly.

■ The set of objects able to handle the request is to be specified dynamically.

FIGURE 5-13

UML for the Chain of Responsibility pattern

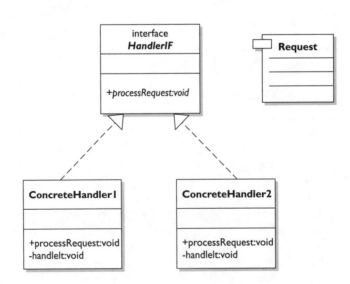

J2EE Technology Feature   The J2EE technology feature associated with the
Chain of Responsibility pattern is *RequestDispatcher* in the servlet/JSP API.

Example Code   The following example Java code demonstrates the Chain of
Responsibility pattern:

```java
package j2ee.architect.ChainOfResponsibility;
public class ChainOfResponsibilityPattern {
  public static void main(String[] args) {
    System.out.println("Chain Of Responsibility Pattern Demonstration.");
    System.out.println("----------------------------------------------");
    try {
      // Create Equity Order request.
      System.out.println("Creating Equity Order request.");
      Request equityOrderRequest = new Request(Request.EQUITY_ORDER);
      // Create Bond Order request.
      System.out.println("Creating Bond Order request.");
      Request bondOrderRequest = new Request(Request.BOND_ORDER);
      // Create a request handler.
      System.out.println("Creating 1st handler.");
      HandlerIF handler = new ConcreteHandler1();
      // Process the Equity Order.
      System.out.println("Calling 1st handler with Equity Order.");
      handler.processRequest(equityOrderRequest);
      // Process the Bond Order.
      System.out.println("Calling 1st handler with Bond Order");
      handler.processRequest(bondOrderRequest);
    } catch (Exception e) {System.out.println(e.getMessage());}
    System.out.println();
  }
}


package j2ee.architect.ChainOfResponsibility;
public class ConcreteHandler1 implements HandlerIF {
  public void processRequest(Request parm) {
    // Start the processing chain here...
    switch (parm.getType()) {
      case Request.EQUITY_ORDER: // This object processes equity orders
        handleIt(parm);          // so call the function to handle it.
        break;
      case Request.BOND_ORDER:   // Another object processes bond orders so
        System.out.println("Creating 2nd handler."); // pass request along.
        new ConcreteHandler2().processRequest(parm);
        break;
```

```
    }
  }
  private void handleIt(Request parm) {
    System.out.println("ConcreteHandler1 has handled the processing.");
  }
}


package j2ee.architect.ChainOfResponsibility;
public class ConcreteHandler2 implements HandlerIF {
  public void processRequest(Request parm) {
    // You could add on to the processing chain here...
    handleIt(parm);
  }
  private void handleIt(Request parm) {
    System.out.println("ConcreteHandler2 has handled the processing.");
  }
}


package j2ee.architect.ChainOfResponsibility;
public interface HandlerIF {
  public void processRequest(Request request);
}


package j2ee.architect.ChainOfResponsibility;
public class Request {
  // The universe of known requests that can be handled.
  public final static int EQUITY_ORDER = 100;
  public final static int BOND_ORDER  = 200;
  // This objects type of request.
  private int type;
  public Request(int parm) throws Exception {
    // Validate the request type with the known universe.
    if ((parm == EQUITY_ORDER) || (parm == BOND_ORDER))
      // Store this request type.
      this.type = parm;
    else
      throw new Exception("Unknown Request type "+parm+".");
  }
  public int getType() {
    return type;
  }
}
```

Command

The Command pattern's intent is to encapsulate a request as an object, thereby letting you parameterize clients with different requests, queue or log requests, and support rollback types of operations.

The Command pattern is also known as Action or Transaction. The UML is shown in Figure 5-14.

Benefits   Following is a list of benefits of using the Command pattern:

- It separates the object that invokes the operation from the object that actually performs the operation.

- It simplifies adding new commands, because existing classes remain unchanged.

Applicable Scenarios   The following scenarios are most appropriate for the Command pattern:

- You need to parameterize objects according to an action to perform.

- You create, queue, and execute requests at different times.

- You need to support rollback, logging, or transaction functionality.

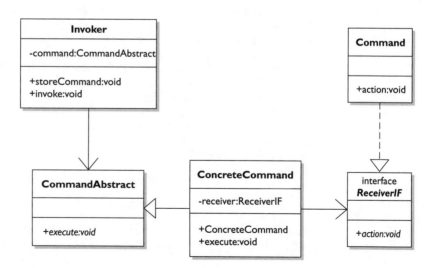

FIGURE 5-14

UML for the Command pattern

J2EE Technology Feature   The J2EE technology features associated with the Command pattern are

- MessageBeans invoke business logic based on content of messages dispatched to them.
- Servlets/JSPs are invoked based on the type of HTTP request that is received by the web container.

Example Code   The following example Java code demonstrates the Command pattern:

```
package j2ee.architect.Command;
public class CommandPattern {
  public static void main(String[] args) {
    System.out.println("Command Pattern Demonstration.");
    System.out.println("-----------------------------");
    // Create receiver objects.
    System.out.println("Creating receivers.");
    ReceiverIF order = new Order();
    ReceiverIF trade = new Trade();
    // Create commands passing in receiver objects.
    System.out.println("Creating commands.");
    CommandAbstract cmdOrder = new ConcreteCommand(order);
    CommandAbstract cmdTrade = new ConcreteCommand(trade);
    // Create invokers.
    System.out.println("Creating invokers.");
    Invoker invOrder = new Invoker();
    Invoker invTrade = new Invoker();
    // Storing commands in invokers respectively.
    System.out.println("Storing commands in invokers.");
    invOrder.storeCommand(cmdOrder);
    invTrade.storeCommand(cmdTrade);
    // Call invoke on the invoker to execute the command.
    System.out.println("Invoking the invokers.");
    invOrder.invoke();
    invTrade.invoke();
    System.out.println();
  }
}

package j2ee.architect.Command;
abstract class CommandAbstract {
```

```
    public abstract void execute();
}

package j2ee.architect.Command;
public class ConcreteCommand extends CommandAbstract {
  // The binding between action and receiver
  private ReceiverIF receiver;
  public ConcreteCommand(ReceiverIF receive) {
    this.receiver = receive;
  }
  public void execute() {
      receiver.action();
  }
}

package j2ee.architect.Command;
public class Invoker {
  private CommandAbstract command;
  public void storeCommand(CommandAbstract cmd) {
    this.command = cmd;
  }
  public void invoke() {
    command.execute();
  }
}

package j2ee.architect.Command;
public class Order implements ReceiverIF {
  public void action() {
    System.out.println("Order.action() called.");
  }
}

package j2ee.architect.Command;
public interface ReceiverIF {
  public void action();
}

package j2ee.architect.Command;
public class Trade implements ReceiverIF {
  public void action() {
    System.out.println("Trade.action() called.");
  }
}
```

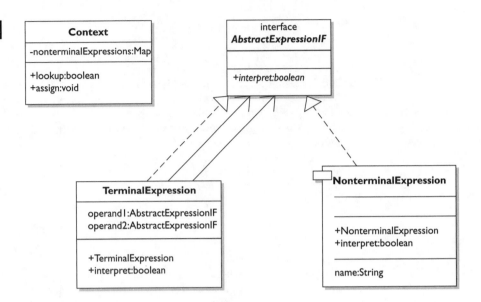

FIGURE 5-15

UML for the
Interpreter
pattern

Interpreter

The Interpreter pattern's intent is to define a representation of the grammar of a
given language, along with an interpreter that uses this representation to interpret
sentences in the language. The UML is shown in Figure 5-15.

Benefits   Following is a list of benefits of using the Interpreter pattern:

- It is easier to change and extend the grammar.
- Implementing the grammar is straightforward.

Applicable Scenarios   The following scenarios are most appropriate for the
Interpreter pattern:

- The grammar of the language is not complicated.
- Efficiency is not a priority.

Example Code   The following example Java code demonstrates the Interpreter
pattern:

```java
package j2ee.architect.Interpreter;
import java.util.ArrayList;
import java.util.ListIterator;
import java.util.StringTokenizer;
public class InterpreterPattern {
  public static void main(String[] args) {
    System.out.println("Interpreter Pattern Demonstration.");
    System.out.println("--------------------------------");
    BookInterpreterContext bookInterpreterContext = new BookInterpreterContext();
    bookInterpreterContext.addTitle("Pickwick Papers");
    bookInterpreterContext.addTitle("Great Expectations");
    bookInterpreterContext.addTitle("Wuthering Heights");
    bookInterpreterContext.addTitle("Crossfile");
    bookInterpreterContext.addAuthor("William Shakespeare");
    bookInterpreterContext.addAuthor("Emily Bronte");
    bookInterpreterContext.addAuthor("James Marathon");
    bookInterpreterContext.addTitleAndAuthor(
      new TitleAndAuthor("Pickwick Papers", "William Shakespeare"));
    bookInterpreterContext.addTitleAndAuthor(
      new TitleAndAuthor("Great Expectations", "William Shakespeare"));
    bookInterpreterContext.addTitleAndAuthor(
      new TitleAndAuthor("Wuthering Heights", "Emily Bronte"));
    bookInterpreterContext.addTitleAndAuthor(
      new TitleAndAuthor("Crossfire", "James Marathon"));
    BookInterpreterClient bookInterpreterClient
      = new BookInterpreterClient(bookInterpreterContext);
    System.out.println("show author ->"
      + bookInterpreterClient.interpret("show author"));
    System.out.println("show title ->"
      + bookInterpreterClient.interpret("show title"));
    System.out.println("show author for title <Crossfire> ->"
      + bookInterpreterClient.interpret("show author for title <Crossfire>"));
    System.out.println("show title for author <William Shakespeare> ->"
      + bookInterpreterClient.interpret(
        "show title for author <William Shakespeare>"));
    System.out.println();
  }
}
class BookInterpreterClient {
  BookInterpreterContext bookInterpreterContext;
  public BookInterpreterClient(BookInterpreterContext parm) {
    bookInterpreterContext = parm;
  }
  // language syntax:
```

```
// show title
// show author
// show title for author <author-name>
// show author for title <title-name>
public String interpret(String expression) {
  StringTokenizer expressionTokens = new StringTokenizer(expression);
  String currentToken;
  char mainQuery = ' ';
  char subQuery = ' ';
  String searchString = null;
  boolean forUsed = false;
  boolean searchStarted = false;
  boolean searchEnded = false;
  StringBuffer result = new StringBuffer();
  while (expressionTokens.hasMoreTokens()) {
    currentToken = expressionTokens.nextToken();
    if (currentToken.equals("show")) {
      continue;//show in all queries, not really used
    } else if (currentToken.equals("title")) {
      if (mainQuery == ' ') {
        mainQuery = 'T';
      } else {
        if ((subQuery == ' ') && (forUsed)) {
          subQuery = 'T';
        }
      }
    } else if (currentToken.equals("author")) {
      if (mainQuery == ' ') {
        mainQuery = 'A';
      }  else {
        if ((subQuery == ' ') && (forUsed)) {
          subQuery = 'A';
        }
      }
    } else if (currentToken.equals("for")) {
      forUsed = true;
    } else if ((searchString == null) && (subQuery != ' ')
        && (currentToken.startsWith("<"))) {
      searchString = currentToken;
      searchStarted = true;
      if (currentToken.endsWith(">")) {
        searchEnded = true;
      }
    } else if ((searchStarted) && (!searchEnded)) {
      searchString = searchString + " " + currentToken;
```

```java
            if (currentToken.endsWith(">")) {
              searchEnded = true;
            }
          }
        }
        if (searchString != null) {
          searchString
            = searchString.substring(1,(searchString.length() - 1));//remove <>
        }
        BookAbstractExpression abstractExpression;
        switch (mainQuery) {
          case 'A' : {
            switch (subQuery) {
              case 'T' : {
                abstractExpression = new BookAuthorTitleExpression(searchString);
                break;
              } default : {
                abstractExpression = new BookAuthorExpression();
                break;
              }
            }
            break;
          } case 'T' : {
            switch (subQuery) {
              case 'A' : {
                abstractExpression = new BookTitleAuthorExpression(searchString);
                break;
              } default : {
                abstractExpression = new BookTitleExpression();
                break;
              }
            }
            break;
          } default : return result.toString();
        }
        result.append(abstractExpression.interpret(bookInterpreterContext));
        return result.toString();
      }
}
class BookInterpreterContext {
  private ArrayList titles = new ArrayList();
  private ArrayList authors = new ArrayList();
  private ArrayList titlesAndAuthors = new ArrayList();
  public void addTitle(String title) {titles.add(title);}
  public void addAuthor(String author) {authors.add(author);}
```

```
public void addTitleAndAuthor(TitleAndAuthor titleAndAuthor)
  {titlesAndAuthors.add(titleAndAuthor);}
public ArrayList getAllTitles() {return titles;}
public ArrayList getAllAuthors() {return authors;}
public ArrayList getAuthorsForTitle(String titleIn) {
  ArrayList authorsForTitle = new ArrayList();
  TitleAndAuthor tempTitleAndAuthor;
  ListIterator titlesAndAuthorsIterator = titlesAndAuthors.listIterator();
  while (titlesAndAuthorsIterator.hasNext()) {
    tempTitleAndAuthor = (TitleAndAuthor)titlesAndAuthorsIterator.next();
    if (titleIn.equals(tempTitleAndAuthor.getTitle())) {
      authorsForTitle.add(tempTitleAndAuthor.getAuthor());
    }
  }
  return authorsForTitle;
}
public ArrayList getTitlesForAuthor(String authorIn) {
  ArrayList titlesForAuthor = new ArrayList();
  TitleAndAuthor tempTitleAndAuthor;
  ListIterator authorsAndTitlesIterator = titlesAndAuthors.listIterator();
  while (authorsAndTitlesIterator.hasNext()) {
    tempTitleAndAuthor = (TitleAndAuthor)authorsAndTitlesIterator.next();
    if (authorIn.equals(tempTitleAndAuthor.getAuthor())) {
      titlesForAuthor.add(tempTitleAndAuthor.getTitle());
    }
  }
  return titlesForAuthor;
}
}
abstract class BookAbstractExpression {
  public abstract String interpret(BookInterpreterContext parm);
}
class BookAuthorExpression extends BookAbstractExpression {
  public String interpret(BookInterpreterContext parm) {
    ArrayList authors = parm.getAllAuthors();
    ListIterator authorsIterator = authors.listIterator();
    StringBuffer titleBuffer = new StringBuffer("");
    boolean first = true;
    while (authorsIterator.hasNext()) {
      if (!first) {titleBuffer.append(", ");}
      else {first = false;}
      titleBuffer.append((String)authorsIterator.next());
    }
    return titleBuffer.toString();
  }
```

```
  }
class BookAuthorTitleExpression extends BookAbstractExpression {
  String title;
  public BookAuthorTitleExpression(String parm) {title = parm;}
  public String interpret(BookInterpreterContext parm) {
    ArrayList authorsAndTitles = parm.getAuthorsForTitle(title);
    ListIterator authorsAndTitlesIterator = authorsAndTitles.listIterator();
    StringBuffer authorBuffer = new StringBuffer("");
    boolean first = true;
    while (authorsAndTitlesIterator.hasNext()) {
      if (!first) {authorBuffer.append(", ");}
      else {first = false;}
      authorBuffer.append((String)authorsAndTitlesIterator.next());
    }
    return authorBuffer.toString();
  }
}
class BookTitleExpression extends BookAbstractExpression {
  public String interpret(BookInterpreterContext parm) {
    ArrayList titles = parm.getAllTitles();
    ListIterator titlesIterator = titles.listIterator();
    StringBuffer titleBuffer = new StringBuffer("");
    boolean first = true;
    while (titlesIterator.hasNext()) {
      if (!first) {titleBuffer.append(", ");}
      else {first = false;}
      titleBuffer.append((String)titlesIterator.next());
    }
    return titleBuffer.toString();
  }
}
class BookTitleAuthorExpression extends BookAbstractExpression {
  String title;
  public BookTitleAuthorExpression(String parm) {title = parm;}
  public String interpret(BookInterpreterContext parm) {
    ArrayList titlesAndAuthors = parm.getTitlesForAuthor(title);
    ListIterator titlesAndAuthorsIterator = titlesAndAuthors.listIterator();
    StringBuffer titleBuffer = new StringBuffer("");
    boolean first = true;
    while (titlesAndAuthorsIterator.hasNext()) {
      if (!first) {titleBuffer.append(", ");}
      else {first = false;}
      titleBuffer.append((String)titlesAndAuthorsIterator.next());
    }
    return titleBuffer.toString();
```

```
  }
}
class TitleAndAuthor {
  private String title;
  private String author;
  public TitleAndAuthor(String parm1, String parm2) {
    title = parm1;
    author = parm2;
  }
  public String getTitle() {return title;}
  public String getAuthor() {return author;}
}
```

Iterator

The Iterator pattern's intent is to provide a way to access the elements of an aggregate object sequentially without exposing its underlying implementation. *java.util.Enumeration* and *java.util.Iterator* are examples of the Iterator pattern.

The Iterator pattern is also known as Cursor. The UML is shown in Figure 5-16.

Benefits   Following is a list of benefits of using the Iterator pattern:

■ It supports variations in the traversal of a collection.

■ It simplifies the interface to the collection.

Applicable Scenarios   The following scenarios are most appropriate for the Iterator pattern:

■ Access to a collection object is required without having to expose its internal representation.

■ Multiple traversals of objects need to be supported in the collection.

■ A universal interface for traversing different structures needs to be provided in the collection.

J2EE Technology Feature and J2SE API Association   The J2EE technology feature associated with the Command pattern is *ValueListHandler* in the J2EE Patterns Catalog.

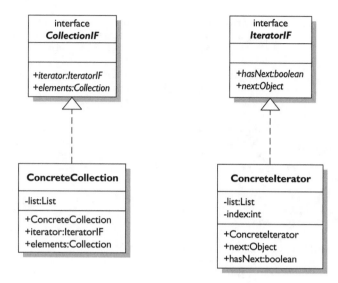

FIGURE 5-16

UML for the
Iterator pattern

The J2SE APIs associated with the Iterator pattern are

■ *java.util.Iterator*

■ *java.util.Enumeration*

Example Code The following example Java code demonstrates the Iterator pattern:

```
package j2ee.architect.Iterator;
public class IteratorPattern {
  public static void main(String[] args) {
    System.out.println("Iterator Pattern Demonstration.");
    System.out.println("----------------------------");
    System.out.println("Building string array of books.");
    String[] books = new String[8];
    books[0] = "PowerBuilder Developers Guide, 1994";
    books[1] = "Informix Developers Guide, 1995";
    books[2] = "Informix Universal Data Option, 1996";
    books[3] = "SQL Server Developers Guide, 1999";
    books[4] = "SilverStream Success I, 1999";
    books[5] = "SilverStream Success II, 2000";
    books[6] = "J2EE Unleashed, 2001";
    books[7] = "Enterprise Architect Study Guide, 2002";
    // Turn the string array into a collection.
```

```
    System.out.println("Turning string array into a collection.");
    CollectionIF collection = new ConcreteCollection(books);
    // Get an iterator for the collection.
    System.out.println("Getting an iterator for the collection..");
    IteratorIF iterator = collection.iterator();
    // Iterate through and print each object in the list.
    System.out.println("Iterate through the list.");
    int i = 0;
    while (iterator.hasNext()) {
      System.out.println((++i)+" "+iterator.next());
    }
    System.out.println();
  }
}

package j2ee.architect.Iterator;
import java.util.*;
public interface CollectionIF {
  // Interface for creating a
  // collection that needs iterating.
  public IteratorIF iterator();
  public Collection elements();

}

package j2ee.architect.Iterator;
import java.util.*;
public class ConcreteCollection implements CollectionIF {
  // Builds an iterable list of elements
  private List list = new ArrayList();
  public ConcreteCollection(Object[] objectList) {
    for (int i=0; i < objectList.length; i++) {
      list.add(objectList[i]);
    }
  }
  public IteratorIF iterator() {
    return new ConcreteIterator(this);
  }
  public Collection elements() {
    return Collections.unmodifiableList(list);
  }
}

package j2ee.architect.Iterator;
import java.util.*;
public class ConcreteIterator implements IteratorIF {
  private List list;
  private int index;
  public ConcreteIterator(CollectionIF parm) {
```

```
      list = (List) parm.elements();
      index = 0;
   }
   public Object next() throws RuntimeException {
      try {
        return list.get(index++);
      } catch (IndexOutOfBoundsException ioobe) {
        throw new RuntimeException("No Such Element");
      }
   }
   public boolean hasNext() {
      return (index < list.size()) ? true : false;
   }
}

package j2ee.architect.Iterator;
public interface IteratorIF {
   // Interface for Iterators.
   public boolean hasNext();
   public Object next();
}
```

Mediator

The Mediator pattern's intent is to define an object that encapsulates how a set of objects interacts. It helps to promote a looser coupling by keeping objects from referring to each other explicitly, therefore allowing any interaction to vary independently. The UML is shown in Figure 5-17.

Benefits   Following is a list of benefits of using the Mediator pattern:

- It decouples colleagues.

- It simplifies object protocols.

- It centralizes control.

- The individual components become simpler and much easier to deal with because they do not need to pass messages to one another.

- The components do not need to contain logic to deal with their intercommunication and are therefore more generic.

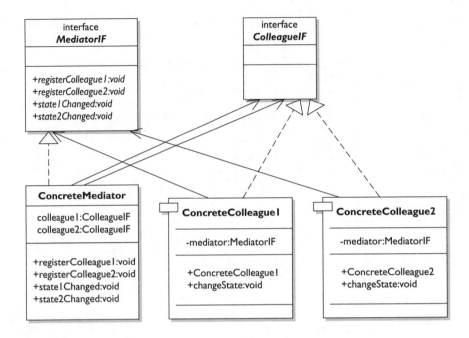

FIGURE 5-17

UML for the
Mediator pattern

Applicable Scenarios   The following scenarios are most appropriate for the
Mediator pattern:

- A set of objects communicates in complex but well-defined ways.

- Custom behavior distributed between several objects is required without
  subclassing. It is commonly used structurally in message-based systems. The
  messages themselves are the means by which related objects are decoupled.

Example Code   The following example Java code demonstrates the Mediator
pattern:

```
package j2ee.architect.Mediator;
public class MediatorPattern {
  public static void main(String[] args) {
    System.out.println("Mediator Pattern Demonstration.");
    System.out.println("--------------------------------");
    // Construct mediator and colleagues
    System.out.println("Constructing mediator and colleagues.");
```

```
      MediatorIF  mediator   = new ConcreteMediator();
      ColleagueIF colleague1 = new ConcreteColleague1(mediator);
      ColleagueIF colleague2 = new ConcreteColleague2(mediator);
      // Display colleague values.
      System.out.println("Displaying colleague states.");
      System.out.println("colleague1.toString()="+colleague1);
      System.out.println("colleague2.toString()="+colleague2);
      // Change state on colleague1 and the mediator
      // will coordinate the change with colleague2.
      System.out.println("Calling colleague1.changeState()");
      ((ConcreteColleague1) colleague1).changeState();
      // Display colleague values now.
      System.out.println("Displaying colleague states now.");
      System.out.println("colleague1.toString()="+colleague1);
      System.out.println("colleague2.toString()="+colleague2);
      // Change state on colleague2 and see what happens.
      System.out.println("Calling colleague2.changeState()");
      ((ConcreteColleague2) colleague2).changeState();
      // Display colleague values now.
      System.out.println("Displaying colleague states again.");
      System.out.println("colleague1.toString()="+colleague1);
      System.out.println("colleague2.toString()="+colleague2);
      System.out.println();
   }
}

package j2ee.architect.Mediator;
public interface ColleagueIF { }

package j2ee.architect.Mediator;
public class ConcreteColleague1 implements ColleagueIF {
  private MediatorIF mediator;
  // This colleague uses a boolean for it's state.
  private boolean state;
  public ConcreteColleague1(MediatorIF parm) {
    this.mediator = parm;
    this.mediator.registerColleague1(this);
  }
  public void setState(boolean parm) {
    this.state = parm;
  }
  public void changeState() {
```

```
    state = state ? false : true;
    mediator.state1Changed();
  }
  public String toString() {
    return new Boolean(state).toString();
  }
}

package j2ee.architect.Mediator;
public class ConcreteColleague2 implements ColleagueIF {
  private MediatorIF mediator;
  // This colleague uses a string for its state.
  private String state = "false";
  public ConcreteColleague2(MediatorIF parm) {
    this.mediator = parm;
    this.mediator.registerColleague2(this);
  }
  public void setState(String parm) {
    this.state = parm;
  }
  public void changeState() {
    state = state.equals("false") ? "true" : "false";
    mediator.state2Changed();
  }
  public String toString() {
    return state;
  }
}

package j2ee.architect.Mediator;
public class ConcreteMediator implements MediatorIF {
  ColleagueIF colleague1;
  ColleagueIF colleague2;
  public void registerColleague1(ColleagueIF parm) {
    this.colleague1 = (ConcreteColleague1) parm;
  }
  public void registerColleague2(ColleagueIF parm) {
    this.colleague2 = (ConcreteColleague2) parm;
  }
  public void state1Changed() {
    String s = (colleague2.toString().equals("true")) ? "false" : "true";
```

```
      ((ConcreteColleague2) colleague2).setState(s);
  }
  public void state2Changed() {
    boolean b = (colleague1.toString().equals("true")) ? false : true;
    ((ConcreteColleague1) colleague1).setState(b);
  }
}

package j2ee.architect.Mediator;
public interface MediatorIF {
  //Interface for communicating with colleagues
  public void registerColleague1(ColleagueIF parm);
  public void registerColleague2(ColleagueIF parm);
  public void state1Changed();
  public void state2Changed();
}
```

Memento

The Memento pattern's intent is to capture and internalize an object's internal state so that objects can be restored to this state later. It must do this without violating encapsulation.

The Memento pattern is also known as Token. The UML is shown in Figure 5-18.

Benefits   Following is a list of benefits of using the Memento pattern:

■ It preserves encapsulation boundaries.

■ It simplifies the originator.

FIGURE 5-18

UML for the
Memento pattern

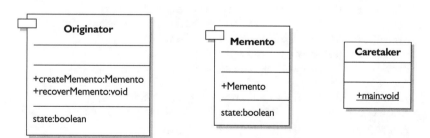

Applicable Scenarios   The following scenarios are most appropriate for the Memento pattern:

- A snapshot containing enough information regarding the state of an object can be saved so that it can be restored to the complete state using the snapshot information later.

- Using a direct interface to obtain the state would impose implementation details that would break the rules of encapsulation for the object.

J2EE Technology Feature   The J2EE technology feature associated with the Memento pattern is EntityBeans using Bean-Managed Persistence (BMP).

Example Code   The following example Java code demonstrates the Memento pattern:

```java
package j2ee.architect.Memento;
public class MementoPattern {
  public static void main(String[] args) {
    System.out.println("Memento Pattern Demonstration.");
    System.out.println("------------------------------");
    // Run the caretaker
    Caretaker.run();
    System.out.println();
  }
}


package j2ee.architect.Memento;
public class Caretaker {
  public static void run() {
    // Create originator and set initial values.
    System.out.println("Creating originator and setting initial values.");
    Originator originator = new Originator();
    originator.setState(true);
    originator.setName("The Originator");
    // Create memento.
    System.out.println("Creating memento.");
    Memento memento = originator.createMemento();
    System.out.println(originator);
    // Change originator values.
    System.out.println("Changing originator values.");
    originator.setState(false);
```

```
    originator.setName("To be undone.");
    System.out.println(originator);
    // Recover state from memento.
    System.out.println("Recovering originator values from memento.");
    originator.recoverFromMemento(memento);
    System.out.println(originator);
  }
}

package j2ee.architect.Memento;
public class Memento {
  private boolean state;
  private String  name;
  Memento(boolean parm1, String parm2) {
    this.state = parm1;
    this.name  = parm2;
  }
  boolean getState() {return this.state;}
  String getName()   {return this.name;}
}

package j2ee.architect.Memento;
public class Originator {
  private boolean state;
  private String  name;
  private String  other;
  // Create memento, save critical data in it.
  public Memento createMemento() {
    return new Memento(state, name);
  }
  // Recover critical data from memento.
  public void recoverFromMemento(Memento memento) {
    this.state = memento.getState();
    this.name  = memento.getName();
  }
  public void setState(boolean parm) {
    this.state = parm;
  }
  public void setName(String parm) {
    this.name = parm;
  }
  public String toString() {
    return "Originator.toString() state="+state+", name="+name;
  }
}
```

Observer

The Observer pattern's intent is to define a one-to-many dependency so that when one object changes state, all its dependents are notified and updated automatically. Java provides support for implementing the Observer pattern via the *java.util.Observer* interface and the *java.util.Observable* class.

The Observer pattern is also known as Dependents or Publish-Subscribe. The UML is shown in Figure 5-19.

Benefits   Following is a list of benefits of using the Observer pattern:

■ It abstracts the coupling between the subject and the observer.

■ It provides support for broadcast type communication.

Applicable Scenarios   The following scenarios are most appropriate for the Observer pattern:

■ A change to an object requires changing other objects, and the number of objects that need to be changed is unknown.

■ An object needs to notify other objects without making any assumptions about the identity of those objects.

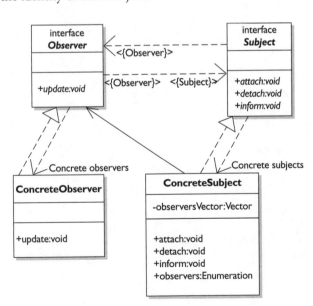

FIGURE 5-19

UML for the
Observer pattern

J2EE Technology Feature and J2SE API Association   The J2EE
technology feature associated with the Observer pattern is JMS (Java Message
Server) Publish/Subscribe Model.

The J2SE APIs associated with the Observer pattern are

- *java.lang.Observable*
- *java.lang.Observer*

Example Code   The following example Java code demonstrates the Observer
pattern:

```
package j2ee.architect.Observer;
public class ObserverPattern {
  public static void main(String[] args) {
    System.out.println("Observer Pattern Demonstration.");
    System.out.println("----------------------------");
    // Constructing observers.
    System.out.println("Constructing observer1 and observer2.");
    ObserverIF observer1 = new ConcreteObserver();
    ObserverIF observer2 = new ConcreteObserver();
    // Constructing observable (subject).
    System.out.println("Constructing observerable (subject).");
    ConcreteSubject subject = new ConcreteSubject();
    // Add observer object references to the subject.
    System.out.println("Registering observers with subject.");
    subject.addObserver(observer1);
    subject.addObserver(observer2);
    System.out.println("Doing something in the subject over time...");
    System.out.println();
    System.out.println("                     Observable  Observer1   Observer2");
    System.out.println("Iteration   changed?   notified?   notified?");
    // Use loop to simulate time.
    for(int i=0;i < 10;i++) {
      System.out.print(i+":              ");
      subject.doSomething();
      System.out.println();
    }
    System.out.println();
    System.out.println("Removing observer1 from the subject...repeating...");
    System.out.println();
    subject.removeObserver(observer1);
    // Another loop to simulate time.
    for(int i=0;i < 10;i++) {
```

```java
      System.out.print(i+":                    ");
      subject.doSomething();
      System.out.println();
    }
  }
}

package j2ee.architect.Observer;
public class ConcreteObserver implements ObserverIF {
  private ConcreteSubject subject; // Reference to subject
  public void update() {
    if (subject == null) { subject = new ConcreteSubject(); }
    System.out.print("        Yes!");
  }
}

package j2ee.architect.Observer;
import java.util.*;
public class ConcreteSubject implements SubjectIF {
  List observers = new ArrayList();
  public void addObserver(ObserverIF parm) {observers.add(parm);}
  public void removeObserver(ObserverIF parm)
{observers.remove(observers.indexOf(parm));}
  public void notifyObservers() {
    for (Iterator i = observers.iterator(); i.hasNext();) {
      ((ObserverIF) i.next()).update();
    }
  }
  public void doSomething() {
    double d = Math.random();
    if (d<0.25 || d>0.75) {
      System.out.print("Yes");
      notifyObservers();
    } else {
      System.out.print("No");
    }
  }
}

package j2ee.architect.Observer;
public interface ObserverIF {
  public void update();
}

package j2ee.architect.Observer;
public interface SubjectIF {
```

```
    public void addObserver(ObserverIF parm);
    public void removeObserver(ObserverIF parm);
    public void notifyObservers();
}
```

State

The State pattern's intent is to allow an object to alter its behavior when its internal state changes, appearing as though the object itself has changed its class.

The State pattern is also known as Objects for States and acts in a similar way to the Receiver in the Command pattern. The UML is shown in Figure 5-20.

Benefits   Following is a list of benefits of using the State pattern:

- It keeps state-specific behavior local and partitions behavior for different states.

- It makes any state transitions explicit.

Applicable Scenarios   The following scenarios are most appropriate for the State pattern:

- The behavior of an object depends on its state and it must be able to change its behavior at runtime according on the new state.

- Operations have large, multipart conditional statements that depend on the state of the object.

FIGURE 5-20

UML for the
State pattern

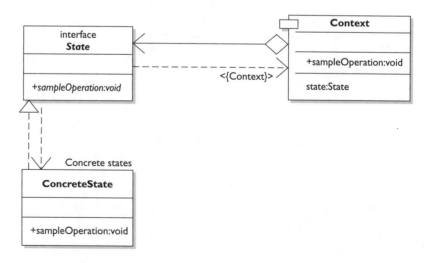

Example Code   The following example Java code demonstrates the State pattern:

```
package j2ee.architect.State;
public class StatePattern {
  public static void main(String[] args) {
    System.out.println("State Pattern Demonstration.");
    System.out.println("--------------------------");
    // Construct context.
    System.out.println("Constructing context.");
    Context context = new Context();
    // Call request, make state handle the request.
    System.out.println("Calling context.request().");
    context.request();
    // Flip state.
    System.out.println("Calling context.changeState().");
    context.changeState();
    // call request.
    System.out.println("Calling context.request().");
    context.request();
    System.out.println();
  }
}

package j2ee.architect.State;
public class ConcreteState1 implements StateIF {
  public void handle() {
    System.out.println("ConcreteState1.handle() called.");
  }
}

package j2ee.architect.State;
public class ConcreteState2 implements StateIF {
  public void handle() {
    System.out.println("ConcreteState2.handle() called.");
  }
}

package j2ee.architect.State;
public class Context {
  // Initial state.
  private StateIF state = new ConcreteState1();
  // Request operation.
  public void request() {
    state.handle();
  }
  // Switch states
```

```
    public void changeState() {
        if (state instanceof ConcreteState1)
        state = new ConcreteState2();
      else
        state = new ConcreteState1();
    }
}

package j2ee.architect.State;
public interface StateIF {
  public void handle();
}
```

Strategy

The Strategy pattern's intent is to define a family of functionality, encapsulate each one, and make them interchangeable. The Strategy pattern lets the functionality vary independently from the clients that use it.

The Strategy pattern is also known as Policy. The UML is shown in Figure 5-21.

Benefits   Following is a list of benefits of using the Strategy pattern:

- It provides a substitute to subclassing.

- It defines each behavior within its own class, eliminating the need for conditional statements.

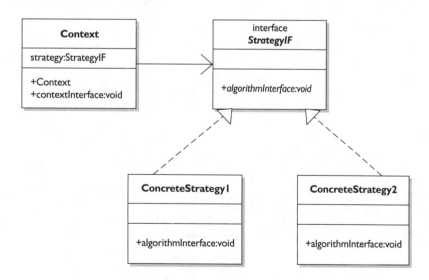

FIGURE 5-21

UML for the Strategy pattern

■ It makes it easier to extend and incorporate new behavior without changing the application.

Applicable Scenarios   The following scenarios are most appropriate for the Strategy pattern:

■ Multiple classes differ only in their behaviors. The servlet API is a classic example of this.

■ You need different variations of an algorithm.

■ An algorithm uses data that is unknown to the client.

Example Code   The following example Java code demonstrates the Strategy pattern:

```
package j2ee.architect.Strategy;
public class StrategyPattern {
  public static void main(String[] args) {
    System.out.println("Strategy Pattern Demonstration.");
    System.out.println("----------------------------");
    // Construct strategies.
    System.out.println("Constructing strategies.");
    StrategyIF strategy1 = new ConcreteStrategy1();
    StrategyIF strategy2 = new ConcreteStrategy2();
    // Construct contexts.
    System.out.println("Constructing contexts.");
    Context context1 = new Context(strategy1);
    Context context2 = new Context(strategy2);
    // Execute contextInterface.
    System.out.println("Constructing context interfaces.");
    context1.contextInterface("J2EE Unleashed");
    context2.contextInterface("J2EE Unleashed");
    context1.contextInterface("The Secret Commissions");
    context2.contextInterface("The Secret Commissions");
    System.out.println();
  }
}

package j2ee.architect.Strategy;
public class ConcreteStrategy1 implements StrategyIF {
  // Switch text to all upper case.
  public void algorithmInterface(String parm) {
    System.out.println(parm.toUpperCase());
  }
}
```

```
package j2ee.architect.Strategy;
public class ConcreteStrategy2 implements StrategyIF {
  // Switch text beginning with "the".
  public void algorithmInterface(String parm) {
    System.out.println((parm.toLowerCase().startsWith("the "))
      ? parm.substring(4) + ", " + parm.substring(0,4)
      : parm);
  }
}

package j2ee.architect.Strategy;
public class Context {
  // Reference to the strategy.
  StrategyIF strategy;
  // Register reference to strategy on construction.
  public Context(StrategyIF parm) {this.strategy = parm;}
  // Call strategy's method.
  public void contextInterface(String parm) {strategy.algorithmInterface(parm);}
}

package j2ee.architect.Strategy;
public interface StrategyIF {
  public void algorithmInterface(String parm);
}
```

Template Method

The Template Method pattern's intent is to define the skeleton of a function in an operation, deferring some steps to its subclasses. The Template Method lets subclasses redefine certain steps of a function without changing the structure of the function. The HttpServlet does this in the servlet API. The UML is shown in Figure 5-22.

Benefit   The Template Method pattern is a very common technique for reusing code.

Applicable Scenarios   The following scenarios are most appropriate for the Template Method pattern:

- You want to implement the nonvarying parts of an algorithm in a single class and the varying parts of the algorithm in subclasses.

- Common behavior among subclasses should be moved to a single common class, avoiding duplication.

FIGURE 5-22

UML for the
Template Method
pattern

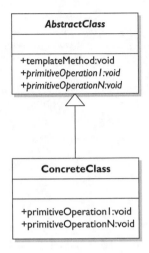

Example Code   The following example Java code demonstrates the Template Method pattern:

```
package j2ee.architect.TemplateMethod;
public class TemplateMethodPattern {
  public static void main(String[] args) {
    System.out.println("TemplateMethod Pattern Demonstration.");
    System.out.println("------------------------------------");
    // Construct concrete classes.
    System.out.println("Constructing concrete classes.");
    AbstractClass class1 = new ConcreteClass1();
    AbstractClass class2 = new ConcreteClass2();
    // Call template method.
    System.out.println("Calling template methods.");
    class1.templateMethod();
    class2.templateMethod();
    System.out.println();
  }
}

package j2ee.architect.TemplateMethod;
public abstract class AbstractClass {
  public void templateMethod() {
    System.out.println("AbstractClass.templateMethod() called.");
    primitiveOperation1();
    primitiveOperationN();
  }
  public abstract void primitiveOperation1();
  public abstract void primitiveOperationN();
}
```

```
package j2ee.architect.TemplateMethod;
public class ConcreteClass1 extends AbstractClass {
  public void primitiveOperation1() {
    System.out.println("ConcreteClass1.primitiveOperation1() called.");
  }
  public void primitiveOperationN() {
    System.out.println("ConcreteClass1.primitiveOperationN() called.");
  }
}

package j2ee.architect.TemplateMethod;
public class ConcreteClass2 extends AbstractClass {
  public void primitiveOperation1() {
    System.out.println("ConcreteClass2.primitiveOperation1() called.");
  }
  public void primitiveOperationN() {
    System.out.println("ConcreteClass2.primitiveOperationN() called.");
  }
}
```

Visitor

The Visitor pattern's intent is to represent an operation to be performed on elements of an object structure. The Visitor pattern allows for the addition of a new operation without changing the classes of the elements on which it is to operate. Figure 5-23 shows the UML.

Benefits   Following are the benefits of using the Visitor pattern:

- It simplifies the addition of new operations.
- It gathers related operations while separating unrelated ones.

Applicable Scenarios   The following scenarios are most appropriate for the Visitor pattern:

- An object structure contains many objects with differing interfaces and there is a need to perform operations on these objects in a way that depends on their concrete classes.
- Many distinct and unrelated operations need to be performed on objects in a structure and there is a need to avoid cluttering the classes with these operations.
- The classes defining the object structure rarely change but you frequently need to define new operations that perform over the structure.

FIGURE 5-23

UML for the
Visitor pattern

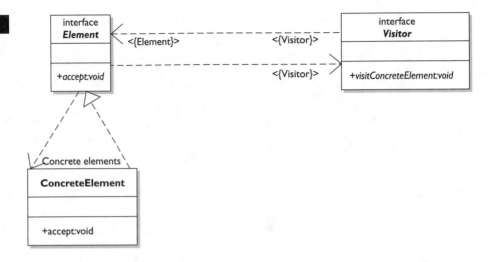

Example Code   The following example Java code demonstrates the Visitor
pattern:

```
package j2ee.architect.Visitor;
public class VisitorPattern {
  public static void main(String[] args) {
    System.out.println("Visitor Pattern Demonstration.");
    System.out.println("---------------------------");
    // Construct list of elements.
    System.out.println("Constructing two elements.");
    ElementIF[] elements = new ElementIF[2];
    elements[0] = new ConcreteElementA();
    elements[1] = new ConcreteElementB();
    // Construct object structure.
    System.out.println("Constructing object structure.");
    ObjectStructure objectStructure = new ObjectStructure(elements);
    // Visit elements in object structure.
    System.out.println("Visiting elements in object structure.");
    objectStructure.visitElements();
    System.out.println();
  }
}

package j2ee.architect.Visitor;
public class ConcreteElementA implements ElementIF {
  public void accept(VisitorIF parm) {
    parm.visitConcreteElementA(this);
  }
  public void operationA() {
```

```java
        System.out.println("ConcreteElementA.operationA() called.");
    }
}


package j2ee.architect.Visitor;
public class ConcreteElementB implements ElementIF {
  public void accept(VisitorIF parm) {
    parm.visitConcreteElementB(this);
  }
  public void operationB() {
    System.out.println("ConcreteElementB.operationB() called.");
  }
}


package j2ee.architect.Visitor;
public class ConcreteVisitor implements VisitorIF {
  public void visitConcreteElementA(ConcreteElementA parm) {
    parm.operationA();
  }
  public void visitConcreteElementB(ConcreteElementB parm) {
    parm.operationB();
  }
}


package j2ee.architect.Visitor;
public interface ElementIF {
  public void accept(VisitorIF parm);
}


package j2ee.architect.Visitor;
import java.util.*;
public class ObjectStructure {
  private List objectStruct;
  private VisitorIF visitor;
  public ObjectStructure(ElementIF[] parm) {
    objectStruct = Arrays.asList(parm);
  }
  public void visitElements() {
    if (visitor == null) { visitor = new ConcreteVisitor(); }
    for (Iterator i = objectStruct.iterator(); i.hasNext();) {
      ((ElementIF) i.next()).accept(visitor);
    }
  }
}


package j2ee.architect.Visitor;
public interface VisitorIF {
  public void visitConcreteElementA(ConcreteElementA parm);
  public void visitConcreteElementB(ConcreteElementB parm);
}
```

Now that we've covered each of the GoF Design Patterns, let's review scenarios and also identify the Design Pattern that is most appropriate as a solution.

SCENARIO & SOLUTION

Given Scenarios	Appropriate Design Pattern
The system needs to be independent of how its objects are created, composed, and represented. The system needs to be configured with one of a multiple family of objects. The family of related objects is intended to be used together and this constraint needs to be enforced. You want to provide a library of objects that does not show implementations and only reveals interfaces.	Abstract Factory
The algorithm for creating a complex object needs to be independent of the components that compose the object and how they are assembled. The construction process is to allow different representations of the constructed object.	Builder
A class is not able to anticipate the class of objects it needs to create. A class wants its subclasses to specify the objects it instantiates. Classes delegate responsibility to one of several helper subclasses, and you want to localize the knowledge of which helper subclass is the delegate.	Factory Method
The classes to instantiate are specified at runtime. You want to avoid building a class hierarchy of factories that parallels the hierarchy of objects. Instances of the class have one of only a few different combinations of state.	Prototype
A single instance of a class is needed, and it must be accessible to clients from a well-known access point.	Singleton
You want to utilize an existing class with an incompatible interface. You want to create a reusable class that cooperates with classes that don't necessarily have compatible interfaces. You need to use several existing subclasses but do not want to adapt their interfaces by subclassing each one.	Adapter
You want to avoid a permanent binding between the functional abstraction and its implementation. Both the functional abstraction and its implementation need to be extended using subclasses. Changes to the implementation should not impact the client (not even a recompile).	Bridge

SCENARIO & SOLUTION

Given Scenarios	Appropriate Design Pattern
You want to represent a full or partial hierarchy of objects. You want clients to be able to ignore the differences between the varying objects in the hierarchy. The structure is dynamic and can have any level of complexity.	Composite
You want to transparently and dynamically add responsibilities to objects without affecting other objects. You want to add responsibilities to an object that you may want to change in the future. Extending functionality by subclassing is no longer practical.	Decorator
You want to provide a simpler interface to a more complex subsystem. Several dependencies exist between clients and the implementation classes of an abstraction. You want to layer the subsystems.	Facade
The application uses a considerable number of objects. The storage costs are high because of the quantity of objects. The application does not depend on object identity.	Flyweight
You need a more versatile or sophisticated reference to an object, rather than a simple pointer.	Proxy
More than one object can handle a request and the handler is unknown. A request is to be issued to one of several objects and the receiver is not specified explicitly. The set of objects able to handle the request is to be specified dynamically.	Chain of Responsibility
You need to parameterize objects by an action to perform. You specify, queue, and execute requests at different times. You need to support rollback, logging, or transaction functionality.	Command
The grammar of the language is not complicated and efficiency is not a priority.	Interpreter
Access to a collection object is required without having to expose its internal representation. You need to support multiple traversals of objects in the collection. You need to provide a universal interface for traversing different structures in the collection.	Iterator
A set of objects communicates in complex but well-defined ways. Custom behavior distributed between several objects is required without subclassing.	Mediator

SCENARIO & SOLUTION

Given Scenarios	Appropriate Design Pattern
A snapshot containing enough information regarding the state of an object can be saved so that it can be restored to the complete state using the snapshot information later. Using a direct interface to obtain the state would impose implementation details that would break the rules of encapsulation for the object.	Memento
A change to an object requires changing other objects, and the number of objects that need to be changed is unknown. An object needs to notify other objects without making any assumptions about the identity of those objects.	Observer
The behavior of an object depends on its state and it must be able to change its behavior at runtime according on the new state. Operations have large multipart conditional statements that depend on the state of the object.	State
Multiple classes differ only in their behavior. You need different variations of an algorithm. An algorithm uses data that is unknown to the client.	Strategy
You want to implement the nonvarying parts of an algorithm in a single class and the varying parts of the algorithm in subclasses. Common behavior among subclasses should be moved to a single common class, avoiding duplication.	Template Method
An object structure contains many objects with differing interfaces and you need to perform operations on these objects in a way that depends on their concrete classes. Many distinct and unrelated operations need to be performed on objects in a structure and you need to avoid cluttering the classes with these operations. The classes defining the object structure rarely change but you frequently need to define new operations that perform over the structure.	Visitor

J2EE Patterns

Part I of the certification exam requires that you know the Gang of Four Design Patterns only, but for Parts II and III, you may find it helpful to study and then include in your solution some of the new J2EE Patterns from Sun. Although we do not go into great detail on these patterns, the next few sections will at least serve as an introduction by covering the scenarios for which they are potential solutions.

exam

W a t c h

You may find it helpful to study and then include in your solutions some of the new J2EE Patterns from Sun. For complete details of the emerging J2EE Patterns, refer to the following web site: http://java.sun.com/blueprints/ corej2eepatterns/index.html.

Similar to the GoF Design Patterns, the J2EE Patterns are broken down into the various sections that address the tiers (or layers) that make up an application:

- Presentation Tier
- Business Tier
- Integration Tier

Presentation Tier Patterns

The presentation tier encapsulates the logic required to service the clients accessing a system. Presentation tier patterns intercept a client request and then provide facilities such as single sign-on, management of the client session, and access to services in the business tier before constructing and delivering the response back to the client.

The patterns currently available for the presentation layer follow:

- Composite View
- Dispatcher View
- Front Controller
- Intercepting Filter
- Service To Worker
- View Helper

The next table lists scenarios along with suggestions of one or more of the J2EE presentation tier patterns to aid in the solution.

Business Tier Patterns

The business tier provides the services required by application clients and contains the business data and logic. All business processing for the application is gathered and placed into this tier. Enterprise JavaBean (EJB) components are one of the ways to implement business processing in this tier.

SCENARIO & SOLUTION

You have an application that needs to preprocess and/or post-process a client request…	Intercepting Filter
You have an application that requires centralized control for client request handling…	Front Controller and Intercepting Filter
You need to add logging, debugging, or some other behavior to be carried out for each client request…	Front Controller and Intercepting Filter
You want to create a generic command interface for delegating processing from the controller to the helper components…	Front Controller
You want to delegate processing to a JSP or servlet and you want to implement your Model View Controller (MVC) Controller as a JSP or servlet…	Front Controller
You want to create an MVC View from multiple subviews…	Composite View
You need to implement an MVC View as a JSP or servlet…	View Helper
You would like to partition your MVC Model and MVC View…	View Helper
Your application needs to encapsulate presentation-related data formatting logic…	View Helper
You want to implement your Helper components as Custom tags or JavaBeans…	View Helper
Your application needs to combine multiple presentation patterns…	Service To Worker and Dispatcher View
You want to encapsulate MVC View management and navigation logic…	Service To Worker and Dispatcher View

Here are the patterns available for the business tier:

- Aggregate Entity
- Business Delegate
- Composite Entity
- Service Locator
- Session Façade
- Transfer Object
- Transfer Object Assembler

- Value List Handler
- Value Object Assembler
- Value Object

The following table is a list of scenarios along with suggestions of one or more of the J2EE business tier patterns to aid in the solution.

Integration Tier Patterns

This tier is responsible for accessing external resources and systems, such as relational and nonrelational data stores and any legacy applications. A business tier object uses the integration tier when it requires data or services that reside at the resource level.

SCENARIO & SOLUTION

You need to minimize coupling between presentation and business layers…	Business Delegate
You need to cache business services for clients…	Business Delegate
Your application needs a simpler interface to clients…	Business Delegate
Within the business tier you want to shield the client from implementation (lookup/creation/access) details of business services…	Business Delegate and Service Locator
Your application needs to separate the lookup for vendor or other technology dependencies for services…	Service Locator
You need to provide a uniform method for service lookup and creation…	Service Locator
You want to shield the complexity and dependencies for EJB and JMS component lookup…	Service Locator
You need to transfer data between application tiers…	Value Object
You have to reduce network traffic between clients and EJBs…	Session Facade
You want to minimize the number of remote method invocations by providing more coarser grained method access to business tier components…	Session Facade
You want to manage relationships between EJB components and hide the complexity of their interactions…	Session Facade

SCENARIO & SOLUTION

You need to shield components in the business tier from clients…	Session Facade and Business Delegate
You want to provide uniform access to components in the business tier…	Session Facade
You need to design complex, coarser grained EJB entity beans…	Aggregate Entity
You have to identify coarse grained objects and dependent objects for EJB entity bean design…	Aggregate Entity
You want to minimize or eliminate the EJB entity bean clients' dependency on the actual database schema…	Aggregate Entity
You have to improve manageability and minimize number of EJB entity beans…	Aggregate Entity
You want to minimize (or eliminate) EJB entity bean to entity bean relationships…	Aggregate Entity and Session Facade
You need to get the data model for the application from various business tier components…	Value Object Assembler (This could also be a DataAccessObject as well)
You want on the fly data model construction…	Value Object Assembler
You want to shield the data model construction complexity from clients…	Value Object Assembler
Your application needs to provide query and list processing facilities…	Value List Handler
You want to reduce the overhead of using EJB finder methods…	Value List Handler
You need to facilitate server-side caching of query results, with forward and backward navigation, for clients …	Value List Handler

The components in this tier can use JDBC, J2EE connector technology, or some other proprietary software to access data at the resource level.

Here are the patterns available for the integration tier:

- Data Access Object
- Service Activator

The following table is a list of scenarios along with suggestions of one or more of the J2EE integration tier patterns to aid in the solution.

SCENARIO & SOLUTION

You want to reduce the amount of coupling between business and resource tiers (layers)…	Data Access Object
You need to centralize the access to resource tiers (layers) …	Data Access Object
You must reduce complexity for accessing resource from the business tier (layer) …	Data Access Object
You want to provide asynchronous processing for EJB components…	Service Activator
You need to send a message to an EJB…	Service Activator

exam
⍟atch
The level of detail that we've provided on Sun's core J2EE patterns is somewhat cursory. Although you will not need to have knowledge of them for Part I, you will find it useful to learn more about them and then use them in Parts II and III.

CERTIFICATION OBJECTIVE 5.03

State the Name of a Gamma et al. Design Pattern Given the UML Diagram and/or a Brief Description of the Pattern's Functionality

Study each design pattern diagram shown earlier. The following table has a brief description of each pattern's functionality:

Pattern's Functionality	Pattern Name
Provides an interface for creating families of related or dependent objects without specifying the concrete classes.	Abstract Factory
Separates construction of a complex object from its representation so that the construction process can create different representations.	Builder

Pattern's Functionality	Pattern Name
Defines an interface for creating an object, letting subclasses decide which class to instantiate. Allows a class to defer the actual instantiation to subclasses.	Factory Method
Specifies the kinds of objects to create using a prototypical instance, and creates new objects by copying this prototype.	Prototype
Ensures a class has only one instance, and provides a global point of access to it.	Singleton
Converts the class's interface into another interface that the client expects. Lets classes work together that couldn't otherwise do so because of incompatible interfaces.	Adapter
Decouples abstraction from its implementation so that the two can vary independently.	Bridge
Composes objects into tree structures to represent part-whole hierarchies. Lets clients treat individual objects and compositions of objects in a uniform manner.	Composite
Attaches added responsibilities to an object dynamically. Provides flexible alternative to subclassing to extend functionality.	Decorator
Provides a unified interface to a set of interfaces in one or more subsystems. Defines a higher level interface that makes the subsystems easier to use.	Facade
Uses sharing to support large numbers of fine-grained objects in an efficient manner.	Flyweight
Provides a placeholder or surrogate for another object to control access to it.	Proxy
Avoids coupling the sender of a request to its receiver by giving more than one object a chance to handle the request. The receiving objects are chained together and pass the request along the chain until it is handled.	Chain Of Responsibility
Encapsulates a request as an object, allowing the client to be parameterized with different requests, queue or log requests, and to be able to support undo operations.	Command
Given a language, defines a representation for its grammar along with an interpreter of the grammar that uses the representation to interpret sentences in the language.	Interpreter
Provides a way to access the elements of a collection (aggregate) object sequentially without having to expose the underlying representation.	Iterator
Defines an object that encapsulates how a set of objects interacts. Promotes loose coupling by keeping objects from referring to each other directly and varying their interaction independently.	Mediator
Without violating encapsulation, captures and externalizes an object's internal state so that the object's essential state can be restored later.	Memento

Pattern's Functionality	Pattern Name
Defines a one-to-many dependency among objects so that when one object changes state, all its dependents (subscribers) are notified and updated automatically.	Observer
Allows an object to alter its behavior when its internal state changes; the object will appear to change its class.	State
Defines a family of algorithms, encapsulating each one, and makes them interchangeable. Lets the algorithm vary independently from clients that use it.	Strategy
Defines the skeleton of an algorithm (function) in an operation, deferring some steps to subclasses. Lets subclasses redefine certain steps of an algorithm without changing the algorithm's structure.	Template Method
Represents an operation to be performed on the elements of an object structure. Lets you define a new operation without changing the classes of the elements on which it operates.	Visitor

The following table shows the alternate names for the Gamma et al. Design Patterns:

Pattern Name	Also Known As
Abstract Factory	Kit
Factory Method	Virtual Constructor
Adapter	Wrapper
Bridge	Handle/Body
Decorator	Wrapper
Proxy	Surrogate
Command	Action or Transaction
Iterator	Cursor
Memento	Token
Observer	Dependents or Publish-Subscribe
State	Objects for States
Strategy	Policy

CERTIFICATION OBJECTIVE 5.04

Identify Benefits of a Specified Gamma et al. Design Pattern

Here is a list of the benefits for each of the Gamma et al. Design Patterns:

GoF Design Pattern	Benefits
Abstract Factory	Isolates client from concrete (implementation) classes. Makes the exchanging of object families easier. Promotes consistency among objects.
Builder	Permits you to vary an object's internal representation. Isolates the code for construction and representation. Provides finer control over the construction process.
Factory Method	Removes the need to bind application-specific classes into the code. The code interacts solely with the resultant interface and so will work with any classes that implement that interface. Because creating objects inside a class is more flexible than creating an object directly, it enables the subclass to provide an extended version of an object.
Prototype	Allows adding or removing objects at runtime. Specifies new objects by varying its values or structure. Reduces the need for subclassing. Allows dynamic configuring of an application with classes.
Singleton	Controls access to a single instance of the class. Reduces name space usage. Permits refinement of operations and representation. Permits a variable number of instances. Is more flexible than class methods (operations).
Adapter	Allows two or more previously incompatible objects to interact. Allows reusability of existing functionality.
Bridge	Enables the separation of implementation from the interface. Improves extensibility. Allows the hiding of implementation details from the client.
Composite	Defines class hierarchies consisting of primitive and complex objects. Makes it easier to add new kinds of components. Provides the flexibility of structure with a manageable interface.

GoF Design Pattern	Benefits
Decorator	Provides greater flexibility than static inheritance. Avoids the need to place feature-laden classes higher-up the hierarchy. Simplifies coding by allowing you to develop a series of functionality-targeted classes, instead of coding all of the behavior into the object. Enhances the extensibility of the object, because changes are made by coding new classes.
Facade	Provides a simpler interface to a complex subsystem without reducing the options provided by the subsystem. Shields clients from the complexity of the subsystem components. Promotes looser coupling between the subsystem and its clients. Reduces the coupling between subsystems provided that every subsystem uses its own Facade pattern and other parts of the system use the Facade pattern to communicate with the subsystem.
Flyweight	Reduces the number of objects to deal with. Reduces memory and storage devices if the objects are persisted.
Proxy	Remote proxy shields the fact that the implementation resides in another address space. Virtual proxy performs optimizations—e.g., by creating objects on demand.
Chain of Responsibility	Reduces coupling. Adds flexibility when assigning responsibilities to objects. Allows a set of classes to act as one; events produced in one class can be sent to other handler classes within the composition.
Command	Separates the object that invokes the operation from the object that performs the operation. Simplifies adding new commands, because existing classes remain unchanged.
Interpreter	Makes it easier to change and extend the grammar. Makes implementing the grammar straightforward.
Iterator	Supports variations in the traversal of a collection. Simplifies the interface to the collection.
Mediator	Decouples colleagues. Simplifies object protocols. Centralizes control. Individual components become simpler and much easier to deal with because they do not need to pass messages to one another. Components do not need to contain logic to deal with their intercommunication and are therefore more generic.
Memento	Preserves encapsulation boundaries. Simplifies the originator.

GoF Design Pattern	Benefits
Observer	Abstracts the coupling between the subject and the observer. Provides support for broadcast type communication.
State	Keeps state-specific behavior local and partitions behavior for different states. Makes any state transitions explicit.
Strategy	Provides a substitute to subclassing. Defines each behavior within its own class, eliminating the need for conditional statements. Makes it easier to extend and incorporate new behavior without changing the application.
Template Method	Lets code be reused.

CERTIFICATION OBJECTIVE 5.05

Identify the Gamma et al. Design Pattern Associated with a Specified J2EE Technology Feature

Here is a list of J2EE technology features and the associated Gamma et al. Design Patterns that are used to implement them:

J2EE Technology Feature	Associated GoF Design Pattern
EJB Factory (*javax.ejb.EJBHome, javax.ejb.EJBLocalHome*) JMS Connection Factory (*javax.jms.QueueConnectionFactory, javax.jms.TopicConnectionFactory*)	Factory Method
EJB remote reference (*javax.ejb.EJBObject*)	Proxy
JMS Publish/Subscribe Model	Observer

CERTIFICATION SUMMARY

By studying this chapter, you now have an understanding of the Gang of Four's Design Patterns and some introductory material on J2EE patterns. You should also understand which are the most appropriate patterns to use for given scenarios.

TWO-MINUTE DRILL

Here are some of the key points from each certification objective in Chapter 5.

Identify the Benefits of Using Design Patterns

❑ Help designers to focus on solutions quicker if they recognize patterns that have been successful in the past.

❑ Give new ideas to designers who have studied patterns.

❑ Provide a common language for design discussions.

❑ Provide a solution to a real-world problem.

❑ Capture knowledge and document the best practices for a domain.

❑ Document decisions and the rationale that lead to the solution.

❑ Reuse the experience of predecessors.

❑ Communicate the insight already gained previously.

❑ Describe the circumstances (when and where), the influences (who and what), and the resolution (how and why it balances the influences).

Identify the Most Appropriate Design Pattern for a Given Scenario

❑ The Abstract Factory is most appropriate when the system needs to be independent of how its objects are created, composed, and represented.

❑ The Adapter is most appropriate when you want to utilize an existing class with an incompatible interface.

❑ The Bridge is most appropriate when you want to avoid a permanent binding between the functional abstraction and its implementation.

❑ The Builder is most appropriate when the algorithm for creating a complex object needs to independent of the components that compose the object and how they are assembled.

❑ The Chain of Responsibility is most appropriate when more than one object can handle a request and the handler is unknown.

❑ The Command is most appropriate when you need to parameterize objects by an action to perform.

❑ The Composite is most appropriate when you want to represent a full or partial hierarchy of objects.

❑ The Decorator is most appropriate when you want to transparently and dynamically add responsibilities to objects without affecting other objects.

❑ The Facade is most appropriate when you want to provide a simpler interface to a more complex subsystem.

❑ The Factory Method is most appropriate when a class is not able to anticipate the class of objects it needs to create.

❑ The Flyweight is most appropriate when the application uses a considerable number of objects.

❑ The Interpreter is most appropriate when the grammar of the language is not complicated and efficiency is not a priority.

❑ The Iterator is most appropriate when access to a collection object is required without having to expose its internal representation.

❑ The Mediator is most appropriate when a set of objects communicates in complex but well-defined ways.

❑ The Memento is most appropriate when a snapshot containing enough information regarding the state of an object can be saved so that it can be restored to the complete state using the snapshot information later.

❑ The Observer is most appropriate when a change to an object requires changing other objects, and the number of objects that need to be changed is unknown.

❑ The Prototype is most appropriate when the classes to instantiate are to be specified at runtime.

❑ The Proxy is most appropriate when you need a more versatile or sophisticated reference to an object, rather than a simple pointer.

❑ The Singleton is most appropriate when a single instance of a class is needed, and it must be accessible to clients from a well-known access point.

❑ The State is most appropriate when the behavior of an object depends on its state and it must be able to change its behavior at runtime according to the new state.

❑ The Strategy is most appropriate when multiple classes differ only in their behavior.

❑ The Template Method is most appropriate when you want to implement the nonvarying parts of an algorithm in a single class and the varying parts of the algorithm in subclasses.

❑ The Visitor is most appropriate when an object structure contains many objects with differing interfaces and you need to perform operations on these objects in a way that depends on their concrete classes.

State the Name of a Gamma et al. Design Pattern Given the UML Diagram and/or a Brief Description of the Pattern's Functionality

Review the Gang of Four (Gamma et al.) diagrams and associated descriptions that appear earlier in the chapter:

Identify Benefits of a Specified Gamma et al. Design Pattern

Here are the benefits for each of the Gamma et al. Design Patterns:

GoF Design Pattern	Benefits
Abstract Factory	Isolates client from concrete (implementation) classes. Makes the exchanging of object families easier. Promotes consistency among objects.
Builder	Permits you to vary an object's internal representation. Isolates the code for construction and representation. Provides finer control over the construction process.
Factory Method	Removes the need to bind application-specific classes into the code. The code interacts solely with the resultant interface and so will work with any classes that implement that interface. Because creating objects inside a class is more flexible than creating an object directly, it enables the subclass to provide an extended version of an object.
Prototype	Allows adding or removing objects at runtime. Specifies new objects by varying its values or structure. Reduces the need for subclassing. Allows dynamic configuring of an application with classes.
Singleton	Controls access to a single instance of the class. Reduces name space usage. Permits refinement of operations and representation. Permits a variable number of instances. Is more flexible than class methods (operations).

GoF Design Pattern	Benefits
Adapter	Allows two or more previously incompatible objects to interact. Allows reusability of existing functionality.
Bridge	Enables the separation of implementation from the interface. Improves extensibility. Allows the hiding of implementation details from the client.
Composite	Defines class hierarchies consisting of primitive and complex objects. Makes it easier to add new kinds of components. Provides the flexibility of structure with a manageable interface.
Decorator	Provides greater flexibility than static inheritance. Avoids the need to place feature-laden classes higher-up the hierarchy. Simplifies coding by allowing you to develop a series of functionality-targeted classes, instead of coding all of the behavior into the object. Enhances the extensibility of the object, because changes are made by coding new classes.
Facade	Provides a simpler interface to a complex subsystem without reducing the options provided by the subsystem. Shields clients from the complexity of the subsystem components. Promotes looser coupling between the subsystem and its clients. Reduces the coupling between subsystems provided that every subsystem uses its own Facade pattern and other parts of the system use the Facade pattern to communicate with the subsystem.
Flyweight	Reduces the number of objects to deal with. Reduces memory and storage devices if the objects are persisted.
Proxy	Remote proxy shields the fact that the implementation resides in another address space. Virtual proxy performs optimizations—e.g., by creating objects on demand.
Chain of Responsibility	Reduces coupling. Adds flexibility when assigning responsibilities to objects. Allows a set of classes to act as one; events produced in one class can be sent to other handler classes within the composition.
Command	Separates the object that invokes the operation from the object that performs the operation. Simplifies adding new commands, because existing classes remain unchanged.
Interpreter	Makes it easier to change and extend the grammar. Makes implementing the grammar straightforward.
Iterator	Supports variations in the traversal of a collection. Simplifies the interface to the collection.

GoF Design Pattern	Benefits
Mediator	Decouples colleagues. Simplifies object protocols. Centralizes control. Individual components become simpler and much easier to deal with because they do not need to pass messages to one another. Components do not need to contain logic to deal with their intercommunication and are therefore more generic.
Memento	Preserves encapsulation boundaries. Simplifies the originator.
Observer	Abstracts the coupling between the subject and the observer. Provides support for broadcast type communication.
State	Keeps state-specific behavior local and partitions behavior for different states. Makes any state transitions explicit.
Strategy	Provides a substitute to subclassing. Defines each behavior within its own class, eliminating the need for conditional statements. Makes it easier to extend and incorporate new behavior without changing the application.
Template Method	Lets you reuse code.

Identify the Gamma et al. Design Pattern Associated with a Specified J2EE Technology Feature

Here is a list of J2EE technology features and the associated Design Patterns that are used to implement them:

❑ The EJB Factory (javax.ejb.EJBHome, javax.ejb.EJBLocalHome) and JMS Connection Factory (javax.jms.QueueConnectionFactory, javax.jms.TopicConnectionFactory) use the Factory Method pattern.

❑ The EJB remote reference (javax.ejb.EJBObject) uses the Proxy pattern.

❑ The JMS Publish/Subscribe Model uses the Observer pattern.

SELF TEST

The following questions will help you measure your understanding of the material presented in this chapter. Read all the choices carefully because there may be more than one correct answer. Choose all correct answers for each question.

Identify the Benefits of Using Design Patterns

1. Which of the following is not a benefit of using Design Patterns?

   A. They provide a common language for design discussions

   B. They provide solutions to "real-world" problems

   C. They communicate the insight already gained previously

   D. They provide solutions to totally novel problems

Identify the Most Appropriate Design Pattern for a Given Scenario

2. The Factory Method design pattern is useful when a client must create objects having different

   A. Subclasses

   B. Ancestors

   C. Sizes

   D. Similarities

3. What design pattern limits the number of instances a class can create?

   A. Command

   B. Limiter

   C. Strategy

   D. Singleton

4. Iterators are useful when dealing with which of the following types of classes?

   A. Dynamic

   B. Collection

   C. Singleton

   D. Small

State the Name of a Gamma et al. Design Pattern Given the UML Diagram and/or a Brief Description of the Pattern's Functionality

5. What is the Abstract Factory pattern also known as?

  A. Kit

  B. Wrapper

  C. Cursor

  D. Virtual Constructor

6. Which pattern is shown in the diagram?

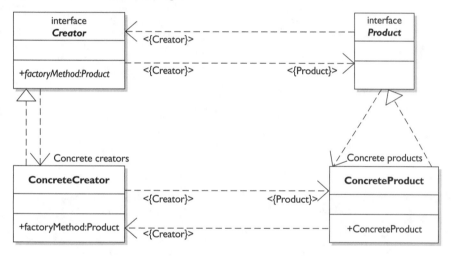

  A. Abstract Factory

  B. Factory Method

  C. Command

  D. Chain of Responsibility

7. What pattern is also known as Virtual Constructor?

  A. Abstract Factory

  B. Memento

  C. Wrapper

  D. Factory Method

8. Which pattern is shown in the diagram?

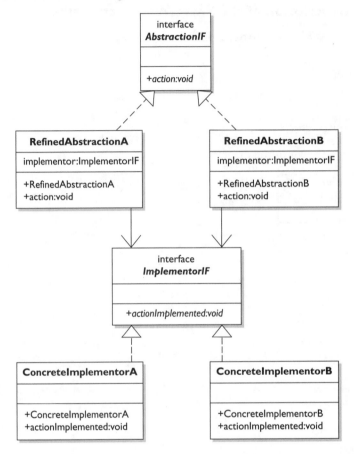

A. Proxy

B. Decorator

C. Bridge

D. Observer

9. What is the Adapter pattern also known as?

A. Surrogate

B. Wrapper

C. Token

D. Proxy

10. Which pattern is shown in the diagram?

A. Proxy

B. Facade

C. Adapter

D. Bridge

11. What pattern is also known as Handle/Body?

A. Proxy

B. Adapter

C. Abstract Factory

D. Bridge

12. Which pattern is shown in the diagram?

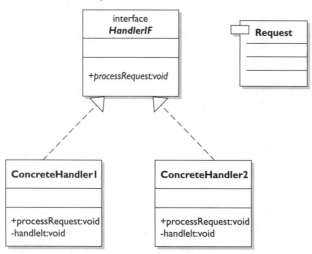

    A. Chain of Responsibility

    B. Command

    C. Memento

    D. Factory Method

13. What is the Decorator pattern also known as?

    A. Wrapper

    B. Adapter

    C. Composite

    D. Strategy

14. Which pattern is shown in the diagram?

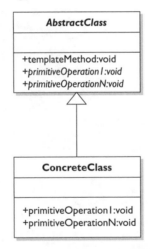

    A. Template Method

    B. Command

    C. Singleton

    D. State

15. What pattern is also known as Surrogate?

    A. Observer

    B. Bridge

    C. Proxy

    D. Decorator

16. What is the Command pattern also known as?

    A. Action

    B. Transaction

    C. Wrapper

    D. Surrogate

17. The Command design pattern _____ a request in an object.

    A. Separates

    B. Encapsulates

    C. Processes

    D. Decouples

Identify Benefits of a Specified Gamma et al. Design Pattern

18. Which of the following elements are parts of the Gang of Four (GoF) Design Pattern format?

    A. Problem

    B. Solution

    C. Consequences

    D. Intent

Identify the Gamma et al. Design Pattern Associated with a Specified J2EE Technology Feature

19. The Decorator pattern appears in which of the following Java packages?

    A. *java.io*

    B. *java.awt*

    C. *java.lang*

    D. *java.util*

20. Which Java package contains classes that implement the Iterator design pattern?

    A. *java.enumeration*

    B. *java.util*

    C. *java.math*

    D. *java.text*

21. What two methods are defined by the Enumeration interface?

    A. `hasMoreElements()`

    B. `getElement()`

    C. `nextElement()`

    D. `nextelement()`

SELF TEST ANSWERS

Identify the Benefits of Using Design Patterns

1. ☑ D. Design patterns do not address totally novel problems, so this cannot be a benefit gained.
   ☒ A, B and C are real benefits gained by using Design patterns.

Identify the Most Appropriate Design Pattern for a Given Scenario

2. ☑ A. The Factory Method design pattern is useful when a client must create objects having different subclasses.
   ☒ B, C, and D. The Factory Method design pattern is not useful with these situations.

3. ☑ D. The Singleton pattern limits the number of instances a class can create.
   ☒ A, B, and C do not limit the number of instances a class can create.

4. ☑ B. Iterators are useful when dealing with Collection classes.
   ☒ A, C, and D are not appropriate for the Iterator pattern.

State the Name of a Gamma et al. Design Pattern Given the UML Diagram and/or a Brief Description of the Pattern's Functionality

5. ☑ A. The Abstract Factory pattern is also known as Kit.
   ☒ B, C, and D are not valid aliases for Abstract Factory.

6. ☑ B. The diagram depicts the Factory Method pattern.
   ☒ A, C, and D are not depicted in the diagram.

7. ☑ D. The Factory Method pattern is also known as the Virtual Constructor.
   ☒ A, B, and C are not valid aliases for Virtual Constructor.

8. ☑ C. The diagram depicts the Bridge pattern.
   ☒ A, B, and D are not depicted in the diagram.

9. ☑ B. The Adapter pattern is also known as the Wrapper.
   ☒ A, C, and D are not valid aliases for Adapter.

10. ☑ B. The diagram depicts the Facade pattern.
    ☒ A, C, and D are not depicted in the diagram.

11. ☑ D. The Bridge pattern is also known as Handle/Body.

☒ A, B, and C are not valid aliases for Handle/Body.

12. ☑ A. The diagram depicts the Chain of Responsibility pattern.

☒ B, C, and D are not depicted in the diagram.

13. ☑ A. The Decorator pattern is also known as the Wrapper.

☒ B, C, and D are not valid aliases for Decorator.

14. ☑ A. The diagram depicts the Template Method pattern.

☒ B, C, and D are not depicted in the diagram.

15. ☑ C. The proxy pattern is also known as Surrogate.

☒ A, B, and D are not valid aliases for Surrogate.

16. ☑ A and B. The Command pattern is also known as Action or Transaction.

☒ C and D are not valid aliases for Command.

17. ☑ B. The Command design pattern encapsulates a request in an object.

☒ A, C, and D are not valid descriptions of the Command pattern.

Identify Benefits of a Specified Gamma et al. Design Pattern

18. ☑ C and D. Consequences and Intent are valid elements in the (GoF) Design Pattern format.

☒ A and B are not valid elements in the (GoF) Design Pattern format.

Identify the Gamma et al. Design Pattern Associated with a Specified J2EE Technology Feature

19. ☑ A and B. The Decorator pattern appears in the *java.io* and *java.awt* packages.

☒ C and D do not contain the Decorator pattern.

20. ☑ B. The *java.util* package contains classes that implement the Iterator design pattern.

☒ A, C, and D do not implement the Iterator design pattern.

21. ☑ A and C. The Enumeration interface contains `hasMoreElements()` and `nextElement()` methods.

☒ B and D are not valid methods in the Enumeration interface.

6

Legacy
Connectivity

The capacity and capability to migrate legacy systems to Java 2 Enterprise Edition (J2EE) is on the increase as the need to web-enable legacy systems increases. A growing number of legacy systems, including IBM mainframe, UNIX, and client-server, can now be migrated to J2EE to take advantage of its security, speed, reliability, and cross-platform capabilities. Some of the benefits of this are freedom from obsolete software, return on the original investment in legacy systems (especially after Y2K) via extended life of these systems, and opportunities for e-commerce using legacy systems and databases. To that end, this chapter will cover the following topics:

- Engineering the Enterprise Information Systems (EIS) Integration Tier
- Best practices for EIS integration
- Guidelines for data access
- EIS access objects and connections
- Java Enterprise Engineering: Services
- Role of transactions
- Best practices relating to transactions in each tier
- Appropriate and inappropriate use for given situations

Introduction to Legacy Connectivity

As businesses move toward an e-business strategy, the challenge of legacy connectivity is to enable each enterprise to integrate new e-business applications with existing Enterprise Information Systems (EISs). Enterprise applications require access to applications running on EIS. These systems provide the information infrastructure for an enterprise—the so-called "books and records," as they say on Wall Street.

EISs include enterprise mainframe transaction processing systems, relational database management systems (RDBMS), and other legacy information systems. Enterprises run their businesses using the information stored in these systems, and the success of an enterprise critically depends on this information. Enterprises with successful e-businesses need to integrate their EISs with web-based applications. They need to extend the reach of their EISs to support business-to-business (B2B) transactions.

Before the J2EE Connector Architecture (JCA) was defined, no specification for the Java platform addressed the problem of providing a standard architecture for integrating EIS. We used JNI (Java Native Interface) and RMI (Remote Method Invocation) to create a Java interface to a process running in its native domain. For example, a Java program using JNI, RMI, or CORBA (Common Object Request Broker) can call a C++ program running on a Windows NT machine. Most EIS vendors as well as application server vendors use nonstandard proprietary architectures to provide connectivity between application servers and enterprise information systems that provide services such as messaging, legacy database access, and mainframe transaction or batch processing. Figure 6-1 illustrates the complexity of an EIS environment.

Legacy Connectivity Using Java: the Classic Approach

Thus far, the classic approach to legacy connectivity is based on the two-tier client-server model, which is typical of applications that are not based on the web. With this approach, an EIS provides an adapter that defines an application programming interface (API) for accessing the data and functions of the EIS—basically, you "black box" the target system and create a Java API. A typical client application accesses data and functions exposed by an EIS through this adapter interface. The client uses the programmatic API exposed by the adapter to connect to and access the EIS. The adapter implements the support for communication with the EIS and provides access to EIS data and functions.

Communication between an adapter and the EIS typically uses a protocol specific to the EIS. This protocol provides support for security and transactions, along with support for content propagation from an application to the EIS. Most adapters expose an API to the client that abstracts out the details of the underlying protocol and the distribution mechanism between the EIS and the adapter. In most cases, a resource adapter is specific to a particular EIS. However, an EIS may provide more than one adapter that a client can use to access the EIS. Because the key to EIS adapters is their reusability, independent software vendors try to develop adapters that employ a widely used programming language to expose a client programming model that has the greatest degree of reusability.

FIGURE 6-1 EIS environments: legacy applications with an e-business front end

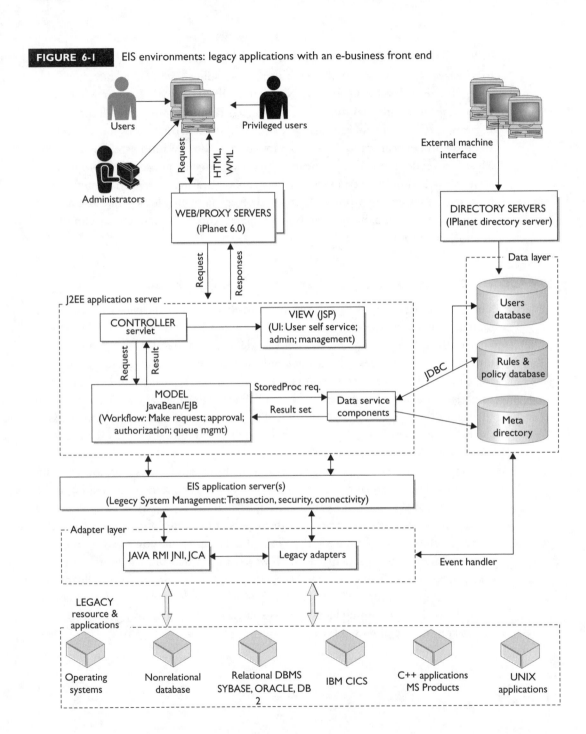

Using a Simple EIS Java Adapter

An EIS may provide a simple form of an adapter, where the adapter maps an API that is specific to the EIS to a reusable, standard API. Often, such an adapter is developed as a *library*, whereby the application developer can use the same programming language to access the adapter as she uses to write the application, and no modifications are required to the EIS. For example, a Java application developer can use a Java-based adapter—an adapter written in the Java programming language—to access an EIS that is based on some non-Java language or platform.

An EIS adapter may be developed as a C library, for example. See the following code listing, which shows a Java application that uses a JNI to access this C library or C-based resource adapter. The JNI is the native programming interface for Java, and it is part of the Java Developers Kit (JDK). The JNI allows Java code that runs within a Java Virtual Machine (JVM) to operate with applications and libraries written in other languages, such as C and C++. Programmers typically use the JNI to write native methods when they cannot write the entire application in Java. This is the case when a Java application needs to access an existing library or application written in another programming language. While the JNI was especially useful before the advent of the J2EE platform, some of its uses may now be replaced by the J2EE Connector architecture. As you can see in Figure 6-2, the JNI to the resource adapter enables the Java application to communicate with the adapter's C library. While this approach does work, it is complex to use. The Java application has to understand how to invoke methods through the JNI. This approach also provides none of the J2EE support for transactions, security, and scalability. The developer is exposed to the complexity of managing these system-level services, and must do so through the complex JNI.

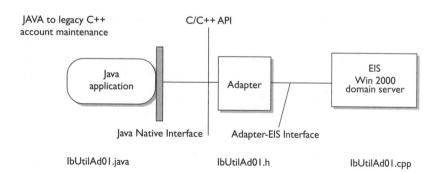

FIGURE 6-2

Java JNI application

```
public class lbUtilAd01  {
public native String createUser  (String pszUIDName, String pszUIDPassword,
String pszFirstName,String pszLastName,
 String pszOrg,String pszRoot,
 String pszAdminName, String pszAdminPassword);
  static
  {
      // Load the C++ DLL
      System.loadLibrary("lbUtilAD01");
  }
  public static void main(String args[])
  {
    lbUtilAd01 AD01 = new lbUtilAd01();
  AD01.createUser("Jbambara", "test1234", "Joe", "Bambara", "ou=Test OU",
 "dc=TRADING, dc=bank, dc=com", "administrator", "pw1234$!");
Output of JAVAH compiler: javah lbUtilad01
/* DO NOT EDIT THIS FILE - it is machine generated */
#include <jni.h>
/* Header for class tacadapter_lbUtilAd01 */
#ifndef _Included_tacadapter_lbUtilAd01
#define _Included_tacadapter_lbUtilAd01
#ifdef __cplusplus
extern "C" {
#endif
JNIEXPORT jstring JNICALL Java_tacadapter_lbUtilAd01_createUser
  (JNIEnv *, jobject, jstring, jstring, jstring, jstring, jstring, jstring,
 jstring,
string);
```

Here's the C++ program *lbUtilAD01.cpp*, which is called by *lbUtilAD01.java*:

```
// lbUtilAD01.cpp: implementation of the lbUtilAD01 class.
// This will CREATE user WINNT account for MS ADSI
….
#include "tacadapter_lbUtilAd01.h"
#define _WIN32_WINNT 0x0500
extern "C" __declspec( dllexport ) LPWSTR CharStringToUnicodeString
(const char *string);
char *GetSID(const char *szDomainName,LPWSTR,LPWSTR,const
char *szUserName,VARIANT *);
// JAVA JNI interface call signature
JNIEXPORT jstring JNICALL Java_tacadapter_lbUtilAd01_createUser
  (JNIEnv *env, jobject obj, jstring pszUIDName, jstring pszUIDPassword,jstring
szFirstName,jstring pszLastName,jstring pszOrg,jstring pszRoot,jstring
 pszAdminName, jstring pszAdminPassword)
  {
```

```
char strORG[1024],strRDN[1024], strFullName[1024];
HRESULT result;
jstring rMessage;
// convert call signature args to use in program
const char *szUIDName       = env -> GetStringUTFChars(pszUIDName, 0);
const char *szUIDPassword   = env -> GetStringUTFChars(pszUIDPassword, 0);
const char *szOrg   = env -> GetStringUTFChars(pszOrg, 0);
const char *szRoot  = env -> GetStringUTFChars(pszRoot, 0);
const char *szAdminName     = env -> GetStringUTFChars(pszAdminName, 0);
const char *szAdminPassword = env -> GetStringUTFChars(pszAdminPassword, 0);
const char *szFirstName     = env -> GetStringUTFChars(pszFirstName, 0);
const char *szLastName      = env -> GetStringUTFChars(pszLastName, 0);
IADsContainer *pContainer;
IADs *pServer=NULL;
IADsUser *pADuserpw=NULL;
IDispatch *pDisp=NULL;
LPWSTR lpADSIPath,lpUIDName,lpUIDPasswd,lpFirstName,lpLastName;
LPWSTR lpOrg,lpFullName, lpRDNName;
// GET ADSIPATH
lpADSIPath = CharStringToUnicodeString(strORG);
result = ADsOpenObject(lpADSIPath,lpAdminID,lpAdminPasswd,
 ADS_SECURE_AUTHENTICATION, IID_IADsContainer,(void**)&pContainer);
// CREATE USER
lpRDNName = CharStringToUnicodeString(strRDN);
 result= pContainer->Create(L"user",lpRDNName,&pDisp);
 result = pADuserpw->SetPassword(lpUIDPasswd);
//  COMMIT the changes
 result=pADuserpw->SetInfo();
    if (!SUCCEEDED(result))
    {
 rMessage = env -> NewStringUTF(GetErrorCode(result));
 cout << "Fail to pw set info" << endl;
 return(rMessage);
    }
```

Distributed EIS Adapters

Another, more complex, form of an EIS adapter might do its "adaptation"
work across diverse component models, distributed computing platforms, and
architectures. For example, an EIS may develop a distributed adapter that includes
the ability to perform remote communication with the EIS using Java RMI. This
type of adapter exposes a client programming model based on component-model
architecture. Adapters use different levels of abstraction and expose different APIs

based on those abstractions, depending on the type of the EIS. For example, with certain types of EISs, an adapter may expose a remote function call API to the client application. If so, a client application uses this remote function call API to execute its interactions with the EIS. An adapter can expose either a synchronous or an asynchronous mode of communication between the client applications and the EIS.

In the following code, the *lbUtilAd01* C++ program illustrates the use of adapters designed for synchronous communication using Java RMI. Adapters designed for this approach provide a synchronous request-reply communication model for use between an application and an EIS. In the following example and Figure 6-3, when an application wants to interact with the EIS to create an Windows 2000 account, it invokes this remote function on the EIS. The application that initiated the call then waits until the function completes and returns its reply to the caller. The reply contains the results of the function's execution on the EIS. An interaction such as this is considered *synchronous* because the execution of the calling application waits synchronously during the time the function executes on the EIS. One form of synchronous adapter allows bidirectional synchronous communication between an application and an EIS. This type of adapter enables an EIS to call an application synchronously.

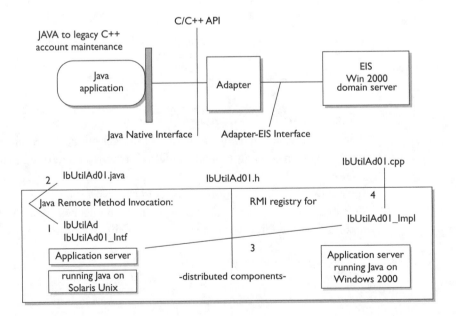

FIGURE 6-3	
Java RMI application	

```
import java.rmi.*;
import java.rmi.Naming;
import java.rmi.RemoteException;
public class lbUtilAd {
  String Win2KServer;
  lbUtilAd01Intf obj;
  public lbUtilAd(String server) throws Exception {
        Win2KServer = server;
     obj = (lbUtilAd01Intf)Naming.lookup("//"+Win2KServer+"/lbUtilAd01");
  }
public String createUser
 (String pszUIDName, String pszUIDPassword,
 String pszFirstName,String pszLastName,
 String pszOrg,String pszRoot,
 String pszAdminName, String pszAdminPassword)
throws RemoteException
  {
        return (obj.createUser(pszUIDName, pszUIDPassword,
 pszFirstName, pszLastName, pszOrg, pszRoot,  pszAdminName, pszAdminPassword));
  }
public static void main(String args[]) throws Exception
{
lbUtilAd obj = new lbUtilAd("ADSISERVER");
obj.createUser("jbambara", "pw", "Joe","Bambara", "org1","root1","administrator",
"admpw12$!"));
}
}
```

Legacy Connectivity Using J2EE Connector

The emerging JCA standard will obviate most of the need to build JNI and RMI code by providing a mechanism to store and retrieve enterprise data in J2EE. It is, however, important to keep in mind that a lot of developers use Java Database Connectivity (JDBC) to access data sources that are the underlying data store for such products as PeopleSoft and SAP to avoid using adapters that don't work with older versions of these products. In some cases, they will need to write their own adapters.

The latest versions of many application servers, including BEA WebLogic and IBM WebSphere, support JCA adapters for enterprise connectivity. Using JCA to access an EIS is analogous to using JDBC to access a database. By using the JCA, EIS vendors no longer need to customize their products for each application server. Application server vendors who conform to the JCA need not add custom code whenever they want to obtain connectivity to a new EIS.

Before JCA, each enterprise application integration (EAI) vendor created a proprietary resource adapter interface for its own EAI product, requiring a resource adapter to be developed for each EAI vendor and EIS combination (for instance, you need a SAP resource adapter to use the messaging tools of Tibco). To solve that problem, as one of its main thrusts, JCA attempts to standardize the resource adapter interfaces. The JCA provides a Java solution to the problem of connectivity between the many application servers and EISs already in existence. The JCA is based on the technologies that are defined and standardized as part of J2EE.

The JCA defines a standard architecture for connecting the J2EE platform to heterogeneous EISs. Examples of EISs include mainframe transaction processing, such as IBM CICS; database systems, such as IBM DB2; and legacy applications not written in the Java programming language, such as IBM COBOL. By defining a set of scalable, secure, and transactional mechanisms, the JCA enables the integration of EISs with application servers and enterprise applications.

The JCA enables a vendor to provide a standard resource adapter for its EIS. The resource adapter is integrated with the application server, thereby providing connectivity between the EIS and the enterprise application. An EIS vendor provides a standard resource adapter that has the ability to plug into any application server that supports the JCA. Multiple resource adapters, i.e., one per type of EIS, can be added into an application server. This ability enables application components deployed on the application server to access the underlying EISs. Figure 6-4 illustrates the JCA.

Resource Adapter

A resource adapter manifests itself as an implementation of interfaces in the *javax.resource.cci* and *javax.resource.spi* package. It will require a system-level software library when you are accessing a resource that uses native libraries to connect to an EIS. EIS vendors, middleware or application server vendors, or even end users of legacy systems provide a resource adapter. A resource adapter implements the EIS adapter-side of the connector system contracts. These contracts include connection management, transaction management, and security. A resource adapter also provides a client-level API that applications use to access an EIS. The client-level API can be the common client interface (CCI) or an API specific to the resource adapter or the EIS.

A resource adapter can also be used within an application server environment, which is referred to as a *managed* environment. The application server interacts with

FIGURE 6-4

J2EE Connector
Architecture

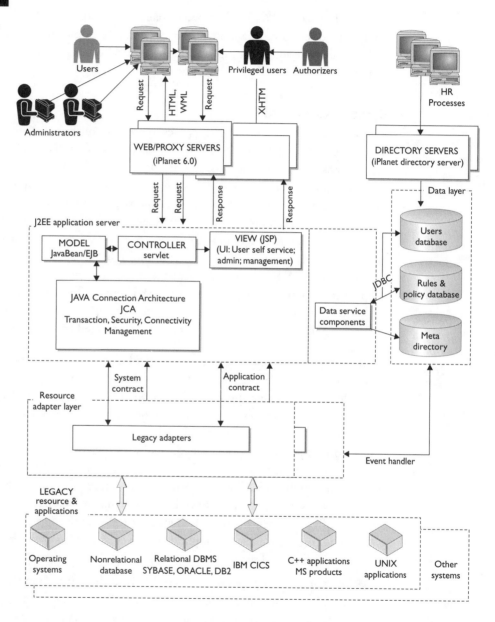

the resource adapter using the system contracts, while J2EE components use the client API to access the EIS. A resource adapter can also be used in a two-tier or nonmanaged scenario. In a nonmanaged scenario, an application directly interacts with the resource adapter using both the system contracts and the client API to connect to the EIS.

System Contract

A *contract* is an agreement between parties to provide collaborative mutually beneficial interaction. An application server and an EIS collaborate to keep all system-level mechanisms, such as transactions, security, and connection management, transparent from the application components. As a result, an application component provider can focus on the development of business and presentation logic for its application components and need not resolve at the system-level, issues related to EIS integration. This facilitates development of scalable, secure, and transactional enterprise applications that require connectivity with multiple EISs.

The benefits of the system contract are the *quid pro quo* provided by the resource adapter. It is the set of functionality you get to help perform the business task. The JCA defines the following set of system-level contracts between an application server and EIS. Table 6-1 shows system contracts implemented by resource adapters.

- *Connection management contracts* provide for pool connections to an underlying EIS and let application components connect to an EIS. This leads to a scalable application environment that can support a large number of clients requiring access to EISs. Connection management enables the application server to maintain back-end system connections. Support for connection pooling is provided, since creating connections to back-end systems is expensive. Connection pooling enables an EJB server to pool connections to back-end systems, so rather than opening connections on an as-needed basis, connections with data and services are established, configured, cached, and reused automatically by the application server. The contract enables an application server to offer its own services for transaction and security management.

- A *transaction management contract* between the transaction manager and an EIS that supports transactional access to EIS resource managers lets an application server use a transaction manager to manage transactions across multiple resource managers. The contract also supports transactions that are managed internal to an EIS resource manager without the necessity of involving an external transaction manager. The transaction management contract supports transactional access to underlying resource managers. The service enables the transaction manager provided within the Enterprise JavaBeans (EJB) server to manage transactions across multiple back-end systems. Connector developers define what level of transaction support they need—none, local (with a single back-end system and its resource manager), or the other end of the spectrum, XA—with either single or two-phase commit for working across multiple back-end systems and their associated resource managers.

■ A *security contract* enables a secure access to an EIS and provides support for a secure application environment, which reduces security threats to the EIS and protects valuable information resources managed by the EIS. The service enables the developer to define security between the EJB server and the back-end system. The specific security mechanism that is used is dependent on the security mechanism provided by the back-end system. For example, if a system requires Kerberos, the connection developer will include it. Under the contract, the connector provider must also support user authentication and any specific security contracts required by the back-end system.

TABLE 6-1	System Contracts Implemented by Resource Adapters

Interface Name	Description
ConnectionManager	Implemented by a resource adapter to provide connection management support in a nonmanaged environment.
ConnectionRequestInfo	Encapsulates security and client-specific information. A connection factory creates an object that implements this interface and passes it unmodified to a managed connection factory.
LocalTransaction	Provides methods for local transaction demarcation. Resource adapters at *LocalTransaction* and *XATransaction* levels must implement this interface.
ManagedConnection	Represents a physical connection to an EIS.
ManagedConnectionFactory	Represents a factory for managed connections.
ManagedConnectionMetaData	Package *javax.transaction.xa, Javax.resource.spi.*
XAResource	Provides methods for distributed XA transaction demarcation. Provides support for two-phase commit.

Common Client Interface

The JCA also defines a CCI for EIS access. The CCI defines a client API that is a standard for application components. It is analogous to the JDBC API standard. The CCI enables application components and EAI frameworks to drive interactions across heterogeneous EISs using a common client API. The CCI is intended as a standard for use by EAI and tools vendors.

Java Connector Architecture

With that background in mind, let's consider how the current version of the JCA specification as well as J2EE in general compare to some of the features found in EAI vendors' products. Many EAI vendors, Tibco for example, have either announced JCA support or are in the process of releasing products that incorporate JCA-based adapters. In light of this, and before we can discuss how JCA fits into the EAI picture, it's important that you first understand some basic EAI features:

- Resource adapters
- Data mapping
- Messaging brokers

Typical EAI vendors include proprietary adapters built to work with their products. These adapters allow for synchronous and asynchronous communication to an EIS. JCA adapters resemble those adapters, except JCA adapters include only a synchronous communication channel. Resource adapters represent the EAI feature JCA most directly matches, although most EAI vendors' adapters offer more features than JCA adapters—for example, asynchronous capability. Obviously, JCA is in its infancy, but just like JDBC, it is a standard and when it matures it will be more desirable than having to maintain in-house domain knowledge on the plethora of vendor EAI software. However, for now, JCA is deficient.

Data mapping means that data acquired in one format (for instance in the EIS's native format—such as an EBCDIC (extended binary code format) byte stream) by the resource adapter may have to be transformed into the format required for the business object. Mapping data from one system to another is time consuming because you must map each business object in both systems. In response, EAI vendors provide visual tools to enable a developer to set up such mapping. While JCA does not offer a data-mapping facility, EJB container-managed persistence (CMP) facility provides similar functionality. However, currently, not all EJB containers can use EJB CMP with JCA. This will change as JCA use increases.

Messaging brokers, another feature common to many EAI products, usually enable both point-to-point (PTP) and publish/subscribe messaging. EAI products employ messaging as the connectivity layer to tie together disparate systems. Currently, JCA does not address connectivity to an EIS in a message-oriented manner. It is possible, however, to implement some of a message broker's feature set by using J2EE's Java Message Service (JMS).

J2EE Connector Architecture: a General Integration Strategy

The majority of the work developers do today is creating new systems that must integrate with other systems. Integration can be simple to conceive but hard to accomplish; you can look at it in two ways:

- **Inbound integration** Outside systems initiate data requests to your system.
- **Outbound integration** Your system initiates data requests to other systems.

All of the following integration types are applicable in an inbound and an outbound manner. User interface (UI) integration, or "screen scraping" as it is known, represents a coarse type of integration. With UI-level integration, the data passed between systems will exist in the form of a UI representation. An outbound integration at the UI level entails requesting the UI as perhaps a web page from a remote system, and then possibly manipulating it before displaying it as if it were part of your system's UI. An inbound integration at the UI level entails allowing an outside system to request UI pages from your system for inclusion on a remote system.

on the **Job**

You should choose UI integration over other options when it is unimportant to distinguish the data type being retrieved. UI integration often requires the least amount of effort to implement. UI integration is also least likely to scale well, because the original system may not be able to handle the load inflicted on it by a heavily used J2EE application.

Message-level integration is growing in popularity, especially with the advent of web services. It implies that the data passed between systems will be in the form of a message (a defined, data-driven text format). Outbound message integration involves requesting data from a remote system in a message form—for example, a Simple Object Access Protocol (SOUP) message. With an inbound integration, your system receives a request for data via a message and responds with a message. Message-oriented integration lends itself to loose coupling between systems because the systems remain unaware of the object types that exist on the remote system. That type of loose coupling works well with applications that wish to communicate over the Internet.

Object or remote procedure call (RPC) integration implies integrating systems using distributed objects (that is, using EJB calls to integrate). With object-level integration, data passes between systems as parameters to method calls. In an outbound object-level integration, your system invokes objects on remote systems, while in an inbound object-level integration, a remote system calls objects on your system to retrieve data. One of the main advantages of object-level integration is that you can call detailed APIs with full type safety and easily propagate the error codes and exceptions between systems.

Data-level integration implies that the data passed between systems will be in a data/record-oriented manner. In an outbound data-level integration, your system requests data in a record-oriented fashion from other systems. With an inbound data-level integration, a remote system requests data from your system in a record-oriented manner.

The advantage of a data-level integration is that it lends itself to data mapping from one system onto the business objects in another system.

The Structure of the JCA

As mentioned, JCA's main components include the resource adapter, system contracts, and the CCI, which together give JCA the ability to access data in enterprise systems.

Resource Adapters and System Contracts

To use JCA in a J2EE container, you must have a JCA resource adapter, which resembles a JDBC driver. A JCA adapter is specific to an EIS (for example, Tibco) and is contained in a Resource Adapter Archive (RAR) file composed of the jar files and native libraries necessary to deploy the resource adapter on a J2EE container. A JCA adapter interacts with a J2EE server via system contracts. They enable the J2EE server to propagate the context in which a JCA adapter is being called.

There are three types of system contracts:

■ Connection management

■ Transaction management

■ Security

Connection Management   The connection management contract describes the agreement a J2EE container has with the adapter regarding establishing, pooling, and tearing down connections. This contract allows listeners created on a connection to respond to events. (Also note that the underlying protocol an adapter uses to connect to an EIS is outside the scope of the JCA specification.)

JCA resource adapters must supply two implementations with the adapter. First, a *ConnectionFactory* provides a vehicle for creating connections. Second, the *Connection* class represents this particular resource adapter's underlying connection.

Transaction Management   The transaction management contract controls transactions in two different ways. First, it allows distributed transactions that provide a mechanism to propagate transactions that originate from inside an application server to an EIS system. For example, in an EJB, a transaction may be created. If this EJB then employs a JCA resource adapter, the transaction management contract enables the transaction to propagate to the EIS. In that circumstance, the transaction manager on the application server would control multiple resources to conduct distributed transaction coordination—for example, a two-phase commit.

In the second way, the transaction management contract can control transactions by creating *local transactions*. Local transactions are local in the sense that they exist only on a particular EIS resource. The contract provides transactions control, but they are related to any transaction that exists on the application server where the JCA resource adapter is running. Note that the resource adapter need not implement the transaction management contract. Making this optional allows for resource adapters in non-transaction resources.

Security   The security contract enables the application server to connect to an EIS system using security properties. The application server authenticates with the

EIS system by using security properties composed of a principle (a user ID) and credentials (a password). An application server can employ two methods to authenticate to an EIS system (via a resource adapter).

With the first method, container-managed sign-on, the security credentials configure when the resource adapter is deployed on the application server. You can choose from several ways to configure security properties when using container-managed sign-on:

- **Configured identity**   All resource adapter connections use the same identity when connecting to the EIS system.

- **Principal mapping**   The principal used when connecting to the EIS system is based on a combination of the current principal in the application server and the mapping.

- **Caller impersonation**   The principal used in the EIS system exactly matches the principal in the application server.

- **Credentials mapping**   Similar to caller impersonation, except the type of credentials must be mapped from application server credentials to EIS credentials.

While it's simple to configure the security properties at deployment time, this strategy proves less flexible because the security properties cannot change at runtime. Alternatively, you can configure security properties by component-managed sign-on, which allows you to pass security properties each time a connection is acquired from the resource adapter.

Common Client Interface

To retrieve and update data, you employ JCA's CCI layer, a method set resembling the type of commands used in JDBC to call a stored procedure. A JCA resource adapter is not required to support the CCI layer (the resource adapter creators can choose their own API set), and even if the resource adapter does support CCI, it may also support an API specific for that particular adapter. This owes to the diverse functionality contained in EIS software. Database operations boil down to add, update, delete, and inquire. EIS software may be more process oriented and hence would include a larger set of functionality.

Just like the JDBC API, the CCI APIs can be divided into four sections:

- APIs related to establishing a connection to an EIS, also referred to as the *connection interfaces.*
- CCI APIs cover command execution on an EIS, referred to as the *interaction interfaces.*
- Record/ResultSet interfaces, which encapsulate the query results to an EIS.
- *Metadata interfaces*, which allows the ability to examine EIS's metadata—for example, the attributes or type of EIS data to be queried.

The code that follows illustrates a JCA CCI query of a client count from an EIS:

```
Public class JCAclass1...
int count;
try {
// obtain the connection

ConnectionSpec spec = new CciConnectionSpec(user, password);
Connection con = cf.getConnection(spec);
Interaction ix = con.createInteraction();
CciInteractionSpec iSpec = new CciInteractionSpec();

// command execution
iSpec.setSchema(user);
iSpec.setFunctionName("CLIENTCOUNT");

// handle the result set
RecordFactory rf = cf.getRecordFactory();
IndexedRecord iRec = rf.createIndexedRecord("InputRecord");
Record rec = ix.execute(iSpec, iRec);
Iterator iter = ((IndexedRecord)rec).iterator();
while(iter.hasNext())

{
   Object obj = iter.next();
if(obj instanceof Integer) count = ((Integer)obj).intValue();"
}
/ close the connection
con.close();
}
```

```
catch(Exception e)
 {
  e.printStackTrace();
 }
System.out.println(the count is  " "+ count);
...
```

Limitations of the JCA 1.0 and JCA 2.0

As mentioned, the JCA is early in its evolution and as such lacks support for more exotic adapter types. With respect for support of bidirectional, asynchronous adapters, the JCA 1.0 event model does not support same—asynchronous—communications. It supports only the synchronous request/reply model. This means a resource adapter can call a remote system and wait for response, but the remote system can't initiate a call back to an adapter at a later point.

Although this is common in the application server world, it is not well suited for more complex integration scenarios. For example, JCA 1.0 is useful in a business-to-consumer (B2C) scenario where the application needs to check availability on a certain item in inventory before processing the order. However, it is limiting in a high-volume EAI and business-to-business scenario involving many disparate systems and where an immediate response from an external system is not critical, or where it is difficult to ensure an external system is up and running. These situations tend to benefit from the flexibility offered by loosely coupled asynchronous connections.

The CCI is designed to work with hierarchical and tabular data. Although CCI can be used to support XML, there is no built-in support for XML records. BEA's adapter framework *forces* you to use XML, yet it retains JCA compatibility (as long as you include their JAR files). It would be useful to be able to transform records retrieved from interactions with the back-end system into XML inside of the resource adapter. JCA does not provide any built-in support for working with application metadata. Developers, however, can use whatever metadata API and repository they want.

Basic JCA Adapter Implementation

Let's quickly explore the steps required to implement a JCA adapter—that is, a set of classes with which a J2EE application server targets a particular enterprise system. As mentioned, a JCA adapter functions in much the same way as a JDBC driver connects to databases. We will describe the adapter's capabilities, as well as how to deploy and run it. We will see what occurs when the adapter executes in the container. It's important to frame the sample-adapter discussion by describing its functionality. Moreover, the example adapter implements only those classes required for the JCA specification's connection management section. Further, most of the adapter's method implementations contain print statements that let you see the method calls' order, without hooking up a debugger. The example adapter does not, however, address transaction and security contacts.

To use a JCA adapter, you need a J2EE application server with JCA 1.0 specification support. You upload the resource adapter archive—for example, the *Ucnyadapter.rar* file. The adapter includes two class categories:

- **Managed classes**   The application server calls managed classes to perform the connection management. They're needed only if the application server is managing the connection via a connection pool, which is probably the case.

- **Physical connection classes**   These required classes, which the aforementioned managed classes may call, establish the connection to the EIS.

ManagedConnectionFactory

With the *UCManagedConnectionFactory* class, which implements the *ManagedConnectionFactory* interface, you create the *UCConnectionFactory* and *UCManagedConnection* classes. The *UCManagedConnectionFactory* class acts as the main entry point for the application server to call into the adapter:

```
package ucnyjca;

import java.io.PrintWriter;
import java.io.Serializable;
import java.sql.DriverManager;
import java.util.Iterator;
import java.util.Set;
import javax.resource.ResourceException;
import javax.resource.spi.*;
import javax.security.auth.Subject;

public class UCManagedConnectionFactory
implements ManagedConnectionFactory, Serializable
{

    public UCManagedConnectionFactory() {
        System.out.println("We are executing
UCManagedConnectionFactory.constructor");
```

```
    }

    public Object createConnectionFactory(ConnectionManager cxManager)
throws ResourceException {
        System.out.println("We are executing
UCManagedConnectionFactory.createConnectionFactory,1");
        return new UCDataSource(this, cxManager);
    }

    public Object createConnectionFactory() throws ResourceException {

            System.out.println("We are executing
UCManagedConnectionFactory.createManagedFactory,2");
        return new UCDataSource(this, null);
    }

    public ManagedConnection createManagedConnection
(Subject subject, ConnectionRequestInfo info) {
        System.out.println("We are executing
UCManagedConnectionFactory.createManagedConnection");
        return new UCManagedConnection(this, "test");
    }

    public ManagedConnection matchManagedConnections
(Set connectionSet, Subject subject, ConnectionRequestInfo info)
        throws ResourceException
    {
        System.out.println("We are executing
UCManagedConnectionFactory.matchManagedConnections");
        return null;
    }

    public void setLogWriter(PrintWriter out) throws ResourceException {
        System.out.println("We are executing
UCManagedConnectionFactory.setLogWriter");
    }

    public PrintWriter getLogWriter() throws ResourceException {
        System.out.println("We are executing
 UCManagedConnectionFactory.getLogWriter");
        return DriverManager.getLogWriter();
    }

    public boolean equals(Object obj) {
        if(obj == null)
            return false;
        if(obj instanceof UCManagedConnectionFactory)
        {
            int hash1 = ((UCManagedConnectionFactory)obj).hashCode();
```

```
            int hash2 = hashCode();
            return hash1 == hash2;
        }
        else
        {
            return false;
        }
    }

    public int hashCode()
    {
            return 1;
    }
}
```

ManagedConnection

The *UCManagedConnection* class implements the *ManagedConnection* interface. *UCManagedConnection* encapsulates the adapter's physical connection, in this case the *UCConnection* class:

```java
package ucnyjca;

import java.io.PrintWriter;
import java.sql.Connection;
import java.sql.SQLException;
import java.util.*;
import javax.resource.NotSupportedException;
import javax.resource.ResourceException;
import javax.resource.spi.*;
import javax.security.auth.Subject;
import javax.transaction.xa.XAResource;


public class UCManagedConnection
  implements ManagedConnection
{
    private UCConnectionEventListener UCListener;
    private String user;
    private ManagedConnectionFactory mcf;
    private PrintWriter logWriter;
    private boolean destroyed;
    private Set connectionSet;

  UCManagedConnection(ManagedConnectionFactory mcf, String user)
  {
    System.out.println("We are executing UCManagedConnection");
    this.mcf = mcf;
```

```
    this.user = user;
    connectionSet = new HashSet();
    UCListener = new UCConnectionEventListener(this);
  }

  private void throwResourceException(SQLException ex)
    throws ResourceException
  {
    ResourceException re = new ResourceException("SQLException: " +
ex.getMessage());
    re.setLinkedException(ex);
    throw re;
  }

  public Object getConnection(Subject subject, ConnectionRequestInfo
connectionRequestInfo)
    throws ResourceException
  {
    System.out.println("We are executing UCManagedConnection.getConnection");
    UCConnection UCCon = new UCConnection(this);
    addUCConnection(UCCon);
    return UCCon;
  }

  public void destroy()
  {
        System.out.println("We are executing UCManagedConnection.destroy");
        destroyed = true;
  }

  public void cleanup()
   {
        System.out.println("We are executing UCManagedConnection.cleanup");
  }

  public void associateConnection(Object connection)
   {
        System.out.println("We are executing
UCManagedConnection.associateConnection");
  }

  public void addConnectionEventListener(ConnectionEventListener listener)
   {
        System.out.println("We are executing
UCManagedConnection.addConnectionEventListener");
    UCListener.addConnectorListener(listener);
  }

  public void removeConnectionEventListener(ConnectionEventListener listener)
```

```
    {
        System.out.println("We are executing
CManagedConnection.removeConnectionEventListener");
      UCListener.removeConnectorListener(listener);
    }

  public XAResource getXAResource()
    throws ResourceException
    {
        System.out.println("We are executing
UCManagedConnection.getXAResource");
      return null;
    }

  public LocalTransaction getLocalTransaction()
    {
          System.out.println("We are executing
UCManagedConnection.getLocalTransaction");
        return null;
    }

  public ManagedConnectionMetaData getMetaData()
    throws ResourceException
    {
    System.out.println("We are executing UCManagedConnection.getMetaData");
    return new UCConnectionMetaData(this);
    }


  public void setLogWriter(PrintWriter out)
    throws ResourceException
    {
        System.out.println("We are executing UCManagedConnection.setLogWriter");
      logWriter = out;
    }

  public PrintWriter getLogWriter()
    throws ResourceException
    {
        System.out.println("We are executing UCManagedConnection.getLogWriter");
      return logWriter;
    }

  Connection getUCConnection()
    throws ResourceException
    {
        System.out.println("We are executing
UCManagedConnection.getUCConnection");
      return null;
```

```
  }

  boolean isDestroyed()
  {
        System.out.println("We are executing UCManagedConnection.isDestroyed");
     return destroyed;
  }

  String getUserName()
  {
        System.out.println("We are executing UCManagedConnection.getUserName");
     return user;
  }

  void sendEvent(int eventType, Exception ex)
  {
        System.out.println("We are executing UCManagedConnection.sendEvent,1");
     UCListener.sendEvent(eventType, ex, null);
  }

  void sendEvent(int eventType, Exception ex, Object connectionHandle)
  {
        System.out.println("We are executing UCManagedConnection.sendEvent,2 ");
     UCListener.sendEvent(eventType, ex, connectionHandle);
  }

  void removeUCConnection(UCConnection UCCon)
  {
        System.out.println("We are executing
UCManagedConnection.removeUCConnection");
     connectionSet.remove(UCCon);
  }

  void addUCConnection(UCConnection UCCon)
  {
        System.out.println("We are executing
UCManagedConnection.addUCConnection");
     connectionSet.add(UCCon);
  }

  ManagedConnectionFactory getManagedConnectionFactory()
  {
        System.out.println("We are executing
UCManagedConnection.getManagedConnectionFactory");
     return mcf;
  }

}
```

UCConnectionEventListener

The *UCConnectionEventListener* class allows the application server to register callbacks for the adapter. The application server can then perform operations—connection-pool maintenance, for example—based on the connection state:

```
package ucnyjca;

import java.util.Vector;
import javax.resource.spi.ConnectionEvent;
import javax.resource.spi.ConnectionEventListener;
import javax.resource.spi.ManagedConnection;

public class UCConnectionEventListener
    implements javax.sql.ConnectionEventListener
{
    private Vector listeners;
    private ManagedConnection mcon;


    public UCConnectionEventListener(ManagedConnection mcon)
    {
        System.out.println("We are executing UCConnectionEventListener");
        this.mcon = mcon;
    }

    public void sendEvent(int eventType, Exception ex, Object connectionHandle)
    {
        System.out.println("We are executing
UCConnectionEventListener.sendEvent");
    }

    public void addConnectorListener(ConnectionEventListener l)
    {
        System.out.println("We are executing
UCConnectionEventListener.addConnectorListener");
    }

    public void removeConnectorListener(ConnectionEventListener l)
    {
        System.out.println("We are executing
UCConnectionEventListener.removeConnectorListener");
    }

    public void connectionClosed(javax.sql.ConnectionEvent connectionevent)
    {
        System.out.println("We are executing
UCConnectionEventListener.connectorClosed");
```

```
    }

    public void connectionErrorOccurred(javax.sql.ConnectionEvent event)
    {
        System.out.println("We are executing
UCConnectionEventListener.connectorErrorOccurred");
    }

}
```

UCConnectionMetaData

The *UCConnectionMetaData* class provides meta information—for example, the maximum number of connections allowed, and so on—regarding the managed connection and the underlying physical connection class:

```
package ucnyjca;

import javax.resource.ResourceException;
import javax.resource.spi.*;


public class UCConnectionMetaData
    implements ManagedConnectionMetaData
{

    private UCManagedConnection mc;

    public UCConnectionMetaData(UCManagedConnection mc)
    {
        System.out.println(We are executing UCConnectionMetaData.constructor);
        this.mc = mc;
    }"
    public String getEISProductName()
        throws ResourceException
    {
        System.out.println(We are executing
UCConnectionMetaData.getEISProductName);
        return "ucnyjca";
    }

    public String getEISProductVersion()
        throws ResourceException
    {
        System.out.println(We are executing
UCConnectionMetaData.getEISProductVersion);
        return "1.0";
```

```
    }

    public int "etMaxConnections()
        throws ResourceException
    {
            System.out.println(We are executing
UCConnectionMetaData.getMaxConnections);
            return 5;
    }

    public String getUserName()
        throws ResourceException
    {
            return mc.getUserName();
    }

}
```

UCConnection

The *UCConnection* class represents the "handle" to the underlying physical connection to the EIS. *UCConnection* is one of the few classes that does not implement an interface in the JCA specification. The implementation that follows is simple, but a working implementation might contain connectivity code using sockets, as well as other functionality:

```
package ucnyjca;

public class UCConnection
{
    private UCManagedConnection mc;

    public UCConnection(UCManagedConnection mc)
    {
        System.out.println("We are executing UCConnection");
        this.mc = mc;
    }
}
```

UCConnectionRequestInfo

The *UCConnectionRequestInfo* class contains the data (such as the username, password, and other information) necessary to establish a connection:

```
package ucnyjca;

import javax.resource.spi.ConnectionRequestInfo;
```

```
public class UCConnectionRequestInfo
    implements ConnectionRequestInfo
{

    private String user;
    private String password;

    public UCConnectionRequestInfo(String user, String password)
    {
        System.out.println(We are executing UCConnectionRequestInfo);
        this.user = user;
        this.password = password;
    }

    public String getUser()
    {
        System.out.println(We are executing UCConnectionRequestInfo.getUser);
        return user;
    }

    public String getPassword()
    {
        System.out.println(We are executing
UCConnectionRequestInfo.getPassword);
        return password;
    }

    public boolean equals(Object obj)
    {
        System.out.println(We are executing UCConnectionRequestInfo.equals);
        if(obj == null)
            return false;
        if(obj instanceof UCConnectionRequestInfo)
        {
            UCConnectionRequestInfo other = (UCConnectionRequestInfo)obj;
            return isEqual(user, other.user) &&
isEqual(password, other.password);
        } else
        {
            return false;
        }
    }

    public int hashCode()
    {
        System.out.println(We are executing UCConnectionRequestInfo.hashCode);
        String result = " + user + password;
```

```
        return result.hashCode();
    }

    private boolean isEqual(Object o1, Object o2)
    {
        System.out.println(We are executing UCConnectionRequestInfo.isEqual);
        if(o1 == null)
            return o2 == null;
        else
            return o1.equals(o2);
    }

}
```

UCDataSource

The *UCDataSource* class serves as a connection factory for the underlying connections. Because the example adapter does not implement the CCI interfaces, it implements the *DataSource* interface in the *javax.sql* package:

```
package ucnyjca;

import java.io.PrintWriter;
import java.io.Serializable;
import java.sql.*;
import javax.naming.Reference;
import javax.resource.Referenceable;
import javax.resource.ResourceException;
import javax.resource.spi.ConnectionManager;
import javax.resource.spi.ManagedConnectionFactory;
import javax.sql.DataSource;
public class UCDataSource
    implements DataSource, Serializable, Referenceable
{
    private String desc;
    private ManagedConnectionFactory mcf;
    private ConnectionManager cm;
    private Reference reference;
    public UCDataSource(ManagedConnectionFactory mcf, ConnectionManager cm)
    {
        System.out.println(We are executing UCDataSource);
        this.mcf = mcf;
        if(cm == null)
            this.cm = new UCConnectionManager();
        else
            this.cm = cm;
    }
```

```
        public Connection getConnection(String username, String password)
            throws SQLException
    {
        System.out.println(We are executing UCDataSource.getConnection,2);
        try
        {
            javax.resource.spi.ConnectionRequestInfo
info = new UCConnectionRequestInfo(username, password);
            return (Connection)cm.allocateConnection(mcf, info);
        }
        catch(ResourceException ex)
        {
            throw new SQLException(ex.getMessage());
        }
    }

    public int getLoginTimeout()
        throws SQLException
    {
        return DriverManager.getLoginTimeout();
    }

    public void setLoginTimeout(int seconds)
        throws SQLException
    {
        DriverManager.setLoginTimeout(seconds);
    }

    public PrintWriter getLogWriter()
        throws SQLException
    {
        return DriverManager.getLogWriter();
    }

    public void setLogWriter(PrintWriter out)
        throws SQLException
    {
        DriverManager.setLogWriter(out);
    }

    public String getDescription()
    {
        return desc;
    }

    public void setDescription(String desc)
    {
        this.desc = desc;
```

```
    }

    public void setReference(Reference reference)
    {
        this.reference = reference;
    }

    public Reference getReference()
    {
        return reference;
    }
}
```

Build the RAR File

The next step is to build the *ucnyjca.rar* file. Typically you would have a source directory containing two subdirectories: *ucnyjca* containing the *.java* files, and *META-INF* containing the configuration files.

To compile and build the rar file:

1. Compile the class files: *javac *.java* in the *ucnyjca* directory.

2. Build the *ucnyjca.jar*:

   ```
   jar cvf ucnyjca.jar ucnyjca
   ```

3. Create the *rar* file using the *ucnyjca.jar* and the *META-INF* directory:

   ```
   jar cvf ucnyjca.rar ucnyjca.jar META-INF
   ```

If you were to execute the example code in this chapter, you would see the following sequence of *System.out.println*:

```
We are executing UCManagedConnectionFactory.constructor
We are executing UCManagedConnectionFactory.createManagedConnection
We are executing UCManagedConnection
We are executing UCConnectionEventListener
We are executing UCManagedConnection.getMetaData
We are executing UCConnectionMetaData.constructor
We are executing UCConnectionMetaData.getEISProductName
We are executing UCConnectionMetaData.getEISProductVersion
We are executing UCConnectionMetaData.getMaxConnections
```

The audit trail shows the *ManagedConnectionFactor*'s creation, which then invoked the *ManagedConnection*, which in turn created the *ConnectionEventListener*. You also see that the application server called the *ConnectionMetaData*.

The JCA specification's complexity makes implementing even basic adapters a difficult task. Moreover, the task grows when you add the transaction and security contracts (not implemented for this example), as well as the CCIs. The complexity shows that the JCA specification is oriented toward commercial software vendors implementing adapters and their customers using them. In this arena, the JCA makes sense, although a less flexible, simpler interface version would be nice. Therefore, if you are considering using JCA to connect to a legacy system in your enterprise, you would make the implementation more likely by leveraging an off-the-shelf adapter rather than developing your own. If the system to which you need connectivity does not have a JCA adapter, consider an alternative approach. Perhaps the old style for a workaround or using web services may provide the best solution.

For its part, while JCA is still a new standard, it shows promise for making the task of integrating with an EIS less daunting. It is, however, still a ways off in terms of general availability for most vendors. The economy, when it eventually upturns, will create opportunities for J2EE architects to apply JCA to reface the enterprise.

CERTIFICATION OBJECTIVE 6.01

Distinguish Appropriate from Inappropriate Techniques for Providing Access to a Legacy System from Java Technology Code Given an Outline Description of That Legacy System

The following nine exercises are in the form of practice essay questions:

1. Read the question.
2. Develop an essay style answer.
3. Review the draft and finalize your response.
4. Review the answer in the book.

EXERCISE 6-1

Techniques and Best Practices

Question   As an enterprise architect who is commissioned to J2EE technology–enable a set of existing legacy or EIS systems, what are some of the techniques and best practices that you might incorporate?

Answer   When integrating existing EIS with any new technology, especially J2EE, it's a given that EIS integrates more easily when using proven guidelines and standards. Following are some tried-and-true concepts.

J2EE systems that access existing or external information resources should avoid accessing those resources directly from multiple locations—that is, they should avoid a one-stop-shopping bean piece of API code. Otherwise, multiple access entwines your business logic with the implementation details of an external resource. If the API to that resource changes (when, for example, you change resource vendors, a new version is released, or for other reasons), changes to your J2EE application source code will be necessary throughout the application, and the resulting testing burden can be considerable.

Per our desire to adhere to standards for some resources, an EIS resource vendor or some third party may provide a J2EE connector extension, an adapter that allows J2EE systems to interoperate with other EIS resources transparently and with transaction management capability.

For database access, a standard in the JDBC API makes vendors' proprietary technology accessible in an open way. Switching database implementations, even at runtime, is facilitated with JDBC, which provides a standard API to mask the vendor-specific implementation details in connection configuration data and access and transaction functionality.

In addition, it is a good practice to use the data access object (DAO) design pattern to encapsulate access to EIS resources and prepare for eventual migration to a JCA-based interface. If no J2EE connector extension is available for your EIS resource, a good alternative is to use DAO classes to represent the EIS system as an abstract resource. Instead of calling the EIS system directly from the enterprise bean, create a DAO class that represents the services your bean needs. This is an application of the Bridge design pattern, which makes an interface's implementation transparently replaceable by decoupling the implementation from the interface. A DAO class that wraps an EIS resource insulates the enterprise bean from changes in that resource. New versions of the EIS resource can then be implemented and the change control will be the only necessary modifications to the DAO layer of the J2EE application. Another benefit of this practice is experienced when a connector becomes available for your EIS resource. The enterprise can replace the existing DAO implementation with one that simply dispatches calls to the connector.

Imagine that the enterprise is using a custom legacy system to which your enterprise bean needs access. A DAO class can provide a vendor-agnostic API interface to the enterprise bean, while handling the details of service requests from the enterprise bean to the legacy system. This scheme is advantageous when a single service request from your J2EE server's perspective requires access to a number of existing EIS resources—that is, a DAO can be used to facade multiple EIS resources. This use of the façade pattern facilitates changes to these EIS services. When an existing EIS service is replaced, the existing DAO class can be replaced with a new DAO class that presents the new service to the enterprise bean in terms of the existing DAO interface. Isolating your enterprise bean functionality with a DAO layer makes it easier for your J2EE system design to evolve with time.

The DAO class(es) should reflect the functional requirements of the services your enterprise beans need, not necessarily the structure of the existing system. A DAO class's interface should reflect a current view. Analyze what the existing EIS system does, determine what needs to be done today and tomorrow, and create methods in the DAO classes that provide the most frequently required functionality. If multiple EIS resources are required to perform a single task, the DAO class can combine access to these systems and present them to the EJB as a single service. So as an EIS integration best practice, we should avoid letting the structure of existing EIS resources dictate the structure of the integrated system. Instead, architect and design with your new requirements and goals in mind. Use existing legacy resources as services to meet those requirements.

A DAO class should be neither a collection of unrelated tools nor a tool designed for one application, but something that cleanly and completely represents a clear and reusable abstraction. UML diagrams such as collaboration, statechart, activity, and package diagrams can be a help in the analysis.

EXERCISE 6-2

Implementing Data Validation and Referential Integrity Constraints

Question   As an architect integrating a J2EE system with an existing EIS database system, where should data validation and referential integrity constraints be implemented?

Answer   This is a difficult call. The practical aspects of the decision revolve around the following:

- How much will it ultimately cost?
- How much is already invested in the database application?
- How long is it expected to be functional?

If the DBMS is relational and was implemented after the mid 1980s, it is typically best to use the DBMS functionality to enforce value and referential integrity. Sybase, Oracle, SQL Server, DB2, and Informix—to mention the most popular DBMS's—have had these abilities for many years. These DBMSs include declarative value and referential integrity constraint features, integrated with the Data Description Language (DDL), and they provide built-in declarative triggers to handle cascading actions required for referential integrity, such as deleting all item rows in a cancelled order. Implementing these in the enterprise bean layer would duplicate logic, making maintenance difficult. Any change to the database constraints would require making the change to enterprise beans and to the database.

The architectural benefits and capabilities maintaining data integrity constraints in the database layer include the following:

- *Facilitates use by multiple applications.* If for some reason multiple applications are responsible for maintaining database integrity, every application creates an opportunity for bugs that would violate that integrity. Furthermore, other applications that may want to access the database are relieved of the duty of maintaining integrity constraints. They still must, of course, deal with error conditions that result if they violate those constraints.

- *Centralization.* If the constraints are maintained only in the database, the database is the one place where data can be considered consistent by definition. If data inconsistencies exist, either the integrity constraints are incorrect or the design has flaws.

- *Portability.* Simple value and integrity constraints, such as primary keys, simple foreign keys, uniqueness, value range checking, and so on, are reasonably portable.

- *Performance and reliability.* Database vendors that offer database constraints features have invested a great deal of time and money in ensuring that those features operate correctly and efficiently.

The drawbacks of using the DBMS built-in database integrity constraints mechanisms and the EJB can include the following:

- *Possible duplication of logic.* Enterprise beans generally need reasonable data to perform properly. Therefore, most well-designed enterprise beans do a reasonably good job of checking data values and existence constraints. Database integrity violation errors usually indicate a bug or a problem with the design. Nevertheless, the logic enforcing value and referential integrity is necessarily duplicated. Changing the integrity rules in the database will usually also entail changes to the code, and keeping the two synchronized can be a problem.

- *Potential non-portability of DBMS constraints.* While simple value and referential integrity constraints are fairly portable, databases differ in coverage and syntax for more involved mechanisms such as composite foreign keys, database triggers, and procedural triggers. Procedural triggers in particular are portability concerns, because, when offered, they are often written in the database vendor's product-specific proprietary language. For example, Sybase Transact SQL is very different from the Oracle PL/SQL procedure language.

- *Database definition and configuration is uncontrolled.* Because database constraint and trigger configuration are performed with the database vendor's tools, such constraints are maintained outside of the J2EE server framework. Because the data model constraints are specified not in the deployment descriptor, but in the persistence layer, such constraints are not part of a J2EE server deployment. They must therefore be managed separately, complicating deployment and maintenance and providing another possible avenue for system flaws.

Another option is to use the EJB to handle constraints. Referential integrity constraints can be implemented in the EJB tier. The constraints required for an application may not be available in the DBMS chosen. The data model may have constraint requirements that cannot be satisfied using the DBMS constraint language. Such constraints can be implemented in the EJB tier. EJB-tier constraint management also provides portability, since the enterprise beans will operate identically in J2EE-branded containers. Constraints in the EJB tier can also be controlled by way of environment settings in the application deployment descriptor, centralizing constraint management and making it controllable at deploy time.

Yet another option is to implement constraints in both the EJB and database tiers and to configure the constraint implementation at deploy time. This strategy is useful especially when an application must be portable to many different databases, and you want consistent behavior across vendors while optimizing performance by using each database's full power.

You could also create a persistence server for the EIS tier. Constraints should be expressed in a declarative constraint language provided by the database vendor. In their absence the implementation should choose to wrap a layer of integrity management software around the database API. The EIS tier of your application can be an API that you create to wrap the database. Your application accesses the data store only through that server. This application of the decorator design pattern can provide a solution that is portable across databases, is declaratively configurable, and provides a consistent behavior across various clients. As a great deal of design, construction, validation, and maintenance are required, the decorator design pattern should be the solution where ultimate flexibility and portability are required.

Finally, commercial transaction processing (TP) monitors provide the benefits of the persistence server described above. TP monitors can provide scalability and availability. Typically, they work with multiple database vendors. You avoid vendor lock-in by wrapping calls to the monitor in DAO classes.

EXERCISE 6-3

Legacy Mapping

Question What is legacy object mapping?

Answer Legacy object mapping builds wrappers around legacy system interfaces to access elements of the legacy business logic and database tiers directly. Legacy object mapping tools are used to create proxy objects that access legacy system functions and make them available in an object-oriented manner.

EXERCISE 6-4

Transaction Monitors

Question What is the purpose of a transaction monitor?

Answer Transaction monitors are programs, such as IBM CICS, that monitor transactions, to ensure that they are completed in a successful manner. They ensure that successful transactions are committed, that unsuccessful transactions are aborted, and that the in-flight data updates are rolled back to the status quo ante or the state it was in before the attempted change.

EXERCISE 6-5

Off-Board Servers

Question What is an off-board server?

Answer An off-board server is a server that executes as a proxy for a legacy system. It communicates with the legacy system using the custom protocols supported by the legacy system. It communicates with external applications using industry-standard protocols.

EXERCISE 6-6

JDBC vs. ODBC

Question How does Java Database Connectivity (JDBC) differ from Microsoft database connectivity interface (ODBC)?

Answer ODBC is the industry-standard interface by which database clients connect to database servers. JDBC is a pure Java solution that does not follow the ODBC standard. A bridge between JDBC and ODBC allows JDBC to access databases that support ODBC.

EXERCISE 6-7

Accessing Legacy System Software

Question How is Java Native Interface (JNI) used to access legacy system software?

Answer JNI is used to write custom code to interface Java objects with legacy software that does not support standard communication interfaces.

EXERCISE 6-8

Accessing COM Objects

Question How is Java-to-COM bridging used to access COM objects?

Answer A Java-to-COM bridge enables COM objects to be accessed as Java classes and Java classes to be accessed as COM objects, thereby providing some support for using Microsoft software with Java.

EXERCISE 6-9

RMI vs. CORBA

Question What are the primary differences between RMI and CORBA, and for what is Internet Inter-ORB Protocol (IIOP) used?

Answer RMI and CORBA are both distributed-object technologies that support the creation, maintenance, and accessibility of objects. CORBA supports a language-independent approach to developing and deploying distributed objects. RMI is a Java-specific approach. IIOP is used to support communication between object request brokers such as CORBA via TCP/IP. RMI uses a stub that is a proxy for a remote object that runs on the client computer. RMI and CORBA use a skeleton as a proxy for a remote object that runs on the server. Stubs forward a client's RMIs (and their associated arguments) to skeletons, which forward them on to the appropriate server objects. Skeletons return the results of server method invocations to clients via stubs. The difference between RMI and CORBA is that the CORBA stubs access the ORB, and then the CORBA skeleton.

CERTIFICATION SUMMARY

The JCA is a specification for the Java platform that addresses the need to provide a standard architecture for integrating EIS. It complements the use of JNI and RMI to create a Java interface to a process running in its native domain.

TWO-MINUTE DRILL

Distinguish Appropriate from Inappropriate Techniques for Providing Access to a Legacy System from Java Technology Code Given an Outline Description of That Legacy System

❑ The EAI facilitates the integration of EISs, or legacy systems, as they are also known. The classic means of communicating with an existing EIS has been a specialized adapter, which implements the support for communication with the EIS and provides access to EIS data and functions. Communication between an adapter and the EIS typically uses a protocol specific to the EIS.

❑ Another, more complex, form of an EIS adapter might do its adaptation work across diverse component models, distributed computing platforms, and architectures. For example, an EIS may develop a distributed adapter that includes the capability to perform remote communication with the EIS using Java RMI or CORBA.

❑ The JCA puts EAI into mainstream use by establishing a standard.

❑ The JCA comprises a resource adapter, connection management contracts, a transaction management contract, a security contract, and the CCI.

❑ A JCA resource adapter is specific to an EIS (Tibco) and is contained in a RAR file. The RAR is composed of the JAR files and native libraries required to deploy the resource adapter on a J2EE container.

❑ A JCA adapter interacts with a J2EE server via system contracts. Three types of system contracts can be used:

   ❑ Connection management

   ❑ Transaction management

   ❑ Security

❑ The connection management contract describes the interaction between a J2EE container and the adapter with respect to pooling and tearing down connections. All JCA resource adapters supply two implementations with the adapter: a *ConnectionFactory* and a *Connection* class.

❑ The transaction management contract provides a mechanism to propagate transactions that originate from inside an application server to an EIS system. The transaction management contract can control transactions by creating local transactions that exist only on a particular EIS resource.

❑ The security contract enables the application server to connect to an EIS using security properties composed of a principle (a user ID) and credentials (a password, a certificate).

❑ To retrieve and update data, JCA's CCI layer is used. The CCI APIs establishing a connection to an EIS cover command execution on an EIS to provide Record/ResultSet interfaces, which encapsulate the query results and allow EIS metadata (the type of data) to be queried.

SELF TEST

The following questions will help you measure your understanding of the material presented in this chapter. Read all the choices carefully because there might be more than one correct answer. Choose all correct answers for each question.

Distinguish Appropriate from Inappropriate Techniques for Providing Access to a Legacy System from Java Technology Code Given an Outline Description of That Legacy System

1. For a system consisting of exclusively Java objects, which distributed technology would be most appropriate for communication?

   A. CORBA

   B. RMI

   C. JNDI

   D. JavaBeans

2. Which of the following are true about the Interface Definition Language (IDL)?

   A. Interfaces between CORBA objects can be specified using IDL.

   B. Applications can be implemented using IDL.

   C. Interfaces described in IDL can be mapped to other programming languages.

   D. Stubs and skeletons are written in IDL.

3. An object that implements the interfaces *java.rmi.Remote* and *java.io.Serializable* is being sent as a method parameter from one JVM to another. How would it be sent by RMI?

   A. RMI will serialize the object and send it.

   B. RMI will send the stub of the object.

   C. Both A and B throw an exception.

4. The RMI compiler rmic runs on which of the following files to produce the stub and skeleton classes?

   A. On the remote interface class file

   B. On the remote service implementation class file

   C. On the remote service implementation Java file

   D. On the remote interface Java file

5. Which distributed object technology is most appropriate for systems that consist of objects written in different languages and that execute on different operating system platforms?

    A. RMI

    B. CORBA

    C. DCOM

    D. DCE

6. Which of the following can be used by Java RMI?

    A. Stubs

    B. Skeletons

    C. ORBs

    D. IIOP

7. Which of the following is not a tier of a three-tier architecture?

    A. Client interface

    B. Business logic

    C. Security

    D. Data storage

8. Which of the following is *not* true about RMI?

    A. RMI uses the Proxy design pattern.

    B. RMI uses object serialization to send objects between JVMs.

    C. The RMI Registry is used to generate stubs and skeletons.

    D. The RMI client can communicate with the server without knowing the server's physical location.

SELF TEST ANSWERS

Distinguish Appropriate from Inappropriate Techniques for Providing Access to a Legacy System from Java Technology Code Given an Outline Description of That Legacy System

1. ☑ **B** is correct. RMI would be appropriate for communication between Java objects because it is built into the core Java environment. It is a built-in facility for Java, which allows you to interact with objects that are actually running on JVMs on remote machines on the network.
☒ **A, C,** and **D** are incorrect. CORBA is more extensive than RMI. Unlike RMI, objects that are exported using CORBA can be accessed by clients implemented in any language with an IDL binding. RMI is much more simple and straightforward than CORBA because it supports only Java objects. So where the facilities of CORBA are not required, it is preferable to go for RMI. JNDI and JavaBeans are not distributed object technologies.

2. ☑ **A** and **C** are correct. Interfaces between CORBA objects can be specified using IDL, but it is a language that can be used only for interface definitions. It cannot be used to implement applications.
☒ **B** and **D** are incorrect. We use other languages to implement the interfaces written in IDL. Interfaces written in IDL can be mapped to any programming language. CORBA applications and components are thus independent of the language used to implement them. Stubs and skeletons are not written; they are generated by the IDL compiler. Stubs and skeletons would be in the same language as the corresponding client or server.

3. ☑ **B** is correct. When you declare that an object implements the *java.rmi.Remote* interface, RMI will prevent it from being serialized and sent between JVMs as a parameter. Instead of sending the implementation class for a *java.rmi.Remote* interface, RMI substitutes the stub class. Because this substitution occurs in the RMI internal code, one cannot intercept this operation.
☒ **A** and **C** are incorrect. If the object had not implemented *Remote*, it would have been serialized and sent over the network.

4. ☑ **B** is correct. The RMI compiler, rmic, can be used to generate the stub and skeleton files. The compiler runs on the remote service implementation class file.
☒ **A, C,** and **D** are incorrect.

5. ☑ B is correct. CORBA is the most appropriate object technology for systems that use objects written in different languages, and it supports a variety of operating system platforms.
   ☒ A, C, and D each work with specific platforms.

6. ☑ A, B, and D are correct. RMI can use stubs, skeletons, and IIOP.
   ☒ C is incorrect because ORBs are used with CORBA.

7. ☑ C is correct. Security is not a tier of a three-tiered architecture.
   ☒ A, B, and D are tiers of a three-tiered architecture.

8. ☑ C is correct because it is *not* true about RMI. RMI uses the proxy design pattern in the stub and skeleton layer. In the proxy pattern, an object in one context is represented by another (the proxy) in a separate context. The proxy knows how to forward method calls between the participating objects. In RMI's use of the proxy pattern, the stub class plays the role of the proxy. RMI uses a technology called *Object Serialization* to transform an object into a linear format that can then be sent over the network wire. The RMI compiler, rmic, is used to generate the stub and skeleton files.
   ☒ A, B, and D are incorrect.

7

Enterprise JavaBeans and the EJB Container Model

T he Enterprise JavaBeans (EJB) specification is an industry initiative led and driven by Sun Microsystems with participation from many supporting vendors in the industry. Sun owns the process of defining, creating, and publishing the specification while ensuring the incorporation of input and feedback from the industry and the general public.

The EJB requirements enable communication with Java 2 Enterprise Edition (J2EE) clients including JavaServer Pages (JSP), servlets, and application clients as well as with EJBs in other EJB containers. The goal of these features is to allow EJB invocations to work even when client components and EJBs are deployed in J2EE products from different vendors. Support for interoperability among components includes transaction propagation, naming services, and security services.

The term *enterprise* implies that an application will be scalable, available, reliable, secure, transactional, and distributed. To provide these types of features, an enterprise application requires access to a variety of infrastructure services, such as distributed communication services, naming and directory services, transaction services, messaging services, data access and persistence services, and resource-sharing services.

When a *distributed framework* is used, a client makes a call to what appears to be the interface of a business object. What it actually calls, however, is a *stub* that mimics the interface of that business object. This layer between clients and business objects is added because it is more practical to place stubs in the remote and distributed locations of clients than to place complete copies in the location of business objects.

In a distributed framework, the client calls a business method on a stub as if it were the real object. The stub then communicates this request to a *tie*. The tie calls the method on the real business object. A result is returned to the stub and the client (see Figure 7-1).

The J2EE application programming interfaces (API) provide common interfaces that supply easy access to these underlying infrastructure services, regardless of their actual implementation. The J2EE APIs and their vendor implementations provide additional services that are not supplied directly by the Java Virtual Machine (JVM), such as database access, transaction support, security enforcement, caching, and concurrency.

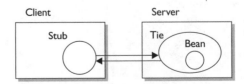

FIGURE 7-1

The distributed processing framework

The following benefits are gained by adhering to the J2EE standard:

■ **Reusable application components**   The productivity benefits of writing components in the Java programming language include component reuse and outsourcing, declarative customization (not programmatic), and the ability for the developer to focus on business logic only.

■ **Portability**   The portability characteristics of EJB components are made possible by J2EE. This platform consists of several standard Java APIs that provide access to a core set of enterprise-class infrastructure services. These standardized APIs ensure that the Java code can be run on any vendor's application server.

■ **Broad industry adoption**   A wide selection of vendor tools and components allow choice and flexibility in server selection.

■ **Application portability**   Code is more than just platform independent; it is also middleware independent.

■ **No vendor lock-in**   Architecture decisions are made at deployment, not at the development phase. Interserver *portability* allows code to be deployed on any EJB server; interserver *scalability* allows servers to be transparently replaced to accommodate changing needs for service level, performance, or security.

■ **Protection of IT investment**   Wraps and integrates with the existing infrastructure, application, and data stores; is portable across multiple servers and databases; serves multilingual clients, such as browsers, Java technology, ActiveX, or Common Object Request Broker (CORBA) clients; EJB framework simplifies and enhances CORBA; and existing middleware solutions are being adapted by the well-established vendors to support the EJB framework via a thin portability layer.

CERTIFICATION OBJECTIVE 7.01

List the Required Classes/Interfaces That Must Be Provided for an Enterprise JavaBeans Component

Here we review the component architecture of EJBs. We also cover the required classes and interfaces for EJB, which include the home and remote interfaces, the

XML deployment descriptor, the business logic (bean) class, and the context objects. While these names may or may not be meaningful to you at this point, you will soon understand how each of these pieces fits into the EJB component model.

e x a m
ⓦ a t c h   *This objective is required by the certification exam.*

Classes and Interfaces for EJB

The components used to create and access EJBs facilitate the creation and execution of business logic on an enterprise system. Each EJB session and entity bean must have the following classes and interfaces:

- Home (EJBHome) interface
- Remote (EJBObject) interface
- XML deployment descriptor
- Bean class
- Context objects

Home (EJBHome) Interface

The EJBHome object provides the lifecycle operations (`create()`, `remove()`, `find()`) for an EJB. The container's deployment tools generate the class for the EJBHome object. The EJBHome object implements the EJB's home interface. The client references an EJBHome object to perform lifecycle operations on an EJBObject interface. The Java Naming and Directory Interface (JNDI) is used by the client to locate an EJBHome object.

The EJBHome interface provides access to the bean's lifecycle services and can be utilized by a client to create or destroy bean instances. For entity beans, it provides finder methods that allow a client to locate an existing bean instance and retrieve it from its persistent data store.

Remote (EJBObject) Interface

The remote (EJBObject) interface provides access to the business methods within the EJB. An EJBObject represents a client view of the EJB. The EJBObject exposes all of the application-related interfaces for the object, but not the interfaces that allow the EJB container to manage and control the object. The EJBObject wrapper allows the EJB container to intercept all operations made on the EJB. Each time a client invokes a method on the EJBObject, the request goes through the EJB container before being delegated to the EJB. The EJB container implements state management, transaction control, security, and persistence services transparently to both the client and the EJB.

XML Deployment Descriptor

The deployment descriptor is an XML (Extensible Markup Language) file provided with each module and application that describes how the parts of a J2EE application should be deployed. The deployment descriptor configures specific container options in your deployment tool of choice.

The rules associated with the EJB that govern lifecycle, transactions, security, and persistence are defined in an associated XML deployment descriptor object. These rules are defined declaratively at the time of deployment rather than programmatically at the time of development. At runtime, the EJB container automatically performs the services according to the values specified in the deployment descriptor object associated with the EJB.

Business Logic (Bean) Class

The bean class is developed by the bean developer and contains the implementation and the methods defined in the remote interface. In other words, the bean class has the basic business logic. For entity and session beans, the bean class extends either *javax.ejb.SessionBean* or *javax.ejb.EntityBean*, depending upon the type of EJB required.

Context Objects for Session and Entity

For each active EJB instance, the EJB container generates an instance context object to maintain information about the management rules and the current state of the instance. A session bean uses a *SessionContext* object, while an entity bean uses an *EntityContext* object. Both the EJB and the EJB container use the context object to coordinate transactions, security, persistence, and other system services.

CERTIFICATION OBJECTIVE 7.02

Distinguish Between Session and Entity Beans

Here we review two of the three types of EJBs: session and entity beans.

Session and Entity Beans

The EJB specification supports both *transient* and *persistent* objects. A transient object is referred to as a *session* bean, and a persistent object is known as an *entity* bean.

A Session Bean

A session bean is an EJB that is created by a client and usually exists only for the duration of a single client-server session. A session bean usually performs operations such as calculations or database access on behalf of the client. While a session bean may be transactional, it is not recoverable if a system crash occurs. Session bean objects can be stateless or they can maintain a conversational state across methods and transactions. If a session bean maintains a state, the EJB container manages this state if the object must be removed from memory. However, persistent data must be managed by the session bean object itself.

The tools for a container generate additional classes for a session bean at deployment time. These tools obtain information from the EJB architecture by examining its classes and interfaces. This information is utilized to generate two classes dynamically that implement the home and remote interfaces of the bean. These classes enable the container to intercede in all client calls on the session bean. The container generates a serializable *Handle* class as well, which provides a way to identify a session bean instance within a specific lifecycle. These classes can be implemented to perform customized operations and functionality when mixed in with container-specific code.

In addition to these custom classes, each container provides a class that provides metadata to the client and implements the SessionContext interface. This provides access to information about the environment in which a bean is invoked.

An Entity Bean

An entity bean is an object representation of persistent data maintained in a permanent data store such as a database. A primary key identifies each instance of an entity bean. Entity beans are transactional and are recoverable in the event of a system crash.

Entity beans are representations of explicit data or collections of data, such as a row in a relational database. Entity bean methods provide procedures for acting on the data representation of the bean. An entity bean is persistent and survives as long as its data remains in the database.

An entity bean can be created in two ways: by direct action of the client in which a `create()` method is called on the bean's home interface, or by some other action

SCENARIO & SOLUTION

You need to maintain non-enterprise data across method invocations for the duration of a session. What kind of EJB would you use?	You should use a session bean, an EJB that is created by a client and usually exists only for the duration of a single client-server session.
You need to create an EJB to represent enterprise data. What kind of EJB should you use?	You should use an entity bean, which is an object representation of persistent data maintained in a permanent data store such as a database.

that adds data to the database that the bean type represents. In fact, in an environment with legacy data, entity objects may exist before an EJB is even deployed.

An entity bean can implement either bean-managed or container-managed persistence. In the case of bean-managed persistence, the implementer of an entity bean stores and retrieves the information managed by the bean through direct database calls. The bean may utilize either Java Database Connectivity (JDBC) or SQL-Java (SQLJ) for this method. (Session beans may also access the data they manage using JDBC or SQLJ.) A disadvantage to this approach is that it makes it more difficult to adapt bean-managed persistence to alternative data sources.

In the case of container-managed persistence, the container provider may implement access to the database using standard APIs. The container provider can offer tools to map instance variables of an entity bean to calls to an underlying database. This approach makes it easier to use entity beans with different databases.

Above are some possible scenario questions that will help you review the differences between session and entity beans.

CERTIFICATION OBJECTIVE 7.03

Recognize Appropriate Uses for Entity, Stateful Session, and Stateless Session Beans

In a enterprise environment, application use may grow to a point at which systems based on such things as Java servlets and Hypertext Markup Language (HTML) are not scalable to provide the required performance. At this point, a distributed solution can provide the scalability needed to meet changing demands. EJB allows the application to be distributed onto as many servers as required.

When to Use Entity and Session JavaBeans

The following details some appropriate scenarios for using EJBs:

- Use entity beans to persist data. An entity bean is a sharable enterprise data resource that can be accessed and updated by multiple users.

- Use stateful session beans when any one of the following conditions is true; otherwise use stateless session beans:

  - The session bean must retain data in its member variables across method invocations.

  - The state of the bean needs to be initialized when the session bean is instantiated.

  - The session bean must retain information about the client across multiple method invocations.

  - The session bean is servicing an interactive client whose presence must be known to the applications server or EJB container.

CERTIFICATION OBJECTIVE 7.04

Distinguish Between Stateful and Stateless Session Beans

Now that you know a little bit about the EJB architecture, session beans, and entity beans, this objective breaks down each of these components in detail and covers using session beans and the differences between stateless session beans and stateful session beans. You'll learn how to define stateless and stateful session bean classes, add methods to them, define the session bean interface, create a remote interface, create a home interface, and create deployment descriptors. We'll talk about the steps required to compile, assemble, and deploy stateless session beans and how to call them from a client.

Using Session Beans

Building a session bean can be quite simple once you have mastered a few basic steps. These steps are explained later in this section by walking you through an example of a session bean that provides validation for fields passed to it in a hash table.

As mentioned, session beans can either be stateful or stateless. With stateful beans, the EJB container saves internal bean data during and in between method calls on the client's behalf. With stateless beans, the clients may call any available instance of an instantiated bean for as long as the EJB container has the ability to pool stateless beans. This enables the number of instantiations of a bean to be reduced, thereby reducing required resources.

Stateless Session Beans

A session bean represents work performed by a *single* client. That work can be performed within a single method invocation, or it may span multiple method invocations. If the work does span more than one method, the object must retain the user's object state across the method calls, and a stateful session bean would therefore be required.

Generally, stateless beans are intended to perform individual operations automatically and don't maintain state across method invocations. They're also *amorphous*, in that any client can use any instance of a stateless bean at any time at the container's discretion. They are the lightest weight and easiest to manage of the various EJB component configurations.

Stateful Session Beans

Stateful session beans maintain state both within and between transactions. Each stateful session bean is therefore associated with a specific client. Containers are able to save and retrieve a bean's state automatically while managing instance pools (as opposed to bean pools) of stateful session beans.

Stateful session beans maintain data consistency by updating their fields each time a transaction is committed. To keep informed of changes in transaction status, a stateful session bean implements the SessionSynchronization interface. The container calls methods of this interface while it initiates and completes transactions involving the bean.

Session beans, whether stateful or stateless, are not designed to be persistent. The data maintained by stateful session beans is intended to be transitional.

It is used solely for a particular session with a particular client. A stateful session bean instance typically can't survive system failures and other destructive events. While a session bean has a container-provided identity (called its *handle*), that identity passes when the client removes the session bean at the end of a session. If a client needs to revive a stateful session bean that has disappeared, it must provide its own means to reconstruct the bean's state.

Stateful vs. Stateless Session Beans

A stateful session bean *will* maintain a conversational state with a client. The state of the session is maintained for the duration of the conversation between the client and the stateful session bean. When the client removes the stateful session bean, its session ends and the state is destroyed. The transient nature of the state of the stateful session bean should not be problematic for either the client or the bean, because once the conversation between the client and the stateful session bean ends, neither the client nor the stateful session bean should have any use for the state.

A stateless session bean *will not* maintain conversational states for specific clients longer than the period of an individual method invocation. Instance variables used by a method of a stateless bean may have a state, but only for the duration of the method invocation. After a method has finished running either successfully or unsuccessfully, the states of all its instance variables are dropped. The transient nature of this state gives the stateless session bean beneficial attributes, such as the following:

- **Bean pooling**   Any stateless session bean method instance that is not currently invoked is equally available to be called by an EJB container or application server to service the request of a client. This allows the EJB container to pool stateless bean instances and increase performance.

- **Scalability**   Because stateless session beans are able to service multiple clients, they tend to be more scalable when applications have a large number of clients. When compared to stateful session beans, stateless session beans usually require less instantiation.

- **Performance**   An EJB container will never move a stateless session bean from RAM out to a secondary storage, which it may do with a stateful session bean; therefore, stateless session beans may offer greater performance than stateful session beans.

Since no explicit mapping exists between multiple clients and stateless bean instances, the EJB container is free to service any client's request with any available instance. Even though the client calls the `create()` and `remove()` methods of the stateless session bean, making it appear that the client is controlling the lifecycle of an EJB, it is actually the EJB container that is handling the `create()` and `remove()` methods without necessarily instantiating or destroying an EJB instance.

Defining the Session Bean Class

The session bean class must be declared with the `public` attribute. This attribute enables the container to obtain access to the session bean. Java gives a developer the ability to extend a base class and inherit its properties. This ability pertains to session beans as well, allowing developers to take full advantage of any object-oriented legacy code that they may wish to reuse.

The following is an example of a session bean extending a base class:

```
public class ValidateInputBean extends TradingBaseClass implements SessionBean
{
    ...
}
```

Session Bean Interface

Session beans are held to the J2EE EJB specification that requires all session beans to implement the *javax.ejb.SessionBean* interface. This requirement forces session beans to contain the following methods:

- `ejbActivate()`
- `ejbPassivate()`
- `ejbRemove()`
- `setSessionContext(SessionContext)`

A minimum sample of how a bean class must look is shown here:

```
public class ValidateInputBean extends TradingBaseClass implements SessionBean
{
    public void ejbActivate  () throws EJBException {..}
    public void ejbPassivate () throws EJBException {..}
    public void ejbRemove    () throws EJBException {..}
    protected   SessionContext m_context;
    public void setSessionContext (SessionContext sc)
                throws EJBException {
        m_context = sc;
    }
}
```

Clients of a session bean may either be *remote* or *local,* depending on what interfaces are implemented.

Remote clients access a session bean via their remote and remote home interfaces (*javax.ejb.EJBObject* and *javax.ejb.EJBHome,* respectively). Remote clients have the advantage of being location independent. They can access a session bean in an EJB container from any Remote Method Invocation-Internet Inter-ORB Protocol (RMI-IIOP)–compliant application, including non-Java programs such as CORBA-based applications. Because remote objects are accessed through standard Java RMI APIs, objects that are passed as method arguments are passed by value. This means that a copy of the object being passed is created and sent between the client and the session bean.

Local clients access a session bean via their local and local home interfaces (*javax.ejb.EJBLocalObject* and *javax.ejb.EJBLocalHome,* respectively). A local client is location dependent. It must reside inside the same JVM as the session bean with which it interfaces. Local clients can have objects passed as arguments to methods by reference. Doing this avoids the overhead of creating copies of objects sent between clients and session beans. Certain applications will perform considerably better without this overhead. The enterprise bean provider should be aware that both the client and the session bean can change common objects.

Both local and remote home interfaces (*javax.ejb.LocalHome* and *javax.ejb.EJBHome,* respectively) provide an interface to the client, allowing the client to create and remove session objects. However, session objects are more commonly removed by using the `remove()` method in the EJBObject interface.

Neither local nor remote clients access session beans directly. To gain access to session bean methods, they use a *component* interface to the session bean. Instances of a session bean's remote interface are called session EJBObjects, while instances of a session bean's local interface are called session EJBLocalObjects.

Both local and remote interfaces provide the following services to a client:

- Delegate business method invocations on a session bean instance
- Return the session object's home interface
- Test to determine whether a session object is identical to another session object
- Remove a session object

Any method on a session bean class that is to be made visible to a client must be added to the bean's remote interface. This makes it possible to hide session bean methods from clients as well as make different methods of a session bean available using different interfaces. Figure 7-2 illustrates how the client will see the EJB session bean interfaces.

When the application is deployed, the container or application server will use the interfaces defined by the enterprise bean provider and create EJBHome, EJBObject, stub, and tie classes:

- The *EJBHome* class is used to create instances of the session bean class and the *EJBObject* class.

- The *EJBObject* class provides access to the desired methods of the session bean.

- The stub classes act as proxies to the remote EJBObjects.

- The tie classes provide the call and dispatch mechanisms that bind the proxy to the EJBObject.

FIGURE 7-2

EJB session bean interface exposed to a client

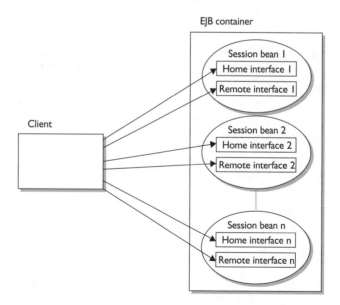

Creating a Remote Interface   All remote interfaces must extend the class *javax.ejb.EJBObject*. The following is an example:

```
public interface ValidateInputRemote extends EJBObject { .. }
```

Methods in Remote Interfaces   The enterprise bean provider provides the session bean's remote interface, which extends *javax.ejb.EJBObject*, and the EJB container implements this interface. An enterprise bean's remote interface provides the client's view of a session object and defines the business methods that are callable by the client.

All business methods declared in the remote interface must have the same parameters and same return value types as the bean class. It is not necessary for all bean class methods to be exposed to the remote client.

All business methods declared in the remote interface must also throw at least the same exceptions as those in the bean class. They must also throw the *java.rmi .RemoteException* exception, because EJBs are dependent on the RMI package, specifically the *java.rmi.Remote* package, for distributed processing.

Normally the container or application server being used will generate the necessary remote interface code. The container should also update this code when changes are made to the bean class.

The method names and the signatures in the remote interface must be identical to the method names and signatures of the business methods defined by the enterprise bean. This is different from the home interface, where method signatures must match, as method names can be different.

In addition to business methods that may be defined in the remote interface, the methods listed here and shown in Figure 7-3 must be contained inside the remote interface:

- **getEJBHome()**   This method returns a reference to the session bean's home interface.

- **getHandle()**   This method returns a handle for the EJB object. This handle can be used at a later time to re-obtain a reference to the EJB object. A session object handle can be serialized to a persistent data store to enable the retrieval of a session object even beyond the lifetime of a client process. This is assuming that the EJB container does not crash or time out the session object, thereby destroying it.

- **getPrimaryKey()** This method is not to be used for session beans. It returns the session bean object's primary key, but since individual session objects are to be used only by the specific client that creates them, they are intended to appear anonymous. If `getPrimaryKey()` is called looking for the identity of a session object, the method will throw an exception. This is different from entity objects, which expose their identity as primary keys.

- **isIdentical()** This method is used to test whether the EJB object passed is identical to the invoked EJB object.

- **remove()** This method is used to remove a session bean object.

Note that these methods are included automatically by virtue of inheritance.

A typical remote interface definition for a session bean looks something like this:

```
import javax.ejb.*;
import java.rmi.*;
import java.util.*;
public interface ValidateInputRemote extends EJBObject
{
    public void isInt (double amount) throws RemoteException;
    public void isNum (double amount) throws RemoteException;
}
```

FIGURE 7-3

Methods in the session bean remote interface

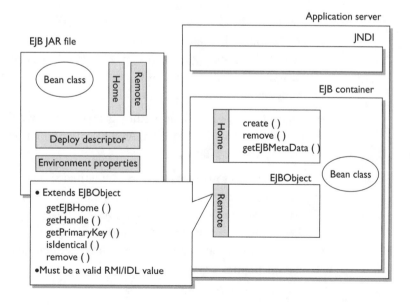

Creating a Home Interface   Session beans are instantiated when a client makes a call to one of the `create()` methods defined in the home interface. The home interface contains a `create()` method for every corresponding `ejbCreate()` method in the bean class.

The home interface is implemented in a container through an object called the *home* object. The container makes visible an instance of the home object to clients that want to instantiate a session bean.

In addition to `create()` methods that are to be defined in the home interface, the methods listed here and shown in Figure 7-4 are to be contained in the home interface:

- **getEJBMetaData()**   This method is used to obtain the *EJBMetaData* interface of an EJB. EJB deployment tools are responsible for implementing classes that provide metadata to the remote client. The *EJBMetaData* interface enables the client to get information about the enterprise bean. This metadata may be used to give access to the enterprise bean clients that use a scripting language to access these enterprise beans. Development tools may also use this metadata. The *EJBMetaData* interface is not a remote interface, so its class must be serializable.

- **getHomeHandle()**   This method is used to obtain a handle of a home object. The EJB specification allows a client to obtain a handle for the remote home interface. The client can use the home handle to store a reference to an entity bean's remote home interface in stable storage and re-create the reference later. This handle functionality may be useful to a client that needs to use the remote home interface in the future but does not know the JNDI name of the remote home interface.

- **remove(Handle h)**   This method is used to remove EJB objects that are identified by their handles. A handle may be retrieved by using the `getHandle()` method.

- **remove(Object primaryKey)**   This method should not be used for session beans. It is used to remove EJB objects that are identified by their primary key. Because session objects do not have primary keys that are accessible to clients, invoking this method on a session bean will result in a *RemoveException*. A container may also remove the session object automatically when the session object's lifetime expires.

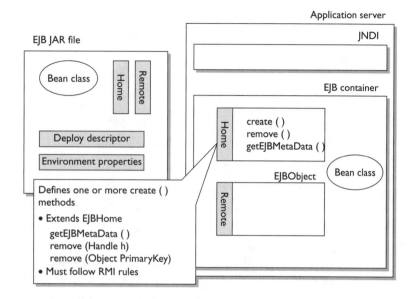

FIGURE 7-4

Methods in the session bean home interface

Since all session objects keep their identity anonymous, `finder()` methods for session beans should not be defined. The `finder()` methods for entity beans are covered later on in this chapter in the section "Home Interfaces and finder() Methods."

Again, note that the methods in the preceding list are included automatically by virtue of inheritance. Here is an example of a home interface definition for an EJB:

```
import javax.ejb.*;
import java.rmi.*;
public interface AccountRemoteHome extends EJBHome
{
  Account create() throws CreateException, RemoteException;
}
```

Session Bean Class Methods

Session bean classes are used as the "molds" for instantiating session bean instances. These instances are indirectly called as local and remote clients via home and remote interfaces. `EJBCreate()` methods correspond with the `create()` methods of the session bean's home interface and are used for initializing the session bean's instance. The business methods created in a session bean class are a superset of those defined for the session bean's local or remote interface. These business methods implement the core business logic for session beans.

create() Methods   The EJB specification requires the session bean class to contain one or more `ejbCreate()` methods. These `ejbCreate()` methods are normally used to initialize the bean.

As many `ejbCreate()` methods as necessary may be added to the bean (only one `ejbCreate()` method for stateless session beans, however), as long as their signatures meet the following requirements:

- They must have a public access control modifier.
- They must have a return type of *void*.
- They must have RMI compliant arguments, in that they are serializable objects.
- They must not have a *static* or *void* modifier.

Several exceptions may be thrown including the *javax.ejb.CreateException* and other application-specific exceptions. The `ejbCreate()` method will usually throw a *CreateException* if an input parameter is not valid.

When a client invokes a `create()` method of a home interface, the `ejbCreate()` method of the session bean is called and the session bean and EJBObject are instantiated. After the session bean and EJBObject have been instantiated, the `create()` method returns a remote object reference of the EJBObject instance associated with the session bean instance to the client. The client can then invoke all of the business methods of this reference.

Because the `ejbCreate()` method is able to throw both *javax.ejb.CreateException* when there is a problem creating an object and the *javax.ejb.EJBException* when there is a system problem, the `create()` methods must be declared to throw both of these exceptions as well. In addition to the two aforementioned exceptions, the `create()` method must also throw any programmer-defined applications exception that may be thrown in the `ejbCreate()` method.

Business Methods   The primary purpose of a session bean is to execute business methods that implement business logic for use by a client. `create()` methods return object references from which clients may invoke business methods. To the client, these business methods appear to be running locally; however, they actually run remotely in the session bean container.

Session bean business methods, like any other Java method, are defined with the following procedures:

■ Add a method to the bean.

■ Write and then save the code.

■ Debug the code.

■ Finish the bean.

It is important to note that the bean class should *not* implement the remote interface. The bean class code is where all of the actual business code exists. This code is not supposed to be called without a proxy; therefore, it cannot be viewed directly by the client.

EXERCISE 7-1

Review Code for a Stateless Session Bean

In the following exercise, the classes and interfaces are provided for a stateless session bean. The exercise is presented step-wise in the order that the classes and interfaces would be created. Your completed code should look something like the code contained in the following sections.

1. Create the Stateless Session Bean Class   Here is an example of a stateless session bean class. As you will see, the only purpose of this bean is to pass back a simple message to the caller. The inline documentation points out the required methods along with the business methods.

```
package j2ee.architect.SLSession;
import javax.ejb.*;
// A stateless session bean.
public class SLSessionBean implements SessionBean {
  SessionContext sessionContext;
  // Bean's methods required by EJB specification.
  public void ejbCreate() throws CreateException {
    log("ejbCreate()");
  }
  public void ejbRemove() {
    log("ejbRemove()");
  }
  public void ejbActivate() {
    log("ejbActivate()");
  }
```

```
public void ejbPassivate() {
  log("ejbPassivate()");
}
public void setSessionContext(SessionContext parm) {
  this.sessionContext = parm;
}
// Bean's business methods.
public String getMsg() {
  log("getMsg()");
  return
    "This is a message from an stateless session bean!";
}
public void log(String parm) {
  System.out.println(new java.util.Date()
    +":SLSessionBean:"+this.hashCode()+" "+parm);
}
}
```

2. Create the Stateless Session Bean Home Interface Here is a home
interface for our stateless session bean example:

```
package j2ee.architect.SLSession;
import javax.ejb.*;
import java.rmi.*;
// This is the remote home interface, used by clients as a
// factory for EJB objects (remote references). The EJB
// container vendor implements this extended interface.
// In this home interface there is a create() method that
// corresponds to the ejbCreate() method in bean code.
public interface SLSessionRemoteHome extends EJBHome {
  // Creates/returns the EJB Object (remote reference).
  public SLSessionRemote create() throws CreateException, RemoteException;
}
```

3. Create the Stateless Session Bean Remote Interface Here is
a remote interface for our stateless session bean example:

```
package j2ee.architect.SLSession;
import javax.ejb.*;
import java.rmi.*;
// This is the remote interface, used by clients when
// they need to call an EJB objects. The EJB container
// vendor implements this extended interface, which is
// responsible for delegating subsequent calls to the
// bean code.
```

```
public interface SLSessionRemote extends javax.ejb.EJBObject {
    // Returns a String to caller.
    public String getMsg() throws RemoteException;
}
```

The following illustration shows how a client will view the remote interface.

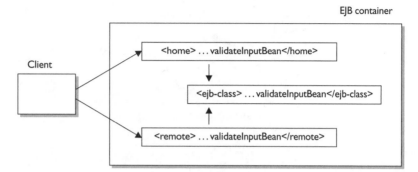

4. Create Deployment Descriptors

A deployment descriptor, located within a Java Archive (JAR) file, allows the properties of an EJB to be maintained outside of Java code. It allows the bean developer to make information about the bean available to the application assembler and the bean deployer. A deployment descriptor also provides runtime information used by the EJB container. The EJB specification is specific with regard to the content and format of deployment descriptors.

The deployment descriptor, written in XML, contains the structural information about the EJB, such as the relative path and name of the bean class file, remote interface, and home interface, as well as the state management type and the transaction management type.

The deployment descriptor file may also contain optional information pertaining to multiple role names, environment entries, and data-source references. Note that all of the attributes of the bean are contained within XML tags.

Here is our deployment descriptor for the stateless session bean:

```
<?xml version="1.0" encoding="UTF-8"?>
<!DOCTYPE ejb-jar PUBLIC
"-//Sun Microsystems, Inc.//DTD Enterprise JavaBeans 2.0//EN"
"http://java.sun.com/dtd/ejb-jar_2_0.dtd">
<ejb-jar>
    <enterprise-beans>
```

```
      <session>
        <display-name>SLSession</display-name>
        <ejb-name>SLSession</ejb-name>
        <home>j2ee.architect.SLSession.SLSessionRemoteHome</home>
        <remote>j2ee.architect.SLSession.SLSessionRemote</remote>
        <ejb-class>j2ee.architect.SLSession.SLSessionBean</ejb-class>
        <session-type>Stateless</session-type>
        <transaction-type>Container</transaction-type>
      </session>
    </enterprise-beans>
    <assembly-descriptor>
      <container-transaction>
        <method>
          <ejb-name>SLSession</ejb-name>
          <method-name>*</method-name>
        </method>
        <trans-attribute>Required</trans-attribute>
      </container-transaction>
    </assembly-descriptor>
  </ejb-jar>
```

Some of the elements in the preceding deployment descriptor sample are described here:

- **ejb-jar** The root element of the EJB deployment descriptor. These files are discussed later in the chapter in the section "The Lifecycle of an EJB."

- **enterprise-beans** Declares the session, entity, and/or message-driven beans.

- **session** Defines the enterprise bean to be a session bean as opposed to an entity or message-driven bean.

- **ejb-name** A unique name of a session, entity, or message-driven bean in an *ejb-jar* file; this element is used to tie EJBs together and for constructing a URL (note that there is no relationship between the element *ejb-name* and the JNDI name that is assigned to an enterprise bean's home).

- **home** The fully qualified name of an enterprise bean's home interface.

- **remote** The fully qualified name of enterprise bean's remote interface.

- **ejb-class** The fully qualified name of the enterprise bean's class.

- **session-type** The session-type element is either stateful or stateless.

■ **transaction-type**   Declares whether transaction demarcation is performed by the enterprise bean or the EJB container.

5. Compile, Assemble, and Deploy Stateless Session Bean   The next steps in the process are to compile, assemble, and then deploy the session bean. The following set of steps is used to complete this process. Although this book is designed for the architect and actual implementation steps are not required, we have added the details of these steps for completeness.

As part of the deployment process, references in the deployment descriptor need to be resolved to actual resources in the container. How these resources are resolved is, at the moment, container specific. In the WebLogic environment, the following file can be used for the stateless session bean example:

```
<?xml version="1.0"?>
<!DOCTYPE weblogic-ejb-jar PUBLIC
"-//BEA Systems, Inc.//DTD WebLogic 6.0.0 EJB//EN"
"http://www.bea.com/servers/wls600/dtd/weblogic-ejb-jar.dtd">
<weblogic-ejb-jar>
    <weblogic-enterprise-bean>
        <ejb-name>SLSession</ejb-name>
        <jndi-name>SLSessionRemoteHome</jndi-name>
    </weblogic-enterprise-bean>
</weblogic-ejb-jar>
```

Here are the remaining steps to complete the compile/package/deployment process:

6. Compile the Java classes.

7. Package the classes and deployment descriptors into a JAR file.

8. Generate stub and tie code for the container and add them to the JAR file.

9. Deploy the JAR file to the application server.

10. Package the required classes for a remote client of the bean.

Here is an example client of the stateless session bean:

```
package j2ee.architect.SLSession;
import javax.naming.Context;
import javax.naming.InitialContext;
import java.util.Properties;
```

```java
// This client calls a method on a stateless session bean.
public class SLSessionClient {
  public static void main(String[] args) throws Exception {
    // Get the JNDI initial context.
    Context ctx = getInitialContext();
    // Get a reference to the home object
    Object obj = ctx.lookup("SLSessionRemoteHome");
    // Narrow (cast) the returned RMI-IIOP object.
    SLSessionRemoteHome home = (SLSessionRemoteHome)
      javax.rmi.PortableRemoteObject.narrow(obj,
      SLSessionRemoteHome.class);
    // Use the home object (factory) to create the
    // SLSB EJB Object (the remote reference).
    SLSessionRemote mySLSessionRemote = home.create();
    // Call the getMsg() method on the EJB object.
    // The remote reference will delegate the call
    // to the bean code, receive the response and
    // then pass it to this client.
    System.out.println(mySLSessionRemote.getMsg());
    // When finished with the remote reference,
    // remove it and the EJB container will then
    // destroy the EJB object.
    mySLSessionRemote.remove();
  }
  private static Context getInitialContext() throws Exception {
    // This implementation is specific to the Weblogic
    // server and will differ for other server vendors.
    String providerUrl = "t3://localhost:7001";
    String icFactory = "weblogic.jndi.WLInitialContextFactory";
    String user = null;
    String password = null;
    Properties properties = null;
    try {
      properties = new Properties();
      properties.put(Context.INITIAL_CONTEXT_FACTORY, icFactory);
      properties.put(Context.PROVIDER_URL, providerUrl);
      if (user != null) {
        properties.put(Context.SECURITY_PRINCIPAL, user);
        properties.put(Context.SECURITY_CREDENTIALS,
          password == null ? "" : password);
      }
      return new InitialContext(properties);
    }
    catch(Exception e) {
      System.out.println(
```

```
                 "Unable to connect to JNDI server at " + providerUrl);
            throw e;
        }
    }
}
```

Here is the output information provided by the client:

```
This is a message from an stateless session bean!
```

Here is the output information provided by the client and the application server console:

```
...when the jar is deployed to the server...
Sat Nov 09 12:58:55 EST 2002:SLSessionBean:4536570 ejbCreate()
Sat Nov 09 12:58:55 EST 2002:SLSessionBean:2076276 ejbCreate()
...when the client application is executed...
Sat Nov 09 12:59:15 EST 2002:SLSessionBean:2076276 getMsg()
...when the server is shut down...
Sat Nov 09 13:01:33 EST 2002:SLSessionBean:2076276 ejbRemove()
Sat Nov 09 13:01:33 EST 2002:SLSessionBean:4536570 ejbRemove()
```

The next section will cover the client side of the calls in a little more detail.

Calling Stateless Session Beans from a Client

When a client calls an EJB, the ultimate goal is to gain the benefits derived from executing the business methods on a bean class. Before the EJB can get access to these methods, it must first find the EJBHome interface necessary to make an instance of the EJB class. The first step in the process of finding the EJBHome starts with creating an InitialContext class.

InitialContext   The *InitialContext* class acts as the client's interface to the JNDI interface. The *InitialContext* may contain information that will allow a client to bind to many naming services such as JNDI, CORBA Common Object Service ("COS"), and Domain Naming Service (DNS). Using the *InitialContext* class allows a client to have to maintain only a single interface to any naming service in the client's environment that supports JNDI. If any problems are encountered with the creation of the *InitialContext* object or with calling one of its methods, the *javax.naming.NamingException* will be thrown.

More on Type Narrowing In a stand-alone Java application, if a Java object such as *Object* is returned from a *Hashtable*, the return type of the method `get()` will be the supertype *Object* instead of the derived type *String*. Here's an example:

```
Hashtable hash = ..;
..;
hash.get("keyToAStringElement");
```

It is up to the developer to cast, or narrow, the return value of the method `get()` to the proper object type. For example:

```
String aString = (String) hash.get("keyToAStringElement");
```

In the EJB application, once an object reference is obtained by a client, the method `javax.rmi.PortableRemoteObject.narrow()` must be used to perform type-narrowing for its client-side representation of its home and remote interfaces. The *javax.rmi.PortableRemoteObject* class is part of the RMI-IIOP standard extension. Type-narrowing ensures that the client programs are interoperable with different EJB containers.

Once the *InitialContext* has been used as the starting point for looking up a specific JNDI registered object, the `javax.rmi.PortableRemoteObject .narrow()` method should be called to perform type-narrowing of the client-side representations of the home interface.

Finding Objects and Interfaces: The JNDI Clients that have access to the JNDI API may use this API to look up enterprise beans, resources such as databases, and data in environment variables. From the earlier example, the client application locates an EJB with the following:

```
// Get a reference to the home object
Object obj = ctx.lookup("SLSessionRemoteHome");
```

The name that a J2EE client uses to refer to an EJB does not necessarily have to be identical to the JNDI name of the EJB deployed in the EJB container or application server. The level of indirection provided by the ability to map J2EE client names to JNDI registered EJBs gives great flexibility to distributed applications by allowing the client to use names that reference EJBs that make logical sense to the client. The client even has the ability to reference a single EJB with different names, when it makes sense to do so. This flexibility comes in handy when either the client code or the server code changes dynamically. The name that a stand-alone Java client uses to refer to an EJB using a JNDI lookup method must be identical to the EJB's JNDI name in the EJB container or application server.

Creating an Instance Using EJBHome   Finally, after the home reference has been found, narrowed, and called, the home reference's `create()` method can be called, returning the remote reference upon which the desired business methods can be invoked. The syntax for the calling of the `create()` method may look somewhat like this:

```
SLSessionRemote mySLSessionRemote = home.create();
```

Remember that `create()` returns a reference to a remote interface, not the bean object itself. This means that certain programming practices that may be taken for granted in Java may not be used with EJBs. For example, objects are passed to EJBs via the arguments of the method calls and results are passed back to the client via the EJBs return object. It is not possible to maintain a reference to an input argument of an EJB, change that argument's values inside of the EJB, and then have access to those changes at the client.

Calling Session Bean Methods from a Client   After all the components of a session bean have been created and a remote reference to the EJB is made available to a client, the exposed business methods of the EJBObject and the lifecycle methods of the EJBHome are available to the client as if the EJB were local to that client.

Coding Clients to Call EJBs   After the session bean reference has been made available to a client, it is up to the client to instantiate the bean components through the bean's home interface. Only then can the business logic methods of the bean class be accessed via the exposed methods of the EJBObject. For J2EE applications to run in an efficient and stable fashion, both client and server developers should adhere to standard programming policy practices and procedures, two of which are mentioned next.

Session Beans, Reentrance, and Loop-Back Calls   If a bean is allowed to invoke methods on itself or another bean that invokes methods on the initial bean, the initial bean is said to be *reentrant*. This type of self-accessing call is referred to as a *loop-back call*. As opposed to an entity bean, a session bean is never allowed to be reentrant. If a session bean attempts to make a loop-back, the EJB container should throw a *java.rmi.RemoteException*.

Remove the Bean When Done   When a client no longer has use for a session bean, it should remove the session object using the `javax.ejb` `.EJBObject.remove()` method or the `javax.ejb.EJBHome` `.remove(Handle handle)` method. If the `javax.ejb` `.EJBHome.remove(Object primaryKey)` method is called on a session by mistake, the *javax.ejb.RemoveException* will be thrown because session beans, unlike entity beans, do not have a primary key.

Different Types of Clients

The EJB framework allows many different types of clients to instantiate EJBs and takes advantage of the business logic that they implement. For the rest of this section, examples of different types of clients calling a session bean will be presented along with some of the necessary tasks that must be completed to support these different clients. This section concentrates on how clients can be integrated with EJBs.

Servlets Calling Session Beans   A *servlet* is a Java program that runs within a Web or application server and implements the *javax.servlet.Servlet* interface. Servlets are designed to receive and respond to requests from Internet clients or browsers. The standard protocols used for communication between a browser and a servlet are usually Hypertext Transfer Protocol (HTTP) or secure Hypertext Transfer Protocol (HTTPS). Servlets receive and respond to requests from Internet clients using methods defined by the *javax.servlet.Servlet* interface. After the web or application server constructs the servlet, the servlet gets initialized by the lifecycle method `init()`.

EXERCISE 7-2

Review Code for a Stateful Session Bean

To become more familiar with developing and coding, let's review the code for a stateful session bean. Your code should look something like the code shown next. Again, we use a step-wise approach that covers all the steps required to create, package, deploy, and call the bean.

1. Create the Stateful Session Bean Class   Following is an example of a stateful session bean class. The purpose of this bean is to create and initialize a counter and have a business method increment the counter. The inline documentation points out the required methods along with the business methods.

```
package j2ee.architect.SFSession;
import javax.ejb.*;
// A stateful session bean.
// When bean is created a counter is initialized with the
// parameter value. A business method increments the counter.
public class SFSessionBean implements SessionBean {
  private SessionContext sessionContext;
  // The counter.
  private int ctr;
  // Bean's methods required by EJB specification
  public void ejbCreate(int parm) throws CreateException {
    this.ctr = parm;
    log("ejbCreate("+parm+")");
  }
  public void ejbRemove() {
    log("ejbRemove() ctr="+ctr);
  }
  public void ejbActivate() {
    log("ejbActivate() ctr="+ctr);
  }
  public void ejbPassivate() {
    log("ejbPassivate() ctr="+ctr);
  }
  public void setSessionContext(SessionContext parm) {
    this.sessionContext = parm;
  }
  // Bean's business methods
  public int increment() {
    log("increment() ctr="+ctr);
    return ++ctr;
  }
  private void log(String parm) {
    System.out.println(new java.util.Date()
      +":SFSessionBean:"+this.hashCode()+" "+parm);
  }
}
```

2. Create the Stateful Session Bean Home Interface   Here is a home interface for our stateful session bean example:

```
package j2ee.architect.SFSession;
import javax.ejb.*;
import java.rmi.*;
// This is the home interface, used by clients as a
// factory for EJB objects (remote references). The EJB
// container vendor implements this extended interface.
```

```
// In this home interface there is a create() method that
// corresponds to the ejbCreate() method in actual bean code.
public interface SFSessionRemoteHome extends EJBHome {
  public SFSessionRemote create(int ct)
    throws CreateException, RemoteException;
}
```

3. Create the Stateful Session Bean Remote Interface   Here is a remote interface for our stateful session bean example:

```
package j2ee.architect.SFSession;
import javax.ejb.*;
import java.rmi.*;
// This is the remote interface, used by clients when
// they need to call an EJB object. The EJB container
// vendor implements this extended interface, which is
// responsible for delegating subsequent calls to the
// actual bean code.
public interface SFSessionRemote extends EJBObject {
  public int increment() throws RemoteException;
}
```

4. Create Deployment Descriptors   As mentioned in the preceding exercise, the deployment descriptor, located within a JAR file, allows the properties of an EJB to be maintained outside of Java code.

Here is our deployment descriptor for the stateful session bean:

```
<!DOCTYPE ejb-jar PUBLIC
    "-//Sun Microsystems, Inc.//DTD Enterprise JavaBeans 2.0//EN"
    "http://java.sun.com/dtd/ejb-jar_2_0.dtd">
<ejb-jar>
 <enterprise-beans>
  <session>
   <display-name>SFSession</display-name>
   <ejb-name>SFSession</ejb-name>
   <home>j2ee.architect.SFSession.SFSessionRemoteHome</home>
   <remote>j2ee.architect.SFSession.SFSessionRemote</remote>
   <ejb-class>j2ee.architect.SFSession.SFSessionBean</ejb-class>
   <session-type>Stateful</session-type>
   <transaction-type>Container</transaction-type>
  </session>
 </enterprise-beans>
 <assembly-descriptor>
  <container-transaction>
   <method>
    <ejb-name>SFSession</ejb-name>
```

```
    <method-name>*</method-name>
  </method>
  <trans-attribute>Required</trans-attribute>
  </container-transaction>
 </assembly-descriptor>
</ejb-jar>
```

5. Compile, Assemble, and Deploy Stateful Session Bean   The next
steps in the process are to compile, assemble, and then deploy the stateful session
bean. In our example, the following list of steps are used to complete the process.
Although this is book is designed for the architect and actual implementation steps
are not required, we have added the details of these steps for completeness.

As part of the deployment process, references in the deployment descriptor need
to be resolved to actual resources in the container. How these resources are resolved is,
at the moment, container specific. In the WebLogic environment, the following file
can be used for the stateful session bean example:

```
<?xml version="1.0"?>
<!DOCTYPE weblogic-ejb-jar PUBLIC
    "-//BEA Systems, Inc.//DTD WebLogic 6.0.0 EJB//EN"
    "http://www.bea.com/servers/wls600/dtd/weblogic-ejb-jar.dtd">
<weblogic-ejb-jar>
  <weblogic-enterprise-bean>
    <ejb-name>SLSession</ejb-name>
    <stateful-session-descriptor>
      <stateful-session-cache>
        <max-beans-in-cache>3</max-beans-in-cache>
        <idle-timeout-seconds>120</idle-timeout-seconds>
        <cache-type>LRU</cache-type>
      </stateful-session-cache>
    </stateful-session-descriptor>
    <jndi-name>SLSessionRemoteHome</jndi-name>
  </weblogic-enterprise-bean>
</weblogic-ejb-jar>
```

Here are the remaining steps to complete the compile/package/deployment
process:

6. Compile the Java classes.

7. Package the classes and deployment descriptors into a JAR file.

8. Generate stub and tie code for the container and add them to the JAR file.

9. Deploy the JAR to the application server.

10. Package the required classes for a remote client of the bean.

Here is an example client of the stateful session bean:

```
package j2ee.architect.SFSession;
import javax.ejb.*;
import javax.naming.*;
import java.util.Properties;
// This client calls a method on 5 instances of a
// stateful session bean. The EJB container is setup
// to allow only 3 in memory.  When executed it will
// demonstrate how beans are passivated to and
// activated from storage.
public class SFSessionClient {
  private static final int NUMBEANS = 5;
  public static void main(String[] args) {
    try {
      // Get the JNDI initial context.
      Context ctx = getInitialContext();
      // Narrow (cast) the returned RMI-IIOP object.
      SFSessionRemoteHome home = (SFSessionRemoteHome)
        javax.rmi.PortableRemoteObject.narrow(
          ctx.lookup("SFSessionRemoteHome"),
          SFSessionRemoteHome.class);
      // Create array to hold EJB Objects
      SFSessionRemote mySFSession[] = new SFSessionRemote[NUMBEANS];
      // Populate array with remote references
      System.out.println("Instantiating beans");
      System.out.println("and calling increment()...");
      for (int i=0; i < NUMBEANS; i++) {
        // Create initialized remote reference
        mySFSession[i] = home.create(((i+1)*10)-1);
        // Call the increment method and print value
        System.out.println(new java.util.Date()
          +" loop1: mySFSession["
          +i+"].increment()="
          +mySFSession[i].increment());
        // Put this thread to sleep for a bit
        Thread.sleep(1000);
      }
      // Now call the increment method and see
      // what happens with passivation/activation
      System.out.println("Calling increment() again.");
      for (int i=0; i < NUMBEANS; i++) {
        // Again call increment and print value
        System.out.println(new java.util.Date()
          +" loop2: mySFSession["
```

```
        +i+"].increment()="
        +mySFSession[i].increment());
      // Sleep for a bit again
      Thread.sleep(1000);
    }
    // Finished with the beans, so remove them
    for (int i=0; i < NUMBEANS; i++) {
      mySFSession[i].remove();
    }
  } catch (Exception e) {
    e.printStackTrace();
  }
}
private static Context getInitialContext() throws Exception {
  // This implementation is specific to the Weblogic
  // server and will differ for other server vendors.
  String providerUrl = "t3://localhost:7001";
  String icFactory = "weblogic.jndi.WLInitialContextFactory";
  String user = null;
  String password = null;
  Properties properties = null;
  try {
    properties = new Properties();
    properties.put(Context.INITIAL_CONTEXT_FACTORY, icFactory);
    properties.put(Context.PROVIDER_URL, providerUrl);
    if (user != null) {
      properties.put(Context.SECURITY_PRINCIPAL, user);
      properties.put(Context.SECURITY_CREDENTIALS,
        password == null ? "" : password);
    }
    return new InitialContext(properties);
  }
  catch(Exception e) {
    System.out.println(
      "Unable to connect to JNDI server at " + providerUrl);
    throw e;
  }
}
}
```

Here is the output information provided by the client:

```
Instantiating beans
and calling increment()...
Sat Nov 09 13:04:09 EST 2002 loop1: mySFSession[0].increment()=10
Sat Nov 09 13:04:10 EST 2002 loop1: mySFSession[1].increment()=20
```

```
Sat Nov 09 13:04:11 EST 2002 loop1: mySFSession[2].increment()=30
Sat Nov 09 13:04:12 EST 2002 loop1: mySFSession[3].increment()=40
Sat Nov 09 13:04:13 EST 2002 loop1: mySFSession[4].increment()=50
Calling increment() again.
Sat Nov 09 13:04:14 EST 2002 loop2: mySFSession[0].increment()=11
Sat Nov 09 13:04:15 EST 2002 loop2: mySFSession[1].increment()=21
Sat Nov 09 13:04:16 EST 2002 loop2: mySFSession[2].increment()=31
Sat Nov 09 13:04:17 EST 2002 loop2: mySFSession[3].increment()=41
Sat Nov 09 13:04:18 EST 2002 loop2: mySFSession[4].increment()=51
```

Here is the output information provided by the client and the application server console:

```
Sat Nov 09 13:04:09 EST 2002:SFSessionBean:4039138 ejbCreate(9)
Sat Nov 09 13:04:09 EST 2002:SFSessionBean:4039138 increment() ctr=9
Sat Nov 09 13:04:10 EST 2002:SFSessionBean:5775816 ejbCreate(19)
Sat Nov 09 13:04:10 EST 2002:SFSessionBean:5775816 increment() ctr=19
Sat Nov 09 13:04:11 EST 2002:SFSessionBean:2897995 ejbCreate(29)
Sat Nov 09 13:04:11 EST 2002:SFSessionBean:2897995 increment() ctr=29
Sat Nov 09 13:04:12 EST 2002:SFSessionBean:6664484 ejbCreate(39)
Sat Nov 09 13:04:12 EST 2002:SFSessionBean:6664484 increment() ctr=39
Sat Nov 09 13:04:13 EST 2002:SFSessionBean:4034480 ejbCreate(49)
Sat Nov 09 13:04:13 EST 2002:SFSessionBean:4034480 increment() ctr=49
Sat Nov 09 13:04:14 EST 2002:SFSessionBean:4039138 increment() ctr=10
Sat Nov 09 13:04:15 EST 2002:SFSessionBean:5775816 increment() ctr=20
Sat Nov 09 13:04:16 EST 2002:SFSessionBean:2897995 increment() ctr=30
Sat Nov 09 13:04:17 EST 2002:SFSessionBean:6664484 increment() ctr=40
Sat Nov 09 13:04:18 EST 2002:SFSessionBean:4034480 increment() ctr=50
Sat Nov 09 13:04:19 EST 2002:SFSessionBean:4039138 ejbRemove() ctr=11
Sat Nov 09 13:04:19 EST 2002:SFSessionBean:5775816 ejbRemove() ctr=21
Sat Nov 09 13:04:19 EST 2002:SFSessionBean:2897995 ejbRemove() ctr=31
Sat Nov 09 13:04:19 EST 2002:SFSessionBean:6664484 ejbRemove() ctr=41
Sat Nov 09 13:04:19 EST 2002:SFSessionBean:4034480 ejbRemove() ctr=51
```

Using Entity Beans

An entity bean is an EJB that models data that is typically stored in a relational database management system (RDBMS). Usually, it exists for as long as the data associated with it exists.

An entity bean is an *object* representation of data. An object is generally considered to be any entity with two specific attributes: *state* and *functionality*.

Entity beans implement this criteria and are therefore considered objects. An entity bean contains a copy of persisted data; therefore, it has a state. It also contains business logic; therefore, it has functionality. With these properties, entity beans can provide the same types of benefits as those of object databases.

Entity beans allow data to be persisted as Java objects as opposed to existing as rows in a table. They enable the enterprise bean provider to associate Java objects abstractly with relational database components (see Figure 7-5). Subsequently, the EJB deployer is able to map these abstract relational components to existing persistence devices.

Entity beans access relational databases as well as enterprise systems or applications used to persist data (see Figure 7-6). Entity beans are able to be written in a robust and object-oriented fashion so that they can be used with a variety of data sources or data streams.

Entity beans are most often used for representing a set of data, such as the columns in a database table, with each entity bean instance containing one element of that data set, such as a row from a database table.

Methods of the entity bean's home interface, as defined in the EJB specification, allow clients to read, insert, update, and delete entities in a database.

FIGURE 7-5

Entity bean representing RDBMS-based data

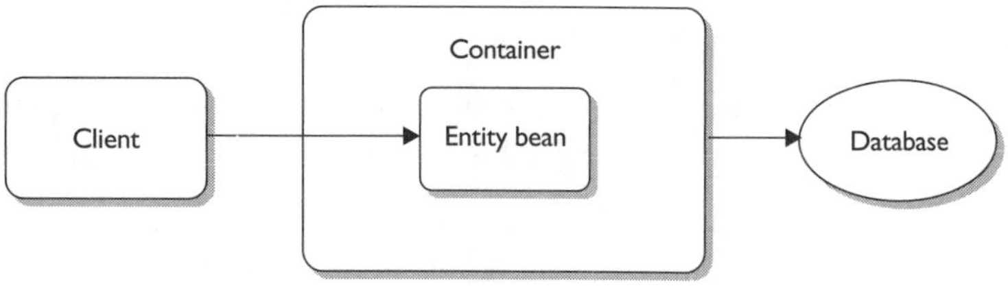

FIGURE 7-6

Entity beans
representing
legacy application–
based data

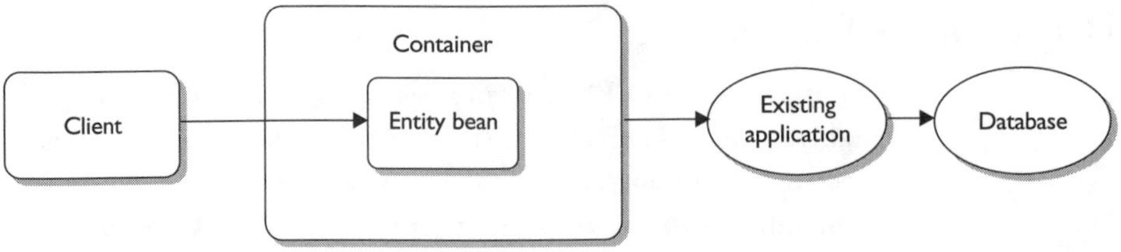

Entity bean instances hold a copy of persisted data. If multiple clients execute the same find operation, for example, all of them will get handles to the same entity bean instance. Each client will get a handle to the same logical instance of the bean, but based on the transactional mode, each client could actually be talking to a different physical instance of the bean class. If contention exists between entity bean calls, it is handled by regarding each call as a separate transaction.

Uses of Entity Beans

The following are common uses of entity beans:

- Entity beans can be used to enforce the integrity of data that will be persisted as well as data that might potentially be persisted.

- Entity beans can be reused to cache data, therefore saving trips to the database.

- Entity beans can be used to model domain objects with unique identities that might be shared by multiple clients.

- Unlike session beans, entity beans are intended to model records in a data set, not to maintain conversations with clients.

- Entity beans can be used for wrapping JDBC code, hence giving the application an object-oriented interface for the data set.

- Entity beans can be wrapped by session beans, giving the developer more control in determining how clients can control data.

- Entity beans can be used in either bean-managed persistence (BMP) or container-managed persistence (CMP) mode. CMP mode should be used if at all possible, allowing the enterprise bean provider to concentrate on writing business logic instead of JDBC logic.

Entity Bean Lifecycle States

As they execute the bean methods described later in this objective, entity bean instances can be in one of three states (see Figure 7-7):

- **Null**   The bean instance doesn't exist.
- **Pooled**   The bean exists but isn't associated with any specific entity object.
- **Ready**   The bean instance has been assigned an entity object identity.

The EJB container invokes the following entity bean interface methods when lifecycle events occur. The enterprise bean provider is responsible for placing business logic in this container to handle the events of the application. The container invokes the following methods:

- **ejbActivate()**   An entity bean instance is chosen, removed from the available pool, and assigned to a specific EJB object.
- **ejbLoad()**   The container synchronizes its state by loading data from the underlying data source.

Various states of
an entity bean

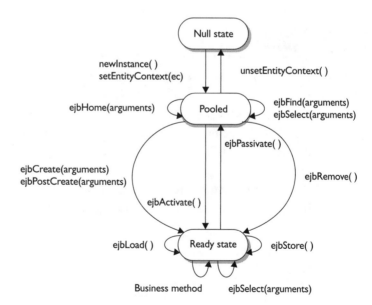

■ **ejbPassivate()** An entity bean instance is about to be disassociated with a specific EJB object and returned to the available pool.

■ **ejbRemove()** An EJB object that is associated with an entity bean instance is removed by a client-invoked remove operation on the entity bean's home or remote interface.

■ **ejbStore()** The container needs to synchronize the underlying data source, or persistent state, with the entity bean instance by storing data to the underlying data source.

Developing Entity Beans

The preceding sections covered most of the components of an entity bean. The following exercise completes a checklist of tasks, annotated with helpful hints, required to develop an entity bean. Often, a development tool will be provided with the particular application or EJB server in use, such as SilverStream, Web Logic, or WebSphere. When using development tools, many of these tasks will be wrapped in a graphical user interface (GUI) integrated development environment (IDE) for creating interfaces and deployment descriptor files.

EXERCISE 7-3

Review Code for Entity Bean Using Container-Managed Persistence

Provide the code for an entity bean. Your code should look similar to the code shown in the following sections. To increase your familiarity with this process, we review the code for an entity bean that uses CMP. We use a step-wise approach that covers all the things required to create, package, deploy, and call the bean.

1. Create the CMP Entity Bean Class The following CMP entity bean class example assumes that the following table definition exists in the database:

```
create table tb_product (
    productId    varchar(64),
    name         varchar(64),
    productPx    numeric(18),
    description  varchar(64)
);
```

The inline documentation points out the required methods along with the business methods:

```
package j2ee.architect.EntityCMP;
import javax.ejb.*;
import java.util.*;
// CMP Entity Bean
abstract public class EntityCMPBean implements EntityBean {
  EntityContext entityContext;
  // Methods required by the EJB specification.
  // They are called by the container only.

  // This method corresponds to the create() method
  // found in the home interface.  Because this
  // is CMP, the method will return void and the
  // EJB Container will make the primary key.
  public java.lang.String ejbCreate(java.lang.String productId,
    java.lang.String name, java.lang.Double productPx,
    java.lang.String description) throws CreateException {
    log("ejbCreate()  [primary key="+productId+"]");
    // However, with CMP we must set the Bean's fields
    // with the parameters passed in, so that the EJB
    // Container is able to inspect our Bean and
    // insert the corresponding database entries.
    setProductId(productId);
    setName(name);
    setProductPx(productPx);
    setDescription(description);
    return null;
  }
  // Called after ejbCreate() method.
  public void ejbPostCreate(java.lang.String productId, java.lang.String name,
  java.lang.Double productPx,
ava.lang.String description) throws CreateException {
    log("ejbPostCreate() [primary key="+getProductId()+"]");
  }
  public void ejbRemove() throws RemoveException {
    log("ejbRemove() [primary key="+getProductId()+"]");
  }
  // Loads/re-loads the entity bean instance with
  // the current value in database. We can leave
  // this basically empty for CMP. The EJB container
  // will set public fields to the current values.
  public void ejbLoad() {
    log("ejbLoad() [primary key="+getProductId()+"]");
  }
  // Updates the database value with the current
  // value of this entity bean instance. We can leave
  // this basically empty for CMP. The EJB container
  // will save public fields to the database.
```

```
  public void ejbStore() {
     log("ejbStore() [primary key="+getProductId()+"]");
  }
  public void ejbActivate() {
     log("ejbActivate() [primary key="+getProductId()+"]");
  }
  public void ejbPassivate() {
     log("ejbPassivate() [primary key="+getProductId()+"]");
  }
  public void unsetEntityContext() {
     log("unsetEntityContext() [primary key="+getProductId()+"]");
     this.entityContext = null;
  }
  public void setEntityContext(EntityContext entityContext) {
     log("setEntityContext() called.");
     this.entityContext = entityContext;
  }
  // No finder methods are required because
  // they are implemented by Container

  // Abstract getters and setters
  public abstract void setProductId(java.lang.String productId);
  public abstract void setName(java.lang.String name);
  public abstract void setProductPx(java.lang.Double productPx);
  public abstract void setDescription(java.lang.String description);
  public abstract java.lang.String getProductId();
  public abstract java.lang.String getName();
  public abstract java.lang.Double getProductPx();
  public abstract java.lang.String getDescription();
 // Log message to console
  public void log(String msg) {
     System.out.println(Calendar.getInstance().getTime()
        +":EntityCMPBean:" + msg);
  }
}
```

2. Create the CMP Entity Bean Home Interface   Here is a home interface for our CMP entity bean example:

```
package j2ee.architect.EntityCMP;
import javax.ejb.*;
import java.util.*;
import java.rmi.*;
// This is the home interface, used by clients as a
// factory for EJB objects (remote references). The EJB
// container vendor implements this extended interface.
// In this home interface there is a create() method that
```

```
// corresponds to the ejbCreate() method in actual bean code.
public interface EntityCMPRemoteHome extends javax.ejb.EJBHome {
  // Finder methods that return one or
  // more EJB Objects (remote reference).
  // The functionality of these finder methods
  //  can be customized at deployment time
  public Collection findByName(String string)
    throws FinderException, RemoteException;
  public Collection findByDescription(String string)
    throws FinderException, RemoteException;
  public Collection findByProductPx(Double dbl)
    throws FinderException, RemoteException;
  public Collection findAllProducts()
    throws FinderException, RemoteException;
  public EntityCMPRemote findByPrimaryKey(String productId)
    throws FinderException, RemoteException;
  // Creates/returns the EJB Object (remote reference).
  public EntityCMPRemote create(String productId, String name,
    Double productPx, String description)
    throws CreateException, RemoteException;
}
```

3. Create the CMP Entity Bean Remote Interface

Here is a remote interface for our CMP entity bean example. It is important to note that the following code is not supposed to demonstrate the *best practice* for the design of the remote interface. An improved implementation would provide access via a session façade (see Chapter 5), which would simplify access and reduce potential network traffic.

```
package j2ee.architect.EntityCMP;
import javax.ejb.*;
import java.util.*;
import java.rmi.*;
// This is the remote interface, used by clients when
// they need to call an EJB objects. The EJB container
// vendor implements this extended interface, which is
// responsible for delegating subsequent calls to the
// actual bean code.
public interface EntityCMPRemote extends EJBObject {
  // Getters and setters for Entity Bean fields.
  public String getProductId() throws RemoteException;
  public void setName(String name) throws RemoteException;
  public String getName() throws RemoteException;
  public void setProductPx(Double productPx) throws RemoteException;
  public Double getProductPx() throws RemoteException;
  public void setDescription(String description) throws RemoteException;
  public String getDescription() throws RemoteException;
}
```

4. Create Deployment Descriptors As mentioned in the first code review exercise in this chapter, the deployment descriptor, located within a JAR file, allows the properties of an EJB to be maintained outside of Java code.

Here is our deployment descriptor (*ejb-jar.xml*) for the CMP entity session bean. You will notice some EJB Query Language (EJB QL), which defines the queries for the finder and select methods of an entity bean with CMP.

```xml
<?xml version="1.0"?><!DOCTYPE ejb-jar PUBLIC
"-//Sun Microsystems, Inc.//DTD Enterprise JavaBeans 2.0//EN"
"http://java.sun.com/j2ee/dtds/ejb-jar_2_0.dtd">
<ejb-jar>
  <enterprise-beans>
    <entity>
      <display-name>EntityCMP</display-name>
      <ejb-name>EntityCMP</ejb-name>
      <home>j2ee.architect.EntityCMP.EntityCMPRemoteHome</home>
      <remote>j2ee.architect.EntityCMP.EntityCMPRemote</remote>
      <ejb-class>j2ee.architect.EntityCMP.EntityCMPBean</ejb-class>
      <persistence-type>Container</persistence-type>
      <prim-key-class>java.lang.String</prim-key-class>
      <reentrant>False</reentrant>
      <cmp-version>2.x</cmp-version>
      <abstract-schema-name>EntityCMP</abstract-schema-name>
      <cmp-field>
        <field-name>productId</field-name>
      </cmp-field>
      <cmp-field>
        <field-name>name</field-name>
      </cmp-field>
      <cmp-field>
        <field-name>productPx</field-name>
      </cmp-field>
      <cmp-field>
        <field-name>description</field-name>
      </cmp-field>
      <primkey-field>productId</primkey-field>
      <query>
        <query-method>
          <method-name>findByName</method-name>
          <method-params>
            <method-param>java.lang.String</method-param>
          </method-params>
        </query-method>
        <ejb-ql>WHERE name = ?1</ejb-ql>
      </query>
```

```xml
      <query>
        <query-method>
          <method-name>findByDescription</method-name>
          <method-params>
            <method-param>java.lang.String</method-param>
          </method-params>
        </query-method>
        <ejb-ql>WHERE description = ?1</ejb-ql>
      </query>
      <query>
        <query-method>
          <method-name>findByProductPx</method-name>
          <method-params>
            <method-param>java.lang.Double</method-param>
          </method-params>
        </query-method>
        <ejb-ql>WHERE productPx = ?1</ejb-ql>
      </query>
      <query>
        <query-method>
          <method-name>findAllProducts</method-name>
          <method-params />
        </query-method>
        <ejb-ql>WHERE productId IS NOT NULL</ejb-ql>
      </query>
    </entity>
  </enterprise-beans>
  <assembly-descriptor>
    <container-transaction>
      <method>
        <ejb-name>EntityCMP</ejb-name>
        <method-name>*</method-name>
      </method>
      <trans-attribute>Required</trans-attribute>
    </container-transaction>
  </assembly-descriptor>
</ejb-jar>
```

5. Compile, Assemble, and Deploy the CMP Entity Bean The next steps in the process are to compile, assemble, and then deploy the entity bean. In our example the following set of steps are used to complete the process. As part of the deployment process, references in the deployment descriptor need to be resolved to actual resources in the container. How these resources are resolved is, at the moment, container specific.

In the WebLogic environment, the following files can be used for the CMP Entity bean example:

Here's the code for the *weblogic-ejb-jar.xml* file:

```
<?xml version="1.0"?><!DOCTYPE weblogic-ejb-jar PUBLIC
"-//BEA Systems, Inc.//DTD WebLogic 6.0.0 EJB//EN"
"http://www.bea.com/servers/wls600/dtd/weblogic-ejb-jar.dtd" >
<weblogic-ejb-jar>
  <weblogic-enterprise-bean>
    <ejb-name>EntityCMP</ejb-name>
    <entity-descriptor>
      <entity-cache>
        <max-beans-in-cache>1000</max-beans-in-cache>
      </entity-cache>
      <persistence>
        <persistence-type>
          <type-identifier>WebLogic_CMP_RDBMS</type-identifier>
          <type-version>6.0</type-version>
          <type-storage>META-INF/weblogic-cmp-rdbms-jar.xml</type-storage>
        </persistence-type>
        <persistence-use>
          <type-identifier>WebLogic_CMP_RDBMS</type-identifier>
          <type-version>6.0</type-version>
        </persistence-use>
      </persistence>
    </entity-descriptor>
    <jndi-name>EntityCMPRemoteHome</jndi-name>
  </weblogic-enterprise-bean>
</weblogic-ejb-jar>
```

Here's the code for the *weblogic-cmp-rdbms-jar.xml* file:

```
<!DOCTYPE weblogic-rdbms-jar PUBLIC
 '-//BEA Systems, Inc.//DTD WebLogic 6.0.0 EJB RDBMS Persistence//EN'
 'http://www.bea.com/servers/wls600/dtd/weblogic-rdbms-persistence.dtd'>
<weblogic-rdbms-jar>
  <weblogic-rdbms-bean>
    <ejb-name>EntityCMP</ejb-name>
    <data-source-name>_dbPool</data-source-name>
    <table-name>tb_product</table-name>
    <field-map>
      <cmp-field>productId</cmp-field>
      <dbms-column>productId</dbms-column>
    </field-map>
    <field-map>
```

```
      <cmp-field>name</cmp-field>
      <dbms-column>name</dbms-column>
    </field-map>
    <field-map>
      <cmp-field>productPx</cmp-field>
      <dbms-column>productPx</dbms-column>
    </field-map>
    <field-map>
      <cmp-field>description</cmp-field>
      <dbms-column>description</dbms-column>
    </field-map>
  </weblogic-rdbms-bean>
</weblogic-rdbms-jar>
```

Here are the remaining steps for completing the compile/package/deployment process:

6. Compile the Java classes.

7. Package the classes and deployment descriptors into a JAR file.

8. Generate stub and tie code for the container and add them to the JAR file.

9. Deploy the JAR file to the application server.

10. Package the required classes for a remote client of the bean.

Here is an example of a client of the CMP entity bean:

```
package j2ee.architect.EntityCMP;
import javax.ejb.*;
import javax.naming.*;
import javax.rmi.*;
import java.rmi.*;
import java.util.*;
// Client application for a CMP Entity Bean.
public class EntityCMPClient {
  public static void main(String[] args) throws Exception {
    EntityCMPRemoteHome home = null;
    try {
      // Lookup and get a reference to the home object
      Context ctx = getInitialContext();
      home = (EntityCMPRemoteHome) PortableRemoteObject.narrow(
          ctx.lookup("EntityCMPRemoteHome"), EntityCMPRemoteHome.class);
      // Create some new EJB Objects
      System.out.println("Adding new products...");
      home.create("10000", "Penne Pasta", new Double(15), "Bowl of pasta");
```

```
    home.create("10001", "Tomato Soup", new Double(2), "Bowl of Tomato soup");
    home.create("10002", "Apple Pie", new Double(3.5), "Large Apple pie");
    home.create("10003", "Milk", new Double(1), "Glass of milk");
    home.create("10004", "Juice", new Double(1), "Carton of apple juice");
    home.create("10005", "Juice", new Double(1), "Carton of cranberry juice");
    // Find a product and display its description
    Iterator i = home.findByName("Juice").iterator();
    System.out.println("Here are the products with name=Juice:");
    while (i.hasNext()) {
      EntityCMPRemote product = (EntityCMPRemote)
        PortableRemoteObject.narrow(i.next(), EntityCMPRemote.class);
      System.out.println(product.getDescription());
    }
    // Find all products that cost $1
    i = home.findByProductPx(new Double(1)).iterator();
    System.out.println("Here are the products that cost $1:");
    while (i.hasNext()) {
      EntityCMPRemote product = (EntityCMPRemote)
        PortableRemoteObject.narrow(i.next(), EntityCMPRemote.class);
      System.out.println(product.getDescription());
    }
  } catch (Exception e) {
    e.printStackTrace();
  } finally {
    if (home != null) {
      // Remove products added by this client
      System.out.println("Deleting products added..");
      Iterator i = home.findAllProducts().iterator();
      while (i.hasNext()) {
        try {
          EntityCMPRemote product = (EntityCMPRemote)
            PortableRemoteObject.narrow(i.next(), EntityCMPRemote.class);
          if (product.getProductId().startsWith("1000")) {
            product.remove();
          }
        }
        catch (Exception e) {
          e.printStackTrace();
        } // end try/catch
      } // end while
    } // end if
  } // end finally
} // end main
private static Context getInitialContext() throws Exception {
  // This implementation is specific to the Weblogic
  // server and will differ for other server vendors.
```

```
    String providerUrl = "t3://localhost:7001";
    String icFactory = "weblogic.jndi.WLInitialContextFactory";
    String user = null;
    String password = null;
    Properties properties = null;
    try {
      properties = new Properties();
      properties.put(Context.INITIAL_CONTEXT_FACTORY, icFactory);
      properties.put(Context.PROVIDER_URL, providerUrl);
      if (user != null) {
        properties.put(Context.SECURITY_PRINCIPAL, user);
        properties.put(Context.SECURITY_CREDENTIALS,
          password == null ? "" : password);
      }
      return new InitialContext(properties);
    }
    catch(Exception e) {
      System.out.println(
        "Unable to connect to JNDI server at " + providerUrl);
      throw e;
    }
  }
} // end class
```

Here is the output information provided by the client:

```
Adding new products...
Here are the products with name=Juice:
Carton of apple juice
Carton of cranberry juice
Here are the products that cost $1:
Toasted Sesame
Almond
Cranberry and Carrot
Glass of milk
Carton of apple juice
Carton of cranberry juice
Deleting products added..
```

Here is the output information provided by the client and the application server console:

```
Sat Nov 09 13:20:42 EST 2002:EntityCMPBean:setEntityContext() called.
Sat Nov 09 13:20:42 EST 2002:EntityCMPBean:ejbCreate()  [primary key=10000]
Sat Nov 09 13:20:42 EST 2002:EntityCMPBean:ejbPostCreate() [primary key=10000]
Sat Nov 09 13:20:42 EST 2002:EntityCMPBean:ejbStore() [primary key=10000]
```

```
Sat Nov 09 13:20:42 EST 2002:EntityCMPBean:setEntityContext() called.
Sat Nov 09 13:20:42 EST 2002:EntityCMPBean:ejbCreate()   [primary key=10001]
Sat Nov 09 13:20:42 EST 2002:EntityCMPBean:ejbPostCreate() [primary key=10001]
Sat Nov 09 13:20:42 EST 2002:EntityCMPBean:ejbStore() [primary key=10001]
Sat Nov 09 13:20:42 EST 2002:EntityCMPBean:setEntityContext() called.
Sat Nov 09 13:20:42 EST 2002:EntityCMPBean:ejbCreate()   [primary key=10002]
Sat Nov 09 13:20:42 EST 2002:EntityCMPBean:ejbPostCreate() [primary key=10002]
Sat Nov 09 13:20:42 EST 2002:EntityCMPBean:ejbStore() [primary key=10002]
Sat Nov 09 13:20:42 EST 2002:EntityCMPBean:setEntityContext() called.
Sat Nov 09 13:20:42 EST 2002:EntityCMPBean:ejbCreate()   [primary key=10003]
Sat Nov 09 13:20:42 EST 2002:EntityCMPBean:ejbPostCreate() [primary key=10003]
Sat Nov 09 13:20:42 EST 2002:EntityCMPBean:ejbStore() [primary key=10003]
Sat Nov 09 13:20:42 EST 2002:EntityCMPBean:setEntityContext() called.
Sat Nov 09 13:20:42 EST 2002:EntityCMPBean:ejbCreate()   [primary key=10004]
Sat Nov 09 13:20:42 EST 2002:EntityCMPBean:ejbPostCreate() [primary key=10004]
Sat Nov 09 13:20:42 EST 2002:EntityCMPBean:ejbStore() [primary key=10004]
Sat Nov 09 13:20:42 EST 2002:EntityCMPBean:setEntityContext() called.
Sat Nov 09 13:20:42 EST 2002:EntityCMPBean:ejbCreate()   [primary key=10005]
Sat Nov 09 13:20:42 EST 2002:EntityCMPBean:ejbPostCreate() [primary key=10005]
Sat Nov 09 13:20:42 EST 2002:EntityCMPBean:ejbStore() [primary key=10005]
Sat Nov 09 13:20:42 EST 2002:EntityCMPBean:setEntityContext() called.
Sat Nov 09 13:20:42 EST 2002:EntityCMPBean:setEntityContext() called.
Sat Nov 09 13:20:42 EST 2002:EntityCMPBean:setEntityContext() called.
Sat Nov 09 13:20:42 EST 2002:EntityCMPBean:ejbActivate() [primary key=10004]
Sat Nov 09 13:20:42 EST 2002:EntityCMPBean:ejbLoad() [primary key=10004]
Sat Nov 09 13:20:42 EST 2002:EntityCMPBean:ejbActivate() [primary key=10005]
Sat Nov 09 13:20:42 EST 2002:EntityCMPBean:ejbLoad() [primary key=10005]
Sat Nov 09 13:20:42 EST 2002:EntityCMPBean:ejbStore() [primary key=10004]
Sat Nov 09 13:20:42 EST 2002:EntityCMPBean:ejbStore() [primary key=10005]
Sat Nov 09 13:20:42 EST 2002:EntityCMPBean:ejbLoad() [primary key=10004]
Sat Nov 09 13:20:42 EST 2002:EntityCMPBean:ejbStore() [primary key=10004]
Sat Nov 09 13:20:42 EST 2002:EntityCMPBean:ejbLoad() [primary key=10005]
Sat Nov 09 13:20:42 EST 2002:EntityCMPBean:ejbStore() [primary key=10005]
Sat Nov 09 13:20:42 EST 2002:EntityCMPBean:setEntityContext() called.
Sat Nov 09 13:20:42 EST 2002:EntityCMPBean:setEntityContext() called.
Sat Nov 09 13:20:42 EST 2002:EntityCMPBean:setEntityContext() called.
Sat Nov 09 13:20:42 EST 2002:EntityCMPBean:setEntityContext() called.
Sat Nov 09 13:20:42 EST 2002:EntityCMPBean:setEntityContext() called.
Sat Nov 09 13:20:42 EST 2002:EntityCMPBean:setEntityContext() called.
Sat Nov 09 13:20:42 EST 2002:EntityCMPBean:ejbActivate() [primary key=10]
Sat Nov 09 13:20:42 EST 2002:EntityCMPBean:ejbLoad() [primary key=10]
Sat Nov 09 13:20:42 EST 2002:EntityCMPBean:ejbActivate() [primary key=40]
Sat Nov 09 13:20:42 EST 2002:EntityCMPBean:ejbLoad() [primary key=40]
Sat Nov 09 13:20:42 EST 2002:EntityCMPBean:ejbActivate() [primary key=50]
Sat Nov 09 13:20:42 EST 2002:EntityCMPBean:ejbLoad() [primary key=50]
Sat Nov 09 13:20:42 EST 2002:EntityCMPBean:ejbActivate() [primary key=10003]
```

```
Sat Nov 09 13:20:42 EST 2002:EntityCMPBean:ejbLoad() [primary key=10003]
Sat Nov 09 13:20:42 EST 2002:EntityCMPBean:ejbActivate() [primary key=10004]
Sat Nov 09 13:20:42 EST 2002:EntityCMPBean:ejbLoad() [primary key=10004]
Sat Nov 09 13:20:42 EST 2002:EntityCMPBean:ejbActivate() [primary key=10005]
Sat Nov 09 13:20:42 EST 2002:EntityCMPBean:ejbLoad() [primary key=10005]
Sat Nov 09 13:20:42 EST 2002:EntityCMPBean:ejbStore() [primary key=10]
Sat Nov 09 13:20:42 EST 2002:EntityCMPBean:ejbStore() [primary key=40]
Sat Nov 09 13:20:42 EST 2002:EntityCMPBean:ejbStore() [primary key=50]
Sat Nov 09 13:20:42 EST 2002:EntityCMPBean:ejbStore() [primary key=10003]
Sat Nov 09 13:20:42 EST 2002:EntityCMPBean:ejbStore() [primary key=10004]
Sat Nov 09 13:20:42 EST 2002:EntityCMPBean:ejbStore() [primary key=10005]
Sat Nov 09 13:20:42 EST 2002:EntityCMPBean:ejbLoad() [primary key=10]
Sat Nov 09 13:20:42 EST 2002:EntityCMPBean:ejbStore() [primary key=10]
Sat Nov 09 13:20:42 EST 2002:EntityCMPBean:ejbLoad() [primary key=40]
Sat Nov 09 13:20:42 EST 2002:EntityCMPBean:ejbStore() [primary key=40]
Sat Nov 09 13:20:42 EST 2002:EntityCMPBean:ejbLoad() [primary key=50]
Sat Nov 09 13:20:42 EST 2002:EntityCMPBean:ejbStore() [primary key=50]
Sat Nov 09 13:20:42 EST 2002:EntityCMPBean:ejbLoad() [primary key=10003]
Sat Nov 09 13:20:42 EST 2002:EntityCMPBean:ejbStore() [primary key=10003]
Sat Nov 09 13:20:42 EST 2002:EntityCMPBean:ejbLoad() [primary key=10004]
Sat Nov 09 13:20:42 EST 2002:EntityCMPBean:ejbStore() [primary key=10004]
Sat Nov 09 13:20:42 EST 2002:EntityCMPBean:ejbLoad() [primary key=10005]
Sat Nov 09 13:20:42 EST 2002:EntityCMPBean:ejbStore() [primary key=10005]
Sat Nov 09 13:20:42 EST 2002:EntityCMPBean:setEntityContext() called.
Sat Nov 09 13:20:42 EST 2002:EntityCMPBean:setEntityContext() called.
Sat Nov 09 13:20:42 EST 2002:EntityCMPBean:setEntityContext() called.
Sat Nov 09 13:20:42 EST 2002:EntityCMPBean:setEntityContext() called.
Sat Nov 09 13:20:42 EST 2002:EntityCMPBean:setEntityContext() called.
Sat Nov 09 13:20:42 EST 2002:EntityCMPBean:setEntityContext() called.
Sat Nov 09 13:20:42 EST 2002:EntityCMPBean:setEntityContext() called.
Sat Nov 09 13:20:42 EST 2002:EntityCMPBean:setEntityContext() called.
Sat Nov 09 13:20:42 EST 2002:EntityCMPBean:setEntityContext() called.
Sat Nov 09 13:20:42 EST 2002:EntityCMPBean:setEntityContext() called.
Sat Nov 09 13:20:42 EST 2002:EntityCMPBean:setEntityContext() called.
Sat Nov 09 13:20:42 EST 2002:EntityCMPBean:setEntityContext() called.
Sat Nov 09 13:20:42 EST 2002:EntityCMPBean:ejbActivate() [primary key=10]
Sat Nov 09 13:20:42 EST 2002:EntityCMPBean:ejbLoad() [primary key=10]
Sat Nov 09 13:20:42 EST 2002:EntityCMPBean:ejbActivate() [primary key=20]
Sat Nov 09 13:20:42 EST 2002:EntityCMPBean:ejbLoad() [primary key=20]
Sat Nov 09 13:20:42 EST 2002:EntityCMPBean:ejbActivate() [primary key=30]
Sat Nov 09 13:20:42 EST 2002:EntityCMPBean:ejbLoad() [primary key=30]
Sat Nov 09 13:20:42 EST 2002:EntityCMPBean:ejbActivate() [primary key=40]
Sat Nov 09 13:20:42 EST 2002:EntityCMPBean:ejbLoad() [primary key=40]
Sat Nov 09 13:20:42 EST 2002:EntityCMPBean:ejbActivate() [primary key=50]
Sat Nov 09 13:20:42 EST 2002:EntityCMPBean:ejbLoad() [primary key=50]
Sat Nov 09 13:20:42 EST 2002:EntityCMPBean:ejbActivate() [primary key=60]
```

```
Sat Nov 09 13:20:42 EST 2002:EntityCMPBean:ejbLoad() [primary key=60]
Sat Nov 09 13:20:42 EST 2002:EntityCMPBean:ejbActivate() [primary key=10000]
Sat Nov 09 13:20:42 EST 2002:EntityCMPBean:ejbLoad() [primary key=10000]
Sat Nov 09 13:20:42 EST 2002:EntityCMPBean:ejbActivate() [primary key=10001]
Sat Nov 09 13:20:42 EST 2002:EntityCMPBean:ejbLoad() [primary key=10001]
Sat Nov 09 13:20:42 EST 2002:EntityCMPBean:ejbActivate() [primary key=10002]
Sat Nov 09 13:20:42 EST 2002:EntityCMPBean:ejbLoad() [primary key=10002]
Sat Nov 09 13:20:42 EST 2002:EntityCMPBean:ejbActivate() [primary key=10003]
Sat Nov 09 13:20:42 EST 2002:EntityCMPBean:ejbLoad() [primary key=10003]
Sat Nov 09 13:20:42 EST 2002:EntityCMPBean:ejbActivate() [primary key=10004]
Sat Nov 09 13:20:42 EST 2002:EntityCMPBean:ejbLoad() [primary key=10004]
Sat Nov 09 13:20:42 EST 2002:EntityCMPBean:ejbActivate() [primary key=10005]
Sat Nov 09 13:20:42 EST 2002:EntityCMPBean:ejbLoad() [primary key=10005]
Sat Nov 09 13:20:42 EST 2002:EntityCMPBean:ejbStore() [primary key=10]
Sat Nov 09 13:20:42 EST 2002:EntityCMPBean:ejbStore() [primary key=20]
Sat Nov 09 13:20:42 EST 2002:EntityCMPBean:ejbStore() [primary key=30]
Sat Nov 09 13:20:42 EST 2002:EntityCMPBean:ejbStore() [primary key=40]
Sat Nov 09 13:20:42 EST 2002:EntityCMPBean:ejbStore() [primary key=50]
Sat Nov 09 13:20:42 EST 2002:EntityCMPBean:ejbStore() [primary key=60]
Sat Nov 09 13:20:42 EST 2002:EntityCMPBean:ejbStore() [primary key=10000]
Sat Nov 09 13:20:42 EST 2002:EntityCMPBean:ejbStore() [primary key=10001]
Sat Nov 09 13:20:42 EST 2002:EntityCMPBean:ejbStore() [primary key=10002]
Sat Nov 09 13:20:42 EST 2002:EntityCMPBean:ejbStore() [primary key=10003]
Sat Nov 09 13:20:42 EST 2002:EntityCMPBean:ejbStore() [primary key=10004]
Sat Nov 09 13:20:42 EST 2002:EntityCMPBean:ejbStore() [primary key=10005]
Sat Nov 09 13:20:42 EST 2002:EntityCMPBean:ejbLoad() [primary key=10]
Sat Nov 09 13:20:42 EST 2002:EntityCMPBean:ejbStore() [primary key=10]
Sat Nov 09 13:20:42 EST 2002:EntityCMPBean:ejbLoad() [primary key=20]
Sat Nov 09 13:20:42 EST 2002:EntityCMPBean:ejbStore() [primary key=20]
Sat Nov 09 13:20:42 EST 2002:EntityCMPBean:ejbLoad() [primary key=30]
Sat Nov 09 13:20:42 EST 2002:EntityCMPBean:ejbStore() [primary key=30]
Sat Nov 09 13:20:43 EST 2002:EntityCMPBean:ejbLoad() [primary key=40]
Sat Nov 09 13:20:43 EST 2002:EntityCMPBean:ejbStore() [primary key=40]
Sat Nov 09 13:20:43 EST 2002:EntityCMPBean:ejbLoad() [primary key=50]
Sat Nov 09 13:20:43 EST 2002:EntityCMPBean:ejbStore() [primary key=50]
Sat Nov 09 13:20:43 EST 2002:EntityCMPBean:ejbLoad() [primary key=60]
Sat Nov 09 13:20:43 EST 2002:EntityCMPBean:ejbStore() [primary key=60]
Sat Nov 09 13:20:43 EST 2002:EntityCMPBean:ejbLoad() [primary key=10000]
Sat Nov 09 13:20:43 EST 2002:EntityCMPBean:ejbStore() [primary key=10000]
Sat Nov 09 13:20:43 EST 2002:EntityCMPBean:ejbLoad() [primary key=10000]
Sat Nov 09 13:20:43 EST 2002:EntityCMPBean:ejbRemove() [primary key=10000]
Sat Nov 09 13:20:43 EST 2002:EntityCMPBean:ejbLoad() [primary key=10001]
Sat Nov 09 13:20:43 EST 2002:EntityCMPBean:ejbStore() [primary key=10001]
Sat Nov 09 13:20:43 EST 2002:EntityCMPBean:ejbLoad() [primary key=10001]
Sat Nov 09 13:20:43 EST 2002:EntityCMPBean:ejbRemove() [primary key=10001]
```

```
Sat Nov 09 13:20:43 EST 2002:EntityCMPBean:ejbLoad() [primary key=10002]
Sat Nov 09 13:20:43 EST 2002:EntityCMPBean:ejbStore() [primary key=10002]
Sat Nov 09 13:20:43 EST 2002:EntityCMPBean:ejbLoad() [primary key=10002]
Sat Nov 09 13:20:43 EST 2002:EntityCMPBean:ejbRemove() [primary key=10002]
Sat Nov 09 13:20:43 EST 2002:EntityCMPBean:ejbLoad() [primary key=10003]
Sat Nov 09 13:20:43 EST 2002:EntityCMPBean:ejbStore() [primary key=10003]
Sat Nov 09 13:20:43 EST 2002:EntityCMPBean:ejbLoad() [primary key=10003]
Sat Nov 09 13:20:43 EST 2002:EntityCMPBean:ejbRemove() [primary key=10003]
Sat Nov 09 13:20:43 EST 2002:EntityCMPBean:ejbLoad() [primary key=10004]
Sat Nov 09 13:20:43 EST 2002:EntityCMPBean:ejbStore() [primary key=10004]
Sat Nov 09 13:20:43 EST 2002:EntityCMPBean:ejbLoad() [primary key=10004]
Sat Nov 09 13:20:43 EST 2002:EntityCMPBean:ejbRemove() [primary key=10004]
Sat Nov 09 13:20:43 EST 2002:EntityCMPBean:ejbLoad() [primary key=10005]
Sat Nov 09 13:20:43 EST 2002:EntityCMPBean:ejbStore() [primary key=10005]
Sat Nov 09 13:20:43 EST 2002:EntityCMPBean:ejbLoad() [primary key=10005]
Sat Nov 09 13:20:43 EST 2002:EntityCMPBean:ejbRemove() [primary key=10005]
```

A Closer Look at Entity Beans

This section provides a more in-depth look at the issues that need to be addressed when you're developing EJB component methods and configuration files.

Primary Keys

As mentioned, primary key classes can map to either a single field or multiple fields of an entity bean.

Single field mappings are the simpler of the two cases. In this scenario, the *primkey-field* element in the deployment descriptor is used to specify which field specified by the container-managed element is to be used as the primary key. The *primkey-field* and the container-managed elements are required to be the same type.

In mapping to multiple fields, the fields of the primary key class must be a subset of the container-managed fields. The primary key class, its parameterless constructor, and all primary key class fields are required to be declared as public.

The Unknown Primary Key Class   If the choice of the primary key field or fields is to be delayed until deployment time, the findByPrimaryKey() method, always a single-object finder, must be declared as *java.lang.Object*. The *prim-key-class* element in the deployment descriptor must also be *java.lang.Object*.

The isIdentical() Method   Client applications can test to determine whether different object references are pointing to the same entity object by using the `isIdentitcal()` method.

The following example uses this method:

```
// Get Home references
CustomerRemoteHome custHome1 = (CustomerRemoteHome)
                    javax.rmi.PortableRemoteObject.narrow(
                    initialContext.lookup("java:ucny/um2z8/customers"),
                    CustomerRemoteHome.class);

CustomerRemoteHome custHome2 = (CustomerRemoteHome)
                    javax.rmi.PortableRemoteObject.narrow(
                    initialContext.lookup("java:ucny/um2z8/customers"),
                    CustomerRemoteHome.class);
// Get Remote references
Customer customer1 = custHome1.findByPrimaryKey(100);
Customer customer2 = custHome2.findByPrimaryKey(100);
if (customer1.isIdentical(customer2))
  System.out.println ("identical objects.");
else
  System.out.println ("non-identical objects");
```

Object Equality   The EJB framework doesn't specify *object equality*—that is, the use of the `==` operator. Instead, the `isIdentical()` method should be used to support this functionality.

The equals() Method   The `java.lang.Object equals()` method relies heavily on memory addresses. For this reason, the enterprise bean provider should either override this method or simply not use it. It is recommended that the `isIdentical()` method be used when possible.

The hashCode() Method   The EJB framework doesn't specify the behavior of the `Object.hashCode()` method on object references pointing to entity objects. Instead, the `isIdentical()` method should be used to determine whether two entity object references refer to the same entity object. If the enterprise bean provider wants to use the `hashCode()` method, the following condition must be enforced:

```
if custHome1.equals(custHome2) {
    if (custHome1.hashCode() == custHome2.hashCode())
        System.out.println(this + " is implemented correctly");
```

```
      else
         System.out.println(this + " is NOT implemented correctly");
   }
```

The EntityBean Class and Lifecycle Event Methods

Much like the primary key class, the bean class can be extended from any Java class. If the enterprise bean provider extends an *EntityBean* class from another Java class, the methods of the base class will be available to the client by defining the base class's methods in the stub for the *EntityBean*.

The Public Constructor   To control the initial state of all objects, the enterprise bean provider creates a public constructor. This constructor enables the container to create stable instances of the *EntityBean* class. It is specified that this constructor should take no arguments. The container calls the public constructor to create a bean instance. The `ejbCreate()` and `ejbPostCreate()` methods are invoked to initialize that bean instance.

Accessor Methods   When using CMP, the enterprise bean provider doesn't make direct read and write calls to persistent storage devices. Instead, relational data is accessed via `get` and `set` accessor methods. These accessor methods, as well as the persistent fields and relationships, are declared in the abstract persistence schema of the XML deployment descriptor file.

The *cmr-field-name* element in the abstract persistence schema corresponds to the name used for the `get` and `set` accessor methods used for the relationship. The *cmr-field-type* element is used only for collection-valued cmr-fields.

The ejbCreate( ) Method   When you're using the `create()` and `remove()` methods, it is important to note the difference between session beans and entity beans. When these methods are used with session beans, bean objects are being created and destroyed. When these methods are used with entity beans, records in a database are being created and destroyed.

An entity bean can have zero or more `ejbCreate()` methods. However, the signature of each method must map to the entity bean home interface `create()` methods. When a client invokes a `create()` method to create an entity object, the container invokes the appropriate `ejbCreate()` method.

After the `ejbCreate()` method is completed for a CMP entity bean, the EJB container performs a database insert.

The ejbPostCreate( ) Method   For each `ejbCreate()` method declared, a matching `ejbPostCreate()` method with a void return type should be declared. Immediately after the EJB container invokes the `ejbCreate()` method on an EntityBean instance, it will call the corresponding `ejbPostCreate()` method on that same instance. The `ejbPostCreate()` method can be used to refine the instance created by the `ejbCreate()` method before this instance becomes available to the client.

The `ejbCreate()` method can be used to initialize persistent data, whereas the `ejbPostCreate()` method might do initialization involving the entity's context. Context information isn't available while the `ejbCreate()` method is being invoked, but it is available when the `ejbPostCreate()` is being invoked.

After the `ejbPostCreate()` method is invoked, the instance can discover the primary key by calling the `getPrimaryKey()` method on its entity context object.

The ejbRemove( ) Method   When a container invokes the `ejbRemove()` method on a bean instance or a client calls the corresponding `remove()` method in its remote home or remote interface, it not only removes the entity bean instance, but it also destroys physical data that is related to the bean instance.

Another way to destroy an entity object and its corresponding physical data is by use of the deployment descriptor's cascade-delete deployment descriptor element, contained in the *ejb-relationship-role* element.

The ejbFind( ) Method   An `ejbFind()` method is defined for each of the `find()` methods in the home interface. This includes at least an `ejbFindByPrimaryKey()` method, which returns the primary key to the container.

The setEntityContext( ) Method   For an entity bean instance to use its *EntityContext* information during the instance's lifetime, the bean instance must save the state of the *EntityContext* internally. The following code example accomplishes this:

```
EntityContext myContext;
public void setEntityContext(EntityContext ctx)
{
  myContext = ctx;
}
```

The unsetEntityContext( ) Method   The container calls this method before terminating the entity bean instance:

```
public void unsetEntityContext()
{
  myContext = null;
}
```

The ejbLoad( ) Method   When in ready state in the bean pool, an entity bean must keep its state synchronized with underlying data. During the call to the `ejbLoad()` method, the data is read from the database and stored in the instance variables. In addition, calling the `ejbStore()` method results in its saving the entity bean state to the database.

The container invokes the `ejbLoad()` method right after a bean is instantiated or when a transaction begins.

The ejbStore( ) Method   When data is to be persisted to a permanent storage medium, the EJB container invokes the `ejbStore()` method.

The ejbPassivate( ) Method   The EJB container invokes this method on the entity bean instance when the EJB container decides to return that instance to the bean pool. This method allows the entity bean instance to release any resources that shouldn't be held while in the bean pool. Therefore, if resources are created or acquired during the execution of the `ejbActivate()` method, they should be freed in the `ejbPassivate()` method.

The ejbActivate( ) Method   The EJB container invokes this method when an entity bean instance is chosen from the bean pool and is assigned a specific *object identity (OID)*. This method lets the entity bean acquire or create any necessary resources while the bean is in the ready state.

Home Interfaces and create( ) Methods

Two types of home interfaces can be used. The first is the *remote* home interface, which implements the *EJBHome* interface. The second is the *local* home interface, which implements the *EJBLocalHome* interface. The remote interface creates entity beans that can be accessed from outside of the EJB container by clients. The local interface creates entity beans that are accessed inside the EJB container by clients. The performance gained by using local entity beans is significant because clients get access to entity bean objects by *reference* as opposed to getting access to them by *value*. This saves time that would have been spent communicating with RMI-IIOP.

The name of each `create()` method starts with the prefix *create*. Unique signatures for `create()` methods are made using different method names, as long as the prefix starts with *create*, as well as by overloading `create()` methods with different arguments.

When an entity bean is first created, the `ejbCreate()` method creates a primary key that uniquely identifies that entity object. For the life of the entity bean object, the entity bean is associated with this primary key. As a result, the entity bean object can be retrieved by providing this primary key object to the `findByPrimaryKey()` method.

A bean's home interface can declare zero or more `create()` methods. A `create()` method exists for each different way of creating an entity object. Each of these `create()` methods must have corresponding `ejbCreate()` and `ejbPostCreate()` methods in the bean class. These creation methods are linked at runtime; when a `create()` method is invoked on the home interface, the container delegates the invocation to the corresponding `ejbCreate()` and `ejbPostCreate()` methods on the bean class. Here's an example:

```
public interface ShoppingCartHome extends javax.ejb.EJBHome
{
  public ShoppingCart create(String firstName, String lastName,
      int idNumber) throws RemoteException, CreateException;

  public ShoppingCart create(Integer customerNumber, int idNumber)
  throws RemoteException, CreateException;
}
```

A client can create a new entity object with code similar to this:

```
ShoppingCartHome scartHome = ...
ShopingCart scart = scartHome.create("E", "Matias", 641224);
```

Home Interfaces and finder( ) Methods

As mentioned, when an entity bean is first created, the `ejbCreate()` method creates a primary key that uniquely identifies that entity object. For the life of the entity bean object, the entity bean is associated with this primary key. Therefore, the entity bean object can be retrieved by providing the `findByPrimaryKey()` method of the home interface with a unique primary key object. This primary key is defined by the developer and can be of any type as long as it is unique.

One or more `finder()` methods can be defined in the home interface. One method should exist for every way required to find an entity bean object or collection of entity bean objects. `finder()` methods start with a prefix *find*. The arguments of a `finder()` method are used to locate the desired entity objects. The return type of a `finder()` method is an instance of an entity bean or a collection of entity bean instances.

The following example shows the `findByPrimaryKey()` method:

```
public interface ItemHome extends javax.ejb.EJBLocalHome
{
  //...
  public Item findByPrimaryKey(String number)
  throws FinderException, RemoteException;
  public Item findItemByDescription(String description)
  throws FinderException, RemoteException;
  public Collection findAllItems()
  throws FinderException, RemoteException;
}
```

The following example demonstrates how a client uses the `findByPrimaryKey()` method:

```
ItemRemoteHome itemHome = (ItemRemoteHome)
                     javax.rmi.PortableRemoteObject.narrow(
                     initialContext.lookup("java:ucny/um2z8/items"),
                     ItemRemoteHome.class);
Item item = itemHome.findByPrimaryKey("27018301820A");
```

With BMP, the entity bean provider doesn't write the corresponding `ejbFind()` method for `finder()` methods. `finder()` methods are configured by the development tools provided by the EJB container and then created when the entity bean is deployed. With BMP, the bean provider does have to write the `ejbFind()` methods.

Home Interfaces and remove( ) Methods

The `remove()` method of EJBHome interface supports the destruction of entity bean objects using either a handle object or a primary key object.

The `remove()` method of an EJBLocalHome interface supports the destruction of entity bean objects using only the primary key object.

When a `remove()` method is invoked on an entity object, the container invokes the entity bean instance's `ejbRemove()` method. After the `ejbRemove()` method returns from its invocation, but before the `remove()` method acknowledges its completion to the client, the EJB container removes the entity object from all relationships in which it participates and then removes its persistent representation.

Home Interfaces and getEJBMetaData( ) Methods

The `getEJBMetaData()` method returns a reference to an object that implements the EJBMetaData interface. The EJBMetaData interface allows application assembly tools to discover metadata information about an entity bean. This metadata information allows for loose client-server binding.

Remote Interfaces

Remote interfaces extend the EJBObject interface. They specify what methods of an entity object, created by the enterprise bean provider while implementing the EntityBean interface, can be accessed by a client. The client can exist either inside or outside of the EJB container. If the client exists inside the EJB container, such as the case of a servlet application, the local interface should be used instead. Remote interfaces allow clients to

- Obtain the remote home interface for the entity object.
- Remove the entity object.
- Obtain the entity object's handle.
- Obtain the entity object's primary key.

Local Interfaces

Local interfaces extend the EJBLocalObject interface. These interfaces specify which methods of an entity object, created by the enterprise bean provider while implementing the EntityBean interface, can be accessed by a client that is local to the EJB container. The EJBLocalObject interface defines methods that allow the local client to

- Obtain the local home interface for the entity object.
- Remove the entity object.
- Obtain the entity object's primary key.

Local interfaces can be used as a replacement for JDBC—supporting fast calls to a database while the client runs inside the same JVM as the entity bean.

CERTIFICATION OBJECTIVE 7.05

State the Benefits and Costs of Container-Managed Persistence

One of the evolving aspects of the entity bean is its *persistence*. Before this persistence can be meaningful, you need to understand the details of developing entity beans. Here you will learn about the uses of entity beans, the entity bean lifecycle states, and the steps involved in developing entity beans. You will take a close look at developing entity beans and review how to manage persistence. You'll also learn the benefits and drawbacks of both CMP and BMP.

Managing Persistence

Bean persistence can be managed in two ways: You can let the container manage the persistence of the bean via container-managed persistence (CMP), or you can use bean-managed persistence (BMP). This method requires that the developer implement the interaction code between the EJB and the persistence engine. This is a much more complicated task than opting for the first option. This mode should not be seen as a standard development model, but more as a means to get to and implement the lower level persistence mechanism. In other words, *use BMP only when the limits of CMP have been exceeded.* It is not realistic to consider using this far more complicated model for every EJB that you need to build. The CMP model should be considered as the general persistence model for most of an application's development.

When the container handles the overhead necessary to support a bean in a manner that is satisfactory to the enterprise bean provider, it stands to reason that more of the enterprise bean provider's development efforts can be focused on actually writing business logic.

Container-Managed Persistence

In CMP, entity bean data is maintained automatically by the container that uses the mechanism of its choosing. For example, a container implemented on top of a RDBMS may manage persistence by storing each bean's data as a row in a table.

The container may also use the Java programming language serialization functionality for persistence. When a programmer chooses to utilize CMP beans, the programmer specifies which fields are to be retained.

A persistence manager is used to separate the management of bean relationships from the container. With this separation, a container has the responsibility for managing security, transactions, and so on, while the persistence manager is able to manage different databases via different containers. Using this architecture allows entity beans to become more portable across EJB vendors.

Entity beans are mapped to the database using a bean-persistence manager contract called the *abstract persistence schema*. The persistence manager is responsible for implementing and executing find methods based on EJB QL.

The persistence manager generates a mapping of CMP objects to a persistent data store's objects based on the information provided by the deployment descriptor, the bean's abstract persistence schema, and settings set by the deployer. Persistent data stores may include relational databases, flat files, Enterprise Resource Planning (ERP) systems, and so on.

A contract between the CMP entity bean and the persistence manager allows for defining complex and portable bean-to-bean, bean-to-dependent, and even dependent-to-dependent object relationships within an entity bean. For the persistence manager to be separated from the container, a contract between the bean and the persistence manager is defined.

When EJB is deployed, the persistence manager is used to generate an instantiated implementation of the EJB class and its dependent object classes. It does this based on its XML deployment descriptor and the bean class. The instantiated implementation will include the data access code that will read and write the state of the EJB to the database at runtime. When this happens, the container uses the subclasses generated by the persistence manager instead of the EJBs abstract classes defined by the bean provider. The persistence manager of the EJB container is also used to manage the persistence of the bean state or data. As previously mentioned, the enterprise bean provider in this scenario is able to concentrate on implementing business logic with Java code. A bean using CMP is simpler than one that uses BMP; however, it is also dependent on a container for database access.

Using CMP, the EJB container is responsible for saving the bean's state. Because the persistence process is container managed, the Java code used to retrieve and store data is independent of the data source. On the other hand, the container-managed fields do need to be specified in the deployment descriptor file so the EJB container's persistence manager can automatically handle the persistence process.

Some benefits and drawbacks of CMP are detailed next.

CMP Pros   Benefits of container-managed persistence include the following:

- **Database-independence**   The container, not the enterprise bean provider, maintains database access code to most popular databases.

- **Container-specific features**   Features such as full text search are available for use by the enterprise bean provider.

CMP Cons   Drawbacks to container-managed persistence include the following:

- **Algorithms**   Only container-supported algorithms persistence can be used.

- **Portability**   Portability to other EJB containers may be lost.

- **Access**   The developer has no access to the view and cannot modify the actual code.

- **Efficiency**   Sometimes the generated SQL is not the most efficient with respect to performance.

Bean-Managed Persistence

When using BMP, the bean is responsible for storing and retrieving persisted data. The entity bean interface provides methods for the container to notify an instance when it needs to store or retrieve data.

In BMP mode, the EJB must implement persistence. To do this, methods such as `ejbStore` and `ejbLoad` must be created and used, and communication with SQL databases must be implemented manually using JDBC.

BMP works well when data is being persisted to something other than a relational database, such as file system or a legacy enterprise application. When a bean manages its own persistence, it must also define its own JDBC calls. In this case, the entity bean is directly responsible for saving its own state. On the other hand, the container isn't required to make any database calls. Some benefits and drawbacks of BMP are detailed next.

BMP Pros   Benefits of bean-managed persistence include the following:

- **Container independent**   Entity bean code written for one EJB container should be easily portable to any other certified EJB container.

- **Standards based** The standard EJB and JDBC APIs can be used for data access calls.

- **Datatype access** The ability to access nonstandard datatypes and legacy applications is supported.

- **Maximum flexibility** Data validation logic of any complexity is supported.

- **Database specific features** The application is able to take advantage of nonstandard SQL features of different SQL servers.

BMP Cons Drawbacks to bean-managed persistence include the following:

- **Database specific** Because entity bean code is database specific, if access to multiple databases is required, the enterprise bean provider will have to account for this in its data access methods.

- **Knowledge of SQL** The enterprise bean provider must have knowledge of SQL.

- **Development time** These beans on average take much longer time to develop—as much as five times longer.

The Composition of a CMP Entity Bean

The many components of EJB entity beans must interact with each other and with their container. The following is a summary of the *javax.ejb* package entity bean components and the methods they use. The enterprise bean provider creates some of these components. The EJB container, building on what the enterprise bean provider created, generates the remainder of the required components.

Components Created by the Enterprise Bean Provider The enterprise bean provider is responsible for the creation of classes and interfaces. Business logic is placed in classes. Interfaces are used to define how the EJB container should build supporting objects as well as to define what business methods are to be visible to clients. The following sections describe varieties of these components in further detail.

The Primary Key Class The *primary key* is a unique identifier of an object. The primary key class doesn't necessarily have to relate directly to the primary key of a database table. Quite often, it isn't necessary to create a primary key class because you can use Java objects already defined in the entity bean class (for example, *strings* or *integers*) as primary keys. Note that Java's primitive datatypes (such as *int*) can be used only when wrapped by Java objects. A primary key class is defined within the deployment descriptor file. Although an entity bean class can define a unique class as its primary key, it is still possible for several entity beans to share the same primary key class.

The Remote Home Interface—Interface EJBHome   The enterprise bean provider creates the remote home interface so that the EJB container can create an EJBHome object. The EJBHome object can be used to create, destroy, and find entity bean objects inside a home domain. When the EJB container implements the remote home interface, it enables clients to

- Create new entity objects within a home domain
- Find existing entity objects within a home domain
- Remove an entity object from a home domain
- Execute a home instance business method
- Obtain a handle to the home interface
- Get metadata information allowing for loose client-server binding and scripting

Zero or more `create()` methods, with the prefix name *create*, can be defined in the EJBHome Interface. Each entity object should have one or more `create()` methods. Each method's argument should be used to initialize the state of the entity object.

One `finder()` method should be defined for each different way of finding an entity object or a collection of entity objects within a home domain. The name of a `finder()` method should begin with the prefix *find*. The arguments of the method are used to locate desired entity objects. The return type must be either the entity bean's remote interface or a type that is a collection of objects implementing the entity bean's remote interface.

`remove()` methods can also be defined to remove entity objects that are qualified by either a handle or a primary key. `home()` methods are static methods provided by the enterprise bean provider for global business logic that isn't specific to any bean instance. `home()` methods can have any name that doesn't begin with *create*, *find*, or *remove*.

The Home Handle—Interface HomeHandle   A client can use the home handle after it loses the JNDI name of a remote home interface. If a home handle is returned as the result of a `getEJBHome()` method, the client will be required to narrow the results to get the remote home interface.

The Handle—Interface Handle   The handle object created according to this interface is an abstraction on top of a network reference to an EJB object. It can be used as a persistent reference to that object.

The Remote Interface—Interface EJBObject   An entity bean's remote interface is used to define which methods in the abstract entity bean class will be visible to the client, the so-called *business methods*. In addition, other required methods of the remote interface allow the client to

- Obtain the handle of an entity object
- Obtain the home interface of an entity object
- Remove an entity object

The Local Home Interface—Interface EJBLocalHome   The local home interface is similar to the remote home interface; however, it is faster because the local objects and the clients that call them are inside the same EJB container. As a result, these local objects don't need to support the overhead associated with distributed applications.

The Local Interface—Interface EJBLocalObject   Local interfaces are similar to the remote interface, having the benefit of speed like that of the local home interface when the bean and the client are executing within the same JVM instance.

The Remote Client   A remote client accesses an entity bean via methods defined in both the remote interface and remote home interface of the entity bean. The EJB container provides remote Java objects that implement those interfaces. These objects are accessible from a client through the standard Java APIs for remote object invocation. A remote client of an entity object can be another enterprise bean deployed in either the same or in a different container. A client can also be an arbitrary Java program, such as an application, applet, or servlet. In addition, the remote client view of an entity bean can be mapped to non-Java client environments such as CORBA.

The Local Client   A local client resides in the same JVM and EJB container as the entity bean it uses. In the interest of speed, a local client should access an entity bean through that entity bean's local and local home interfaces. Processing speed is gained because arguments of the methods of the local interface and local home interface are passed by reference instead of by value.

The EntityContext   The EJB container provides entity bean instances with an EntityContext. This EntityContext gives an instance access to the references of any objects associated with the instance, including EJBLocalObjects, EJBObjects, and primary key objects. This access is provided by the `getEJBLocalObject()`, `getEJBObject()`, and `getPrimaryKey()` methods, respectively.

The instance is also given access to information returned by the following methods, which are inherited from the EJBContext object:

- **getEJBHome()**   Returns the remote home interface of the entity bean.
- **getEJBLocalHome()**   Returns the local home interface of the entity bean.
- **getCallerPrincipal()**   Returns the *java.security.Principal*, identifying the invoker of the bean instance's EJB object.
- **isCallerInRole()**   Tests whether the caller of the entity bean instance has a particular role.
- **setRollbackOnly()**   Marks the current transaction so that a rollback is the only outcome of that transaction.
- **getRollbackOnly()**   Tests to see whether the current transaction of an instance has been marked for rollback.
- **getUserTransaction()**   Entity bean instances must not call this method, which returns the *javax.transaction.UserTransaction* interface.

The XML Deployment Descriptor   The *deployment descriptor* is used to declare entity bean persistent fields (cmp-fields) as well as field relationships (cmr-fields). It contains information about entity bean persistence and container-managed relationships in the form of XML elements. This information, known as the *abstract persistence schema*, includes the following:

- The ejb-name for each entity bean, which must be unique within an ejb-jar file.

- The abstract-schema-name for each entity bean, which must be unique within an ejb-jar file. This name can be used when specifying EJB QL queries.

- The ejb-relation set, containing a pair of ejb-relationship-role elements.

- The ejb-relationship-role, which describes a relationship role including its name, its multiplicity within a relation, and its navigability. The name of the cmr-field is specified from the perspective of the relationship participant. Each relationship role refers to an entity bean via an ejb-name element contained in the relationship-role-source element.

Container-Created Objects

After all the required interfaces and abstract classes are designed and developed by the enterprise bean provider, they are introspected by EJB container. It examines the entity bean's deployment descriptor to create concrete objects that have the additional functionality required to integrate the business logic with the requirements of the EJB distributed object framework. These classes include the following:

- **Bean class**   Extends the abstract entity bean class, which implements the EntityBean interface.

- **EJBHome class**   Implements the remote home interface EJBHome. The EJB container makes these instances accessible to the clients through JNDI.

- **EJBObject class**   Implements the remote interface EJBObject.

- **EJBLocalHome class**   Implements the local home interface EJBLocalHome.

- **EJBLocalObject class**   Implements the local interface EJBLocalObject.

Figure 7-8 illustrates EJB objects provided by beans and containers. Entity bean objects are considered to be *persistent objects*; their lifetime isn't limited by the lifetime of the JVM process in which the entity bean instance executes. To illustrate, a JVM crash might result in a rollback of a transaction, but it will neither destroy previously created entity objects nor invalidate references interfaces held by clients.

FIGURE 7-8

EJB objects
provided by
enterprise bean
provider and
EJB container

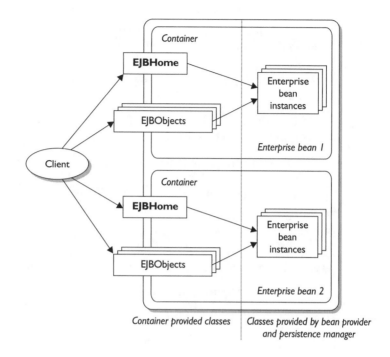

EJB Clients

Two types of EJB clients exist: *remote* clients that exist outside of an EJB container
and *local* clients that exist inside of an EJB container.

Multiple clients can access an entity object simultaneously while the EJB container
synchronizes access to the entity objects via a *transaction manager*.

EJB containers make home interfaces available in a JNDI name space, therefore
making these home interfaces available to clients. The home interfaces of entity beans
allow clients to create, find, and remove entity objects within the enterprise bean's
home domain. These interfaces also allow clients to execute static home business
methods that aren't specific to a particular entity bean object.

Remote Clients

Remote clients can be enterprise beans deployed in the same or different EJB
containers, stand-alone Java applications or applets via Java APIs for remote object
invocation, or non-Java clients such as CORBA clients.

A remote client can get a reference to an existing entity object's remote interface in any of the following ways:

■ Receive the reference as a parameter in a method call as an input parameter or a result.

■ Find the entity object using a `finder()` method defined in the entity bean's remote home interface.

■ Obtain the reference from the entity object's handle.

A client that has a reference to an entity object's remote interface can do the following:

■ Invoke business methods on the entity object through the remote interface.

■ Obtain a reference to the enterprise bean's remote home interface.

■ Pass the reference as a parameter or return value of a method call.

■ Obtain the entity object's primary key.

■ Obtain the entity object's handle.

■ Remove the entity object.

The physical location of the EJB container is usually transparent to the client. A client locates an entity bean's home interface by using the JNDI, which enables applications to access multiple naming and directory services using a single interface. A client's JNDI name space can be configured to contain the home interfaces of enterprise beans located on multiple EJB containers on multiple machines on a network.

A client that is to be interoperable with compliant EJB containers must use the `javax.rmi.PortableRemoteObject.narrow()` method to perform type-narrowing of the client-side representations of the remote home and remote interfaces.

The remote home interface *ItemRemoteHome* for the *ItemMasterBean* entity bean can be located using the following code segment:

```
Context  initialContext = new InitialContext();
ItemRemoteHome itemHome = (ItemRemoteHome)
 javax.rmi.PortableRemoteObject.narrow(
initialContext.lookup("java:ucny/um2z8/items"), ItemRemoteHome.class);
```

Locating an entity bean's local home interface using JNDI is accomplished in a similar manner. It doesn't, however, involve the APIs for remote access. For example, if the *Item* entity bean provided a local home interface rather than a remote home interface, a local client might use the following code segment:

```
Context initialContext  = new InitialContext();
ItemLocalHome itemHome = (ItemLocalHome)
initialContext.lookup("java:ucny/um2z8/items");
```

Local Clients

Local clients access entity beans through local and local home interfaces with the arguments of the local and local home methods being passed by reference. The enterprise bean provider should be aware that argument objects shared between local clients and entity beans can be modified by either the local clients or the entity beans.

A local client can get a reference to an existing entity object's local interface in either of the following ways:

- Receive the reference as a result of a method call.

- Find the entity object using a `finder()` method defined in the entity bean's local home interface.

A local client that has a reference to an entity object's local interface can invoke business methods on the entity object through the local interface.

CERTIFICATION OBJECTIVE 7.06

State the Transactional Behavior in a Given Scenario for an Enterprise Bean Method with a Specified Transactional Attributed as Defined in the Deployment Descriptor

In this section, we review transactions, transaction management, and distributed transactions. Then we discuss the objective concerning transaction attribute settings as well as multiple transactions, the Java Transaction Service (JTS), the Java Transaction API (JTA), and the effect of the transaction attribute on entity and session bean methods.

Transactions and Transaction Management

A *transaction* is one or more tasks that execute as a single atomic operation or unit of work. If all tasks involved in a transaction do not proceed successfully, an inverse task or rollback procedure for all tasks is performed, setting all resources back to their original state. Transactions are characterized by the acronym *ACID*, which stands for Atomic, Consistent, Isolated, and Durable.

The EJB container provides the services and management functions required to support transaction demarcation, transactional resource management, synchronization, and transaction context propagation.

Since JDBC operates at the level of an individual database connection, it does not support transactions that span across multiple data sources. To compensate for this, the JTA provides access to the services offered by a transaction manager. If an EJB requires control of global transaction, it can get access to JTA via the container.

Distributed Transactions

Although the EJB framework can be used to implement a nontransactional system, the model was designed to support distributed transactions. EJB framework requires the use of a distributed transaction management system that supports two-phase commit protocols for flat transactions.

In addition to container-managed transactions, an EJB may participate in client-managed and bean-managed transactions.

The EJB architecture provides automatic support for distributed transactions in component-based applications. Such distributed transactions can automatically update data in multiple databases or even data distributed across multiple sites. The EJB model shifts the complexities of managing these transactions from the application developer to the container provider.

Transaction-Management Paradigms   The J2EE platform supports two transaction-management paradigms: *declarative transaction demarcation* and *programmatic transaction demarcation*.

Declarative transaction management refers to a nonprogrammatic demarcation of transaction boundaries, achieved by specifying within the deployment descriptor the transaction attributes for the various methods of the container-managed EJB component. This is a flexible approach that facilitates changes in the application's transactional characteristics without modifying any code. Container-managed transaction demarcation must be used by entity EJB components.

Transaction Attribute Settings

A transaction attribute supports declarative transaction demarcation and conveys to the container the intended transactional behavior of the associated EJB component's method. Six transaction attributes are possible for container-managed transaction demarcation:

- **NotSupported**   The bean runs outside the context of a transaction. Existing transactions are suspended during method calls. The bean cannot be invoked within a transaction. An existing transaction is suspended until the method called in this bean completes.

- **Required**   Method calls require a transaction context. If a transaction already exists, the bean will use it; if a transaction does not exist, it will be created. The container starts a new transaction if no transaction exists.

- **Supports**   Method calls use the current transaction context if one exists but they don't create one if none exists. The container will not start a new transaction. If a transaction already exists, the bean will be included in that transaction. Note that with this attribute, the bean can run without a transaction.

- **RequiresNew**   Containers create new transactions before each method call on the bean and commit transactions before returning. A new transaction is always started when the bean method is called. If a transaction already exists, that transaction is suspended until the new transaction completes.

- **Mandatory**   Method calls require a transaction context. If one does not exist, an exception is thrown. An active transaction must already exist. If no transaction exists, the *javax.ejb.TransactionRequired* exception is thrown.

- **Never**   Method calls require that no transaction context be present. If one exists, an exception is thrown. The bean must never run with a transaction. If a transaction exists, the *java.rmi.RemoteException* exception is thrown.

Multiple Transactions

A container can manage multiple transactions in two different ways: The container could instantiate multiple instances of the bean, allowing the transaction management of the DBMS to handle any transaction processing issues. Conversely, the container could acquire an exclusive lock on the instance's state in the database, serializing access from multiple transactions to this instance.

Java Transaction Service

The JTS specifies the implementation of a transaction manager supporting the JTA. JTS also implements the Java mapping of the Object Management Group's (OMG) Object Transaction Service (OTS). The EJB specification suggests but does not require transactions based on the JTS API. JTS supports distributed transactions, which have the ability to span multiple databases on multiple systems coordinated by multiple transaction managers. By using JTS, an EJB container ensures that its transactions can span multiple EJB containers.

Java Transaction API

EJB applications communicate with a transaction service using the JTA, which provides a programming interface to start transactions, join existing transactions, commit transactions, and roll back transactions.

When a bean with bean-managed transactions is invoked, the container suspends any current transaction in the client's context. In its method implementation, the bean will initiate the transaction through the JTA *UserTransaction* interface. In stateful beans, the container will associate the bean instance with the same transaction context across subsequent method calls until the transaction is explicitly completed by the bean. However, stateless beans aren't allowed to maintain transaction context across method calls. Each method invocation is required to complete any transaction it initiates.

Entity Bean Methods and Transaction Attributes

All developer-defined methods in the remote interface as well as all methods defined in the home interface (such as `create()`, `remove()`, and `finder()` methods) require transaction attributes. Note that entity beans have to use Container Managed Transactions (CMTs).

Session Bean Methods and Transaction Attributes

All developer-defined methods in the remote interface require transaction attributes. Transaction attributes are *not* needed for the methods in the home interface.

Methods in the remote interface run with the *NotSupported* attribute by default. Transaction attributes are also not needed for the methods in a session bean if you're using Bean Managed Transactions (BMTs).

CERTIFICATION OBJECTIVE 7.07

Given a Requirement Specification Detailing Security and Flexibility Needs, Identify Architectures that Would Fulfill Those Requirements

Here we provide a basic review of security and the EJB framework as an architecture, including containers and their functionality.

Security

To simplify the development process for the enterprise bean provider, the implementation of the security infrastructure is left to the EJB container provider and the task of defining security policies is left to the bean deployer. By avoiding putting hard-coded security policies inside bean code, EJB applications gain flexibility when configuring and reconfiguring security policies for complex enterprise applications. Applications also gain portability across different EJB servers that may use different security mechanisms.

The EJB framework specifies flexibility with regard to security management, allowing it to be declarative (container-managed) or programmatic (bean-managed).

Container-Managed or Declarative Security

The security management that defines method permissions is usually declared in the enterprise bean's deployment descriptor. Container-managed security makes an enterprise bean more flexible, since it isn't tied to the security roles defined by a particular application.

A *security role* is a name given to a grouping of information resource access permissions that are defined for an application. Associating a principal with this security role grants the associated access permissions to that principal as long as the principal is "in" the role.

Here is an excerpt from a deployment descriptor (*ejb-jar.xml*) for an entity bean that is using container-managed security:

```
<assembly-descriptor>
...
  <security-role>
    <role-name>adm_role</role-name>
  </security-role>
  <method-permission>
    <description>only remote access</description>
    <role-name>adm_role</role-name>
    <method>
      <ejb-name>EntityBMP</ejb-name>
      <method-intf>Remote</method-intf>
      <method-name>withdraw</method-name>
    </method>
  </method-permission>
...
</assembly-descriptor>
```

The <method-permission> element identifies the only security role that is allowed to invoke the withdraw method on the remote interface. The <method-permission> element consists of an optional description, a list of security role names, and a list of method elements. The <security-role> element contains the definition of a security role used by the bean. The security roles used in the <method-permission> element must be defined in the <security-role> elements of the deployment descriptor, and the methods must be defined in the enterprise bean's interfaces.

You should also note that errors in bean code programming are less likely to be a factor in causing security holes when using container-managed security, because the container implements the security mechanism. These features make container-managed method access the preferred security method.

Bean-Managed or Procedural Security

However, programmatic (procedural) access control is sometimes necessary
to satisfy fine-grained or application-specific conditions. Enterprise beans can
programmatically manage their own security by using the `isCallerInRole()`
and `getCallerPrincipal()` methods contained on the EJB's context object.
The `isCallerInRole()` method tests whether the caller has a given security
role, returning true if the caller has and false if not. The `getCallerPrincipal()`
method returns the *java.security.Principal* that identifies the caller.

Here is an excerpt of code from a EJB that uses these methods in a bean-managed
security situation:

```
...
  public void deposit(double amt) {
    if (amt >= 10000) {
      if (entityContext.isCallerInRole("admin")) {
        this.balance += amt;
      } else {
        log("REJECTED deposit(" + amt + ") by user "
          +entityContext.getCallerPrincipal().getName());
        throw new EJBException(
          "You do not have permission to deposit $10,000 or more");
      }
    } else {
      this.balance += amt;
    }
    log("deposit(" + amt + ") by user "
      +entityContext.getCallerPrincipal().getName()
      +" balance="+this.balance);
  }
...
```

The `deposit()` method above uses the `isCallerInRole()` method to
determine whether the caller depositing more than $10,000 is in the "admin" role.
If the caller is in this role, the operation is accepted and the balance is updated. If
the caller is not in the "admin" role, the operation is rejected and an exception
is thrown.

The enterprise bean developer is responsible for defining all the security role
names that are used in the bean code. Each of these role names must be added to
the deployment descriptor in the form of a `<security-role-ref>` element.
Part of this element is the `<role-link>` element that associates the role name
to a security role defined elsewhere in the descriptor file.

Security roles are defined with the element `<role-name>`. The following deployment descriptor fragment defines a role name *admin*, which is associated via a `<role-link>` element to role *adm_role*.

```
....
<enterprise-beans>
    ...
    <entity>
        <ejb-name>EntityBMP</ejb-name>
        <ejb-class>EntityBMPBean.class</ejb-class>
        ...
        <security-role-ref>
            <role-name>admin</role-name>
            <role-link>adm_role</role-link>
        </security-role-ref>
        ...
    </entity>
</enterprise-beans>
    .....
```

In this EJB deployment descriptor, the *EntityBMPBean* class uses the symbolic name *admin* to check permissions. In the assembly descriptor section of the deployment descriptor, the security role *adm_role* is defined as follows:

```
....
<assembly-descriptor>
    <security-role>
        <role-name>adm_role</role-name>
    </security-role>
</assembly-descriptor>
....
```

For completeness, here is an excerpt from the WebLogic deployment descriptor *<weblogic-ejb-jar.xml>* file that resolves the role to an actual principal:

```
<weblogic-ejb-jar>
....
  <security-role-assignment>
    <role-name>adm_role</role-name>
    <principal-name>system</principal-name>
  </security-role-assignment>
....
</weblogic-ejb-jar>
```

This use of the deployment descriptor to define a role name and associating it with a role link allows different enterprise beans to use different internal names to refer to the same cluster of permissions. For example, another bean can still refer to the *adm_role* internally using the string *adm* instead of *admin*. A `<security-role-ref>` is able to associate that bean's *adm* reference to the security role *adm_role*.

You should also note that a user or principal is allowed to belong to multiple roles simultaneously. In doing so, the user/principal will benefit from the union set of permissions that those roles grant.

Security Not Covered by the EJB Specification

As opposed to access control, authentication and communication security are not specified in the EJB security guidelines. These aspects of security are left to the proprietary application server or the container.

EJB Framework

The EJB components are declaratively customized. Customizable traits include transactional behavior, security features, lifecycle, state management, and persistence. Figure 7-9 demonstrates how the home interface, remote interface, EJBHome object, and EJBObject of the EJB framework fit into the generic distributed programming model.

Containers

The application server provides a container that supports services for components. A container is an entity that provides lifecycle management, security, deployment, and runtime services to components. Each container type (including EJB, web, JSP, servlet, applet, and application client) provides component-specific services as well.

FIGURE 7-9

Distributed programming with EJB

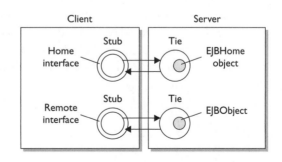

After a client invokes a server component, the container will automatically allocate a process thread and initiate the component. The container manages all resources on behalf of the component and interactions between the component and the external systems. A container provides EJB components with services such as the following:

- **Bean lifecycle management and instance pooling**   These services include creation, activation, passivity, and destruction. Individual EJBs do not need to explicitly manage process allocation, thread management, object activation, or object destruction. The EJB container automatically manages the object lifecycle on behalf of the EJB.

- **State management**   Individual EJBs do not need to explicitly save or restore the conversational object state between method calls. The EJB container automatically manages the object state on behalf of the EJB.

- **Bean transaction management**   This service intercedes between client calls on the remote interface and the corresponding methods in a bean to enforce transaction and security constraints. It can provide notification at both the beginning and the ending of each transaction that involves a bean instance. Individual EJBs do not need to explicitly specify the transaction demarcation code to participate in distributed transactions. The EJB container can automatically manage the start, enrollment, commitment, and rollback of transactions on behalf of the EJB.

- **Security constraint enforcement**   EJBs do not need to explicitly authenticate users or check authorization levels. The EJB container automatically performs all security checking on behalf of the EJB.

- **Distributed remote access**   EJBs use technologies and protocols that are commonly used in distributed programming, such as RMI and IIOP.

- **Container-managed persistence**   EJBs do not need to explicitly retrieve or store persistent object data from a database. The EJB container can automatically manage persistent data on behalf of the EJB. Entity beans can either manage their own persistence or delegate those persistence services to their container. If persistence is delegated to the container, that container will also perform all data retrieval and storage operations automatically on behalf of the bean.

(Note that the majority of the changes made between EJB 1.1 and EJB 2.0 are found in the definition of a new CMP component model. The new CMP model is extremely different from the previous CMP model because it introduces an entirely new entity, the persistence manager, and a completely new way of defining container-managed fields, as well as relationships with other beans and dependent objects.)

■   **Generated remote stubs**   The container will create remote stubs for wrappers such as RMI and CORBA.

Additional Functionality   The EJB server provides an environment that supports the execution of applications developed using EJB architecture, managing and coordinating allocation of resources to the applications. The EJB server must provide one or more EJB containers, which provide homes for the EJBs. EJB containers manage the EJBs contained within them. For each EJB, the container is responsible for registering the object, providing a remote interface for the object, creating and destroying object instances, checking security for the object, managing the active state for the object, and coordinating distributed transactions. In addition, the container has the ability to manage all persistent data within the object.

Vendor-Specific Containers   The exact environment for process and resource management, concurrency control, and thread pooling has not been defined in the EJB specification. So vendors can differentiate their products based on the simplicity or sophistication of the services provided by proprietary containers. A software vendor may choose to create a new application server to support EJB components specifically, or what is more likely, to adapt their existing servers.

Container Location   Several EJB classes can be installed in a single EJB container. The physical implementation of an EJB container is not described in the EJB specification, so even though a particular class of EJB is assigned to a single EJB container, the container may not necessarily represent a physical location. The EJB container can be implemented as a physical unit, such as a single multithreaded process within a server, or it can be implemented as a logical unit that can be replicated and distributed across multiple systems and processes.

Benefits of J2EE and the EJB Framework as an Architecture

The use of the J2EE and EJB framework as an architecture has the following primary benefits:

- EJB components are *server-side components* written entirely with the Java programming language; therefore, applications based on EJB components are not only platform independent but also middleware independent. They can run on any operating system and on any middleware that supports EJB.

- EJB components contain *business logic* only, giving developers freedom from maintaining system-level code that would be integrated with their business logic. The EJB server automatically manages system-level services such as transactions, security, lifecycle, threading, and persistence for the EJB component.

- EJB architecture is inherently *transactional, distributed, portable, multi-tiered, scalable,* and *secure.*

- J2EE architecture provides *authentication,* the means by which communicating entities prove to one another that they are acting on behalf of specific identities (for example, client to server and/or server to client).

- J2EE architecture provides *authorization* (access control), the means by which interactions with resources are limited to collections of users or programs for the purpose of enforcing integrity, confidentiality, or availability constraints.

- J2EE architecture provides *data integrity* (MAC, or message authentication check), which is the means used to prove that information could not have been modified by a third party (for example, the recipient of data must be able to detect and discard messages that were modified after they were originally sent over an open network).

- J2EE architecture provides *confidentiality* (data privacy), the means used to ensure that information is made available only to users who are authorized to access it.

- J2EE architecture provides *non-repudiation,* the means used to prove that a user performed some action such that the user cannot reasonably deny having done so.

- J2EE architecture provides *auditing,* the means used to capture a tamper-resistant record of security related events for the purpose of evaluating the effectiveness of security policies and mechanisms.

CERTIFICATION OBJECTIVE 7.08

Identify Costs and Benefits of Using an Intermediate Data Access Object Between an Entity Bean and the Data Resource

Here we review data access objects for entity beans. This is covered in greater detail in Chapter 5.

Using Data Access Objects for Entity Beans

Sometimes if you decide that BMP is your best approach for entity beans, you must code the SQL into your entity beans. In a large development environment, it is sometimes a good idea to reduce the coupling of entity beans with the SQL necessary to select, insert, update, and delete data using EJB. To achieve reusability, developers create intermediate data access objects that contain implementation code to update and access the data source. The downside to the ease of reuse using a data access object is the additional layer and overhead of creation and garbage collection. Data access objects are typically developed in situations in which the developer is familiar with SQL and performance gains can be achieved over CMP, which sometimes does not provide the best performing SQL.

Why Use a Data Access Object?

The data access object (DAO) pattern separates the interface to a system resource from the underlying code used to access that resource. This allows the benefit of database vendor independence and the ability to represent XML data sources as objects.

Each enterprise bean that accesses a persistent data resource can have an associated DAO class, which defines an abstract API of operations on the resource. This abstract API will make no reference to the resource implementation. The DAO needs to know only how to load itself from a persistent store based on some identity information (such as a primary key) and how to store itself back to the persistent store. Therefore, an enterprise bean uses data it obtains from the DAO, defers the persistence responsibilities to the DAO, and can concentrate entirely on implementing business methods.

A DAO provides resource functionality for a particular resource, implemented for a particular persistence mechanism. For example, a class can be created to encapsulate the database resource access for both single as well as multiple rows. The benefits are independence achieved at a small cost (the development required to build the DAO) that ultimately may save development time.

For CMP entity beans, the EJB container automatically services all persistent storage access; therefore, applications using CMP entity beans do not need a DAO layer, since the application server transparently provides this functionality. However, DAOs may still be useful when an application has a combination of CMP for entity beans and BMP for session beans and/or servlets.

DAOs add a layer of objects between the data client and the data source that requires extra effort to be designed and implemented. However, the benefit realized by choosing this approach makes up for the added effort.

When a factory strategy is used, the hierarchy of concrete factories and concrete products produced by the factories requires additional design and implementation.

CERTIFICATION OBJECTIVE 7.09

State the Benefits of Bean Pooling in an EJB Container

Here we review the concept of pooling resources. We explain how the EJB container uses this concept for EJBs.

Bean Pooling in the EJB Container

Given that the EJB container cannot handle an unlimited number of EJBs, the classic concept of *pooling* is used to share the resources among multiple users. When the EJB is deployed, the deployment descriptor specifies the number of instances to pool and reuse. The cost of creating and destroying an EJBObject can be expensive. The application server manages a pool of EJBs that can be used throughout the application. This pool allows the application server to handle more requests since the server does not have to spend time creating and destroying EJBObjects. Note that stateful session beans cannot be a part of this bean pool.

Benefits of Bean Pooling in an EJB Container

Bean pooling is similar to *connection pooling*, a technique that was pioneered by the DBMS vendors to allow multiple clients to share a cached set of connections that provide access to a database resource.

Bean pooling is used in J2EE for stateless session beans. To implement bean pooling, the application server, as part of a startup process, must create a pool manager object to control access to the stateless session beans. The client asks the pool manager to allocate a bean. If a bean is available in the pool, it is made available to the client immediately; otherwise, a bean is created. When a client no longer needs the bean, it returns the bean to the pool manager for reuse. This strategy allows beans to be quickly allocated to clients, avoiding the expense of setup and initialization.

CERTIFICATION OBJECTIVE 7.10

Explain How the Enterprise JavaBeans Container Does Lifecycle Management and Has the Capability to Increase Scalability

Here we review the lifecycle of EJBs. We also describe their deployment, which is determined by the deployment descriptors settings.

The Lifecycle of an EJB

Detailed documentation describing the lifecycle of an EJB can be found in the EJB specifications on the Sun web site and is illustrated in Figure 7-10. The following list provides a general description of the lifecycle states of an EJB session bean:

1. The client locates the bean's home reference using the JNDI services provided by the application server.

2. The JNDI service returns a home interface reference to the client.

3. The client uses the home interface reference to call the `home.create()` method. In response, the home object then creates an EJBObject. A new instance of the code in the bean class is also instantiated by the `newInstance()` method.

FIGURE 7-10   Lifecycle for an EJB session bean

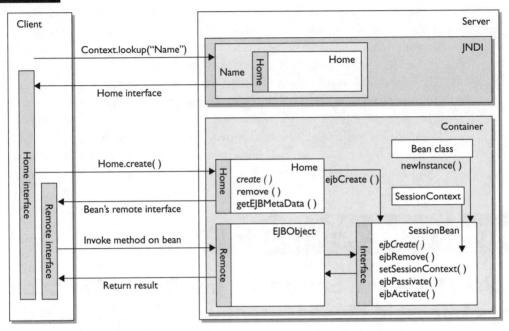

4. The new instance of the bean class, called a session bean, is allocated a session context.

5. The home object passes a reference to the EJBObject in the container to the client's remote interface.

6. The client's remote interface is now able to invoke methods on the EJBObject in the container. This EJBObject will pass these method calls to the session bean.

7. The session bean returns a result to the EJBObject, which in turn returns it to the client's remote interface.

How the EJB Container Manages Lifecycle and How This Allows for Increased Scalability

Here are the steps that the container takes to manage the lifecycle of an entity bean:

1. The container populates the free pool with a working set of bean instances.

2. A client calls the `create()` method on a home object.

3. The home object obtains a bean instance from the free pool.

4. The home object forwards the `create()` arguments (if any) to the `ejbCreate()` method on the bean class.

5. The bean class inserts a row into the table in the database.

6. The bean class returns the primary key of the row to the home object.

7. The container creates an EJB object for the bean class and sets its primary key.

8. The home object invokes the `ejbPostCreate()` method on the bean class to finish the initialization process now that the EJB object can be referenced, because it now exists.

9. The home object returns the remote reference to the EJB object back to the client.

10. The client can now invoke the business methods on the bean class (via the remote reference) that have been defined as available.

11. When the client is finished, the container moves the bean back to the free pool list after calling `ejbPassivate` (for an entity bean).

Note that a substantial overhead is incurred when instantiating bean instances. Scalability within the EJB container environment is increased by preinstantiating a pool of bean instances (bean pool) and allowing them to be quickly utilized by clients.

Deployment

When an EJB application is ready to be deployed to an EJB container, the desired beans and deployment information must be placed in a JAR file. The deployment information that is also placed in this JAR file is contained in an XML file called a *deployment descriptor*.

Deployment Descriptors As mentioned earlier, the deployment descriptor is an XML file containing elements that specify how to create and maintain EJB components and how to establish runtime service settings. The deployment descriptor contains settings that are not to be hard coded inside EJB components. These settings tell the EJB container how to manage and control EJB components and can be set at application assembly time or at application deployment time.

Two basic types of elements are contained inside the deployment descriptor file:

- **Bean elements**   These elements declare the internal structure and external dependencies of EJB components. The descriptor defines, among other things, the EJB class names, the JNDI namespace that represents the container, home interface names, and remote interface names.

- **Application assembly elements**   These elements describe how EJB components are to be integrated into larger applications. Some of the application assembly elements describe environment values, security roles, and transaction attributes.

Packaging Hierarchies   An important attribute of the EJB specification is that it not only provides the programming interfaces but also defines how the component/ application has to be packaged. The deployment descriptor that has to go into the packaging is the standard way of customizing parameters of a specific installation.

EJB components can be packaged as individual EJBs, as a collection of EJBs, or as a complete application system. EJB components are distributed in a JAR file called an *ejb-jar* file. The ejb-jar file contains Java class files, as well as home and remote interfaces for EJBs. It also contains the XML deployment descriptor for the EJB.

Home and Remote Interfaces   The client view is provided through the home interface and the remote interface. Classes constructed by the container when a bean is deployed, based on information provided by the bean, provide these interfaces. The home interface provides methods for creating a bean instance, while the remote interface provides the business logic methods for the component. By implementing these interfaces, the container can intercede in client operations of an EJB. This offers the client a simplified view of the component.

CERTIFICATION SUMMARY

If you have studied this chapter diligently, you should have an understanding of session and entity EJBs. You should also understand when it is appropriate to implement the different EJBs.

TWO-MINUTE DRILL

List the Required Classes/Interfaces That Must Be Provided for an Enterprise JavaBeans Component

❑ The required classes/interfaces that must be provided for an EJB component are the home (EJBHome) interface, the remote (EJBObject) interface, business logic (bean) class, context objects, and the XML deployment descriptor.

Distinguish Between Session and Entity Beans

❑ A *session bean* is an EJB that is created by a client and usually exists only for the duration of a single client-server session.

❑ An *entity bean* is an object representation of persistent data maintained in a permanent data store such as a database. A primary key identifies each instance of an entity bean.

Recognize Appropriate Uses for Entity, Stateful Session, and Stateless Session Beans

❑ Use *stateful* session beans for functionality that requires data to be maintained across business logic method invocations.

❑ Use *stateless* session beans for functionality that does not requires data to be maintained across business logic method invocations.

Distinguish Between Stateful and Stateless Session Beans

❑ Stateful session beans maintain data (state) across business logic method invocations.

❑ Stateless session beans do not maintain data (state) across business logic method invocations.

❑ Stateless session beans can utilize the bean-pooling feature of the EJB container.

State the Benefits and Costs of Container-Managed Persistence

❏ The benefits of CMP include database independence and container-specific features (such as full text search). CMP has drawbacks, as only container-supported algorithms persistence can be used, and portability to other EJB containers may be lost.

State the Transactional Behavior in a Given Scenario for an Enterprise Bean Method with a Specified Transactional Attributed as Defined in the Deployment Descriptor

The following transactional behaviors can be identified for an enterprise bean method:

❏ In NotSupported transactional behavior, existing transactions are suspended during method calls. An existing transaction is suspended until the method called in this bean completes.

❏ In Required transactional behavior, if an enterprise bean method already exists, it will be used. If one does not exist, it will be created.

❏ In Supports transactional behavior, the container will not start a new transaction, but if a transaction already exists, the bean will be included in that transaction.

❏ In RequiresNew transactional behavior, a new transaction is always started when the bean method is called. If a transaction already exists, that transaction is suspended until the new transaction completes.

❏ In Mandatory transactional behavior, if a transaction does not exist, an exception is thrown.

❏ In Never transactional behavior, if a transaction exists, an exception is thrown.

❏ To encapsulate access to data, an application can use intermediate data access objects.

❏ The benefits of bean pooling in an EJB container include lowered cost, specific rates of pool reuse, and increased request handling by the application server.

Identify Costs and Benefits of Using an Intermediate Data Access Object Between an Entity Bean and the Data Resource

To encapsulate access to data an application can use intermediate data access objects. The use of separate objects to access data results in the following:

- ❏ Keeps entity bean code clear and simple
- ❏ Ensures easier migration to container-managed persistence for entity beans
- ❏ Allows for cross-database and cross-schema portability
- ❏ Provides a mechanism that supports tools from different vendors
- ❏ Not useful for CMP entity beans
- ❏ Adds an extra layer
- ❏ Needs more class hierarchy design when using a factory strategy

State the Benefits of Bean Pooling in an EJB Container

- ❏ The cost of creating and destroying an EJBObject can be expensive, so the concept of pooling is used to share the resources among multiple users.
- ❏ The external deployment descriptor specifies the number of instances to pool and re-use.
- ❏ This pool allows the application server to handle more requests since the server does not have to spend time creating and destroy EJBObjects.

Explain How the Enterprise JavaBeans Container Does Lifecycle Management and Has the Capability to Increase Scalability

- ❏ In the EJB container's lifecycle management, while the container handles naming, management, transactional integrity, security, and persistence for the bean developer, the architect needs to determine the settings to tell the container how these concepts apply to a specific bean. This provides greater scalability.
- ❏ The mechanism for creating the deployment descriptors varies from application server to application server, but they all contain the same basic information.

SELF TEST

The following questions will help you measure your understanding of the material presented in this chapter. Read all the choices carefully because there might be more than one correct answer. Choose all correct answers for each question.

List the Required Classes/Interfaces That Must Be Provided for an Enterprise JavaBeans Component

1. Which of the following is not true about EJB objects?

   A. The home interface is responsible for locating or creating instances of the desired bean and returning remote references.

   B. The remote interface, or the EJBObject interface, typically provides method signatures for business methods.

   C. The bean implements either the EntityBean interface or the SessionBean interface but need not implement all the methods defined in the remote interface.

   D. The bean must implement one `ejbCreate()` method for each `create()` method in the home interface.

Distinguish Between Session and Entity Beans

2. Which statement is not true when contrasting the use of entity beans and JDBC for database operations?

   A. Entity beans represent real data in a database.

   B. The bean managed entity bean functionally replaces the JDBC API.

   C. The container-managed entity bean automatically retrieves the data from the persistent storage (database).

   D. When using JDBC, you must explicitly handle the database transaction and the database connection pooling.

Recognize Appropriate Uses for Entity, Stateful Session, and Stateless Session Beans

3. Suppose that the business logic of an existing application is implemented using a set of CGI programs. Which Java technologies can be used to implement the CGI programs as a Java-based solution?

    A. JMAPI

    B. Screen scrapers

    C. Enterprise JavaBeans

    D. Servlets

Distinguish Between Stateful and Stateless Session Beans

4. Which of the following is not true about EJB session bean objects?

    A. A session bean can be defined without an `ejbCreate()` method.

    B. Stateful beans can contain multiple `ejbCreate()` methods as long as they match the home interface definition.

    C. The home interface of a stateless session bean must include a single `create()` method without any arguments.

    D. The stateless session bean class must contain exactly one `ejbCreate()` method without any arguments.

State the Benefits and Costs of Container-Managed Persistence

5. If you try to create an entity bean (CMP)-based table that does not have a primary key, which of the following statements is not true?

    A. You cannot create CMP entity beans without a database primary key.

    B. Duplicate records may be entered in the table.

    C. You can create CMP entity beans without primary keys, but the `findByPrimaryKey()` method will be unreliable.

6. Can you update the primary key field in an entity bean (CMP)?

    A. No; you cannot update the primary key field in a CMP entity bean.

    B. Yes; you can update the primary key field in a CMP entity bean by using accessor methods for the primary key cmp-fields in the component interface of the entity bean.

    C. Yes; you can update the primary key field in a CMP entity bean by calling `ejbStore()`.

State the Transactional Behavior in a Given Scenario for an Enterprise Bean Method with a Specified Transactional Attributed as Defined in the Deployment Descriptor

7. In an application with several stateless session EJBs, in terms of performance ramifications of storing the remote reference to a stateless session bean, which of the following statements is *least* accurate?

    A. You can cache the stateless session bean reference using the `EJBObject.getHandle()`.

    B. You can use the handle (SSB reference) when attempting to access the bean from here on.

    C. The cost for a remote lookup on a stateless session bean is insignificant and generally does not justify using a handle (SSB reference) to access the bean.

    D. The stateless session bean has no concurrency problems—that is, there is no shared data to be corrupted.

Given a Requirement Specification Detailing Security and Flexibility Needs, Identify Architectures That Would Fulfill Those Requirements

8. Which distributed object technology is most appropriate for systems that consist entirely of Java objects?

    A. RMI

    B. CORBA

    C. DCOM

    D. DCE

9. Which distributed object technology is most appropriate for systems that consist of objects written in different languages and that execute on different operating system platforms?

    A. RMI

    B. CORBA

    C. DCOM

    D. DCE

10. Which of the following are used by Java RMI?

    A. Stubs

    B. Skeletons

    C. ORBs

    D. IIOP

11. Which of the following is not a tier of a three-tier architecture?

    A. Client interface

    B. Business logic

    C. Security

    D. Data storage

12. Which of the following Java technologies implements transaction management?

    A. RMI

    B. JTS

    C. JMAPI

    D. JTA

13. Which of the following is not true when discussing application servers and web servers?

    A. A web server understands and supports only the HTTP protocol.

    B. An application server supports HTTP, TCP/IP, and many more protocols.

    C. A web server does not support caching, clustering, and load balancing.

    D. We can configure application servers to work as web servers.

14. Which statement is not true when discussing serialization in EJB?

    A. Serialization means that a machine A's object passed as part of a method call is flattened into a byte stream that can be sent over a network connection.

    B. All EJB methods arguments and return values must be serializable.

    C. Developers should make sure all objects passed as arguments implement *java.io.Serializable*.

    D. Serialization is not possible in EJB.

Explain How the Enterprise JavaBeans Container Does Lifecycle Management and Has the Capability to Increase Scalability

15. Which of the following are true about EJB components, containers, and application servers?

    A. Components run in containers.

    B. Containers are hosted by application servers.

    C. Containers run in components.

    D. Application servers run in containers.

16. Which objects would you find in a directory service?

    A. An EJB home interface

    B. An EJB component

    C. The EJB API

    D. An EJB object interface

17. Containers and servers have the same function. What is the difference between an Enterprise JavaBeans container and an Enterprise JavaBeans server?

    A. Containers run within servers.

    B. Servers run within containers.

    C. Only one server can run in a container.

    D. Only one container can run in a server.

18. Which of the following CMP entity bean methods are used by the container to alert the bean when its state is synchronized with the database?

    A. `ejbLoad()`

    B. `ejbStore()`

    C. `ejbCreate()`

    D. `ejbActivate()`

19. What happens if `remove()` is not invoked on a stateful EJB session bean?

    A. Nothing happens; the bean will last forever.

    B. The container will not honor any more requests for the bean.

    C. An exception occurs in the session bean.

    D. The bean is removed after the session timeout has been reached.

20. With respect to stateful session EJBs, which of the following statements is *not* true?

    A. Stateful session beans support instance pooling.

    B. The lifecycle of a stateful session bean is strictly connected with its client.

    C. When the client removes the bean, it cannot be used by another client without being reinitialized.

    D. A stateful session bean has three states: Does not exist, Method Ready, and Passivated.

SELF TEST ANSWERS

List the Required Classes/Interfaces That Must Be Provided for an Enterprise JavaBeans Component

1. ☑ **C** is correct. The bean or enterprise bean is not the EJB object. It extends either the EntityBean interface or the SessionBean interface. It *must* implement all the methods defined in the remote interface.

   ☒ **A**, **B**, and **D** are incorrect because the EJB object or remote object is a wrapper residing inside the container, between the client and the code. It performs setup and shutdown tasks pre and post bean call. The EJBObject is generated by the EJB server tools. The developer must write another interface, called the remote interface or the EJBObject interface, that extends the interface EJBObject and provides method signatures for all the business methods. The server automatically generates a Java class that implements the remote interface. The home interface is a factory object responsible for locating and creating instances of the bean. The developer must code for the EJB home interface (that is, extend the interface EJBHome), and provide method signatures for all the desired `create()` and `find()` methods.

Distinguish Between Session and Entity Beans

2. ☑ **B** is correct. Entity beans represent the data in a data store. Entity beans do not obviate the JDBC API; they merely provide an alternative.

   ☒ **A**, **C**, and **D** are incorrect because in container-managed entity beans, when the bean is created, the container automatically retrieves the data from the persistent storage (for example, database) and assigns it to the bean's object variables for the user to manipulate or use it. The bean-managed entity bean for the class specifically has to obtain a database connection, retrieve the row/column values, and assign them to the objects in the `ejbLoad()`, which will be called by the container when it instantiates a bean object.

Recognize Appropriate Uses for Entity, Stateful Session, and Stateless Session Beans

3. ☑ **C** and **D** are correct. Both Enterprise JavaBeans and servlets may be used to upgrade CGI programs to Java-based solutions.

   ☒ **A** and **B** are incorrect. JMAPI and screen scrapers are not Java technology.

Distinguish Between Stateful and Stateless Session Beans

4. ☑ A is correct. The J2EE specification requires that the home interface of a Stateless session bean must include a single `create()` method without any arguments.

   ☒ B, C, and D are all true statements.

State the Benefits and Costs of Container-Managed Persistence

5. ☑ A is correct. Yes, you can create CMP entity beans without primary keys.

   ☒ B, C, and D are incorrect because duplicate records may be entered in the table and the `findByPrimaryKey()` method may return varying rows.

6. ☑ A is correct. You cannot change the primary key field of an entity bean.

   ☒ B and C are incorrect because, according to the EJB 2.0 specification, "Once the primary key for an entity bean has been set, the Bean Provider must not attempt to change it by use of set accessor methods on the primary key cmp-fields. The Bean provider should therefore not expose the set accessor methods for the primary key cmp-fields in the component interface of the entity bean." You can effect an update of a primary key field by removing (deleting) and then re-creating (inserting) the bean.

State the Transactional Behavior in a Given Scenario for an Enterprise Bean Method with a Specified Transactional Attributed as Defined in the Deployment Descriptor

7. ☑ C is correct. The cost for a remote lookup on a stateless session bean can be significant and can justify using a handle (SSB reference) to access the bean.

   ☒ A, B, and D are all true statements.

Given a Requirement Specification Detailing Security and Flexibility Needs, Identify Architectures That Would Fulfill Those Requirements

8. ☑ A is correct. RMI is the most appropriate distributed object technology for pure Java applications.

   ☒ B, C, and D are incorrect because they can work with non-Java objects.

9. ☑ B is correct. CORBA is the most appropriate object technology for systems that use objects written in different languages, and it supports a variety of operating system platforms.

   ☒ A, C, and D each work with specific platforms.

10. ☑   A and B are correct. RMI uses stubs and skeletons.
    ☒   C and D are incorrect because ORBs and IIOP are used with CORBA.

11. ☑   C is correct. Security is not a tier of a three-tiered architecture.
    ☒   A, B, and D are tiers of a three-tiered architecture.

12. ☑   B is correct. JTS provides an implementation of transaction management.
    ☒   A, C, and D. These do not implement transaction management. JTA defines an API for transaction management; it does not implement it.

13. ☑   C is correct. A web server understands and supports only the HTTP protocol, whereas an application server supports HTTP,TCP/IP, and many more protocols.
    ☒   A, B, and D are incorrect because web servers and application servers both support features such as caching, clustering, and load balancing. We can also configure an application server to work as web server.

14. ☑   D is correct. Serialization is possible.
    ☒   A, B, and C are incorrect because a good portion of EJB is the framework for underlying remote method invocation. To allow one JVM space A the ability to invoke methods remotely on objects that are in JVM space B (objects running on another machine on the network), all arguments of each method call and their results must be serializable (that is, classes must implement *java.io.Serializable*).

Explain How the Enterprise JavaBeans Container Does Lifecycle Management and Has the Capability to Increase Scalability

15. ☑   A and B are correct because components run in containers that are hosted by application servers.
    ☒   C and D are not true. Containers do not run in components. Application servers do not run in containers.

16. ☑   A is correct. EJB home interfaces are placed in a directory service to facilitate access to an EJB component. The EJB home interface is used to obtain access to an EJB object interface.
    ☒   B, C, and D are incorrect because EJB components are never accessed directly, but only through their EJB home and EJB object interfaces.

17. ☑   A is correct. Enterprise JavaBeans containers run within the context of servers.
    ☒   B, C, and D are incorrect. Servers do not run within containers. A server does not run in a container. Many containers can run in a server.

18. ☑ **A** and **B** are correct. The container notifies the bean using the `ejbLoad()` and `ejbStore()` methods. The `ejbLoad()` method alerts the bean that its container-managed fields have just been populated with data from the database. This gives the bean an opportunity to do any postprocessing before the data can be used by the business methods. The `ejbStore()` method alerts the bean that its data is about to be written to the database. This give the bean an opportunity to do any preprocessing to the fields before they are written to the database.
     ☒ **C** and **D** have nothing to do with data persistence.

19. ☑ **D** is correct. A stateful session bean would be put in an EXIST state until any of the following occurs:
     Call `remove()` on the EJBObjects's stub from the client
     Call `remove(handleToEJBObject)` on EJBHome's stub from the client
     System exception in bean
     Session timeout
     Container failure
     ☒ **A**, **B**, and **C** are not true.

20. ☑ **A** is correct. There is no clear indication that a stateful session bean is or is not pooled, while for the stateless session bean there is a specific paragraph that discusses the sequence for adding or removing a pooled bean instance. Performance reasons may motivate some containers to pool stateful session beans and avoid the overhead of re-creating the entire object. In the black box, it may be pooled, hence the methods `ejbActivate()` and `ejbPassivate()` are included.
     ☒ **B**, **C**, and **D** are all true statements.

8

Messaging

T his chapter is organized a little differently from other chapters in the book. Before we look at the certification objectives, we are going to cover material that will help you to understand the basics of messaging and the Java Message Service (JMS) API. This material provides a valuable and necessary context for the objectives, particularly if you are new to messaging and or JMS.

Messaging Basics

The main subject areas in the messaging arena with which you need to be familiar are messages, message-oriented middleware, JMS, message types, and communication modes. We'll take a look at each of these subject areas before looking at the scenarios that are appropriate for messaging.

Messages

A *message* is a unit of data that is sent from one process to another processes running on either the same or a different machine. The data in the message can range from simple text to a more complex data structure (such as a Java HashMap, which can be used to store name value pairs). The only restriction is that the object must be *serializable* so that it can be easily transformed into a sequence of bytes, transmitted across a network, and then re-created into a copy of the original object.

Middleware

Companies that create large transaction processing solutions to serve their customers, suppliers, or internal users swiftly become aware of the fact that a poorly designed system will not be able to keep pace with an ever-increasing transaction volume. They also quickly realize that just adding new hardware to the mix does not necessarily solve the problem.

These ever-increasing-in-volume types of applications are created using a three-tier instead of a two-tier approach. The existing two tiers, containing the presentation tier and the persistence tier, are supplemented with a middle tier that contains an application commonly known as *middleware*. Figure 8-1 depicts these three tiers.

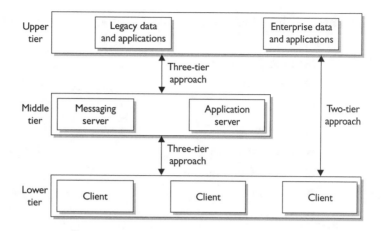

FIGURE 8-1

Three tiers of an application

The middleware provides business solutions and services, such as these:

- **Database management**   The ability to access a database server such as DB/2, Oracle, or SQL Server
- **Messaging**   The ability to send and receive data between applications
- **Naming**   The ability to find a resource by name instead of by location
- **Security**   The ability to authenticate and authorize a user (note that this is not solely a middle tier responsibility)

The Java 2 Enterprise Edition (J2EE) APIs extend standard Java and provide access to these services. The middleware is loosely coupled with the parts of the application that are running in the presentation and persistence tiers. This loose coupling improves the reliability of middleware by isolating it from failures that may occur on either of the other tiers.

Message-Oriented Middleware

Message-oriented middleware, also known as MOM, is middleware that is used for messaging. This middleware is the infrastructure that provides dependable mechanisms that enable applications to create, send, and receive messages within an enterprise environment.

The advantage of message-based applications is that they are event driven. They exchange messages in a wide variety of formats and deliver messages quickly and reliably. Here is a list of the enterprise messaging vendors available at the time of writing:

- BEA Systems, Inc.
- Hewlett-Packard
- IBM
- iPlanet
- Macromedia
- Oracle Corporation
- Pramati
- SilverStream Software, Inc.
- Sonic Software
- SpiritSoft, Inc.
- Talarian Corp.
- TIBCO Software, Inc.

Communication Modes

Typically, applications use *synchronous* method calls for communication. In this type of communication, the requester is blocked from processing any further commands until the response (or a time out) is received.

Synchronous communication is conducted between two active participants. The receiver has to acknowledge receipt of the message before the sender can proceed. From the sender's perspective, this is known as a *blocking* call. As the volume of traffic increases, more bandwidth is required, and the need for additional hardware becomes critical. These implementations are more easily directly affected by hardware, software, and network failures. When capacities are exceeded, the opportunity to process the information is typically lost.

An example of synchronous communication is credit card authorization. When your card is swiped through a card reader and the details of the purchase are entered, the machine dials the authorization computer and waits for a response (approval or denial of the purchase).

In *asynchronous* communication, the parties are peers and can send and receive messages at will. Asynchronous communication does not require real-time acknowledgment of a message; the requester can continue with other processing once it sends the message. From the sender's perspective, this is known as a *non-blocking* call.

An example of asynchronous communication is e-mail. Even if your computer is switched off or your e-mail client is not running, other people can still send e-mail messages to you. When you start your e-mail client, you will be able to view the e-mail messages that have accumulated in your inbox.

Message Models

JMS supports two basic message models known as *publish/subscribe* (pub/sub), in which messages are published on a one or more-to-many basis, and *point-to-point* (PTP), in which messages are sent on a one-to-one basis. The JMS specification requires that the messaging vendor product support at least one of these models in order to be compliant. An in-depth explanation of these two models appears later in this chapter in the sections, "How the Point-to-Point Message Model Works" and "How the Publish/Subscribe Message Model Works."

CERTIFICATION OBJECTIVE 8.01

Identify Scenarios That Are Appropriate to Implementation Using Messaging

The following table shows some example messaging implementations that can be used as solutions to the given scenarios.

SCENARIO & SOLUTION	
You need to call a validation application to approve a customer's credit card purchases. Which type of messaging model is best used for this type of communication, and what type of communication works best in such a scenario?	Point-to-point model messaging is best because the message only needs to be processed one time by the validation system. Synchronous communication works best because the results are required before the customer is allowed to use the merchandise.
You are using an e-mail application, and you want to send a message to several recipients and receive replies from them all. Which type of communication is best for this type of application?	Asynchronous communication is best suited to an e-mail application because the recipients are not required to be online for the sender to send the message.
You need to broadcast information to many recipients…	The publish/subscribe messaging model is best because the broadcast capability is part of its design.
What messaging technology is most appropriate for guaranteeing the delivery of a message to a single recipient and to multiple recipients?	For the single recipient, use the point-to-point messaging model with persistent delivery mode. For multiple recipients, use the publish/subscribe model with a persistent delivery mode and a durable subscriber.
What messaging technology is most appropriate for sending and receiving messages in a transactional way?	Use the point-to-point model. Create transacted sessions and process messages with commit and rollback methods.

List Benefits of Synchronous and Asynchronous Messaging

The benefits of synchronous messaging follow:

- Because both parties must be active to participate in synchronous messaging, if either party is not active, the message transaction cannot be completed.
- A message must be acknowledged before proceeding to the next message. If it is not acknowledged, the message cannot be considered processed.

The benefits of asynchronous messaging are as follows:

- As the volume of traffic increases, asynchronous messaging is better able to handle the spike in demand by keeping a backlog of requests in its queue and then operating at maximum capacity over a period of time instead of needing to service the requests instantaneously.
- Asynchronous messaging is less affected by failures at the hardware, software, and network levels.
- When capacities are exceeded, information is not lost; instead, it is delayed.

Identify Scenarios That Are More Appropriate to Implementation Using Asynchronous Messaging, Rather Than Synchronous

The following scenarios are more appropriate to implementation using asynchronous messaging:

SCENARIO & SOLUTION

You need to implement a messaging system in which a response is not required or not immediately required. Which messaging system is most appropriate?	Asynchronous messaging
You need a high-volume transaction processing capability for sending messages. Which type of messaging is best suited for this use?	Asynchronous messaging
You want a messaging system that uses your system hardware in an efficient manner. Which type of messaging should be used?	Asynchronous messaging

CERTIFICATION OBJECTIVE 8.04

Identify Scenarios That Are More Appropriate to Implementation Using Synchronous Messaging, Rather Than Asynchronous

The following scenario is more appropriate to implementation using synchronous messaging:

SCENARIO & SOLUTION

You are using a credit card authorization/user login authentication system to send a message in which the response to the message is required before the transaction can be completed. Which type of messaging are you using?	Synchronous messaging

Java Message Service

Message-oriented middleware products allow a developer to couple applications loosely together. However, these products are proprietary and quite often complex and expensive. The JMS provides a standard Java interface to these messaging middleware products, freeing developers from having to write low-level infrastructure code, or "plumbing," and allowing solutions to be built quickly and easily. In short, the JMS API provides a convenient and easy way to create, send, receive, and read an enterprise messaging system's messages using Java.

JMS applications can use databases to provide the storage to support message persistence that is necessary for guaranteeing delivery and order of messages. With the arrival of the Enterprise JavaBeans (EJB) 2.0 specification, the EJB message-driven bean (MDB) has been able to receive and process messages asynchronously within the EJB container. These message-driven beans can be instantiated multiple times to provide concurrent (therefore faster throughput) processing of a message queue.

JMS provides an interface from Java applications to messaging products. JMS enables clients (or peers) to exchange data in the form of messages.

Following are the major advantages of using messaging for this exchange:

- Easy integration of incompatible systems

- Asynchronous communications

- One-to-many communications

- Guaranteed messaging

- Transactional messaging

Table 8-1 shows the various components of a JMS messaging application.

TABLE 8-1	Components of a JMS Messaging Application

Component	Function
JMS provider	The host application on which the JMS application runs. The JMS provider converses with JMS applications and supplies the underlying mechanisms required for a messaging application.
Administered objects	JMS objects that are created and maintained by an administrator to be used by JMS clients.
Clients	Applications that can send and/or receive messages.
Messages	Bundles of information that are passed between applications. Each application defines the types of information a message can contain.

Handling Exceptions

If a problem occurs, an application can be notified asynchronously via the *ExceptionListener* interface. This interface identifies the JMS provider problem details to the JMS client. To handle exceptions, the developer must create a listening object that implements the *ExceptionListener* interface and codes the `onException (JMSException exception)` method. The listening object must register itself with the JMS provider by calling the `setExceptionListener (listenerobject)` method on the session.

Managing Sessions

Table 8-2 describes the details of a JMS session. Unless noted otherwise, this information applies to both the pub/sub and PTP models.

Components of a JMS Message

JMS messages have a simple and flexible format that allows the sender to create message formats used by non-JMS applications. The message can contain *simple* or *complex* datatypes. A JMS message is made up of one required component, called the *header*, and two optional components, called *properties* and a *body*. Figure 8-2 illustrates the structure of a JMS message.

Header Fields

The JMS message header includes a number of fields that contain information that can be used to identify and route messages. Each of these header fields includes the appropriate get/set methods. Most of the values are automatically set by the `send` or `publish` method, but the client can set some of them.

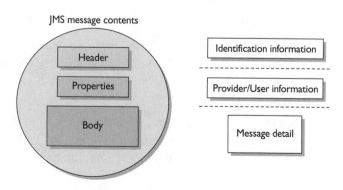

FIGURE 8-2

Structure of a JMS message

TABLE 8-2	JMS Session Details

Session Detail	Description
Transacted session	A related group of messages that are treated as a single work unit. The transaction can be either committed or rolled back. When a message *sender* uses a transacted session and calls the `commit` method, the messages it produces are accepted for delivery. If it calls the `rollback` method, the messages it produces are destroyed. When a message *receiver* uses a transacted session and calls the `commit` method, the messages it consumes are acknowledged. If it calls the `rollback` method, the messages it consumes are recovered (not acknowledged).
Duplicate messages	Clients send messages knowing that JMS will deliver them only once. Therefore, the JMS provider must never deliver a message more than once or deliver a copy of a message that has already been acknowledged. When a copy of a message is delivered, the message header contains a redelivery flag field that will be set, telling the client that this message may have been received before but that, for whatever reason, the JMS server did not receive the client's acknowledgment of receipt. The redelivery flag is set by the JMS provider application, usually as the result of a recovery operation.
Message acknowledgment	If a JMS session is transacted, messages are acknowledged automatically by the commit mechanism and recovered by the rollback mechanism. If a session is not transacted, recovery must be handled manually, and messages are acknowledged in one of three ways: *AUTO_ACKNOWLEDGE*: For each message, the session automatically acknowledges that a client has received the message when the client returns from a call to receive a message or the *MessageListener* called by the session to process the message returns successfully. *CLIENT_ACKNOWLEDGE*: Client acknowledges the message by calling the `acknowledge` method on the message. This also acknowledges all messages that were processed during the session. *DUPS_OK_ACKNOWLEDGE*: Because the session lazily acknowledges the delivery of messages, duplication of messages may result if the JMS provider fails. This mode should be used only if consumers can tolerate duplicate messages. This mode reduces session overhead by minimizing the work the session does to prevent duplicate messages.

Table 8-3 describes a few header fields. For a complete list, refer to the JMS specification at the Sun web site (*http://java.sun.com/products/jms*).

Properties

Properties are values that can add to the information contained in header fields. The JMS API provides some predefined property names that the JMS provider can support (these properties have a *JMS_* prefix).

TABLE 8-3	JMS Message Headers

Header Field	Description
JMSMessageID	Unique identifier for every message.
JMSDeliveryMode	*PERSISTENT* means that delivery of a message is guaranteed. It will continue to exist until all subscribers who requested it receive it. The message is delivered only once. *NON-PERSISTENT* delivery means that every reasonable attempt is made to deliver the message. But in the event of some kind of system failure, the message may be lost. These messages are delivered at most once.
JMSExpiration	The length of time, in milliseconds, that a message will exist before it is removed. Setting this to zero will prevent the message from being removed.
JMSPriority	Although it is not guaranteed, messages with a higher priority are generally delivered before messages with a lower priority. Priority 0 is the lowest and 9 is the highest. Priority 4 is the default. Priorities of 0–4 are grades of normal priority, and priorities of 5–9 are grades of higher priority.
JMSRedelivered	Notifies the client that it probably received this message at least once earlier, but for whatever reason, the client did not acknowledge its receipt. The JMS provider sets this flag, typically during a recovery operation after a failure.

The use of properties is optional. If you decide to use them, they can be of the type *boolean, byte, double, float, int, long, short,* or *String.* They can be set by the producer when the message is sent or by consumers upon receipt of the message. These properties, along with the header field, can be used in conjunction with a *MessageSelector* to filter and route messages based on the criteria specified.

Body

Five different message body formats, or types, allow a JMS client to send and receive data in many different forms and provide compatibility with existing messaging formats. Table 8-4 describes these message body formats.

TABLE 8-4	JMS Message Body Formats

Message Body Format	Content
ByteMessage	A stream of uninterpreted bytes. This type of message body should be used to match most legacy messages.
MapMessage	A set of name/value pairs, similar to a HashMap. The name part is a *String* object and the value is a Java primitive type.
ObjectMessage	A single serializable Java object or a collection of objects.
StreamMessage	A stream of Java primitive values that are entered and read sequentially.
TextMessage	Text formatted as a *String.* This form is well suited to exchanging XML data.

Required Components of a JMS Application

Several main components are required by an application that uses JMS. The first type is known as an *administered object*, because the administrator of the JMS provider application creates them. These objects are placed in a Java Naming and Directory Interface (JNDI) namespace and are administered from either a command-line program, GUI, or an HTML-based management console.

JMS has two types of administered objects: *Destination* and *ConnectionFactory*. The *Destination* object contains configuration information supplied by the JMS provider. The client uses this object to specify a destination for messages that it wishes to send and/or a location from which to receive messages. Two types of *Destination* interfaces can be used: a *Queue* for the PTP model and a *Topic* for the pub/sub model. The *ConnectionFactory* is obtained via a JNDI lookup, and it contains the connection configuration information, or handle containing the IP address, enabling a JMS client application to create a connection with the JMS server.

The other main components required by an application that uses JMS are the *Connection* and *Session*. The *Connection* component provides the physical connection to the JMS server and the *Session* component is responsible for sending and receiving messages, managing transactions, and handling acknowledgments. Figure 8-3 shows the relationships between the JMS components.

Objects Used to Create and Receive Messages in a JMS Client Application

Four objects are used to create and receive messages in a JMS client application:

- *MessageProducer*
- *MessageConsumer*
- *MessageListener*
- *MessageSelector*

FIGURE 8-3

JMS component relationships

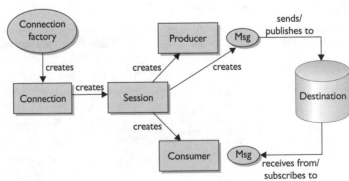

MessageProducer

A *MessageProducer* is created by a session and used to send messages to a destination. In the PTP model, the destination is called a *queue*. For the pub/sub model, the destination is called a *topic*.

When creating a *MessageProducer*, you can also specify the default delivery mode (*setDeliveryMode*). This can be either *NON_PERSISTENT*, which has a lower overhead because the message is not logged, or *PERSISTENT*, which requires the message to be logged, typically to a database. You can also specify the priority of the message (*setPriority*). Priority 0 is the lowest priority and 9 is the highest priority (4 is the default). Priorities of 0–4 are grades of normal priority and priorities of 5–9 are grades of higher priority. You can also specify the expiration time (*setTimeToLive*), which is the amount of time, in milliseconds, that a message should be available (set to 0 for unlimited time).

MessageConsumer

A *MessageConsumer* is created by a session and used to receive messages sent to the destination. The messages can be received in one of two ways: synchronously, where the client calls one of the receive methods (`receive` and `receiveNoWait`) after the consumer is started, or asynchronously, where the client registers a *MessageListener* and then starts the consumer.

The following code is an example of a synchronous connection. (Asynchronous connections are covered in the next section.)

```
// start the connection
queueConn.start();
// receive the first message (wait for a message)
Message message = queueReceiver.receive();
// receive the next message (wait for a minute only)
Message message = queueReceiver.receive(60000);
```

on the
job

All messages in JMS are exchanged asynchronously between the clients, in that the producer does not receive acknowledgment from the consumer that it has processed the message. As soon as the message is sent or published, the producer is not blocked from sending or publishing another message immediately.

MessageListener

A *MessageListener* is an interface that needs to be implemented to process messages in an asynchronous fashion. To receive and process an asynchronous message, you must do the following:

- Create an object that implements the *MessageListener* interface. This includes coding the `onMessage()` method.

■ Register the object with the session via the `setMessageListener()` method.

■ Call the `Start()` method on the *Connection* object to begin receiving messages.

MessageSelector

A *MessageSelector* is an *java.lang.String* object specified by the client by the `createSubscriber()` method. The *MessageSelector* filters out messages that do not meet the criteria specified. The *MessageSelector* examines the message header and properties fields and compares them to an expression contained in a string. The syntax of this expression is based on a subset of SQL92 conditional expression syntax. SQL92 is a standard published by the SQL Standards committee formed by the American National Standards Institute and the International Standards Organization.

Table 8-5 shows some examples of these expressions, and the PTP example that is covered next shows a receiver that reads the queue with and without a *MessageSelector.*

exam
ⓦatch

A message digest is a digital fingerprint value that is computed from a message, file, or byte stream.

TABLE 8-5   JMS Message Selector Examples

Value	Example
Arithmetic operators	`+, -, *, /`
Comparison operators	`<, >, <=, >=, IS NULL, IS NOT NULL, BETWEEN`

Expressions	`(Qty * Price) >= 12300`
	`Day = 'Tuesday'`
	`Month NOT IN ('June', 'July', 'August')`
	`Description LIKE 'UNITED%'`

Identifiers	`$name, JMSPriority, JMSXId, JMS_timeout`
Literals	`'string literal', 64, FALSE`
Logical operators	`AND, OR, NOT`

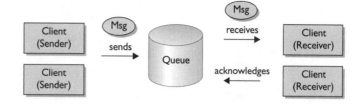

FIGURE 8-4

Point-to-Point model

How the Point-to Point Message Model *Works*

The PTP message model sends messages to a receiver on a one-to-one basis. Figure 8-4 is a diagram showing the PTP model.

Examples of PTP implementation include the following:

- Instant messaging
- Receiving a transaction from another system
- Sending an order to another system
- Supply-chain processing

A message is delivered to a destination, known as a *queue*. Messages in a queue are processed on a first-in, first-out (FIFO) basis. In other words, the subscriber is guaranteed to get each message in the order in which it was sent. The first available receiver processes each message once. This differs from the pub/sub model, in which a single message can be published to one or more subscribers. In addition to processing the next message in a queue, the receiver is also able to browse through the messages in a queue (for example, to count them), but the receiver is unable to process the messages in any other order than FIFO.

The following is a list of the steps and interface classes required for the PTP model of communication:

1. Obtain the *QueueConnectionFactory* object via a JNDI lookup (the JNDI name will vary depending on the messaging vendor and site naming conventions).

2. Obtain a *QueueConnection* to the provider via the *QueueConnectionFactory*. (If security is enabled, pass a user ID and password to the `createQueueConnection` method.)

3. Obtain a *QueueSession* with the provider via the *QueueConnection*.

4. Obtain the queue via a JNDI lookup (the JNDI name will vary depending on the messaging vendor and site naming conventions).

5. Create either a *QueueSender* or a *QueueReceiver* via the *QueueSession* for the required queue.

6. Send and/or receive messages.

7. Close the *QueueConnection* (this will also close the *QueueSender* or *QueueReceiver*, and the *QueueSession*).

In the following example code, a JMS client sends a variety of *TextMessages* and *ObjectMessages* to a queue. Some of these messages are marked with a property called Interesting that is set to true. The sending client finishes up by sending text messages containing the text finish to indicate to the receiver that it can stop processing. The receiving JMS client is started with or without a command-line argument, and it will process the messages in the queue according to this argument setting.

on the job *The JNDI name for the connection factory and the queue will differ across messaging vendor implementations and also depend on your site's naming conventions.*

Here is the code for the sending client:

```
package j2ee.architect;
import java.util.*;
import javax.naming.*;
import javax.jms.*;
public class PTPSend {
  private static final String THIS = "PTPSend";
  public static final String JMS_FACTORY = "myQueueConnectionFactory";
  public static final String QUEUE = "myQueue1";
  public static void main(String[] args) throws Exception {
    // get the initial context
    InitialContext ctx = new InitialContext(System.getProperties());
    // lookup the queue connection factory
    QueueConnectionFactory qconnf =
      (QueueConnectionFactory) ctx.lookup(JMS_FACTORY);
    // create a queue connection
    QueueConnection qconn = qconnf.createQueueConnection();
    // create a queue session
    QueueSession qsess = qconn.createQueueSession(
      false, Session.AUTO_ACKNOWLEDGE);
    // lookup the queue object
    Queue queue = (Queue) ctx.lookup(QUEUE);
    // create a queue sender
    QueueSender qsend = qsess.createSender(queue);
```

```
qsend.setDeliveryMode(DeliveryMode.NON_PERSISTENT);
// start the connection
qconn.start();
// get the number of messages to send
int numMsgs = (args.length > 0) ? new Integer(args[0]).intValue() : 10;
// create messages
Message msg = qsess.createMessage();
TextMessage tmsg = qsess.createTextMessage();
ObjectMessage omsg = qsess.createObjectMessage();
Hashtable hTable = new Hashtable();
log("Started.");
// send the messages
for (int i=0,j=0,k=0; i < numMsgs; i++) {
  j++;k++;      //Increment counters
  if (k == 1) {
    tmsg.setText("News item #"+(i+1));
    // randomly set the Interesting property to true or false
    tmsg.setBooleanProperty("Interesting",((j==3)?true:false));
    log(tmsg.getText()+((j==3)?" (Interesting)":""));
    qsend.send(tmsg);
  } else {
    hTable.clear();
    hTable.put("symbol","ucny");
    hTable.put("bid",new String(""+(100+i)));
    hTable.put("ask",new String(""+(100+i+1)));
    omsg.setObject(hTable);
    // randomly set the Interesting property to true or false
    omsg.setBooleanProperty("Interesting",((j==3)?true:false));
    log(hTable+((j==3)?" (Interesting)":""));
    qsend.send(omsg);
    k=0; //reset counter
  }
  if (j==3) j=0;
}
// create a couple of close messages
tmsg.setText("***CLOSE***");
// set the Interesting property to true on this one
tmsg.setBooleanProperty("Interesting", true);
log(tmsg.getText()+" (Interesting)");
qsend.send(tmsg);
// set the Interesting property to false on this one
tmsg.setBooleanProperty("Interesting", false);
log(tmsg.getText());
qsend.send(tmsg);
// close up
qsend.close();
qsess.close();
```

```
      qconn.close();
      ctx.close();
      log("Finished.");

  }
  private static void log(String msg) {
      System.out.println(new java.util.Date()+" "+THIS+" "+msg);
  }
}
```

Here is the code for the receiving client. Note that the receiving client has been coded by implementing a message listener:

```
package j2ee.architect;
import javax.naming.*;
import javax.jms.*;
public class PTPReceive implements MessageListener {
  private static final String THIS = "PTPReceive";
  public static final String JMS_FACTORY = "myQueueConnectionFactory";
  public static final String QUEUE = "myQueue1";
  private InitialContext ctx;
  protected QueueConnectionFactory qconnf;
  protected QueueConnection qconn;
  protected QueueSession qsess;
  protected Queue queue;
  protected QueueReceiver qrecv;
  private boolean quit = false;
  public boolean ready;
  public static void main(String[] args) throws Exception {
    // instantiate the receiver, if there is no argument
    // pass a null to the constructor.
    PTPReceive rec = new PTPReceive(args.length>0?args[0]:null);
    // if constructor code does not initialize, we exit.
    if (!rec.ready) {
      log("Not ready to receive messages.");
      System.exit(-1);
    }
    log("Started"+(args.length>0?
      " with filter ("+args[0]+").":" with no filter."));
    // Start the thread.
    rec.run();
    // We're done, so clean up.
    rec.close();
    log("Finished.");
  }
  public PTPReceive(String filter) {
    try {
```

```
      // get the initial context
      ctx = new InitialContext(System.getProperties());
      // lookup the queue connection factory
      qconnf = (QueueConnectionFactory) ctx.lookup(JMS_FACTORY);
      // create a queue connection
      qconn = qconnf.createQueueConnection();
      // create a queue session
      qsess = qconn.createQueueSession(false, Session.AUTO_ACKNOWLEDGE);
      // lookup the queue object
      queue = (Queue) ctx.lookup(QUEUE);
      // create a queue receiver
      if (filter == null)
        // this is a queue receiver WITHOUT a filter
        qrecv = qsess.createReceiver(queue);
      else
        // this is a queue receiver WITH a filter
        qrecv = qsess.createReceiver(queue, filter);
      // set the message listener
      qrecv.setMessageListener (this);
      // start the connection
      qconn.start();
      ready = true;
    } catch (Exception e) {
      ready = false;
      log("Initialization failed. "+e);
      close();
    }
  }
  /*
   * The following loop suspends the main thread
   * until the quit boolean is set to true by the
   * onMessage method. While the main thread is
   * suspended the JMS provider calls the onMessage
   * method with its thread.
   */
  public void run() {
    if (!ready) return;
    synchronized (this) {
      while (!quit) {
        try { wait(); }
        catch (InterruptedException ie) { }
      }
    }
  }
  public void onMessage (Message msg) {
    String text;
    try
```

```
  {
    if(msg instanceof ObjectMessage) {
      // we received an object message
        ObjectMessage objmsg = (ObjectMessage)msg;
        log(objmsg.getObject().toString());
    } else if(msg instanceof TextMessage) {
      // we received a text message
        text = ((TextMessage) msg).getText();
      log(text);
      if (text.equals("***CLOSE***")) {
        // we've received the close down message
        // so set the quit boolean to true and
        // wake up all threads that are waiting on
        // this object's monitor (i.e. the main thread)
        synchronized(this) {
          quit = true;
          this.notifyAll();
        }
        }
    } else log("message type not supported");
    } catch (JMSException e) {
      e.printStackTrace ();
    }
  }
  public void close () {
    try { if (qrecv != null) qrecv.close();
    } catch (Exception e) { log("Can't close queue receiver. "+e); }
    try { if (qsess != null) qsess.close();
    } catch (Exception e) { log("Can't close session. "+e); }
    try { if (qconn != null) qconn.close();
    } catch (Exception e) { log("Can't close connection. "+e); }
    try { if (ctx != null) ctx.close();
    } catch (Exception e) { log("Can't close context. "+e); }
  }
  private static void log(String msg) {
    System.out.println(new java.util.Date()+" "+THIS+" "+msg);
  }
}
```

When executed, the following output is from the sending client:

```
Sun Sep 01 17:28:48 EDT 2002 PTPSend Started.
Sun Sep 01 17:28:48 EDT 2002 PTPSend News item #1
Sun Sep 01 17:28:48 EDT 2002 PTPSend {bid=101, symbol=ucny, ask=102}
Sun Sep 01 17:28:48 EDT 2002 PTPSend News item #3 (Interesting)
```

```
Sun Sep 01 17:28:48 EDT 2002 PTPSend {bid=103, symbol=ucny, ask=104}
Sun Sep 01 17:28:48 EDT 2002 PTPSend News item #5
Sun Sep 01 17:28:48 EDT 2002 PTPSend {bid=105, symbol=ucny, ask=106} (Interesting)
Sun Sep 01 17:28:48 EDT 2002 PTPSend News item #7
Sun Sep 01 17:28:48 EDT 2002 PTPSend {bid=107, symbol=ucny, ask=108}
Sun Sep 01 17:28:48 EDT 2002 PTPSend News item #9 (Interesting)
Sun Sep 01 17:28:48 EDT 2002 PTPSend {bid=109, symbol=ucny, ask=110}
Sun Sep 01 17:28:48 EDT 2002 PTPSend ***CLOSE*** (Interesting)
Sun Sep 01 17:28:48 EDT 2002 PTPSend ***CLOSE***
Sun Sep 01 17:28:48 EDT 2002 PTPSend Finished.
```

When executed, here is the output from the receiving client when it is executed with an argument `Interesting=true`, which becomes the message filter, and when it is executed with no argument, which means it must read all items in the queue:

```
Sun Sep 01 17:28:56 EDT 2002 PTPReceive Started with filter (Interesting=true).
Sun Sep 01 17:28:57 EDT 2002 PTPReceive News item #3
Sun Sep 01 17:28:57 EDT 2002 PTPReceive {ask=106, symbol=ucny, bid=105}
Sun Sep 01 17:28:57 EDT 2002 PTPReceive News item #9
Sun Sep 01 17:28:57 EDT 2002 PTPReceive ***CLOSE***
Sun Sep 01 17:28:57 EDT 2002 PTPReceive Finished.

Sun Sep 01 17:29:02 EDT 2002 PTPReceive Started with no filter.
Sun Sep 01 17:29:02 EDT 2002 PTPReceive News item #1
Sun Sep 01 17:29:02 EDT 2002 PTPReceive {ask=102, symbol=ucny, bid=101}
Sun Sep 01 17:29:02 EDT 2002 PTPReceive {ask=104, symbol=ucny, bid=103}
Sun Sep 01 17:29:02 EDT 2002 PTPReceive News item #5
Sun Sep 01 17:29:02 EDT 2002 PTPReceive News item #7
Sun Sep 01 17:29:02 EDT 2002 PTPReceive {ask=108, symbol=ucny, bid=107}
Sun Sep 01 17:29:02 EDT 2002 PTPReceive {ask=110, symbol=ucny, bid=109}
Sun Sep 01 17:29:02 EDT 2002 PTPReceive ***CLOSE***
Sun Sep 01 17:29:02 EDT 2002 PTPReceive Finished.
```

How the Publish/Subscribe Message Model Works

The pub/sub message model allows an application to publish messages on a one-to-many or a many-to-many basis. Figure 8-5 is a diagram depicting the pub/sub model.

Following are some examples of a pub/sub implementation:

- Sending sales forecasts to various people in an organization
- Sending news items to interested parties
- Sending stock prices to traders on the trading floor

FIGURE 8-5

Pub/sub model

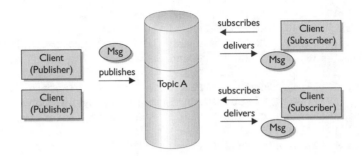

Messages are published to a *topic* (or subject). One or more publishers can publish messages to the same topic. Any client application that wants to receive messages on this topic must first subscribe to the topic. Multiple clients can subscribe to the topic and subsequently receive a copy of the message.

In the nondurable subscription model, the subscriber must be connected at the time a message is published to receive that message. If no subscribers are online, the messages will be published and destroyed soon thereafter. The subscriber can also use a durable subscription model, in which case the messages will be received when the subscriber is reconnected to the topic. Durable subscriptions come with greater overhead because they require additional resources to persist the messages until they can be delivered to all of the known durable subscribers.

The following is a list of the steps and interface classes required for the pub/sub model of communication:

1. Obtain the *TopicConnectionFactory* object via a JNDI lookup (the JNDI name will vary depending on the messaging vendor and site naming conventions).

2. Obtain a *TopicConnection* to the provider via the *TopicConnectionFactory*. (If security is enabled, pass a user ID and password to the `createTopicConnection` method.)

3. Obtain a *TopicSession* with the provider via the *TopicConnection*.

4. Obtain the topic via a JNDI lookup. (The JNDI name will vary depending on the messaging vendor and site naming conventions.)

5. Create either a *TopicPublisher* or a *TopicSubscriber* via the *TopicSession* for the required topic.

6. Publish and/or receive messages.

7. Close the *TopicPublisher* or *TopicSubscriber*, the session, and the connection.

In this example, the publishing client publishes text and object messages to the topic. The subscribing client receives the text and object messages from the topic. The text messages are displayed, and the object messages are executed. Note that the JNDI name for the connection factory and the queue will differ according to the messaging vendor and site naming convention.

Here is the code for the publishing client:

```
package j2ee.architect;
import java.io.*;
import java.util.*;
import javax.naming.*;
import javax.jms.*;
public class PSPublish {
  private static final String THIS = "PSPublish";
  public static final String JMS_FACTORY = "myTopicConnectionFactory";
  public static final String TOPIC = "myTopic1";
  public static void main(String[] args) throws Exception {
    // get the initial context
    InitialContext ctx = new InitialContext(System.getProperties());
    // lookup the topic connection factory
    TopicConnectionFactory tconnf =
      (TopicConnectionFactory) ctx.lookup(JMS_FACTORY);
    // create a topic connection
    TopicConnection tconn = tconnf.createTopicConnection();
    //tconn.setClientID(THIS);
    // create a topic session
    TopicSession tsess = tconn.createTopicSession(false,
      Session.AUTO_ACKNOWLEDGE);
    // lookup the topic object
    Topic topic = (Topic) ctx.lookup(TOPIC);
    // create a topic publisher
    TopicPublisher tpublish = tsess.createPublisher(topic);
    tpublish.setDeliveryMode(DeliveryMode.PERSISTENT);
    // start the connection
    tconn.start();
    log("Started.");
    ObjectMessage omsg = tsess.createObjectMessage();
    TextMessage tmsg = tsess.createTextMessage();
    publishText(tpublish, tmsg, "Market open.");
    publishObject(tpublish, omsg, new PSOrder("BUY", "200", "UCNY"));
    publishObject(tpublish, omsg, new PSOrder("BUY", "100", "UCUS"));
    publishObject(tpublish, omsg, new PSOrder("SELL", "50", "UC"));
    publishText(tpublish, tmsg, "Market closed.");
    publishText(tpublish, tmsg, "After hours market open.");
```

```
    publishObject(tpublish, omsg, new PSOrder("SELL", "25", "UC"));
    publishObject(tpublish, omsg, new PSOrder("BUY", "150", "UCUS"));
    publishText(tpublish, tmsg, "After hours market closed.");
    publishText(tpublish, tmsg, "***CLOSE***");  // Close message
    // close up
    tpublish.close();
    tsess.close();
    tconn.close();
    ctx.close();
    log("Finished.");
  }
  public static void publishObject(TopicPublisher tpublish,
    ObjectMessage omsg, Serializable obj) {
    try {
      log(obj.toString());
      omsg.setObject(obj);
      tpublish.publish(omsg);
      sleep(1000);
    } catch (Exception e) { log("Can't publish message: " + e); }
  }
  public static void publishText(TopicPublisher tpublish,
    TextMessage tmsg, String s) {
    try {
      log(s.toString());
      tmsg.setText(s);
      tpublish.publish(tmsg);
      sleep(1000);
    } catch (Exception e) { log("Can't publish message: " + e); }
  }
  private static void log(String msg) {
    System.out.println(new java.util.Date()+" "+THIS+" "+msg);
  }
  private static void sleep(int m) {
    try { Thread.currentThread().sleep( m );
    } catch (Exception e) {}
  }
}
```

Here is the code for the object that is published:

```
package j2ee.architect;
import java.io.Serializable;
// The object implements 'Runnable' so that the receiver
// can call the run() method. This is not a typical use
```

```java
// of messaging nor of runnable objects.
public class PSOrder implements Runnable, Serializable {
  String side;
  String security;
  String quantity;
  /* constructor methods */
  public PSOrder() {
      setSide("<side not set>");
      setQuantity("<quantity not set>");
      setSecurity("<security not set>");
  }
  public PSOrder(String t, String q, String s) {
      setSide(t);
      setQuantity(q);
      setSecurity(s);
  }
  /* run method */
  public void run() {
    System.out.println(new java.util.Date()+" PSOrder "+this.toString());
  }
  /* toString method */
  public String toString() {
    return getSide()+" "+getQuantity()+" "+getSecurity();
  }
  /* get/set methods */
  public String getSide() {
    return side;
  }
  public void setSide(String t) {
    side = t;
  }
  public String getSecurity() {
    return security;
  }
  public void setSecurity(String s) {
    security = s;
  }
  public String getQuantity() {
    return quantity;
  }
  public void setQuantity(String s) {
    quantity = s;
  }
}
```

Here is the code for the subscribing client. Note that the subscribing client has been coded by implementing a message listener:

```
package j2ee.architect;
import java.util.*;
import javax.naming.*;
import javax.jms.*;
public class PSSubscribe implements MessageListener {
  private static String THIS = "PSSubscribe";
  public static final String JMS_FACTORY = "myTopicConnectionFactory";
  public static final String TOPIC = "myTopic1";
  private InitialContext ctx;
  private TopicConnectionFactory tconnf;
  private TopicConnection tconn;
  private TopicSession tsess;
  private TopicSubscriber tsubscribe;
  private Topic topic;
  private boolean quit = false;
  public boolean ready;
  public static void main(String[] args) {
    PSSubscribe sub = new PSSubscribe(args.length>0?args[0]:"");
    if (!sub.ready) {
      log("Not ready to subscribe to messages.");
      System.exit(-1);
    }
    log("Started.");
    sub.run();
    sub.close();
    log("Finished.");
  }
  public PSSubscribe(String durable) {
    THIS = THIS+durable;
    try {
      ctx = new InitialContext(System.getProperties());
      tconnf = (TopicConnectionFactory) ctx.lookup(JMS_FACTORY);
      tconn = tconnf.createTopicConnection();
      tconn.setClientID(THIS);
      tsess = tconn.createTopicSession(false, Session.AUTO_ACKNOWLEDGE);
      topic = (Topic) ctx.lookup(TOPIC);
      // Create a durable or non-durable based on argument
      if (durable.equalsIgnoreCase("durable"))
        tsubscribe = tsess.createDurableSubscriber(topic,
                        tconn.getClientID());
      else
        tsubscribe = tsess.createSubscriber(topic);
      tsubscribe.setMessageListener(this);
      // start the connection
```

```
        tconn.start();
        ready = true;
    } catch (Exception e) {
        ready = false;
        log("Initialization failed. "+e);
        close();
    }
}
public void run() {
    if (!ready) return;
    synchronized (this) {
        while (!quit) {
            try { wait(); }
            catch (InterruptedException ie) { }
        }
    }
}
public void onMessage(Message msg) {
    if (!ready) return;
    // Declare a reference for the 'Runnable' object messages
    Runnable obj = null;
    try {
        if (msg instanceof ObjectMessage) {
            try {
                obj = (Runnable) ((ObjectMessage) msg).getObject();
            } catch (Exception e) {
                log("Message is not an object!");
                return;
            }
            // The object messages implement 'Runnable'. This is not
            // a typical use of messaging nor of runnable objects.
            try { if (obj != null) { obj.run(); }
            } catch (Exception e) {
                log("Can't run the object.");
            }
        } else if (msg instanceof TextMessage) {
            String text = ((TextMessage) msg).getText();
            log(text);
            if (text.equals("***CLOSE***")) {
                synchronized (this) {
                    quit = true;
                    notifyAll();
                }
            }
        } else {
            log("Message must be ObjectMessage or TextMessage.");
            log(msg.toString());
```

```
        }
    } catch (Exception e) {
        log("Can't receive message:  " + e);
    }
  }
  public void close() {
    try {
      if (tsubscribe != null) tsubscribe.close();
      if (tsess != null) tsess.close();
      if (tconn != null) tconn.close();
      if (ctx != null) ctx.close();
    } catch (Exception e) {
      log("Can't close up. "+e);
    }
  }
  private static void log(String msg) {
    System.out.println(new java.util.Date()+" "+THIS+" "+msg);
  }
}
```

When executed, here is the output from the publishing client:

```
Sun Sep 01 17:25:25 EDT 2002 PSPublish Started.
Sun Sep 01 17:25:25 EDT 2002 PSPublish Market open.
Sun Sep 01 17:25:27 EDT 2002 PSPublish BUY 200 UCNY
Sun Sep 01 17:25:28 EDT 2002 PSPublish BUY 100 UCUS
Sun Sep 01 17:25:29 EDT 2002 PSPublish SELL 50 UC
Sun Sep 01 17:25:30 EDT 2002 PSPublish Market closed.
Sun Sep 01 17:25:31 EDT 2002 PSPublish After hours market open.
Sun Sep 01 17:25:32 EDT 2002 PSPublish SELL 25 UC
Sun Sep 01 17:25:34 EDT 2002 PSPublish BUY 150 UCUS
Sun Sep 01 17:25:35 EDT 2002 PSPublish After hours market closed.
Sun Sep 01 17:25:36 EDT 2002 PSPublish ***CLOSE***
Sun Sep 01 17:25:37 EDT 2002 PSPublish Finished.
```

When executed, here is the output from the subscribing client:

```
Sun Sep 01 17:25:18 EDT 2002 PSSubscribe Started.
Sun Sep 01 17:25:26 EDT 2002 PSSubscribe Market open.
Sun Sep 01 17:25:27 EDT 2002 PSOrder BUY 200 UCNY
Sun Sep 01 17:25:28 EDT 2002 PSOrder BUY 100 UCUS
Sun Sep 01 17:25:29 EDT 2002 PSOrder SELL 50 UC
Sun Sep 01 17:25:30 EDT 2002 PSSubscribe Market closed.
Sun Sep 01 17:25:31 EDT 2002 PSSubscribe After hours market open.
Sun Sep 01 17:25:33 EDT 2002 PSOrder SELL 25 UC
Sun Sep 01 17:25:34 EDT 2002 PSOrder BUY 150 UCUS
Sun Sep 01 17:25:35 EDT 2002 PSSubscribe After hours market closed.
Sun Sep 01 17:25:36 EDT 2002 PSSubscribe ***CLOSE***
Sun Sep 01 17:25:36 EDT 2002 PSSubscribe Finished.
```

Message-Driven Bean (MDB) Component

The message-driven bean (MDB) is a stateless component that is invoked by the EJB container when a JMS message arrives for the destination (topic or queue) for which the bean has registered. An MDB is a message consumer, and like other JMS message consumers, it receives messages from a destination because it implements the *javax.jms.MessageListener* interface. It is then able to perform business logic based on the message contents.

MDBs receive JMS messages from clients in the same manner as any other JMS servicing object. A client that writes to a destination has no knowledge of the fact that an MDB is acting as the message consumer. MDBs were created to have an EJB that can be asynchronously invoked to process messages, while receiving all of the same EJB container services that are provided to session and entity beans.

When a message is sent to a destination, the EJB container ensures that the MDB registered to process the destination exists. If the MDB needs to be instantiated, the container will do this. The onMessage() method of the bean is called, and the message is passed in as an argument. MDBs and stateless session EJBs are similar in the sense that they do not maintain state across invocations. MDBs differ from stateless session beans and entity beans in that they have no home or remote interface. Internal or external clients cannot directly access the MDBs methods. Clients can only indirectly interact with MDBs by sending a message to the destination.

The EJB *deployer* is the person responsible for assigning MDBs to a destination at deployment time. The EJB container provides the service of creating and removing MDB instances as necessary or as specified at deployment time.

EJB Container and Message-Driven Beans

The EJB container allows for the concurrent consumption of messages and provides support for distributed transactions. This means that database updates, message processing, and connections to Enterprise Information Systems using the J2EE Connector Architecture (JCA) can all participate in the same transaction context.

The EJB container or application server provides many services for MDBs, so the bean developer can concentrate on implementing business logic. Here are some of the services provided by the EJB container:

- Handles all communication for JMS messages
- Checks the pool of available bean instances to see which MDB is to be used
- Enables the propagation of a security context by associating the role specified in the deployment descriptor to the appropriate execution thread

- Creates associates a transactional context if one is specified in the deployment descriptor
- Passes the message as an argument to the `onMessage()` method of the appropriate MDB instance
- Reallocates MDB resources to a pool of available instances

The EJB container also provides the following services based on the entries in the deployment descriptor file.

MDB Lifecycle Management   The lifecycle of an MDB corresponds to the lifespan of the EJB container in which it is deployed. Since MDBs are stateless, bean instances are usually pooled by the EJB container and retrieved by the container when a message is written to the destination for which it is a message consumer.

The container creates a bean instance by invoking the `newInstance()` method of the bean instance class object. After the instance is created, the container creates an instance of *javax.ejb.MessageDrivenContext* and passes it to the bean instance via the `setMessageDrivenContext()` method. The `ejbCreate()` method is also called on the bean instance before it is placed in the pool and is then made available to process messages.

Exception Handling   MDBs may not throw application exceptions while processing messages. This means that the only exceptions that may be thrown by a MDB are runtime exceptions indicating a system-level error. The container will handle these exceptions by removing the bean instance and rolling back any transaction started by the bean instance or by the container.

Threading and Concurrency   An MDB instance is assumed to execute in a single thread of control. The EJB container will guarantee this behavior. In addition, the EJB container may provide a mode of operation that allows multiple messages to be handled concurrently by separate bean instances. This deployment option utilizes expert level classes that are defined in the JMS specification. The JMS provider is not required to provide implementations for these classes, so the EJB container may not be able to take advantage of them with every JMS implementation. Using these classes involves a tradeoff between performance and serialization of messages delivered to the server.

Message Acknowledgment   The container always handles message acknowledgment for MDBs. It is prohibited for the bean to use any message acknowledgment methods—for example, `acknowledge()` or `rollback()`.

The message acknowledgment can be set to either *AUTO_ACKNOWLEDGE*, allowing the message to be delivered once, or *DUPS_OK_ACKNOWLEDGE*, allowing the delivery of duplicate messages after a failure. Note that if a bean has the *Required* transaction attribute, it will process the onMessage() method inside a transaction.

Because the MDB has no client, no security principal is propagated to the EJB container on receipt of a message. The EJB framework provides facilities for a bean method to execute in a role specified in the deployment descriptor. As a result, the MDB can be configured to execute within a security context that can then be propagated to other EJBs that are called during the processing of a message.

Example MDB Code

In the following example code, the publishing client publishes simple messages to a topic. The subscribing MDB client receives the simple messages from the topic. Note that the JNDI name for the connection factory and the topic will differ per the messaging vendor and site naming convention.

Here is the code for the publishing client:

```
package j2ee.architect;
import javax.naming.*;
import javax.jms.*;
public class PSMDBPublish {
  private static final String THIS = "PSMDBPublish";
  public static final String JMS_FACTORY = "myTopicConnectionFactory";
  public static final String TOPIC = "myTopic3";
  public static void main(String[] args) throws Exception {
    // get the initial context
    InitialContext ctx = new InitialContext(System.getProperties());
    // lookup the topic connection factory
    TopicConnectionFactory tconnf =
      (TopicConnectionFactory) ctx.lookup(JMS_FACTORY);
    // create a topic connection
    TopicConnection tconn = tconnf.createTopicConnection();
    // create a topic session
    TopicSession tsess = tconn.createTopicSession(false,
        Session.AUTO_ACKNOWLEDGE);
    // lookup the topic object
    Topic topic = (Topic) ctx.lookup(TOPIC);
    // create a topic publisher
    TopicPublisher tpublish = tsess.createPublisher(topic);
    tpublish.setDeliveryMode(DeliveryMode.NON_PERSISTENT);
    // start the connection
    tconn.start();
    log("Started.");
```

```
    // create a simple message
    TextMessage tmsg = tsess.createTextMessage();
    // publish the messages
    tmsg.setText("Market open.");
    tpublish.publish(tmsg);
    log(tmsg.getText());
    tmsg.setText("Market closed.");
    tpublish.publish(tmsg);
    log(tmsg.getText());
    tmsg.setText("After hours market open.");
    tpublish.publish(tmsg);
    log(tmsg.getText());
    tmsg.setText("After hours market closed.");
    tpublish.publish(tmsg);
    log(tmsg.getText());
    // close up
    tpublish.close();
    tsess.close();
    tconn.close();
    ctx.close();
    log("Finished.");
  }
  private static void log(String msg) {
    System.out.println(new java.util.Date()+" "+THIS+" "+msg);
  }
}
```

Here is the code for the subscribing MDB client:

```
package j2ee.architect;
import javax.ejb.*;
import javax.jms.*;
public class PSMDBSubscribe implements MessageDrivenBean, MessageListener {
  private static final String THIS = "PSMDBSubscribe";
  protected MessageDrivenContext ctx;
  // Associate bean instance with a particular context.
  public void setMessageDrivenContext(MessageDrivenContext ctx) {
    this.ctx = ctx;
  }
  // When the bean is initialized.
  public void ejbCreate() { log("ejbCreate()"); }
  // When the bean is destroyed.
  public void ejbRemove() { log("ejbRemove()"); }
  // main business method.
  public void onMessage(Message msg) {
    try {
      // This class processes TextMessages.
```

```
      if (msg instanceof TextMessage) {
        log(((TextMessage) msg).getText());
      }
    } catch (Exception e) { log("Can't receive message:  " + e); }
  }
  private void log(String msg) {
    System.out.println(new java.util.Date()+" "+THIS+" "+msg);
  }
}
```

Here is the deployment descriptor for the subscribing MDB client:

```
<!DOCTYPE ejb-jar PUBLIC "-//Sun Microsystems, Inc.//DTD
Enterprise JavaBeans 2.0//EN"
"http://java.sun.com/j2ee/dtds/ejb-jar_2_0.dtd">
<ejb-jar>
 <enterprise-beans>
  <message-driven>
   <ejb-name>PSMDB</ejb-name>
   <ejb-class>j2ee.architect.PSMDBSubscribe</ejb-class>
   <transaction-type>Container</transaction-type>
   <message-driven-destination>
    <destination-type>javax.jms.Topic</destination-type>
   </message-driven-destination>
  </message-driven>
 </enterprise-beans>
</ejb-jar>
```

Here is the WebLogic deployment descriptor for the subscribing MDB client:

```
<?xml version="1.0"?>
<!DOCTYPE weblogic-ejb-jar PUBLIC "-//BEA Systems, Inc.//DTD
WebLogic 6.0.0 EJB//EN"
"http://www.bea.com/servers/wls600/dtd/weblogic-ejb-jar.dtd">
<weblogic-ejb-jar>
 <weblogic-enterprise-bean>
  <ejb-name>PSMDB</ejb-name>
  <message-driven-descriptor>
   <pool>
    <max-beans-in-free-pool>10</max-beans-in-free-pool>
    <initial-beans-in-free-pool>2</initial-beans-in-free-pool>
   </pool>
   <destination-jndi-name>myTopic3</destination-jndi-name>
  </message-driven-descriptor>
  <jndi-name>PSMDB</jndi-name>
 </weblogic-enterprise-bean>
</weblogic-ejb-jar>
```

When executed, here is the output from the publishing MDB client:

```
Sun Sep 01 17:19:23 EDT 2002 PSMDBPublish Started.
Sun Sep 01 17:19:23 EDT 2002 PSMDBPublish Market open.
Sun Sep 01 17:19:23 EDT 2002 PSMDBPublish Market closed.
Sun Sep 01 17:19:23 EDT 2002 PSMDBPublish After hours market open.
Sun Sep 01 17:19:23 EDT 2002 PSMDBPublish After hours market closed.
Sun Sep 01 17:19:23 EDT 2002 PSMDBPublish Finished.
```

When executed, here is the output from the subscribing MDB client:

```
Sun Sep 01 17:19:23 EDT 2002 PSMDBSubscribe Market open.
Sun Sep 01 17:19:23 EDT 2002 PSMDBSubscribe Market closed.
Sun Sep 01 17:19:23 EDT 2002 PSMDBSubscribe After hours market open.
Sun Sep 01 17:19:23 EDT 2002 PSMDBSubscribe After hours market closed.
```

CERTIFICATION OBJECTIVE 8.05

Identify Scenarios That Are Appropriate to Implementation Using Messaging, Enterprise JavaBeans Technology, or Both

The following table shows messaging and EJB implementations that can be used as solutions for the given scenarios.

SCENARIO & SOLUTION	
You need to perform a transaction that is distributed across multiple applications and systems; which technology is most appropriate for maintaining this type of distributed transaction?	The EJB container provides support for database updates, message processing, and connections to EIS systems using the J2EE Connector Architecture (JCA). This will allow all to participate in the same transaction context. Messaging by itself is not a complete solution for this scenario.
You need to broadcast stock prices to applications executing on a trader's desktop…	A publish/subscribe messaging solution will be sufficient.
You need to send an order request to another system…	Possibly use a combination of EJB for retrieving order data and messaging for sending the data to the other system.
What technology is appropriate for easier integration of incompatible systems?	Use a messaging solution to provide the interface between systems that are not able to communicate directly.

CERTIFICATION SUMMARY

JMS provides a highly flexible and scalable solution for building loosely coupled applications in the enterprise environment. It brings all of the advantages of a messaging-based application into the Java language. JMS links messaging systems with all the benefits of Java technology for rapid application deployment and application maintenance.

This chapter should give you an understanding of the JMS and messaging in general and the appropriate scenarios for using messaging in applications.

TWO-MINUTE DRILL

Here are some of the key points from each certification objective in Chapter 8.

Identify Scenarios That Are Appropriate to Implementation Using Messaging

❑ Scenarios appropriate to implementation using message include asynchronous communication, one-to-many communication, guaranteed messaging, and transactional messaging.

List Benefits of Synchronous and Asynchronous Messaging

❑ Some benefits to synchronous messaging are that both parties must be active to participate and the message must be acknowledged before proceeding to the next.

❑ Asynchronous messaging benefits are that as the volume of traffic increases, more bandwidth or additional hardware is not required; it is less affected by failures at the hardware, software, and network levels; and when capacities are exceeded, information is not lost and is instead only delayed.

Identify Scenarios That Are More Appropriate to Implementation Using Asynchronous Messaging, Rather Than Synchronous

❑ Scenarios more appropriate to asynchronous messaging include those in which a response is not required or not immediately required.

❑ Asynchronous processing is also more appropriate for high volume transaction processing.

Identify Scenarios That Are More Appropriate to Implementation Using Synchronous Messaging, Rather Than Asynchronous

❑ One scenario more appropriate to synchronous messaging includes that in which a response to the message is required before continuing, for example, for transactions requiring credit card or user login authentication.

❑ A second scenario includes a transaction where both parties must be active participants.

Identify Scenarios That Are Appropriate to Implementation Using Messaging, Enterprise JavaBeans Technology, or Both

❑ The scenarios appropriate for messaging technology include broadcasting stock prices to traders, instant messages, and in situations when integration of incompatible systems is necessary.

❑ The scenarios appropriate for EJB technology include those that perform business logic and those that maintain persistent data.

❑ The scenarios appropriate for messaging and EJB technology including those that require maintenance of distributed transactions and those that send an order to another system.

SELF TEST

The following questions will help you measure your understanding of the material presented in this chapter. Read all the choices carefully because there may be more than one correct answer. Choose all correct answers for each question.

Identify Scenarios That Are Appropriate to Implementation Using Messaging

1. Which of the following are characteristics of publish/subscribe message model?

   A. Always use a URL to identify publishers.

   B. Subject-based addressing.

   C. Location-independent publishers.

   D. Only synchronous communication between publishers and subscribers is possible.

2. Which of the following are valid methods for a *TopicSubscriber*?

   A. `receive()`

   B. `receiveNoWait()`

   C. `receiveWait()`

   D. `receiveSync()`

3. What are the types of messaging models supported in JMS?

   A. Point-to-point

   B. Send/receive

   C. Transmit/receive

   D. Publish/subscribe

4. What is a message digest?

   A. A digital fingerprint value that is computed from a message, file, or byte stream

   B. A shortened summary of a message

   C. The subject line of a message

   D. A processing function of the mail server

5. Which of the following scenarios are suitable for publish/subscribe messaging model?

   A. It is used to receive news stories.

   B. It is used for receiving sales forecasts.

   C. It is used for sending stock prices to traders on the trading floor.

   D. It is used to authorize a user ID and password.

6. What deliver modes are available in JMS?

    A. *PERSISTENT*

    B. *NON_PERSISTENT*

    C. *PERMANENT*

    D. *DURABLE*

7. Which of the following are valid message acknowledgment types?

    A. *AUTO_ACKNOWLEDGE*

    B. *CLIENT_ACKNOWLEDGE*

    C. *DUPS_OK_ACKNOWLEDGE*

    D. *NO_ACKNOWLEDGE*

8. Which of the following are *not* valid message body formats?

    A. *MapMessage*

    B. *ObjectMessage*

    C. *TextMessage*

    D. *StringMessage*

9. Which of the following are *not* valid JMS objects?

    A. *MessageProducer*

    B. *MessageConsumer*

    C. *MessageViewer*

    D. *MessageSelector*

10. Which of the following would *not* be used in a client application performing point-to-point messaging?

    A. Topic

    B. *InitialContext*

    C. Queue

    D. Session

List Benefits of Synchronous and Asynchronous Messaging

11. Which of the following are advantages of asynchronous messaging architectures?

    A. Better use of bandwidth

    B. Supports load balancing

    C. Provides sender with instant response

    D. Scalability

12. Which of the following statements are true for asynchronous messaging?

    A. It decouples senders and receivers.

    B. It can increase performance.

    C. It is better suited to smaller message sizes.

    D. It only works with blocking calls.

Identify Scenarios That Are More Appropriate to Implementation Using Asynchronous Messaging, Rather Than Synchronous

13. Which method must be called to receive messages asynchronously?

    A. The `receive` method

    B. The `processMessage` method

    C. The `readMessage` method

    D. The `onMessage` method

14. Which of the following are *not* features of asynchronous messaging?

    A. As the volume of traffic increases, it is better able to handle the spike in demand.

    B. A message must be acknowledged before the producer can send another.

    C. It is less affected by failures at the hardware, software, and network levels.

    D. When capacities are exceeded, information is not lost; instead, it is delayed.

Identify Scenarios That Are More Appropriate to Implementation Using Synchronous Messaging, Rather Than Asynchronous

15. Which method must be called to receive messages synchronously?

    A. The `receive` method

    B. The `processMessage` method

    C. The `readMessage` method

    D. The `onMessage` method

16. Which of the following cases are better suited to synchronous messaging?

    A. Electronic mail

    B. Credit card authorization

    C. Electronic processing of tax return

    D. Validation of a data entered

17. Which of the following are features of synchronous messaging?

    A. Both parties must be active to participate.

    B. Message must be acknowledged before proceeding.

    C. It decouples senders and receivers.

    D. It does not work with blocking calls.

18. Which of the following are *not* features of synchronous messaging?

    A. Both parties must be active to participate.

    B. It is unaffected by increases in traffic volume.

    C. Message must be acknowledged before proceeding to the next.

    D. Message is queued until it is ready for processing.

Identify Scenarios That Are Appropriate to Implementation Using Messaging, Enterprise JavaBeans Technology, or Both

19. Which of the following scenarios are not suitable for publish/subscribe messaging model?

    A. Sending an instant message

    B. Sending an order to another system

    C. Sending news stories to interested parties

    D. Sending a transaction to another system

20. What method must be implemented to receive messages in a Message-Driven Bean (MDB)?

    A. The `receive` method

    B. The `onMessage` method

    C. The `readMessage` method

    D. The `processMessage` method

SELF TEST ANSWERS

Identify Scenarios That Are Appropriate to Implementation Using Messaging

1. ☑ B and C. Publish/subscribe messages use subject-based addressing and provide location-independence for publishers.
  ☒ A and D. URLs are not used to identify publishers. Publish/subscribe is not limited to synchronous communication.

2. ☑ A and B. `receive()` and `receiveNoWait()` are valid methods for *TopicSubscriber.*
  ☒ C and D. `receiveWait()` and `receiveSync()` are not valid methods.

3. ☑ A and D. Point-to-point and publish/subscribe are the messaging models supported in JMS.
  ☒ B and C. Send/receive and transmit/receive are not valid messaging models.

4. ☑ A. A message digest is a digital fingerprint value that is computed from a message, file, or byte stream.
  ☒ B, C, and D are not definitions of a message digest.

5. ☑ D. Authorizing user IDs and passwords must use a synchronous process.
  ☒ A, B, and C. Receiving news stories, sales forecasts, and sending stock prices are suitable for asynchronous messaging.

6. ☑ A and B. *PERSISTENT* and *NON_PERSISTENT* are valid delivery modes.
  ☒ C and D. *PERMANENT* and *DURABLE* are invalid delivery modes.

7. ☑ A, B, and C. *AUTO_ACKNOWLEDGE, CLIENT_ACKNOWLEDGE,* and *DUPS_OK_ACKNOWLEDGE,* are valid.
  ☒ D. *NO_ACKNOWLEDGE* is an invalid message acknowledgement type.

8. ☑ D. *StringMessage* is not a valid message body format.
  ☒ A, B, and C. *MapMessage, ObjectMessage, TextMessage* are valid.

9. ☑ C. *MessageViewer* is not a valid JMS object.
  ☒ A, B, and D. *MessageProducer, MessageConsumer, MessageSelector* are valid.

10. ☑ A. Topics are used in publish/subscribe messaging.
  ☒ B, C, and D are valid classes in point-to-point messaging.

List Benefits of Synchronous and Asynchronous Messaging

11. ☑ **A, B, and D.** Asynchronous architectures make better use of bandwidth, support leveling of workloads, and are more scalable.

    ☒ **C.** Does not provide sender with instant response.

12. ☑ **A, B, and C.** Asynchronous messaging decouples senders and receivers, can increase performance, and is better suited to smaller message sizes.

    ☒ **D.** Asynchronous messaging does not work with blocking calls.

Identify Scenarios That Are More Appropriate to Implementation Using Asynchronous Messaging, Rather Than Synchronous

13. ☑ **D.** The onMessage method must be implemented to receive messages asynchronously.

    ☒ **A, B, and C.** The processMessage and readMessage methods do not exist. The receive method is used for synchronous messaging.

14. ☑ **B.** A message is not acknowledged before a producer can send another in asynchronous messaging.

    ☒ **A, C, and D** are valid features.

Identify Scenarios That Are More Appropriate to Implementation Using Synchronous Messaging, Rather Than Asynchronous

15. ☑ **A.** The receive method must be implemented to receive messages synchronously.

    ☒ **B, C, and D.** The processMessage and readMessage methods do not exist. The onMessage method is used for asynchronous messaging.

16. ☑ **B and D.** Credit card authorization and validation of a data entered are better suited to synchronous messaging because of the need for an instant response.

    ☒ **A and C.** Electronic mail and electronic processing of a tax return do not need instant responses.

17. ☑ **A and B.** Both parties must be active to participate and message must be acknowledged before proceeding.

    ☒ **C and D.** Do not decouple senders and receivers and only work with blocking calls.

18. ☑ **A and C.** Synchronous messaging is not unaffected by volume increase and messages are not queued.

    ☒ **B and D** are valid features.

Identify Scenarios That Are Appropriate to Implementation Using Messaging, Enterprise JavaBeans Technology, or Both

19. ☑ **A, B,** and **D.** Sending an instant message, an order to another system, or a transaction to another system is not suitable for the publish/subscribe message model.
    ☒ **C.** Sending news stories to interested parties is suitable for the publish/subscribe message model.

20. ☑ **B.** The onMessage() method is the correct method.
    ☒ **A, C,** and **D** are incorrect methods to receive messages in a Message-Driven Bean (MDB).

J2EE
SUN® CERTIFIED ENTERPRISE ARCHITECT

9

Internationalization and Localization

CERTIFICATION OBJECTIVES

9.01   State Three Aspects of Any Application That Might Need to Be Varied or Customized in Different Deployment Locales

9.02   List Three Features of the Java Programming Language That Can Be Used to Create an Internationalizable/Localizable Application

✓   Two-Minute Drill

Q&A   Self Test

A pplications often need the flexibility to support the language and presentation customs for several geographic locations. In Java parlance, this process is known as internationalization and localization. This chapter covers the issues surrounding this process and the aspects of an application affected by it.

State Three Aspects of Any Application That Might Need to Be Varied or Customized in Different Deployment Locales

Internationalization is the process of preparing application code to support multiple languages, and *localization* is the process of adapting an internationalized application so that it supports a specific language or locale. A *locale* is an environment that includes regional and language-specific information.

Internationalization and Localization

Internationalization involves isolating portions of the application that present output data to the user so that the data can be converted to the appropriate language and character set. Localization involves translating these strings into a specific language and maintaining them in a file that the application can access—for example, a property file. Thus, internationalizing an application allows it to be adapted to new languages and regions, while localization provides the adaptation of an internationalized application to a specific country or region. It is important to note that the Enterprise JavaBeans (EJB) container need not be running in the same locale as the client browser.

Applications need to customize the presentation of data according to the locale of the user. An application must be internationalized, and then it can be localized. During internationalization (also known as *I18N,* because the number of characters between the first and last character is 18), locale dependencies are separated from an application's source code. Examples of these locale dependencies include user interface labels, messages character set, encoding, and numeric, currency, and time formats. During localization (also known as *L10N*), an internationalized application is adapted to a specific locale. Internationalization and localization make Java 2 Enterprise Edition (J2EE) applications available to a global audience.

Internationalization is typically overlooked when developing an enterprise web application, because these sorts of applications are usually targeted to a particular local user space. When developing an enterprise application that may be used globally, however, you should consider internationalization from the outset. It is easier to design an application that is capable of being internationalized than to redesign an existing application later. As with other redesigns, a great deal of time and money can be saved by planning for internationalization and localization at the outset.

With a web-based enterprise application, the presentation layer is the focus of internationalization and localization efforts. The presentation layer includes JavaServer Pages (JSPs), servlets, and any supporting helper JavaBeans components.

Overview of Internationalizing an Application

Before we get to the details of internationalizing an application, let's review our objectives. After the architectural design and development is completed, an internationalized enterprise application will have the following characteristics:

- With the addition of localization data, the same executable—such as an application Enterprise Archive (file with a .ear extension)—can run worldwide.

- GUI component labels and other textual elements (such as messages) are not hard-coded within the program but are stored outside and retrieved dynamically.

- Regionally dependent data, such as dates and currencies, appear in formats that conform to the end user's region and language.

- Recompilation is not required to support a new language. It can be localized quickly by the addition of the new language property file entries.

So what should you analyze to internationalize your application? Many types of data vary with region or language, so your approach depends on the application being delivered. A non-exhaustive item list of this data includes the following:

messages	labels on GUI components	online help
colors	graphics	icons
dates	times	numbers
currencies	measurements	phone numbers
personal titles	postal addresses	page layouts
legal rules	sounds	

SCENARIO & SOLUTION

You are developing an application that will only execute in a single and very narrow geographic location.	There is no need to develop the application using Java's internationalization feature.
You are creating an application for a company with offices in several countries and time zones. Where possible, the application needs to adapt its functionality and presentation to local customs and language.	Use Java's internationalization feature to develop this application.

CERTIFICATION OBJECTIVE 9.02

List Three Features of the Java Programming Language That Can Be Used to Create an Internationalizable/Localizable Application

Now let's take a look at Java's support for internationalization and localization. We'll look at specific API classes and objects that have been designed to help with I18N and L10N.

Java Support for Internationalization and Localization

An internationalized J2EE application cannot assume that it is being executed from a single locale and often needs to service requests for many locales simultaneously. That is to say that a client request will arrive with an associated locale and consequently expect the response with the same locale. Because internationalization affects all tiers of a J2EE application, it is an architecturally fundamental issue. Unfortunately, on many J2EE projects, application internationalization is an afterthought and usually requires a great deal of refactoring to incorporate it later. As stated previously, internationalization and localization dependencies need to be identified during the project design phase.

Let's review some of the internationalization and localization classes, tools, and features available to use in Java.

Using java.util.Properties for Localization

The *java.util.Properties* class represents a set of properties that can be persisted. The properties can be loaded from or saved to a stream. Both the key and its corresponding lookup value in the list of properties is a string. The properties object typically stores information about the characteristics of an application or its environment, and this can also include information pertaining to internationalization and localization. By creating a properties object and using the `load()` method, a program can read a localized properties file or any arbitrary input stream and then access the appropriate localized values using the same key:

```
Properties props = new Properties();
String myProps = "l10nfile";
props.load(new BufferedInputStream(new FileInputStream(myProps);
String msgvalue = System.getProperty("msgkey");
```

See "ResourceBundle" a little later in this chapter for more advanced uses of properties for localization.

Locale

As mentioned, a locale is a way of identifying and using the exact language and cultural settings for a particular session or user. In Java, a locale is identified by one, two, and occasionally three elements:

- **Language**   This is the basic identifier for a locale. It contains a valid International Standards Organization, ISO 639, two-letter language code. Examples are *en* for English and *es* for Spanish. (A complete list of two-letter language codes can be found at *http://ftp.ics.uci.edu/pub/ietf/http/related/iso639.txt.*)

- **Regional variation**   This is a country code. It contains a valid ISO 3166 two-letter country code. Examples are *GB* for United Kingdom, *CO* for Colombia, and *US* for United States. (A complete list can be found at *http://www.chemie.fu-berlin.de/diverse/doc/ISO_3166.html.*)

- **Variant**   This element is less frequently specified. It is used for creating locales with vendor- or browser-specific code. Examples are *WIN* for Windows, *MAC* for Macintosh, and *POSIX* for POSIX (Linux or UNIX). It is also used to allow for the possibility of more than one locale per country and language combination. Most European countries also now have the *EURO* variant for currency formatting.

Locales are defined with the language and country code separated by an underscore, like so: *es_CO* or *en_US*. The *Locale* class provides a number of constants that you can use to create locale objects for common locales. For example, *Locale.US* creates a locale object for the United States. Other locale names include, for example, *de* for German, *de_CH* for Swiss-style German, and *de_CH_POSIX* for Swiss-style German on a POSIX-compliant platform.

The locale object controls formatting for numeric, data, currency, and percent display. It can affect many other areas, such as how case folding (uppercasing and lowercasing of letters) is handled. It can affect the way a list is sorted (called the *collation sequence*), or which day appears in the leftmost column on a calendar. Based on the locale, Java provides mechanisms for loading the user interface, messages, and specialized code from *resource bundle*s (which are defined next). In short, locales provide a way of configuring classes to match the user requirements dynamically.

Platforms other than Java have slight variations for locale objects, names, and structures. For example, Microsoft Windows uses a proprietary three-letter code to identify a locale.

Many developers confuse character-set problems with locales. Character-set problems are usually the primary aspect that is addressed when internationalizing code. Terms such as *double-byte enabling, kanji,* or *Unicode enabling* are key internationalization discussions. However, the issues surrounding character set are only a part of making a product locale-aware. Without the correct character-set handling, data will not display correctly. However, internationalization and localization goes beyond just manipulating the characters.

In Java, the *java.util.Locale* object represents a specific geographical or cultural region. An operation that requires a locale to perform its task is called *locale-sensitive* and uses the locale to refine information for the user. For example, displaying a number is a locale-sensitive operation—that is, the number should be formatted according to the conventions of the user's native country or region.

Because locale objects are merely region identifiers, no validity check is performed when they are constructed. You can query particular resources to determine whether they are available for your locale. For example, you can call the `getAvailableLocales()` method on *DateFormat* to obtain an array of locales for which *DateFormat*s are installed. When a resource is requested for a particular locale, the best available match is returned, which is not necessarily precisely what was requested.

After you've created a locale, you can access it for information about itself. Use `getCountry()` for the ISO country code and `getLanguage()` for the ISO language code. You can use `getDisplayCountry()` for the name of the country suitable for displaying to the user. Similarly, you can use `getDisplayLanguage()` for the name of the language suitable for displaying to the user. Interestingly, the `getDisplay` accessor methods are locale-sensitive and have two versions: one that uses the default locale and one that uses the locale specified in the argument.

ResourceBundle

The *java.util.ResourceBundle* class defines a naming convention for locales, which should be used whenever organizing resources by locale. Resource bundles hold locale-specific objects. When your class requires a locale-specific resource, for example a string, your class can load it from the resource bundle that matches the current user's locale. Correspondingly, you can write class code that is independent of the user's locale. This allows you to write classes that can do the following:

- Can be localized—translated into different languages
- Can handle multiple locales simultaneously
- Can be modified to support additional locales

A *resource bundle* is a set of related classes that are inherited from *java.util .ResourceBundle*. Each *ResourceBundle* subclass has the same base name plus a component that identifies its locale. For example, suppose your resource bundle is named *UCResources*. The first class you are likely to write is the default resource bundle, which simply has the same name as its family—*UCResources*. You can then create related locale-specific classes as needed—for example, you can provide a German class named *UCResources_de*.

Each subclass of *ResourceBundle* contains the same objects, but the objects have been translated for the locale represented by that subclass of *ResourceBundle*.

The resource bundle lookup searches for classes with a name assembled from the following that are concatenated, separated by underscores. Consider the following example: *UCResources_en_GB_cockney*. This class name includes the following:

- A base class (*UCResources*)
- The desired language (*en*)
- The desired country (*GB*)
- The desired variant (*cockney*)

During runtime, if the class or a properties file of the same name with the properties extension cannot be found, the lookup will review each of the elements in turn until a match is found. By providing a class with no suffixes (that is, the base class), a match will always be found.

The base class must also be fully qualified (for example, *UCPackage.UCResources*, not just *UCResources*). It must also be accessible by your class code; it cannot be a private class to the package where *ResourceBundle.getBundle* is called. While keys must be defined as *java.lang.String*, the lookup values can be any subclass of *java.lang.Object*.

PropertyResourceBundle is a subclass of *ResourceBundle* that handles resources for a locale using a set of static strings from a property object containing the resource data. *ResourceBundle.getBundle* will look for the appropriate properties object and create a *PropertyResourceBundle* that refers to it.

Character Sets

A *character set* is a group of textual or graphical symbols that is mapped to a set of (positive) integers called *code points*. The ASCII (American Standard Code for Information Interchange) character set is commonly used for representing American English. ASCII contains uppercase and lowercase Roman alphabets, European numerals, punctuation, a group of control codes, and some symbols. For example, the ASCII code point for *A* is 65 (hexadecimal 41).

The ISO 8859 character-set series was created because ASCII was not good for supporting languages other than American English. Each ISO 8859 character set can have up to 256 code points. ISO 8859-1, also known as "Latin-1," has the ASCII character set, symbols, and characters with accents, circumflexes, and other diacritics. With the ISO 8859 series of character sets, it is possible to represent texts for dozens of languages.

Unicode (ISO 10646) defines a standard and universal character set. It was designed to represent practically all character sets in use around the world and can be extended. Unicode encompasses alphabetic scripts and ideographic writing systems, and it may be rendered in any direction.

Unicode is an international effort to provide a single character set for everyone. Java uses the Unicode 2.x character-encoding standard. In Unicode, every character uses 2 bytes. Ranges of character encodings represent various writing systems and other special symbols. For example, Unicode characters in the range 0x9FFF through 0xAC00 represent the Han characters used in Asia: China, Japan, Korea, Taiwan, and Vietnam. Despite the obvious advantages of Unicode, it has a big shortcoming: Unicode support is limited on many platforms because of the lack of fonts capable of displaying all the Unicode characters.

The Java programming language internally represents characters and string objects as encoded Unicode. Classes written in the Java programming language can process data in multiple languages, natively performing localized operations such as string comparison, parsing, and collation. Unicode characters in a Java class may be represented as escape sequences, using the notation \u*XXXX*, where *XXXX* is the character's 16-bit code point in hexadecimal. These Unicode-escaped strings are useful for Java source files that are not encoded as Unicode.

Unicode Transformation Format (UTF), where the *U* stands for UCS (Universal Character Set), is a multi-byte encoding format that stores some characters in 1 byte and others in 2 or 3 bytes. If most of the data is ASCII based, UTF is more compact than Unicode, but in a worst-case scenario, the UTF string can be 50 percent larger than the equivalent Unicode string. Overall, UTF is still fairly efficient and is the most widely used character-encoding scheme.

Encoding

An *encoding* will map the code points in a character set to units of a specific width, and it defines byte serialization and ordering rules. Many of these character sets have more than one encoding. The *java.io* package contains classes that support the reading and writing of character data streams using a variety of encoding schemes. Some of these classes are discussed later in this chapter, and they all have names that end in either *Reader* (for example, *BufferedReader* and *InputStreamReader*) or *Writer* (for example, *BufferedWriter*, *PrintWriter,* and *OutputStreamWriter*).

Programmers use *PrintWriter* within JSPs and servlets to produce textual responses, which are automatically encoded. It is possible for servlets to output binary data with no encoding using an *OutputStream* class. You must explicitly set an encoding if you create an application that uses a character set that cannot be handled by the default encoding (ISO 8859-1, *Latin_1*).

UTF-8 is an 8-bit form of UTF, the unification of US-ASCII and Unicode. UTF-8 is a variable-width character encoding that encodes 16-bit Unicode characters into 1 or 2 bytes. Encoding internationalized content in UTF-8 is recommended by Sun because it is compatible with the majority of existing web content and provides access to the Unicode character set. In addition, most current browsers and e-mail clients support it, and it is one of the two required encoding schemes for XML documents (the other being UTF-16).

Handling Text Dates and Numbers with the java.text Package

This package provides several classes and interfaces that can be used for handling text, dates, numbers, and messages in ways that are independent of natural languages. This means that an application can be created in a language-independent manner and can rely on separate, dynamically linked, (and therefore) localized resources.

All of the classes in the *java.text* package are sensitive to either the default or provided locale. This package of classes provides the ability to format numbers, dates, and messages; and to parse, search and sort through strings; and iterate over characters, words, sentences, and line breaks.

This package contains three main groups of classes and interfaces: *iteration, formatting,* and *string collation.* Here is a list of some of the classes in the *java.text* package:

- *Annotation*
- *CollationKey*
- *Collator*
- *Format*

An *annotation* object is a wrapper for a text attribute value if the attribute has annotation characteristics. One characteristic is the text range to which the attribute is applied; this is critical to the semantics of the range. Wrapping the attribute value into an annotation object guarantees that adjacent text does not get merged, even if the attribute values are equal, and it indicates to text containers that the attribute should be discarded if the underlying text is modified.

The different languages of the world use alphabets that differ, and thus they require unique ways to sort strings written in those languages. *Collation* is the process of sorting strings according to locale-specific customs. The *Collator* is an abstract base class that provides locale-sensitive string comparison. Use this class when building search and sort routines for natural-language text. Subclasses implement specific collation requirements. Use the static factory method, `getInstance()`, to obtain the proper collator object for a given locale.

A *CollationKey* represents a string that is controlled by the rules of a specific collator object. Comparing two *CollationKey*s will return the relative order of the strings they represent and is typically faster than using the `Collator.compare()` method when sorting a list of Strings. *CollationKey*s are generated by calling the `getCollationKey()` method on a collator, and they can be compared only when generated from the same collator. The generation process converts the string to a series of bits that can then be compared bitwise. This translates into fast comparisons once the keys are generated. The cost of generating keys is justified in faster comparisons when strings need to be compared many times. Alternatively, the first couple of characters of each string often determine the result of a comparison. `Collator.compare()` examines only as many characters as it needs, and as soon as an inequality is arrived at, the comparison is over.

Format is obviously important. Again, *Format* is an abstract base class for formatting locale-sensitive information such as dates, messages, and numerics. Format defines the programming interface for formatting locale-sensitive objects into strings (use the `format()` method) and for parsing strings into objects (use the `parseObject()` method). Any string formatted by *Format* is parsable by `parseObject()`. *Format* has three concrete subclasses, *DateFormat*, *MessageFormat*, and *NumberFormat*, which will be covered later in this chapter in the sections "Internationalization with Respect to Data Handling," "Message Formatting," and "Date Formatting."

InputStreamReader

An *InputStreamReader* is a mechanism for converting from byte streams to character streams: It reads bytes and converts them into characters according to a specified character encoding. The class has two constructors: one with no arguments will use the platform default encoding and another takes an encoding argument (as a string). The ISO numbers are used to represent an encoding—for example, ISO 8859-9 is represented by *8859_9*.

There is no simple way to determine which encodings are supported, but you can call the `getEncoding()` method to obtain the name of the encoding used by the *InputStreamReader*. Characters that do not exist in a specific character set are substituted with another character, usually a question mark.

OutputStreamWriter

An *OutputStreamWriter* is a mechanism for converting data from character streams to byte streams: Characters written to it are translated into bytes according to a specified character encoding. The encoding that it uses is either specified explicitly by name (again an ISO number), or the default encoding for the platform is the default.

Every invocation of the `write()` method will in turn call the encoding converter for the given character(s). The converted bytes are buffered before being written to the output stream.

Again, as with *InputStreamReader*, you cannot determine which encodings are supported, but calling the `getEncoding()` method will return the encoding used by the *OutputStreamWriter*. Characters that do not exist in a specific character set are substituted with another character, usually a question mark.

Internationalization with Respect to Data Handling

Data handling is the part of a web application most affected by internationalization, with impact in three areas: data input, storage, and presentation.

Data input is typically input to a web application by a Hypertext Transfer Protocol (HTTP) post back to a servlet from a form on an Hypertext Markup Language (HTML) page. Typically, the client platform will provide a means for inputting the data.

The browser running in the client's native locale encodes the form parameter data in the HTTP request so that it is in a readable format for the web application.

When the application receives the data, it is in Unicode format, obviating character-set issues. Word breaking or parsing can be handled with the *BreakIterator* class in the *java.text* package.

Data storage for international applications means setting your database to a Unicode 2.0 character encoding (such as UTF-8 or UTF-16). This allows data to be saved in many different languages. The content you save must be entered properly from the web tier. The Java Database Connectivity (JDBC) drivers must support the encoding you choose.

To enable locale-independent data formatting, an application must be designed to present localized data appropriately for a target locale. The developer must ensure that locale-sensitive text such as dates, times, currency, and numbers are presented in a locale-specific way. If you design your text-related classes in a locale-independent way, they are reusable throughout an application.

The following code demonstrates methods used to format currency in locale-specific and locale-independent ways:

```
package com.ucny.utils;
...
public class Formatter {
...
//Format currency for the default locale.
public static String formatCCY(double amount) {
   String pattern = "$###,###,###.00";
   //Get number format for the default (system) locale.
   NumberFormat nf = NumberFormat.getCurrencyInstance();
   DecimalFormat df = (DecimalFormat)nf;
   df.setMinimumFractionDigits(2);
   df.setMaximumFractionDigits(2);
   df.setDecimalSeparatorAlwaysShown(true);
   df.applyPattern(pattern);
   return df.format(amount);
}
//Format currency for the specified locale.
public static String formatCCY(Locale locale, string prefix, double amount) {
   String pattern = prefix+"###,###,###.00";
   //Get number format for the passed in locale.
   NumberFormat nf = NumberFormat.getCurrencyInstance(locale);
   DecimalFormat df = (DecimalFormat)nf;
   df.setMinimumFractionDigits(2);
   df.setMaximumFractionDigits(2);
   df.setDecimalSeparatorAlwaysShown(true);
   df.applyPattern(pattern);
   return df.format(amount);
} ...
```

In a JSP page, the following code snippet shows calls to the currency format function for the default locale and for the Great Britain locale:

```
...
<%=JSPUtil.formatCCY(Locale.UK, order.getTotal())%>
...
<%=JSPUtil.formatCCY(Locale.UK, "£", order.getTotal())%>
...
```

These JSP expressions use the two versions of the formatCCY() method of the *Formatter* utility. The total that is returned from the order.getTotal() method is a Java double primitive datatype. Note that when using this code, the JSP will need to import the *java.util.Locale* and *com.ucny.utils.Formatter* classes.

Using Java Internationalization APIs in J2EE Applications

Java internationalization APIs include utility classes and interfaces for externalizing application resources, formatting messages, formatting currency and decimals, representing dates and times, and collating. The next sections explain how to use J2SE internationalization APIs in J2EE applications.

Message Formatting

The *java.text.MessageFormat* class provides a generic way to create concatenated message strings. It contains a pattern string that has embedded format specifiers. The MessageFormat.format() method then formats an array of objects using these embedded format specifiers and returns the result in a *StringBuffer*. The *MessageFormat* class is good for formatting system-level messages such as error or logging strings. Here is an example:

```
// Format the message

String pattern =
"Catalog number {0}, item code{1}: has been sent to order processing.";

MessageFormat mf = new MessageFormat(pattern);
Object[] objs =
new Object[] {new Integer(catalogNumber),new Integer(itemNumber)};
StringBuffer result = new StringBuffer();
String message = mf.format(objs,result, new FieldPosition());
```

In this code snippet, the *MessageFormat* holds the pattern and uses it to format the resultant string, substituting formatted objects (integers) in place of the embedded format specifiers ({0} and {1}). The *MessageFormat* class is very effective for internationalizing custom tags for a JSP.

Date Formatting

Typically, enterprise applications store, compare, and perform arithmetic on date values. J2EE applications typically persist date and time values to a JDBC data store using *java.sql.Date;* hold them in memory using *java.util.Date;* manipulate and interpret them using the *java.util.Calendar* class; and parse, format, and present them using the *java.text.DateFormat* class. The *java.text.DateFormat* class is an abstract class that provides a locale-sensitive API for parsing, formatting, and normalizing dates for presentation. The *java.text.SimpleDateFormat* class implements simple date and time value formatting for all supported locales.

Collation

As mentioned, collation is the process of ordering text using language- or script-specific rules, rather than using binary comparison; it is therefore locale-specific. It is possible for a character set to have more than one collating sequences. These lists of characters may be ordered numerically or lexically. For an internationalized application, the abstract class *java.text.Collator* is recommended for use when ordering lists of items. The *java.text.Collator* class and its related classes provide collation facilities that are locale-aware. For example, a component that produces ordered lists of NASDAQ stock issue entries could use *Collator* to place the entries in an order appropriate to the client's locale.

You could rely on the database to provide this collation. However, this may not be a good idea for internationalization, because most databases support a single sort order (typically specified at installation) and may not be portable to another database vendor.

Web Tier Internationalization

The web tier has JSP, JavaBean, and servlet components that need to be designed with internationalization and localization in mind. The essential areas that are covered for I18N and L10N in this layer are

- HTTP requests and responses
- Design of web tier components

HTTP Requests and Responses

For an internationalized web application to work correctly, it must be able to determine the encoding of an incoming request and then ensure that the outgoing response is encoded the same way. However, the default locale for any component in the web tier is not the calling client's locale but the actual web container's default locale. To complicate matters, in a distributed environment, the default locale may differ among containers, making the default locale the locale of the web container servicing the specific part of the request.

The management of locale and encoding can be simplified by a few recommended techniques. The first approach is to choose a single and consistent request encoding. Therefore, if all web components transmit pages using a single encoding, requests from those generated pages will remain in that encoding. As mentioned earlier in this chapter, UTF-8 is considered the best encoding choice because it provides the broadest coverage of character sets, efficient data transmission, and wide browser support. Along with this approach, it is also recommended that you add a servlet filter to compensate for components that do not or forget to set the chosen encoding. The servlet filter sets the response encoding to a single value before a servlet or JSP page receives the request. This provides a single point of control for enforcing (and changing to) the required encoding before a servlet handles the response.

The other approaches are to store the locale and encoding either in hidden variables on HTML forms or in URL parameters, or to store this information on the server in the users' session state or in a stateful session EJB.

As mentioned, the encoding of the responses from JSP pages and servlets determines not only the format of characters in the response but also the encoding of any subsequent request from the served page.

The two attributes in the page directive for a JSP control encoding are

- *contentType*
- *pageEncoding*

Note that when using these attributes, the content type and encoding will be fixed at page translation time. For a more dynamic approach, use either a custom tag or a servlet to set encoding.

For a servlet, the two ways to set encoding of the response are to use the following methods on the *ServletResponse:*

- `setContentType()`
- `setLocale()`

These methods must be called before calling the `Servlet.getWriter()` method to ensure that the writer obtained is formed with the required encoding.

Design of Web Tier Components

The design and implementation of JSPs, custom tags, and JavaBean helper components are affected by I18N and L10N. Any of these components that are responsible for ordering data in a collating sequence or for formatting numbers, dates, currency, or percentages need to take into account the locale to display the data in an appropriate manner for that locale.

The two most common approaches exist for localizing JSP pages are as follows:

- *Creating a JSP for each locale, with each file stored in a separate directory in the server's name space.* Typically, a servlet or servlet filter forwards each request for a JSP page to the appropriate file based on the requesting client's locale. The name of each directory uses the standard resource bundle suffix naming convention.

- *Using resource bundles with a single JSP.* You can put together sets of localized text using locale-aware custom tags. When the page is served, the custom tags grab the necessary text from the resource bundle for the current locale.

The recommendation is to use separate JSP pages for each locale when the structure of the content and display logic differs greatly between locales or when messages depend on the target locale. For all other cases, the recommendation is to use resource bundles, especially for logging and error messages or when content varies in data values and not in content structure.

Here are the advantages to creating a JSP for each locale:

- **Maximum customizability**   This approach also allows for customization of the structure as well as the content for a locale.

- **Source clarity**   Everything is in one place instead of being spread across the JSP file containing the structural tags and a properties file or resource bundle containing named strings.

The disadvantage to creating a JSP for each locale is that it's difficult to keep a consistent look and feel among locales. This approach requires more maintenance because separate files must be maintained consistently for multiple locales.

Here are the advantages to using resource bundles with a single JSP:

- **Easier maintenance**   A change to the JSP page is reflected for all locales.

- **Consistent page structure**   The JSP keeps the same structure in all locales. Only data values, message text, and the language displayed can change.

- **Easy extensibility**   Defining a new resource bundle provides support for a new locale.

Here are the disadvantages to using resource bundles with a single JSP:

- Customizing its structure to locales is more difficult, because a single JSP produces the content for every locale.

- Page encoding must be compatible with the encoding of all application character sets.

Logging and Error Messages

Internationalization and localization are also needed when providing users and administrators with meaningful messages if exceptional conditions occur.

Messages and Exceptions

The presentation layer is responsible for localizing messages for clients of an application. When dealing with exceptions, subclasses of *java.lang.Exception* are recommended for communicating errors. They also need to be serializable so that they can be passed across tiers.

Exception classes should contain information detailing the error and must not already be localized. The presentation tier can use the error information contained in the message to create a message that is appropriate for the client. For the web tier, JSPs are probably the best mechanism for formatting error messages. Uncaught exceptions in a JSP are forwarded to the defined error page, if present. Here is an example:

```
<%@ page language="java" errorPage="jsp/exception/notFound.jsp" %>
```

The *errorPage* element argument defines the URL for the page to be displayed if a JSP page request results in an error.

Message Logging and System Exceptions

Logging messages and system exceptions are intended mostly for support personnel. The recommended approach is to use resource bundles to localize log messages and system exceptions. The easy way to determine a locale for system messages is to use the system default locale. However, if the application happens to be distributed and has differing locales, the locale for all system messages may be defined in an environment entry in the deployment descriptor for the component that creates and outputs the message.

Any system exception should be a subclass of *java.lang.RuntimeException*. With an internationalized design, the exception message should not contain the message itself but a key for the message that can be looked up within a resource bundle. The component that is responsible for writing the message to a log will use the resource bundles and the *MessageFormat* class to build and output a localized exception message. You can create your own subtree below *Exception* and *RemoteException* to indicate exceptions that will return properly localizable error codes.

How Would You Confirm the I18N Status of an Application?

To confirm that I18N validation is successful, you must run the application in another locale where a localized version of it is properly installed and then check that the following statements are true:

■ When the application runs in another locale where translated message files are properly installed, the messages and other values that were localized, such as font names and sizes, come from the message files of that locale and not

SCENARIO & SOLUTION

You need to find a localized value for a given key, for example, an error message.	Use *java.util.Properties* to load values from a stream (e.g. a *java.io.FileInputStream*) and then use a single lookup key to obtain a localized value.
You need to format and present numbers and currencies.	Use *java.text.NumberFormat*.
You need to format and present dates and times.	Use *java.text.DateFormat*.
You need to order and handle text data.	Use *Collator* and *CollationKey* for ordering and *MessageFormat*, *ResourceBundle*, or *PropertyResourceBundle* to handle text.
You need to read and write files.	Use *InputStreamReader* for reading and *OutputStreamWriter* for writing.
You need to create localized JSPs.	Use *Locale*, *contentType*, and *pageEncoding* attributes.
You need to create localized servlets.	Use *Locale* and `ServletResponse.setContentType()` and `ServletResponse.setLocale()` methods.

from any hard-coded defaults. This applies to messages from the message class files, startup message files, and install application messages.

■ The following information and functional items come from the locale that the application is started in and/or from locale-specific files, as applicable:

■ Images

■ Code templates

■ Text files

■ Font names and sizes

■ Date, time, number, and currency formatting

■ Collation

■ Multi-byte characters print correctly from the application.

■ If a user runs the application in a locale that does not have the application installed correctly, the application falls back to using the messages and other nonmessage localizable resources for the default locale. Localizable nonmessage items include window sizes, font names, and help files.

■ Presentation objects resize dynamically to account for both the difference in the size of labels or other information displayed and information that contains multi-byte characters.

■ Presentation objects that receive keyboard input can receive it from different keyboards, and all legal keys are recognized.

■ Browsers, their encoding choices, as well as policies work as expected.

■ For multi-byte and extended ASCII within files and directory names,

■ Directory names with multi-byte as part of the paths to various files used in the application are processed correctly.

■ Multi-byte encoding, where legal in files, is parsed and shown correctly.

■ Message files are reviewed and deemed clear for translation.

■ Any registration, comments, and installation functionality and procedures, including that which involves e-mail or web transmissions of information that may include multi-byte information, was validated to ensure that the information is processed and received correctly.

CERTIFICATION SUMMARY

An application must be internationalized and then it can be localized. The Java APIs provide tools that enable the developer to internationalize a J2EE application. A J2EE application requires the correct behavior for locale and character-set encoding when accepting input, communicating data between tiers, and presenting data back to the client. An application also needs to report system errors in all tiers in a language appropriate for support personnel.

TWO-MINUTE DRILL

Here are some of the key points from each certification objective in Chapter 9.

State Three Aspects of any Application That Might Need to Be Varied or Customized in Different Deployment Locales

❑ Presentation of text, dates, numbers

❑ Labels on presentation components

❑ Sounds

❑ Colors

❑ Images or Icons

❑ Input and output routines that read and write text files

❑ Collation or ordering of data presented in a list

List Three Features of the Java Programming Language That Can Be Used to Create an Internationalizable/Localizable Application

❑ *java.util.Properties* for obtaining localized values using the same key

❑ *java.text.NumberFormat* to handle numbers and currencies

❑ *java.text.DateFormat* to handle date and time

❑ *java.text.Collator* and *java.text.CollationKey* for ordering data

❑ *java.text.MessageFormat, java.util.ResourceBundle,* or *java.util.PropertyResourceBundle* to handle text

❑ *java.io.InputStreamReader* and *java.io.OutputStreamWriter* for reading and writing files

❑ *java.util.Locale* and `contentType` and `pageEncoding` attributes for JSPs

❑ *java.util.Locale* and `ServletResponse.setContentType()` and `ServletResponse.setLocale()` methods for servlets

SELF TEST

The following questions will help you measure your understanding of the material presented in this chapter. Read all the choices carefully because there may be more than one correct answer. Choose all correct answers for each question.

State Three Aspects of Any Application That Might Need to Be Varied or Customized in Different Deployment Locales

1. Why is Internationalization called I18N?

   A. Because the internationalization is just too long to write in a presentation.

   B. The number of characters between the first and last character is 18.

   C. Because I18N is the encoded UTF version of internationalization.

   D. Because I18N is the default ISO code for internationalization.

2. Which of the following application aspects can be customized for different locales?

   A. Labels

   B. Reading a text file

   C. Ordering of data presented in a list

   D. Writing a text file

List Three Features of the Java Programming Language That Can Be Used to Create an Internationalizable/Localizable Application

3. What statement is true with respect to Unicode?

   A. Unicode provides a standard encoding for the character sets of different languages.

   B. Unicode is an encoding that is dependent of the platform, program, or language used to access said data.

   C. Unicode provides a non-unique number for every character.

   D. The Unicode Standard has not been adopted by Microsoft.

4. What statement is true with respect to a *ResourceBundle*?

   A. A *ResourceBundle* allows you to have various lookup tables based on the locale (language/country) upon which the server but not the client is running.

B. Resource bundles support a fourth-level descriptor beyond language/country variants, such that you can have customized messages for people in the northern and people in the southern part of a country, for example.

C. A *ResourceBundle* is a Hashtable that maps strings to values.

D. Resource bundles contain locale-specific objects. When your program needs a locale-specific resource, it can load the resource from the resource bundle that is appropriate for the current user's locale.

5. When using *ResourceBundle*, what is the procedure the system uses to determine which bundle to bind?

A. The resource bundle lookup searches for classes with various suffixes on the basis of the desired locale and the current default locale as returned by `Locale.getDefault()`, and the root resource bundle (base class), in the following order: from parent level to lower level.

B. The resource bundle lookup searches for classes with various suffixes on the basis of the desired locale and the current default locale as returned by `Locale.getHelp()`, and the root resource bundle (base class), in the following order: from lower level (more specific) to parent level (less specific).

C. The resource bundle lookup searches for classes with various suffixes on the basis of the desired locale and the current default locale as returned by `Locale.getDefault()`, and the root resource bundle (base class), in the following order: from lower level (more specific) to parent level (less specific).

D. The resource bundle lookup searches for classes with various suffixes on the basis of the desired locale and the current default locale as returned by `Locale.getDefault()`, and the root resource bundle as returned by `Locale.getBase()`, in the following order: from parent level (less specific) to lower level (more specific).

6. How do you determine the default character encoding for file operations, JDBC requests, and so on?

A. You can identify the default file encoding by checking the *Jvm* property named *default.properties*, as follows:
```
System.out.println(Jvm.getProperty("default.encoding"))
```

B. The default encoding used by locale/encoding-sensitive API in the Java libraries is determined by the system property *defaultfile.encoding*.

C. You can identify the default file encoding by checking the system property named *file.properties*, as follows:
```
System.out.println(System.getProperty("file.encoding"))
```

D. You can set the default file encoding by checking the *Jvm* property named *default.properties*, as follows:

```
System.setProperty("default.encoding"))
```

7. What does UTF stand for?

A. Universal Technical Frontend

B. Unicode Transformation Format

C. United Text Format

D. Universal Transformation Formula

8. What internationalization areas does Java not support?

A. Locales such as country, regional, or area/cultural identifiers

B. Localized resources by virtue of the *ResourceBundle* series of classes

C. Formatting for dates, numbers and decimals, and messages

D. Planetary variants

9. How can you handle input of different decimal symbols—for example, *343,4* as opposed to *343.4*?

A. Use *NumberFormat* and its methods `format()` and `parse()`. This will handle the default locale for you.

B. Use *Format* and its methods `format()` and `parse()`. This will handle the default locale for you.

C. Use *DecimalFormat* and its methods `format()` and `parse()`. This will handle the default locale for you.

D. Use *Format* and its methods `numberformat()` and `numberparse()`. This will handle the default locale for you.

10. What is the difference between UTF-8 and UTF-16?

A. UTF-16 represents every character using 2 bytes. UTF-8 uses the 1-byte ASCII character encodings for all languages except English.

B. UTF-16 represents every character using 2 bytes. UTF-8 uses 3 bytes per character for all languages except English.

C. UTF-16 represents every character using 2 bytes. UTF-8 uses the 1-byte ASCII character encodings for ASCII characters and represents non-ASCII characters using variable-length encoding.

D. UTF-16 represents every character using 1 byte. UTF-8 uses the 2-byte ASCII character encodings for ASCII characters and uses 3 bytes per character for all languages except English.

11. What is a locale and how is it used for I18N?

   A. A locale is an object that represents and provides information about a specific geographical, political, or cultural region. An operation that requires a locale to perform its task is called locale-sensitive and uses the locale to format information correctly for the user.

   B. A locale is an object that represents and provides information about a specific geographical, political, or cultural region. A globale is an object that represents and provides information about a geographical, political, or cultural region.

   C. A locale is an object that Java calls to present information to the user based upon the locale location of the browser.

   D. A locale is an object that represents the supported geographical, political, or cultural regions. An operation that requires a locale to perform its task is called locale-intensive and uses the locale to display information for the user.

12. Which of the following are logical fonts in Java?

   A. Sans-serif

   B. Time New Roman

   C. Monospaced

   D. Dialog

SELF TEST ANSWERS

State Three Aspects of Any Application That Might Need to Be Varied or Customized in Different Deployment Locales

1. ☑ **B.** The number of characters between the first and last character is 18.
   ☒ **A, C,** and **D** are untrue.

2. ☑ **A, B, C** and **D.** All four application aspects can be customized for different locales.

List Three Features of the Java Programming Language That Can Be Used to Create an Internationalizable/Localizable Application

3. ☑ **A.** Unicode provides a standard encoding for the character sets of different languages.
   ☒ **B, C,** and **D** are incorrect. Unicode is an encoding that is independent of the platform, program, or language used to access said data. Unicode provides a unique number for every character. The Unicode Standard has been adopted by Microsoft, as well as by Apple, HP, IBM, JustSystem, Oracle, SAP, Sun, Sybase, Unisys, and others.

4. ☑ **D.** Resource bundles contain locale-specific objects. When your program needs a locale-specific resource, your program can load it from the resource bundle that is appropriate for the current user's locale.
   ☒ **A, B,** and **C.** *ResourceBundle* allows you to have various lookup tables based upon what locale (language/country) the client's browser is running in. Resource bundles also support a third-level descriptor beyond language/country, such that you can have customized messages for presentation beyond just language and country. A *ResourceBundle* is analogous to a Hashtable that maps strings to values.

5. ☑ **C.** The resource bundle lookup searches for classes with various suffixes on the basis of the desired locale, the current default locale as returned by `Locale.getDefault()`, and the root resource bundle (base class), in the following order: from lower level (more specific) to parent level (less specific).
   ☒ **A, B,** and **D** are incorrect as they are at odds with the correct answer **C.**

6. ☑ **C.** You can identify the default file encoding by checking the *System* property named *file.properties*, as follows:
   ```
   System.out.println(System.getProperty("file.encoding"))
   ```
   ☒ **A, B,** and **D** are incorrect as they are at odds with the correct answer **C.**

7. ☑ **B.** UTF stands for Unicode Transformation Format.
☒ **A, C,** and **D** are incorrect.

8. ☑ **D.** Calendar and planetary variants.
☒ **A, B,** and **C** are true. Java internationalization supports locales such as country, regional, or area/cultural identifiers, as well as localized resources by virtue of the *ResourceBundle* series of classes and formatting for dates, numbers and decimals, and messages.

9. ☑ **A** and **C.** Use *NumberFormat* or *DecimalFormat* and its methods `format()` and `parse()`. This will handle the default locale for you.
☒ **B** and **D** are incorrect as they are at odds with the correct answers **A** and **C.**

10. ☑ **C.** UTF-16 represents every character using 2 bytes. UTF-8 uses the 1-byte ASCII character encodings for ASCII characters and represents non-ASCII characters using variable-length encoding.
☒ **A, B,** and **D** are incorrect as they are at odds with the correct answer **C.** UTF-16 represents every character using 2 bytes. UTF-8 uses the 1-byte ASCII character encodings for ASCII characters and represents non-ASCII characters using variable-length encodings. Note that while UTF-8 can save space for Western languages, which are the most common, it can actually use up to 3 bytes per character for other languages.

11. ☑ **A.** A locale is an object that represents and provides information about a specific geographical, political, or cultural region. An operation that requires a locale to perform its task is called locale-sensitive and uses the locale to refine and properly format the date and numeric information for the user.
☒ **B, C,** and **D** are incorrect.

12. ☑ **A, C,** and **D.** Java recognizes five font names—Serif, Sans-serif, Monospaced, Dialog, and DialogInput—along with four font styles—plain, bold, italic, and bolditalic. These are physical fonts but are standard names mapped to physical fonts known to be installed by default on the platform. The mapping is handled by *font.properties*. See the lib/fonts subdirectory of the Java JDK.
☒ **B.** Java does not recognize Times New Roman as platform standard.

J2EE

10

Security

I n an enterprise computing environment, the failure, compromise, or lack of availability of computing resources can jeopardize the life of the enterprise. To survive, an enterprise must identify, minimize, and, where possible, eliminate threats to the security of enterprise computing system resources. *Resources* for our purposes refer to goods and services. A *good* is a tangible property—that is, the physical server. A *service* is an intangible property such as software or data. A threat against a resource is basically an unauthorized use of a good or a service.

Out of the box, Java provides the ability for class code to be easily downloaded and executed. From the point of view of security, the easily downloaded code poses a threat because it may be possible for the code to access enterprise data resources. Therefore, it is important that your system be able to distinguish between code that can be trusted and code that cannot.

The Java security model takes into consideration the origin of the classes, and perhaps who signed them, when it permits or denies operations. This chapter concentrates on threats to services (software and data) and how Java and Java 2 Enterprise Edition (J2EE) fit into the scheme of things. J2EE applications do not obviate existing enterprise security infrastructure; they do, however, have value when integrated with existing infrastructures. The J2EE application model leverages existing security services as opposed to requiring new services.

This chapter begins with a brief review of threats to security, followed by a look at the security restrictions that Java 2 technology environments normally impose on applets running in a browser. Then an overview of Java and some of its security and related APIs is presented. The rest of the chapter describes the security concerns and explores the application of J2EE security mechanisms to the design, implementation, and deployment of secure enterprise applications.

Threats to enterprise resources fall into a few general categories that can overlap, as shown in Table 10-1.

Depending on the environment in which an enterprise application operates, these threats manifest themselves in different forms. For example, in a nondistributed system environment, a threat of disclosure might manifest itself in the vulnerability of information kept in files—for example, a client-server .INI file with user identities, passwords, IP addresses, and listener ports for enterprise databases.

In a distributed system, the code that performs business operations may be spread across multiple servers. A request will trigger the execution of code based on a server, and that code could possibly manipulate enterprise data. To prevent a threat to

TABLE 10-1   Threats to Enterprise Resources

Threat	Description	Example Result of Threat Execution
Compromise of accountability	In legal parlance this is known as "fraud in the impersonation" or "identity theft." Someone is masquerading as another user.	UserX logs on as UserY. UserX uses UserY's identity to make system requests and is afforded all rights and permissions of UserY.
Disclosure of confidential information	Enterprise data is intentionally, negligently, or accidentally made available to parties who have no legal "right to know."	Patient medical record compromised; bank account number compromised.
Modification of information	Enterprise data is intentionally, negligently, or accidentally modified.	Corporate money account balance modified; computer virus stored on a enterprise server.
Misappropriation of protected resources	In legal parlance this is known as "theft of service"; the perpetrator is accessing an enterprise computer system and using the system to perform, on its behalf, services that provide illegal gain or purpose.	UserX gains access to the lottery system and causes the system to create a winning ticket for UserX.
Misappropriation that compromises availability	The service misappropriation or data modification causes an interruption of the enterprise system.	Computer virus causes enterprise server to be unusable; a hacker causes the Amazon.com e-commerce server(s) to be unavailable.

security, it is important that trusted requests be distinguished from those that are not. The server must verify the identity of the caller to evaluate whether the caller is permitted to execute the code. The client may also want to verify the identity of the server before engaging in the transaction—for example, the consumer will not want to send a credit card number to *www.ijuststoleyourid.com*.

A distributed system is typically made up of code executing on behalf of different *principals* (uniquely identified users or machines within the system). To obviate threats, the server requires that the caller provide credentials that are known only to the caller, as proof of identity. The credentials are then checked and verified with an authority, and this is known as the *authentication process*. Authenticated callers are then checked to determine whether they are permitted to access the requested resource; this is known as *authorization*. These are the fundamental phases in security threat prevention.

Obviously, it is impractical to believe that all threats can be eliminated (because new ones are developed every day). The objective is to reduce the exposure to a minimum and therefore acceptable level through using proper authentication and authorization augmented by the use of the security techniques including signing, encryption, and post facto auditing. Java also provides some packages that can facilitate the security techniques used by an enterprise, as shown in Table 10-2.

TABLE 10-2   Security Packages of the Java Platform

Package	Description
java.security	Framework of classes and interfaces for security, including access control and authentication. Also provides support for cryptographic operations, including message digest and signature generation.
java.security.acl	Deprecated as of Java 1.2, replaced by classes in *java.security*.
java.security.cert	Classes and interfaces for parsing and managing X.509 certificates, X.509 certificate revocation lists (CRLs), and certification paths.
java.security.interfaces	Interfaces for RSA (Rivest, Shamir, and Adleman AsymmetricCipher algorithm) and DSA (Digital Signature Algorithm) key encryption.
java.security.spec	Classes and interfaces for DSA, RSA, DER, and X.509 keys and parameters used in public-key cryptography.
javax.crypto	Classes and interfaces for encrypting and decrypting data.
javax.crypto.interfaces	Interfaces for Diffie-Hellman public/private keys.
javax.crypto.spec	Classes and interfaces for key specifications and algorithm parameter specifications used in cryptography.
javax.net.ssl	Classes for encrypted communication across a network using the Secure Sockets Layer (SSL).
javax.security.auth	A framework for authentication and authorization used by Java Authentication and Authorization Service (JAAS).
javax.security.auth.callback	Classes providing low-level functionality that obtains authentication data and displays information to a user.
javax.security.auth.kerberos	Classes that support the Kerberos network authentication protocol.
javax.security.auth.login	Provides a plug-in framework for user authentication.
javax.security.auth.spi	`LoginModule` interface for implementing plug-in user authentication modules.
javax.security.auth.x500	Classes for representing X.500 Principal and X.500 Private Credentials.

Identify Security Restrictions That Java 2 Technology Environments Normally Impose on Applets Running in a Browser

We will now take a look at the restrictions that are normally imposed upon Java Applets that execute within the confines of a browser.

Applets in a Browser

A common misconception of most newcomers to Java is that security restrictions apply only to *applets* (Java classes downloaded and executed within a web browser). In fact, security restrictions can apply to *all* Java classes. (However, they do not apply to classes loaded from the boot *classpath*.) Before the Java API performs an action that is potentially unsafe, it calls the Java Security Manager to determine whether the action is permitted. Here is a partial list of the actions for which checks take place:

- Reading, writing, or deleting a file
- Opening, waiting for, or accepting a socket connection
- Modifying a thread attribute (for example, priority)
- Accessing or updating system properties

If the Java Security Manager does not permit the action, the Java API will not allow the action to take place. Now, you might ask, how is my application able to do one of these so-called unsafe calls, such as read or write a file? The answer is that the Java Security Manager is not installed by default; but it can be by calling it within your class or specifying a parameter to the Java command line. To establish the Java Security Manager within code, place the following as the first line in the `main()` method:

```
System.setSecurityManager( new SecurityManager() );
```

To establish the Java Security Manager via the command line, add the following parameter to the command line:

```
-Djava.security.manager
```

Once installed, the Java Security Manager checks whether a particular permission is granted to the specific requesting class; it throws a *SecurityException* if the permission is denied. The Java Security Manager checks by examining the call trace, so if an untrusted piece of code is invoked as part of a call to a secured method, it will fail because of the presence of the untrusted code. The permission is itself an abstract class representing access to a system resource. The permission can optionally contain a name and an action. When specified, these optional attributes further refine the permission being granted. For example, *java.io.SocketPermission* can be established with a host name of *66.108.43.211:9080* and an action of *accept,connect,listen,* which will allow the code to accept connections on, connect to, or listen on port 9080 on a host specified by IP address 66.108.43.211.

Here is a list of the security restrictions that Java 2 technology environments normally impose on applets running in a browser:

- An applet can utilize only its own code and is not allowed to load libraries or define native methods.

- An applet cannot read or write files on the host that is executing it.

- An applet can make network connections only to the host from which it was downloaded.

- An applet cannot start any program on the local host.

- An applet is restricted from reading the system properties specified in Table 10-3.

TABLE 10-3	Property	Description
System Properties That Cannot Be Accessed by Applets	*java.home*	Java installation directory
	java.class.path	Java classpath
	user.name	User account name
	user.home	User home directory
	user.dir	User's current working directory

CERTIFICATION OBJECTIVE 10.02

Given an Architectural System Specification, Identify Appropriate Locations for Implementation of Specified Security Features and Select Suitable Technologies for Implementation of Those Features

We will now take a look at the authentication and authorization security features that are part of a distributed network environment. We'll look at specific implementations and provide example code for review.

Authentication

In distributed computing, *authentication* is the device used by callers and service providers to prove to one another that they are to be "trusted." When the proof is bidirectional, it is called *mutual* authentication. Authentication establishes an actor's identities and proves that each instance is "authenticated." An entity participating in a call without establishing an identity is "unauthenticated."

Authentication is achieved in phases. Initially, an *authentication context* is established by performing authentication, requiring knowledge of a secret password. The authentication context encapsulates the identity and is able to fabricate an *authenticator*—a proof of identity. The authentication context is then used to provide authentication to other entities with which it interacts. The utility of authentication context should be well planned by the enterprise security team. Of late, security and identity management has become a critical enterprise function. Most large enterprises now have an adjunct group responsible for maintaining a user identity throughout the enterprise environment. Some large enterprises will have thousands of applications, each with its own authentication and identity maintenance. Software such as Thor (*www.thortech.com*) is designed to maintain users, groups, and security policy that provisions authentication for all of the secured resources (programs and data) within an enterprise.

Potential policies for controlling access to an authentication context are listed here:

- Once the user performs an authentication, the processes the user invokes inherit access to the authentication context.

- When a component is authenticated, access to the authentication context may be available to other trusted components.

- When a component is expected to impersonate its caller, the caller delegates its authentication context to the called component.

The whole issue of *propagation* of authentication context from client to the Enterprise JavaBeans (EJB) server to the Enterprise Information System (EIS) server is still evolving, both in terms of the specification as well as vendor offerings. According to the current Java specification, the *container* is the authentication boundary between callers and components hosted by the container. To this end, JAAS is a package that enables services to authenticate and enforce access controls upon clients. It implements a Java version of the standard, plugable authentication module framework and supports client-based authorization. JAAS has been integrated into Java 2 v1.4. The core facilities of Java's security design are intended to protect a client from developers. The client gives permissions to developers to access resources on the client machine. JAAS allows developers to grant or deny access to their programs based on the authentication credentials provided by the client. The JAAS specification extends the types of principals and credentials that can be associated with the client, but it is also evolving.

Java Protection Domains

Some components communicate without the need for authentication. This is because the communication is based on a preestablished trust mechanism. A *protection domain* is the name given to a group of components that have this trust established. Components within the same protection domain do not need to be authenticated with each other, and consequently no constraint is placed on the identity associated during a call. Authentication is required only for components that interact across the boundary of the protection domain. Figure 10-1 illustrates the authentication requirements for interactions that are contained within and that cross the boundary of a protection domain.

The container in the J2EE environment provides the authentication boundary between external and internal components. It is possible that the authentication boundary is not synchronized with the boundaries of protection domains. Even

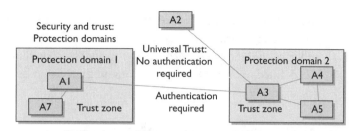

FIGURE 10-1

The Java
protection
domain

though it is the responsibility of the container to enforce the boundaries, you may encounter an environment that contains protection domains that span multiple containers. The issue of protection boundaries is extremely important as enterprise requirements fuse J2EE web and EJB components with back-end EIS resources that have preexisting application security in place—for example, IBM RACF (Resource Access Control Facility) security for CICS (Customer Information Control System) transactions interacting with J2EE.

In general, it is the responsibility of the container to authenticate component calls and police the boundaries of the protection domain. On an inbound call, the container passes the authenticated credentials to the component being called. The credentials can be a simple identity or a more complicated item such as an X.509 certificate. Similarly, when a component makes an outbound call, the container is responsible for establishing the identity of the component making the call. When a call is made across containers and the identity of the calling component has not been authenticated, the containers will check whether an existing trust exists between the interacting containers. If the trust exists, the call is permitted; if not, the call is rejected.

It is important that you differentiate the identity "propagation" model from the "delegation/impersonation" model. In the propagation model, the providers must determine whether or not to accept propagated identities as authentic. In delegation/propagation, the called component is given access to the caller's authentication context, thus enabling the called component to use the passed credentials to act on behalf of (or to impersonate) the caller.

Authentication in J2EE

In a J2EE application, the user's client container communicates with containers in the web, EJB, or EIS layers to access resources in their respective zones. These resources can be either protected or unprotected. A resource is protected when an authorization constraint is defined to the container that hosts it. When a user wishes to access a protected resource, the client container must present credentials (along with, when no trust exists between the containers, an authenticator that proves the caller has a right to use the identity) so that the container can validate them against the defined authorization constraint and then either permit or deny access to the resource.

Authentication in the Web Container

Collections of web resources, such as JSPs, servlets, HTML documents, image files, and compressed archives, are protected in the J2EE environment when the deployer specifies one or more authorization constraints for the collection at deployment time. In the deployed or target environment, when a user of a browser attempts to access protected resources, the web container determines whether the user has been authenticated; if not, the user will be prompted to identify himself using the mechanism specified in the application's deployment descriptor. When the user is successfully authenticated, he still will not be able to access the resource unless his identity is one that is granted permission according to the authorization constraint.

As already mentioned, the deployer specifies the authentication mechanism in the application deployment descriptor. A J2EE web container typically supports the following types of authentication mechanisms:

- HTTP basic
- HTTP digest
- FORM based
- HTTPS mutual

In HTTP basic authentication, the web server authenticates a principal using the user name and password obtained from the web client. The following process shows the conversation between the client browser and the web container to help elaborate on the basic authentication mechanism.

1. Client browser attempts to access a protected resource by sending an HTTP GET request—for example:

    ```
    GET /secure/declarative.html HTTP/1.1 Host: ucny.com
    ```

2. The web container sends back a challenge to the client to authenticate. The `WWW-Authenticate` header within the response contains the type of the authentication mechanism required and the security realm:

```
HTTP/1.1 401 Unauthorized WWW-Authenticate: Basic realm="weblogic"
```

3. The user enters a user ID and a password for the security realm, and the request is resubmitted along with an additional HTTP header whose value contains the authentication mechanism, the security realm, and the credentials. The credentials are formed by concatenating the user ID, a colon, and the password and then encoding this using the base-64 encoding algorithm. The following HTTP GET request contains the base-64 encoded credentials:

```
GET /secure/declarative.html HTTP/1.1 Host: ucny.com
Authorization: Basic c3lzdGVtOnBhc3N3b3Jk
```

4. The server will then attempt to authenticate the credentials within the security realm. If unsuccessful, the server will prompt again for valid credentials. If the credentials are valid, the identity will be checked against the authorization constraint. If the identity is permitted, access to the resource is allowed; otherwise, it is denied.

Basic authentication is limited, because HTTP is a *stateless* protocol. Once authenticated, a browser has to send this authentication data along with each and every client request. This is clearly a security threat because the request is not encrypted and can be captured and then retransmitted by a determined unauthorized individual. What's more, base-64 encoding is simple to decode and gives the hacker a real user ID and password that can be used to gain access to other protected resources. This potentially opens up the enterprise to the threat based upon a "compromise of accountability." For these reasons, it is pragmatic to use basic authentication with an encrypted link and server authentication, more commonly known as *digest authentication*.

Digest authentication is an improvement over basic authentication because it allows the client to prove knowledge of a password without actually transmitting it across the network. The web client authenticates by sending the server a message digest as part of the HTTP request. This message digest is calculated by taking parts of the message along with the client's password and passing them though a one-way hash algorithm. The mechanism works similarly to basic authentication, but in this case, the web container sends back some additional data with the challenge to the client to authenticate.

```
HTTP/1.1 401 Unauthorized WWW-Authenticate: Digest realm="ucny",
qop="auth", nonce="7fef9f6789b0526151d6efbd12196cdc",
opaque="c8202b69f571bdf3eerft43ce6ee2466"
```

The `WWW-Authenticate` header contains the name of the authentication mechanism (`Digest`), the realm (`"ucny"`), and some additional parameters to authenticate. These additional parameters include the `nonce`, or number once, which is a value that is used by the server and is valid for the current authentication sequence only. The browser client must then take the user name, password, realm, nonce, HTTP method, and request Uniform Resource Identifier (URI) and calculate a digest. The digest, a fixed-length encoding, has the properties that hide the actual data. The client will then resubmit the HTTP request along with a response parameter that is the calculated digest:

```
GET /secure/declarative.html HTTP/1.1 Host: ucny.com
Authorization: Digest username="system", realm="weblogic",
qop="auth", nonce="7fef9f6789b0526151d6efbd12196cdc",
opaque="c8202b69f571bdf3eerft43ce6ee2466",
response="5773a30ebe9e6ce90bcb5a535b4dc417"
```

The server in turn calculates the message digest from the inbound request and then compares it to the response value. If the values are not equal, the server responds with a "401 Unauthorized" error. If the values are equal, the credentials are deemed valid and then subsequently used for the authorization check to determine whether the client should have access to the protected resource. If the user is authorized, access to the resource is granted. If the authorization step fails, the server responds with a "403 Access Denied" error.

Form-based authentication allows for the use of a custom HTML form as the user interface for capturing the authentication information. However, as in basic authentication, the target server is not authenticated, and the authentication information is transmitted as plain text and as such is still vulnerable.

With mutual authentication, X.509 certificates are used to establish their identity on the client and on the server. The transmission occurs over a secure channel (SSL) and is much more difficult for a hacker to break into.

Encrypted Communication

Cryptography is a mechanism whereby data is encrypted using a key such that it can be decrypted only with a matching key. The two types of encryption are known as *symmetric* and *asymmetric*. In symmetric encryption, both sender and recipient know a common key, and this is used to encrypt and decrypt messages. In asymmetric encryption, also known as *public-key cryptography,* a key is split into two parts and referred to as a *key pair,* or *private* key and *public* key. Their most interesting feature is that each key is able to decrypt data that was encrypted by the other. The private key is obviously kept private and known only to a single individual or business, and the public key is given to all those who wish to communicate securely back and forth with the private key holder. So the private key holder is the only one who can decrypt data encrypted by the public key holders, and the public key holders are the only ones who can decrypt data encrypted by the private key holder. Figure 10-2 shows how asymmetric cryptography works.

Several choices can be made regarding which type of encryption to use and how much data should be encrypted in any given communication. For example, all the data can be encrypted with a private key so that only the public key holder can decrypt it, or it can be encrypted using a symmetric key known to both sides. Another possibility is to append an encrypted piece on to the communication—in effect, a signature or seal—so that the recipient will know that the sender genuinely sent the data and that the data was not tampered with on the way. In this case, the sender produces a hash code result by executing an algorithm on the complete message. This hash code result then gets encrypted and appended with the original data. Once the message is received, the recipient will attempt to decrypt the encrypted portion of the message to obtain the sender's hash code result. If successful, the recipient knows the message came from the sender. The recipient then executes an

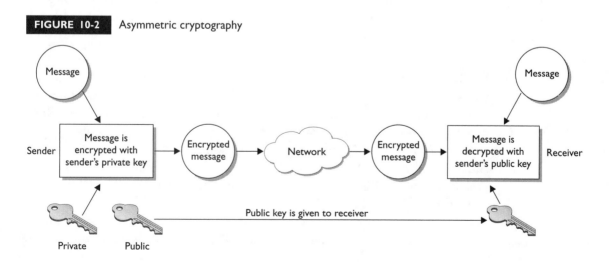

FIGURE 10-2   Asymmetric cryptography

algorithm on the complete message, producing a hash code result to be compared with the sender's hash code. If they are the same, the message has been received without any tampering along the way.

Asymmetric encryption is slower than symmetric encryption when dealing with large amounts of data. This is due in part to the increased length of the keys required in asymmetric cryptography to achieve the same level of protection as the symmetric variety. The longer keys demand more computing resources. Because of this, the bulk of data that needs to be secured is usually encrypted using symmetric cryptography, and a smaller amount is encrypted with asymmetric cryptography. In fact, a large number of hardware manufacturers sell SSL accelerator boards to avoid the overhead of key generation, encryption, and decryption.

Digital Certificates

A big issue with public key (asymmetric) cryptography is the way that recipients obtain the public key. If a public key is received in person, it can be deemed trustworthy. However, if it is received via some other means, it may not be deemed trustworthy. To alleviate the logistical issue of all public keys being handed out in person, a popular solution is for the private key holder to place the public key into a package known as a *digital certificate,* and then sign it with the private key of a trusted authority, known as a *Certificate Authority* (CA). These digital certificates can then be sent securely to recipients that are willing to trust the same CA and have access to the CA's public key. Several CAs are universally trusted, and their public keys are well known. VeriSign (*www.verisign.com*) is a leader in issuing digital certificates globally. The VeriSign public keys get distributed with commercial client and server software such as browsers and web servers.

Secure Sockets Layer

Created by Netscape, SSL is a security protocol that ensures privacy on the Internet. The protocol allows applications to communicate in such a way that eavesdropping cannot easily occur. SSL offers data encryption, server authentication, and message integrity. Servers are authenticated for each request, and clients can be optionally authenticated as well. SSL is independent of the application protocol and as such, protocols such as HTTP or FTP can transparently execute on top of it. All the data is encrypted before it is transmitted.

SSL uses a series of *handshakes* to establish trust between two entities using asymmetric encryption and digital certificates. These handshakes finish with the two entities negotiating a code set, including a set of session keys to be used for bulk encryption and data integrity. SSL has two authentication modes, *mutual* and *server*. In mutual authentication mode, the client and server exchange digital certificates to verify identities. In server authentication mode, the server sends a certificate to the client to establish the identity of the server. Note that HTTPS (HTTP running over SSL) typically uses port 443 instead of HTTP's default port 80. A digital certificate, provided by a CA such as VeriSign, must be installed on the server before server authentication can take place.

Authentication Within the EJB Container

Although EJB containers implement authentication mechanisms, they often rely on the web container to have authenticated a user already. The web container enforces the protection domain for web components and the EJBs that they call. A typical configuration is shown in Figure 10-3.

EJB containers and EJB client containers support version 2 of the Object Management Group's (OMG) Common Secure Interoperability (CSI) protocol. CSIv2 is a standard wire protocol for securing calls over the Internet Inter-ORB Protocol (IIOP). At its core, CSIv2 is an impersonation or "identity assertion" mechanism. It provides the mechanism for an intermediate entity to impersonate, or assert, an identity other than its own. This feature is based on the fact that the target trusts the intermediate entity.

Here is a summary of CSIv2:

■ An Interoperable Object Reference (IOR) holds a component that identifies the security mechanisms supported by the object. The IOR also includes information about the transport, client authentication, and identity and authorization tokens.

FIGURE 10-3

Typical J2EE application configuration

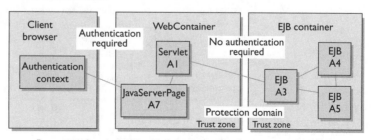

Protection domain: Interaction between application components (A#)

- The security mechanisms contained within the IOR are examined and the mechanism that supports the options required by the client is selected.

- The client uses CORBA's Security Attribute Service (SAS) protocol to set up a security context. This protocol defines messages contained within the service context of requests and replies. The security context established can be either stateful (used for multiple invocation) or stateless (used for a single invocation).

- CSIv2 supports Generic Security Services API (GSSAPI) initial context tokens, but to comply with conformance level 0, only the user name and password must be supported.

CSIv2 is intended for situations where protecting the integrity of data and the authentication of clients are carried out at the transport layer level, along with, for example, SSL. J2EE containers use CSIv2 impersonation to assert the identity of a caller to a component. Figure 10-4 illustrates the CSIv2 architecture components and the enterprise beans that they invoke.

When a J2EE application is deployed to an application server, the deployer defines the CSIv2 security policy to be enforced by the application server. This includes specifying certain security requirements, such as the following: does the target require a protected transport?; does the target require client authentication?; and, if so, what type of authentication is required?

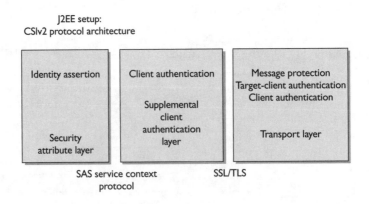

FIGURE 10-4

CSIv2 protocol architecture

Configuring Authentication in J2EE

As part of the web application's authentication mechanism, the servlet container uses the *login-config* element contained in the application deployment descriptor file (*web.xml*). The container performs many checks, some of the most common of which are listed here:

- Does the request need to be decrypted?
- Does the request have authorization constraints?
- Does the request have authentication or authorization requirements?

Typically, resources in an application are protected via a combination of authentication and authorization constraints. Specifying authentication constraints without authorization constraints (and vice versa) does not add any value and therefore does not make sense.

If the container cannot determine the caller's identity, it uses the *<login-config>* element specified in the application deployment descriptor. The following code listing example is an excerpt from an application deployment descriptor. It contains the authentication entries required to enforce the constraint using FORM-based authentication. Note that the associated authorization constraints, specified within the web-resource-collection element, are covered in detail in the "Authorization" section found later in this chapter.

```
<web-app>
  <security-constraint>
    <web-resource-collection>
      ...(resources to be protected)
    </web-resource-collection>
    <auth-constraint>
      <role-name>secure_role</role-name>
    </auth-constraint>
    <user-data-constraint>
      <transport-guarantee>NONE</transport-guarantee>
    </user-data-constraint>
  </security-constraint>
  <login-config>
    <auth-method>FORM</auth-method>
    <form-login-config>
      <form-login-page>login.html</form-login-page>
      <form-error-page>loginError.html</form-error-page>
    </form-login-config>
```

```
    </login-config>
    <security-role>
      <role-name>secure_role</role-name>
    </security-role>
  </web-app>
```

Here is the *<login-config>* excerpt that uses BASIC authentication. Note that the realm-name is used only in BASIC authentication.

```
    ...
      <login-config>
      <auth-method>BASIC</auth-method>
      <realm-name>weblogic</realm-name>
    </login-config>
    ...
```

Here is the *<login-config>* excerpt that uses DIGEST authentication:

```
...
<login-config>
   <auth-method>DIGEST</auth-method>
</login-config>
... Here is the <login-config> excerpt that uses CLIENT-CERT authentication.

...
<login-config>
   <auth-method>CLIENT-CERT</auth-method>
</login-config>
...
```

With BASIC authentication, the browser displays and controls the login process and user interface. The browser will display a simple dialog box prompting for user name and password. With FORM authentication, the web application defines and therefore controls the login process to a greater extent. Here is some example code for a login form:

```
<head><title>Security Demo: login</title></head>
<h2>Login</h2>
Please authenticate yourself:
<form method="POST" action="j_security_check">
Username: <input type="text" name="j_username"><br />
Password: <input type="password" name="j_password"><br />
<br />
<input type="submit" value="Login">
```

```
<input type="reset" value="Reset">
</form>
<p><a href="index.html">home</a>
</html>
```

Here is the code for *loginError.html*:

```
<head><title>Security Demo: login error</title></head>
<h2>Login Error</h2>
<hr width="100%">
Invalid username/password.
<br />
<p><a href="index.html">home</a>
</body>
</html>
```

In FORM-based authentication, the web container performs the authentication check. It does so according to the servlet specification, which specifies that the form method must be a POST, the name of the action must be *j_security_check*, and the names of the user name and password fields must be *j_username* and *j_password*, respectively. When the container sees the *j_security_check* action, it uses an internal mechanism to authenticate the caller. If the logon is authenticated and authorized to access the secured resource, the container produces a session ID to identify a logon session for the caller. The container maintains the logon session ID within a cookie. The server sends the cookie back to the client, and the client caller must then send this cookie back on all subsequent requests. If the authentication fails, the page identified by the `<form-error-page>` is returned to the client.

As mentioned, FORM-based authentication is still not secure by default. But it can be made more secure by conducting it over a secure channel by specifying a transport guarantee for the secured resource. For example, use `<transport-guarantee>SSL</transport-guarantee>`.

Authentication in the Enterprise Information System Layer

When J2EE components need to access and therefore integrate with EISs, they may need to employ alternative mechanisms for security. In addition, they most likely will be operating from protected domains that do not cover the EIS resources they need to access. To provide for these situations, the calling container can be set up to manage the calling component's authentication for the resource. This is known as *container-managed resource manager sign-on*. The J2EE architecture also provides the ability to specify the caller's credentials. This is known as *application-managed resource manager sign-on.*

Within the deployment descriptor, the *<resource-ref>* element specifies a resource called by a component. The *<res-auth>* element specifies whether the resource sign-on is to be handled by the container or application. Components that use application-managed resource manager sign-on can use either the getUserPrincipal() (for web components) or getCallerPrincipal() (for EJB components) method to access the identity of the caller. This identity can then be mapped according to the requirements of the EIS. When container-managed resource manager sign-on is used, the container takes care of the mapping for the component.

Identity Selection

In a J2EE server-side component, the container sets up the identity when the component calls another J2EE component. The identity that is created is dependent on the identity selection policy specified in the deployment descriptor. For the identity selection policy, the deployer can specify either a *<use-caller-identity>* element or a *<run-as>* element. Component identity selection policies may be defined for web and EJB resources. When *<use-caller-identity>* is specified, the container uses the identity of a component's caller in all subsequent calls made by the component. When the *<run-as>* element is specified, the container uses the identity specified within the element. In short, *<use-caller-identity>* maintains accountability and traceability for actions taken by components, and *<run-as>* can quickly give the caller privileges that their own identity lacks.

The following EJB deployment descriptor snippet shows examples of both types of client identity selection policy:

```
//Configuring EJB Component Identity Selection Policies
<enterprise-beans>
  <entity>
    <security-identity>
      <use-caller-identity/>
    </security-identity>
    ...
  </entity>
  <session>
    <security-identity>
      <run-as>
        <role-name>guest</role-name>
```

```
          </run-as>
       </security-identity>
       ...
    </session>
    ...
</enterprise-beans>
```

The following deployment descriptor snippet shows an example of client identity selection policy for a web component. Note that when a *<run-as>* element is not specified, the *use-caller-identity* policy is assumed.

```
//Configuring Web Component Identity Selection Policies
<web-app>
  <servlet>
    <run-as>
      <role-name>guest</role-name>
    </run-as>
    ...
  </servlet>
  ...
</web-app>
```

Authorization

Authorization is the mechanism that controls caller access and interaction with application resources or components. The caller's credentials (identity), which can also be anonymous or arbitrarily set by the caller, can be determined via authentication contexts that are available to the called component. Access can then be determined by comparing the caller's credentials with the access control rules for the required component or resource.

These access control rules are in effect a matching of the application's capabilities with the caller's permissions. The application's capabilities define what can be performed within the application, and the caller's permissions define what the caller is allowed to perform.

In the J2EE architecture, the container provides the "border patrol" between callers requiring access to the target resources and components that execute within the container. So on an inbound call, the container compares the caller's credentials with the access control rules for the target component or resource. If the rules are satisfied, the call will continue; if not, the call is rejected.

Authorization in the J2EE environment can be enforced in two ways: *declaratively*, configured by the deployer and managed by the container, or *programmatically*, embedded in and managed by the component.

Declarative authorization controls access from outside of the application code, whereas programmatic authorization controls access from within the application code. The pros and cons for each technique are detailed in Table 10-4.

The client to a J2EE application typically uses the application container to interact with enterprise resources in the web or EJB layer. Resources that are secured (or protected) have authorization rules that are either declared in deployment descriptors or embedded within component code. These rules control the access to the components, and clients will need to present credentials to be evaluated against the access rules that are in place.

Authorization Enforced by the Container (Declarative)

As mentioned, declarative authorization is established externally to the web or EJB component. It is defined within the deployment descriptor files. Entries within these files map the application permissions (usually defined by the assembler) to the policies or mechanisms that exist in the actual target environment.

The *deployment descriptor* file contains definitions that associate the security roles (logical privileges) with components and the privileges required for permission to access components. The deployer assigns security roles to specific callers, thus establishing the abilities of users in the target environment.

TABLE 10-4	Technique	Pros	Cons
Pros and Cons for Declarative and Programmatic Authorizations	Declarative authorization (external)	Continued flexibility once application is developed. Easily viewed and interpreted by deployer.	May not provide enough fine-grained flexibility.
	Programmatic authorization (internal)	Provides finer grained flexibility.	No flexibility after application is developed. Functionality is buried within code.

Using Declarative Authorization

A client typically uses a J2EE application's container to access enterprise resources in the web or EJB tier. To control access to a web resource declaratively, an application component provider or application assembler must specify the *security-constraint* element along with the *auth-constraint* subelement in the application deployment descriptor. The following deployment descriptor excerpt shows the specification of a protected web resource:

```
<security-constraint>
  <web-resource-collection>
    <web-resource-name>SecurePages</web-resource-name>
    <description>Security constraint for protected resources</description>
    <url-pattern>/secure/*</url-pattern>
    <http-method>POST</http-method>
    <http-method>GET</http-method>
  </web-resource-collection>
  <auth-constraint>
    <description>Users in this role can login</description>
    <role-name>secure_role</role-name>
  </auth-constraint>
  ...
</security-constraint>
```

This excerpt indicates to the container that the URL conforming to the pattern */secure/** can be accessed only by users that are in the *secure_role* role. However, some web content typically does not need to be protected with authorization rules. This unrestricted access is achieved simply by not adding an authentication rule.

To protect or declaratively control access to an enterprise bean resource, the application component provider or application assembler can declare security roles and the methods of the bean's interfaces (remote, home, local, and local home) that each security role is allowed to call. This is declared using *method-permission* elements in the deployment descriptor.

The following deployment descriptor excerpt shows two *method-permission* elements. The first refers to *method2* of all of the interfaces (which could be remote, home, local remote, and local home) of the enterprise bean. The second refers to *method3* on the remote interface of the same enterprise bean.

```
<assembly-descriptor>
  ...
  <security-role>
```

```
        <role-name>usr_role</role-name>
    </security-role>
    <security-role>
        <role-name>adm_role</role-name>
    </security-role>

    ...
    <method-permission>
        <description>remote method2 access</description>
        <role-name>usr_role</role-name>
        <method>
            <ejb-name>DeclarativeSecurity</ejb-name>
            <method-name>method2</method-name>
        </method>
    </method-permission>
    <method-permission>
        <description>remote method3 access</description>
        <role-name>adm_role</role-name>
        <method>
            <ejb-name>DeclarativeSecurity</ejb-name>
            <method-intf>Remote</method-intf>
            <method-name>method3</method-name>
        </method>
    </method-permission>

    ...
</assembly-descriptor>
```

Note that if another method were to use the same name (that is, overloaded methods were in the bean code), this permission scope would refer to both methods. You can refine the scope further by identifying methods with overloaded names by parameter signature, or you can refer to methods of a specific interface of the enterprise bean (such as remote, local).

You can also indicate to the container that it should allow the call to a method to proceed regardless of the caller's identity. By adding the unchecked element to the *method-permission* element, the container authorizes the use of a method to anybody. Here is a deployment descriptor excerpt showing the unchecked element:

```
<assembly-descriptor>
    ...
    <method-permission>
        <unchecked/>
        <method>
```

```
      <ejb-name>DeclarativeSecurity</ejb-name>
      <method-name>method1</method-name>
    </method>
  </method-permission>
  ...
</assembly-descriptor>
```

Additionally, method specifications may be added to an *exclude-list*. This indicates to the container that access to these methods is denied regardless of the caller's identity, even if the methods have been specified in the *method-permission* element. Here is a deployment descriptor excerpt showing the *exclude-list* element:

```
<assembly-descriptor>
  ...
  <exclude-list>
    <method>
      <ejb-name>DeclarativeSecurity</ejb-name>
      <method-name>method4</method-name>
    </method>
  </exclude-list>
  ...
</assembly-descriptor>
```

Authorization Enforced by the Component (Programmatic)

There may be a time when declarative authorization is not sufficient. For example, if a more fine-grained authorization model is required, the developer of a web component can use a combination of the `getUserPrincipal()` and `isUserInRole()` methods that exist on the *HttpServletRequest* object, and the developer of an EJB component can use a combination of the `getCallerPrincipal()` and `isCallerInRole()` methods that exist on the EJB's *context* object, to carry out access control at the component level. This is known as *programmatic* authorization. The web or EJB component can use these methods to determine whether the caller is allowed to perform the functionality that has been called within the component.

Using Programmatic Authorization

As mentioned, the web component developer will use `getUserPrincipal()` and `isUserInRole()` methods within a JSP or servlet to control access to the web resource's functionality. These methods typically require that the client also be authenticated, so it makes sense to use the technique in conjunction with declarative authorization.

The following example shows the use of the programmatic authorization methods `getUserPrincipal()` and `isUserInRole()` in a JSP. The JSP is part of an application that also has some resources protected with declarative authorization. Here is example code for a JSP:

```
<html>
<head><title>Security Demo</title></head>
<body bgcolor="#FFFFFF">
<head><title>Security Demo: programmatically protected page</title></head>
<h2>Programmatically Protected Page</h2>
<hr width="100%">
<%
  java.security.Principal principal = request.getUserPrincipal();
  if (principal != null) {
   boolean inRole = request.isUserInRole("secure_role");
   if (inRole) {
     if ("system".equals(principal.getName())) {
       out.write("<br>You are the correct user ("+principal.getName()
         +") and role, so access is granted!");
       // This is where code for the protected
       // functionality would reside...
     } else {
       out.write("<br>You are NOT the correct user ("+principal.getName()
         +"), so access is denied!");
     }
   } else {
     out.write("<br>You are NOT in the correct role, so access is denied!");
   }
  } else {
    out.write("<p>You are not authenticated, so access is denied!");
  }
%>
<p><a href="../index.html">home</a>
</body>
</html>
```

To control access programmatically to an enterprise bean resource, the enterprise bean provider uses the `isCallerInRole()` and `getCallerPrincipal()` methods to determine whether the caller is within the specified role or is, in fact, a specific user that is authorized to perform the called functionality. Within the EJB deployment descriptor, the assembler must add a *security-role-ref* element for every role that is referred to within the bean code. The assembler must also add a *security-role* element for the *role-link* in every *security-role-ref* element that has been added. Here is an excerpt for an EJB deployment descriptor:

```
<ejb-jar>
  ...
  <enterprise-beans>
    ...
    <ejb-name>ProgrammaticSecurity</ejb-name>
    ...
    <security-role-ref>
      <role-name>programmatic</role-name>
      <role-link>programmatic_role</role-link>
    </security-role-ref>
    ...
  </enterprise-beans>
  ...
  <assembly-descriptor>
    <security-role>
      <role-name>programmatic_role</role-name>
    </security-role>
    ...
  </assembly-descriptor>
  ...
</ejb-jar>
```

When deployed, each *role-name* specified in the *assembly-descriptor* element of the EJB deployment descriptor must be mapped to actual resources in the target server. The following excerpt is from a WebLogic server deployment descriptor that resolves the *role-name* to specific resources within the server:

```
<weblogic-ejb-jar>
  <weblogic-enterprise-bean>
    <ejb-name>ProgrammaticSecurity</ejb-name>
    ...
  </weblogic-enterprise-bean>
  <security-role-assignment>
    <role-name>programmatic_role</role-name>
    <principal-name>system</principal-name>
    <principal-name>auser</principal-name>
  </security-role-assignment>
</weblogic-ejb-jar>
```

In this excerpt, the *security-role-assignment* declares and resolves the *role-name* (*programmatic_role*), specified within the *assembly-descriptor* element of the EJB deployment descriptor, to one or more principal identities (*system* and *auser*) that are known to an authentication realm within the WebLogic server.

Here is an example of enterprise bean code that programmatically determines whether the caller is permitted to execute the method:

```
package j2ee.architect.ProgrammaticSecurity;
import javax.ejb.*;
// A stateless session bean.
public class ProgrammaticSecurityBean implements SessionBean {
  SessionContext sessionContext;
  private static final String ROLE_REQUIRED = "programmatic";
  // Bean's methods required by EJB specification.
  public void ejbCreate() throws CreateException {log("ejbCreate()");}
  public void ejbRemove() {log("ejbRemove()");}
  public void ejbActivate() {log("ejbActivate()");}
  public void ejbPassivate() {log("ejbPassivate()");}
  public void setSessionContext(SessionContext parm) {
    this.sessionContext = parm;
  }
  // Bean's business methods.
  public String method1() {
    log("method1() called by user "
      +sessionContext.getCallerPrincipal().getName());
    return " method1 executed.";
  }
  public String method2() throws EJBException {
    log("method2() called by user "
      +sessionContext.getCallerPrincipal().getName());
    if (!sessionContext.isCallerInRole(ROLE_REQUIRED))
      throw new EJBException ("insufficient permission to access method2");
    // Place method functionality here...
    return " method2 executed.";
  }
  private void log(String parm) {
    System.out.println(new java.util.Date()
      +":ProgrammaticSecurityBean:"+this.hashCode()+" "+parm);
  }
}
```

Authorization Summary

By defining a clear separation of the responsibilities for securing an application among those that develop components, those that assemble components, and those that deploy application components, the J2EE platform achieves its goal of making the details of security much more simple and easy to implement.

The *component-provider* role identifies all the security dependencies embedded in the component, including the following:

- The role names used in method `isUserInRole()` for web components and `isCallerInRole()` for EJB components
- References made by the component to other components
- References to external resources accessed by the component
- The method permission model, including information that identifies the sensitivity of the information exchanged or processing that occurs in individual methods

The *application-assembler* role combines one or more components into an application package and then produces an overall security view for the whole application. The deployer role takes this overall security view and uses it to secure the application for target environment. The deployer does this by mapping the security view elements to the actual policies and mechanisms that exist in the target environment. How this mapping occurs will depend on the vendor for the web and EJB containers. In some cases, additional deployment descriptors resolve this mapping, and in other cases a vendor-specific tool must be used.

CERTIFICATION SUMMARY

The security mechanisms covered in this chapter show how the features of Java and J2EE provide a robust solution for interoperable and distributed security.

TWO-MINUTE DRILL

Here are some of the key points from each certification objective in Chapter 10.

Identify Security Restrictions That Java 2 Technology Environments Normally Impose on Applets Running in a Browser

❑ An applet can utilize only its own code and is not allowed to load libraries or define native methods.

❑ An applet cannot read or write files on the host that is executing it.

❑ An applet can make network connections only to the host from which it was downloaded.

❑ An applet cannot start any program on the local host.

❑ An applet is restricted from reading the following system properties: *java.home, java.class.path, user.name, user.home,* and *user.dir.*

Given an Architectural System Specification, Identify Appropriate Locations for Implementation of Specified Security Features and Select Suitable Technologies for Implementation of Those Features

❑ Authentication

   ❑ Authentication method: BASIC, FORM, DIGEST, and CLIENT-CERT

   ❑ Digital certificates, certificate authorities

   ❑ Secure Sockets Layer (SSL)

   ❑ Common Secure Interoperability (CSIv2)

   ❑ Identity selection: *<run-as>* or *<use-caller-identity>*

   ❑ Security roles

❑ Authorization

   ❑ Authorization enforced by the container (declarative), defined in the deployment descriptor

   ❑ Authorization enforced by the component (programmatic), defined within the application code

SELF TEST

The following questions will help you measure your understanding of the material presented in this chapter. Read all the choices carefully because there may be more than one correct answer. Choose all correct answers for each question.

Identify Security Restrictions That Java 2 Technology Environments Normally Impose on Applets Running in a Browser

1. Which of the following properties cannot be read by an applet?

   A. *os.name*

   B. *file.separator*

   C. *java.home*

   D. *java.version*

Given an Architectural System Specification, Identify Appropriate Locations for Implementation of Specified Security Features and Select Suitable Technologies for Implementation of Those Features

2. What is a message digest?

   A. A digital fingerprint value that is computed from a message, file, or byte stream

   B. A shortened summary of a message

   C. The subject line of a message

   D. A processing function of the mail server

3. What method can be used to help programmatically determine the caller's identity within enterprise bean code?

   A. `getIdentity()`

   B. `getCallerPrincipal()`

   C. `getCallerIdentity()`

   D. `getUserId()`

4. Within enterprise bean code, what method can be used to determine whether the caller is in a security role and authorized to execute the method?

   A. `inRole()`

   B. `isAuthorized()`

C. `isCallerInRole()`

D. `isValid()`

5. What method can be used to help programmatically determine the caller's identity within a JSP?

   A. `getUserPrincipal()`

   B. `getPrincipal()`

   C. `getUser()`

   D. `getIdentity()`

6. Within a JSP, what method can be used to determine whether the caller is programmatically authorized to execute its functionality?

   A. `inRole()`

   B. `okToExecute()`

   C. `isValid()`

   D. `isUserInRole()`

7. What role maps the declarative authorization rules to the target environment?

   A. Deployer

   B. Component provider

   C. Application assembler

   D. Authorizer

8. What role maps the programmatic authorization rules to the target environment?

   A. Application assembler

   B. Component provider

   C. Coder

   D. Deployer

9. For Enterprise JavaBeans (EJBs), where are the declarative authorization rules defined?

   A. Application properties

   B. EJB deployment descriptor

   C. JNDI

   D. Enterprise bean code

10. For web resources, where are the declarative authorization rules defined?

    A. EJB deployment descriptor

    B. Application deployment descriptor

    C. In the web resource

    D. JMS

11. For Enterprise JavaBeans (EJBs), where are the programmatic authorization rules implemented?

    A. JNDI

    B. EJB deployment descriptor

    C. In the enterprise bean code

    D. JMS

12. For web resources, where are the programmatic authorization rules defined?

    A. Java Security Manager

    B. Security policy file

    C. JNDI

    D. Within the JSP or servlet

13. Which of the following is not a valid authentication method (`auth-method`)?

    A. FORM

    B. HTTP

    C. DIGEST

    D. CLIENT-CERT

SELF TEST ANSWERS

Identify Security Restrictions That Java 2 Technology Environments Normally Impose on Applets Running in a Browser

1. ☑ C. A java applet cannot read the *java.home* system property.

   ☒ A, B, and D are incorrect. *os.name*, *file.separator*, and *java.version* can be read by an applet.

Given an Architectural System Specification, Identify Appropriate Locations for Implementation of Specified Security Features and Select Suitable Technologies for Implementation of Those Features

2. ☑ A. A message digest is a digital fingerprint value that is computed from a message, file, or byte stream.

   ☒ B, C, and D are not definitions of a message digest.

3. ☑ B. The getCallerPrincipal() method returns the principal object. The getName() method can then be used to determine the caller's name (identity) from within enterprise bean code.

   ☒ A, C, and D are incorrect because getCallerIdentity() is a deprecated method, and getIdentity() and getUserId() are not valid methods.

4. ☑ C. The isCallerInRole() method can be used to determine if the caller is within the specified role and therefore able to execute the EJB functionality.

   ☒ A, B, and D are incorrect because inRole(), isAuthorized(), and isValid() are not valid methods.

5. ☑ A. The getUserPrincipal() method returns the principal object. The getName() method can then be used to determine the caller's name (identity) from within a JSP.

   ☒ B, C, and D are incorrect because getPrincipal(), getUser(), and getIdentity() are not valid methods.

6. ☑ D. The isUserInRole() method can be used to determine whether the caller is within the specified role and therefore able to execute the JSP functionality.

   ☒ A, B, and C are incorrect because inRole(), okToExecute(), and isValid() are not valid methods.

7. ☑ A. The deployer is responsible for mapping declarative authorization rules to the target environment.

☒ **B, C,** and **D** are incorrect because the Component Provider and Application Assembler are not responsible for providing this mapping. Authorizer is not a J2EE role, so it can't be correct either.

8. ☑ **D.** The deployer is responsible for mapping programmatic authorization rules to the target environment.

☒ **A, B,** and **C** are incorrect because the Application Assembler and Component Provider are not responsible for providing this mapping. Coder is not a J2EE role so it can't be correct either.

9. ☑ **B.** The declarative authorization rules for EJBs are defined within the EJB deployment descriptor.

☒ **A, C,** and **D** are incorrect because EJB authorization rules are not declaratively defined in Application properties, JNDI, or Enterprise bean code.

10. ☑ **B.** The declarative authorization rules for web resources are defined within the application deployment descriptor.

☒ **A, C,** and **D** are incorrect because authorization rules for web resources are not declaratively defined in the EJB deployment descriptor, the web resource, or in JMS.

11. ☑ **C.** The programmatic authorization rules for EJBs are implemented within the enterprise bean code.

☒ **A, B,** and **D** are incorrect because EJB authorization rules are not programmatically implemented in JNDI, the EJB deployment descriptor, or JMS.

12. ☑ **D.** The programmatic authorization rules for web resources are implemented within the JSP or servlet.

☒ **A, B,** and **C** are incorrect because authorization rules for web resources are not programmatically implemented in the Java Security Manager, Security policy file, or JNDI.

13. ☑ **B.** HTTP is not a valid authentication method.

☒ **A, C,** and **D** are incorrect. FORM, DIGEST, and CLIENT-CERT are valid authentication methods.

11

Case Study: Overview of Securities Trading System

his chapter presents a case study that will help you to prepare for and complete Part 2 of the SCEA exam. Here you are presented with a trading application that includes use cases, a domain object model, and additional requirements. Most systems in the real world start off with requirements, and the exam assignment chooses to define the requirements in use cases and a domain model. As the architect for the application, you must develop the class diagram(s), component diagram(s), and sequence or collaboration diagrams to describe your architecture.

This particular case study application was developed for a Wall Street clearing firm, which interacted with hundreds of correspondent trade brokers and their customers. It was intended to help the firm by facilitating the customers' ability to trade securities on the web. To be successful, a trading firm (broker-dealers) must transition their firm to a customer-centric, web-based environment. The Internet was seen as a way to maintain and grow new and existing distribution channels, customers, and strategic partnerships. Basically, the challenge was to determine how this trading firm could develop a winning strategy to compete for customers and brokers who wanted the ease of trading securities via the web.

The solution is the same for all businesses competing in the new e-commerce world—a three-step approach to successful enterprise development:

1. Spend the time to understand what the client needs—in this case, browser-based trading functionality.

2. Choose the right technology—in this case, Java and Java 2 Enterprise Edition (J2EE).

3. Develop a team and teamwork atmosphere to implement the technology—choose architects and developers skilled in trade processing and J2EE design and development.

The Case Study Infrastructure

As with many large organizations, Bank of New Amsterdam (BNA) has several different operating systems running many kinds of software systems. The primary platform for the production business data is the IBM Mainframe S/390 (the mainframe). In addition, Microsoft NT boxes use Internet Information Services (IIS) and other

Microsoft software to provide reporting capabilities, using a SQL Server shadow copy of the business data. BNA also has an investment in Oracle on the S/390. Several preexisting legacy applications provide trade-processing links to the major securities exchanges. These applications work well and have been developed and maintained for the past two decades, during which time a great deal of time and money has been spent. The applications do not need modification; instead, they need a new web front end to make them look good. The development environment is primarily Windows-based.

The advantages of using the mainframe include its reliability, scalability, flexibility, and security. The mainframe has been running continuously for years in BNA without major problems. The mainframe can easily be amended to add hardware resources, such as CPU, memory, disk, or networking hardware, to increase capacity without changing the operating system or application systems. In addition, the CPU, memory, and disk space can be redistributed as application requirements change.

Traditionally, the downside to the mainframe has been the user interface—the 3270 dumb terminal (the green screen), which is not user friendly. Prior to the commencement of BNA's Java project, another group spent a few months trying to develop Windows Active Server Pages (ASPs) to talk to the mainframe. The only solution providing ASP reports, a portfolio management system, solved the interface problem, but it was difficult to connect to the mainframe using ASP for trading.

BNA has experienced difficulty getting the order messages to the mainframe. Along with performance problems, it seemed that every ASP order transaction required multiple dedicated connections to the SQL Server database. Fortunately, Java Database Connectivity (JDBC) connection pooling and Java's platform independence provided the performance and scalability that was needed. Moreover, it allowed us to take advantage of the mainframe for deployment and Windows for development. (Because budget is a limiting factor in an economic downturn, where every developer is competing for business, it is critical that you deliver a solution quickly that will integrate with an organization's existing infrastructure.)

The IBM HTTP server, WebSphere application server, and Oracle 9i Enterprise relational database management system (RDBMS) are all in existence on the company's legacy IBM mainframe enterprise server.

Table 11-1 describes the software components of the web front end.

| TABLE 11-1 | Web Front End Software |

Type of Component	Vendor/Component Name/Version	Description	Software/Hardware Required for Support
Application server	WebSphere Application Server 3/4	Serves up JSPs and servlets, runs EJBs, and provides JDBC connection pools to user data	IBM S/390, Windows NT 4.0 SP4
DBMS	Oracle 9.0i	Database required for application data (orderdb)	Oracle 9i
JavaScript	Netscape/JavaScript	ECMA JavaScript	IE 5 and above or Navigator 4 and above
Browser	Microsoft or Netscape	Web browser required to support JavaScript	IE 5 and above or Navigator 4 and above
XML Tool	IBM/XML Parser for Java/3.1.1	A library for parsing and generating XML documents	Windows NT 4.0 SP4

Figure 11-1 illustrates the enterprise architecture as a diagram, and Figure 11-2 shows a Unified Modeling Language (UML) sequence diagram.

WebSphere Application Server

The WebSphere partition is also connected via TCP/IP sockets to the BNACS API. This API is used to communicate with and retrieve information from the mainframe system via an XML-based message format. Finally, the WebSphere partition is connected to the Stratus TCAM CTPS (the continuous trade processing system from TCAM) application. The WebSphere application sends and maintains orders, and it can look up order status by communicating with CTPS via a proprietary message format.

Continuous Trade Processing

The CTPS system is an order-routing system that is connected to several exchanges and market makers (firms that stand ready to buy and sell a particular stock on a regular and continuous basis at a publicly quoted price). The system receives orders either by direct entry into its terminals or via an in-house–built TCP/IP socket

FIGURE 11-1 Production architecture components

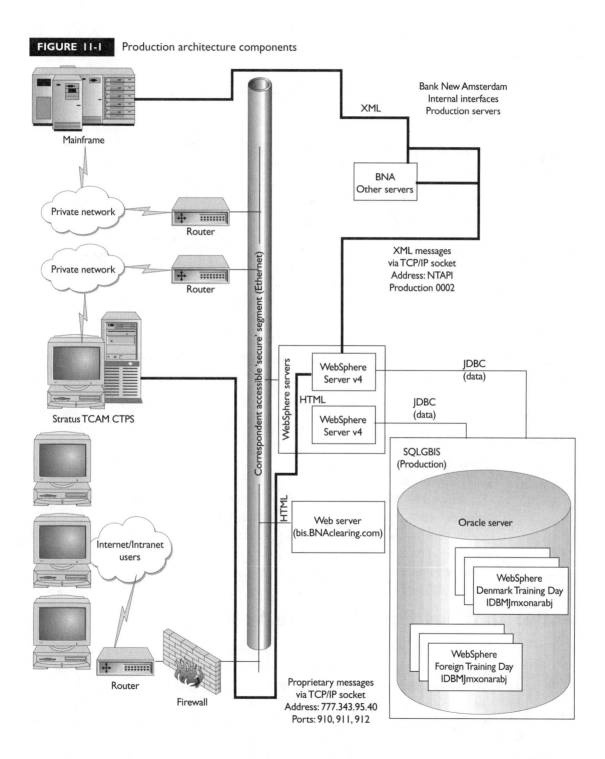

FIGURE 11-2 Production architecture as a UML sequence diagram

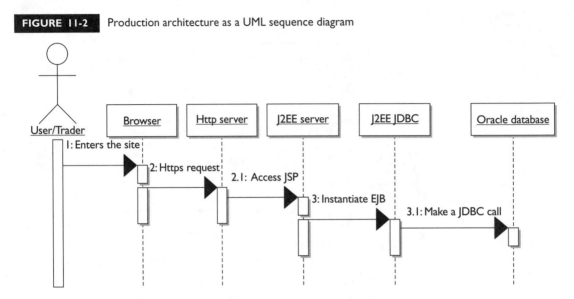

server (sometimes known as the Stratus Gateway Interface). These orders are routed to the appropriate exchange or market maker based on a set of correspondent-defined rules. Executions are then passed back from the exchange or market maker to CTPS, which updates the order file and forwards the result of the execution to the mainframe.

SQLBIS Database Server

The SQLBIS database server was created to service BNA's trading website, Brokerage Information System (BIS). On the database server are several databases (or data *marts*) that are used by BIS and the BIS Trading Area to look up account and application access as well as cross references and other information. The ORDERDB database was created exclusively to support the WebSphere applications. In development, the tables and views were created by developers and migrated to production by the database administration (DBA) group.

Model and Develop the Case Study

This section describes the case study trading application using text and diagrams (mostly UML diagrams). This task is not unlike what you as a SCEA Part 2 test taker must accomplish. As you saw in Chapter 3, UML diagrams and use cases can replace what was formerly called the *functional requirements* in an application development scenario. Moreover, UML is an adopted and widely accepted standard used to describe business processing. UML provides benefits to architects and enterprises by facilitating the construction of robust and maintainable business models, which can support the entire software development lifecycle (SDLC).

The *use case model* describes the target functionality of a new application. A *use case* represents a unit of interaction between an actor and some function. A *use case diagram* describes an interaction between an actor and the system. It presents a collection of use cases and actors and typically specifies or characterizes the functionality and behavior of a enterprise application interacting with one or more external actors. The users and any system that may interact with the system are the *actors*. Actors help delimit the system and give a clearer picture of what it is supposed to do.

Use cases are developed on the basis of the actors' needs. This ensures that the system will turn out to be what the users expected. Use case diagrams contain stick figure icons that represent actors, association relationships, generalize relationships, packages, and use cases. A top-level use case diagram shows the context of a system and the boundaries of the system's behavior. One or more use case diagrams can be drawn to describe a part of an application system. Use cases can include other use cases as part of their behavior. A use case diagram shows the set of external actors and the system use cases in which the actors participate.

After the use case model is completed and signed off by the business managers, development begins in earnest. For the remainder of the chapter, we will mix some of the UML modeling techniques with the actual development product to illustrate the case study.

A use case model typically comprises the following interrelated components:

- Actor definition
- Business process model
- Sequence diagrams
- Class descriptions
- Class diagrams
- State transition (lifecycle) diagrams

Actor Definition

The people involved in the business process are described as a series of actors, who may represent existing jobs or roles in the organization or may be completely new jobs or roles. Table 11-2 shows the various actors involved in a business process and their roles.

Actors and Their Roles

Actor	Description
Customer	Trades with the application based on limits
Trader	Trades with the application based without limits
Continuous trade processing system (CTPS)	Routes orders to the mainframe trading system
Mainframe Trading System	BNACS back office books and records
SQL (Oracle)	Contains the database reference data

Business Process Model

A number of *scenarios*, specific examples of performing the task, are identified for each task that is carried out in the business process.

The *business process*, or task model, describes how the business processes will perform the necessary tasks with or without a computer application. It represents an important aspect of the business requirements, since it describes from a user and business perspective what work is done. The model provides the basis for designing the functionality of the computer application.

A *business process model* is a model of one or more business processes. Each process has a process owner and process goals (such as cycle time, defect rate, and cost) and consists of a set of business activities (in sequence and/or parallel). Figure 11-3 shows an example of a securities trade order and the processing steps it goes through from submission to completion.

Development Environment and Database Design

Before we begin the physical construction of the application components, we must make certain that prerequisite physical items such as infrastructure, development environment, and so on, are in place for use by the development team. In addition to an adequate workstation and the appropriate server(s), the J2EE project libraries and the development GUI presentation tool such as JBuilder are accessible to developers with the appropriate permissions in place. The RDBMS application database, in this case Oracle, with current maintenance and whatever third-party or in-house J2EE development software is ready for use from each workstation. Developers have been availed of the guidelines and naming standards that the project team agreed to use to develop both the database and the application.

Important for development is the preliminary physical database design used for the application. The database design at this point can differ from that of the final

FIGURE 11-3 A trade as a business process

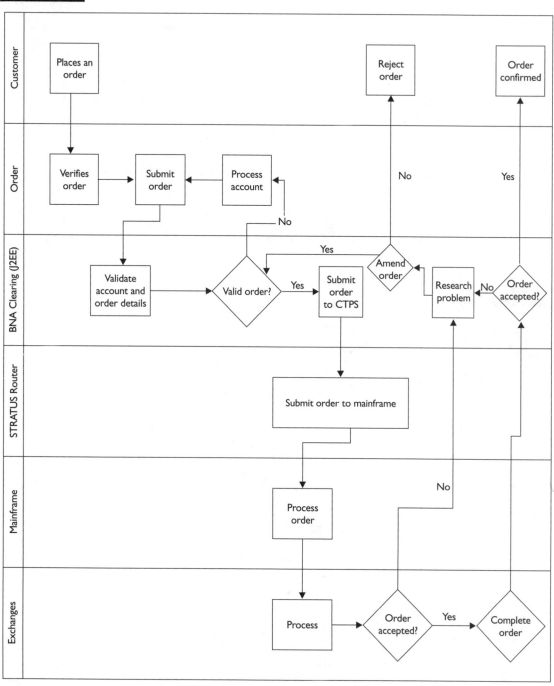

application database design, but it is eventually reconciled in terms of function back to the overall design.

This design of the trade system ORDERDB, shown in Figure 11-4, meets the constraints of the DBMS, and since it is derived directly from a composite data model, it also satisfies the system requirements. The rules ensure that the physical design is valid and that it follows good practice. During development, no attempt is made to achieve good performance. Rather, the design provides a sound starting point for physical tuning when the design of both database and Java classes is adjusted to achieve performance objectives. The database characteristics can vary depending on the DBMS being used.

The key characteristics of many of the popular DBMS engines, such as Oracle, are built according to the following rules:

1. **Entities**   Most entities on the composite data model become a table. The key-only entities may be paired with other key-only entities to form junction tables, which can speed up joins.

FIGURE 11-4   The ORDERDB database

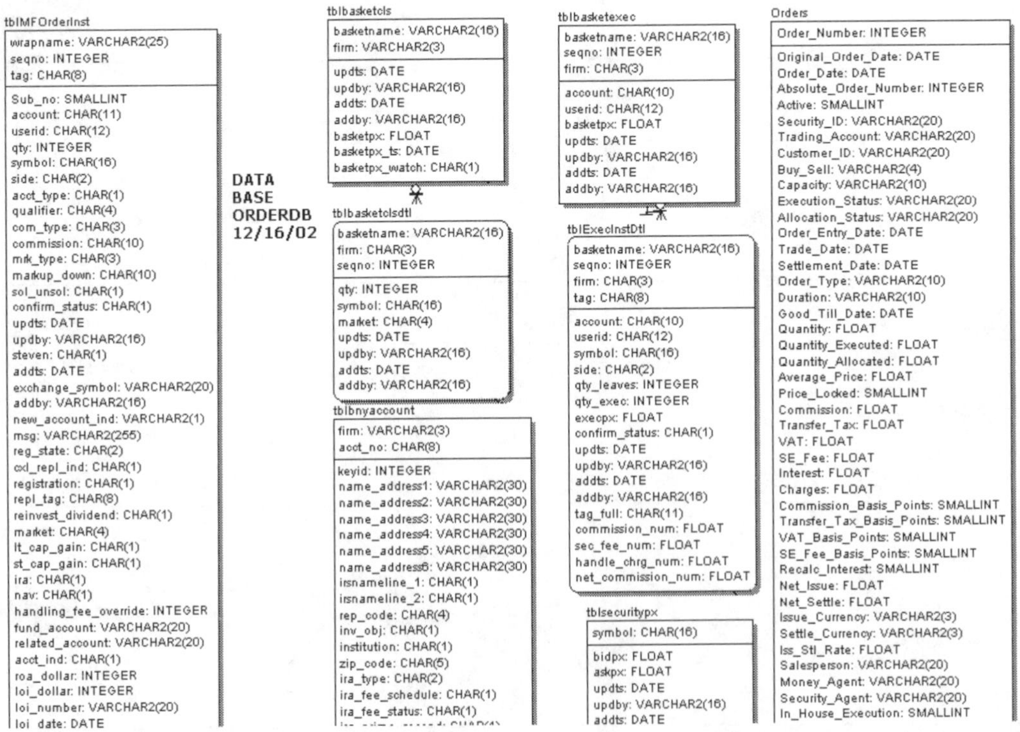

2. **Primary Keys**   The primary key of each entity becomes the primary key of the corresponding table. Specify a UNIQUE index for the entire primary key.

3. **Alternate Keys**   Each alternate key becomes a UNIQUE secondary index.

4. **Foreign Keys**   Indexing each entity foreign key becomes a secondary NON-UNIQUE index.

5. **Referential Integrity**   Make each entity foreign key a FOREIGN KEY for the table, referencing the master of the supported relationship.

6. **Other Non-unique Keys**   Each other non-unique key becomes a NON-UNIQUE index on the corresponding column(s).

7. **Exclusive Relationships**   If a detail entity has two or more mutually exclusive masters:

   ▪ Provide foreign key indexes to support each relationship as defined in Rule 4.

   ▪ The foreign key columns for the relationships should all be defined as NULLS ALLOWED.

   ▪ Maintenance of exclusivity must be handled by program.

Developing the Trading System

The trading system is a browser-based user interface that provides trading functionality—that is, the ability to send trade orders (even baskets of stocks) and view customer account and trade order requests to BNA. Written in Java with J2EE, it provides the customer with an integrated, platform-independent method for accessing account information and submitting and viewing orders via the Internet or a private network. All trading functionality is accessible via a single menu page, which uses a frameset with a header, footer, and a navigation frame on the left to expose the functionality in the right side main frame (no pun intended). Figure 11-5 shows the main trading frameset.

On the left side of the trading page is a frame that exposes the functionality that is currently available for trading—stocks, bonds, mutual funds, as well as baskets and multiple orders—along with some basic operational functionality used to maintain accounts and other external information. The main trading application page and operations page can be depicted as use case diagrams, as shown in Figures 11-6 and 11-7.

FIGURE 11-5 Trading page main menu frameset

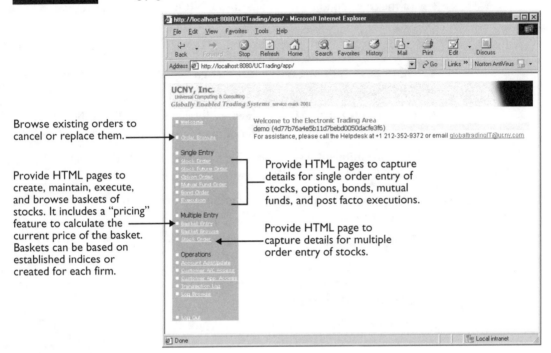

Browse existing orders to cancel or replace them.

Provide HTML pages to create, maintain, execute, and browse baskets of stocks. It includes a "pricing" feature to calculate the current price of the basket. Baskets can be based on established indices or created for each firm.

Provide HTML pages to capture details for single order entry of stocks, options, bonds, mutual funds, and post facto executions.

Provide HTML page to capture details for multiple order entry of stocks.

FIGURE 11-6

Trading page functionality as a use case

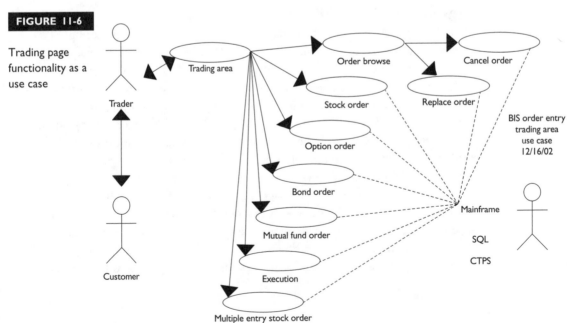

BIS order entry trading area use case 12/16/02

FIGURE 11-7 Operations page functionality as a use case

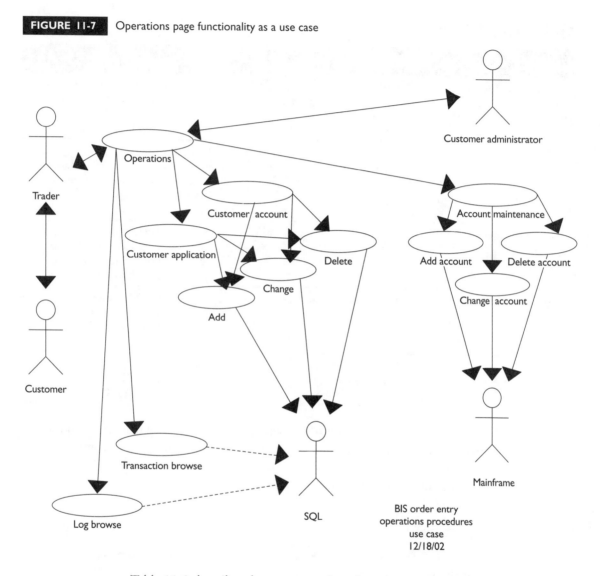

Table 11-3 describes the use case task goals and scenarios.

Sequence Diagrams

Sequence diagrams are models of business processes that represent the different interactions between actors and objects in the system. Each process has a process owner and goals (such as cycle time, defect rate, and cost) and consists of a set of business activities (in sequence and/or in parallel). Figure 11-8 depicts the sequence of a trade order being placed by a customer as it moves through the J2EE application

TABLE 11-3	Tasks and Scenarios	

Task Name	Task Goal	Task Scenarios
All forms of order entry: equity, bonds, mutual funds, baskets	Send order to CTPS routed to the mainframe trading system	Order information is keyed in, and information is edited and routed to CTPS and ultimately to mainframe trading system for processing
Order browse	Review/cancel/replace orders that have been previously sent to CTPS-mainframe trading system	Previously entered order information is edited and sometimes replaced; information is edited and routed to CTPS and ultimately to mainframe trading system for processing
Account maintenance	Add/update/delete retail customer accounts	Account information is edited and sometimes replaced; information is edited and routed to mainframe trading system for processing
Customer application maintenance	Add/update/delete customer application entitlement	Application information is edited and sometimes replaced; information is edited and routed to SQL for processing
Customer account maintenance	Add/update/delete customer account/user entitlement	Account/user information is edited and sometimes replaced; information is edited and routed to SQL for processing

server for verification and onto the trade process router to the mainframe and then to the securities exchange, where the actual trade is executed. After a confirmed execution, each of the front-end processors is notified, and ultimately the customer is availed of the completed order and price.

Class Descriptions

Table 11-4 describes the business classes included in the business process sequence diagram in Figure 11-8.

Class Diagrams

Using the initial list of business classes, you develop class diagrams by identifying and defining the relationships among the classes. This is best done in an interactive

TABLE 11-4	Business Classes and Descriptions
Class	**Description**
Customer	A person who orders securities
Potential Customer	A member of the general public who makes inquiries about our publications to potentially order publications from the company
Order	A request for a security
Order Inquiry	An inquiry from a customer concerning an order that has been placed
Delivery	The security that is purchased is sent to the customer portfolio
Payment	The payment by a customer for securities ordered and/or received
Company	BNACS
Order Browse	A request to view all outstanding security orders
Order Cancel	A request to cancel all outstanding security orders
Order Replace	A request to replace all outstanding security orders

development workshop with business partners. It is also useful to keep these diagrams on display on a whiteboard or other media, and to develop it gradually as the project progresses. The diagrams can also be stored on a UML tool to provide access to all team members and other interested parties.

The class diagrams are also used to show relationships among classes. This aspect of the diagrams will tend to emerge later in the design process, as "lower level" classes are identified. The class diagrams will improve the definition of the classes, which in turn may require changes to the sequence diagrams and, when developed, the state transition diagrams. These other diagrams will also have an impact on the class diagrams.

Two important classes in terms of the back-end processing are the Enterprise JavaBeans (EJB) session beans that process orders: the *AccessOrderBean* will send and track orders, and the *AccessDataBean* will provide associated data pertaining to the customer and the associated order(s). Figures 11-9 and 11-10 are UML class diagrams illustrating the methods and associations for each of these classes.

State Transition (Lifecycle) Diagrams

It is useful to trace what happens to a class through the execution of a business process, or through the computer system that is developed to support the business process.

FIGURE 11-8 Sequence of trade order

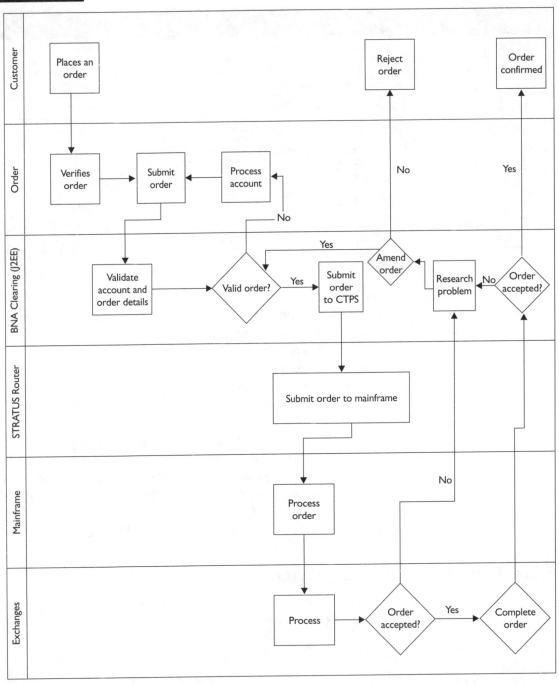

FIGURE 11-9   Class diagram for access order session bean

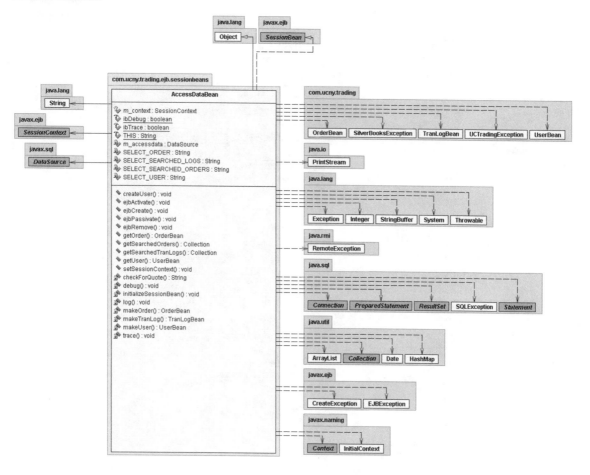

The state transition diagrams show the various states in which a class can exist and the way in which the class changes from one state to another. Figure 11-11 shows a state transition of trade order processing.

FIGURE 11-10 Class diagram for access data session bean

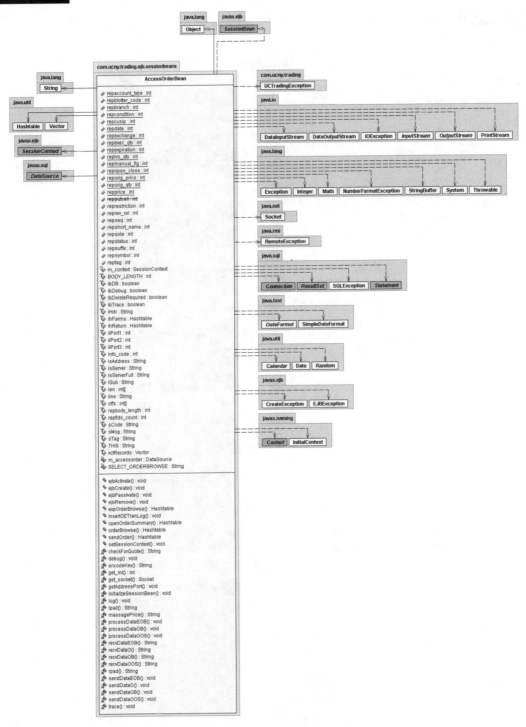

State transition (lifecycle) diagrams

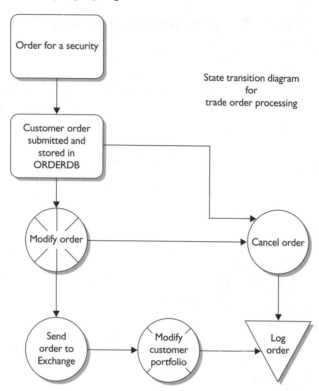

Trade System Design and Implementation

This section describes the user-interface layout, class diagrams, controls, actions, and navigational aspects for the trading application. It is a comprehensive description of how the application works and affects the underlying data elements.

Stock Order Entry *Screen*

Figure 11-12 shows the stock order entry screen, in which a buyer clicks Stock Order and enters information in all the fields.

FIGURE 11-12 Equity trade order screen

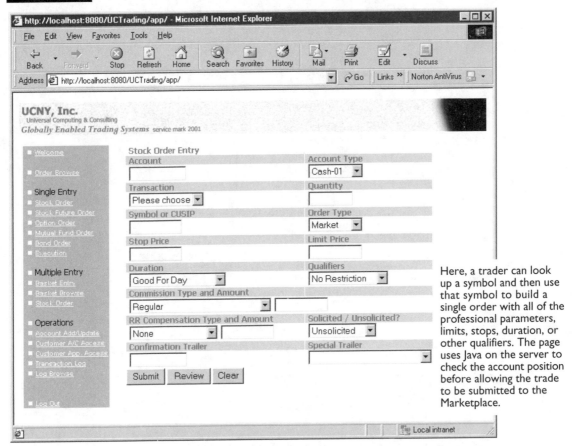

Figure 11-13 shows a class diagram that identifies and defines the relationships between the classes.

In Figure 11-14, you can see that a buy order has been placed for 100 shares of IBM at the market for account 14112345678.

Table 11-5 shows the controls and description of the information entered and validity notes regarding what each control should contain.

FIGURE 11-13 Equity trade order class diagram

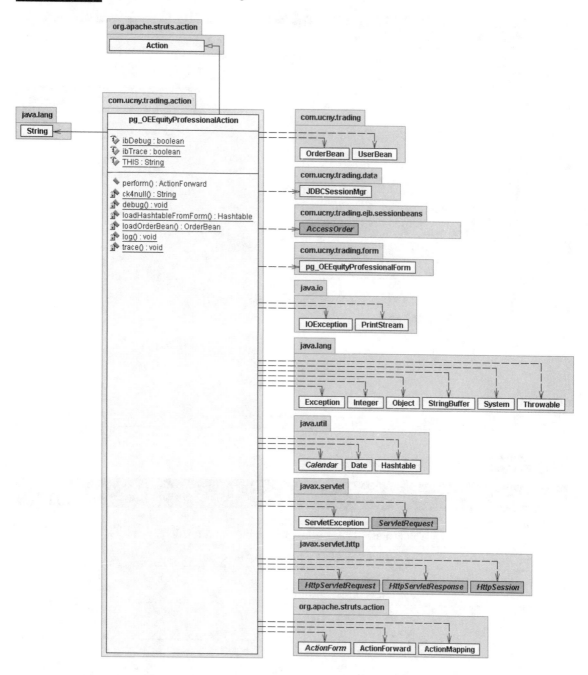

FIGURE 11-14 Submission and execution of trade order

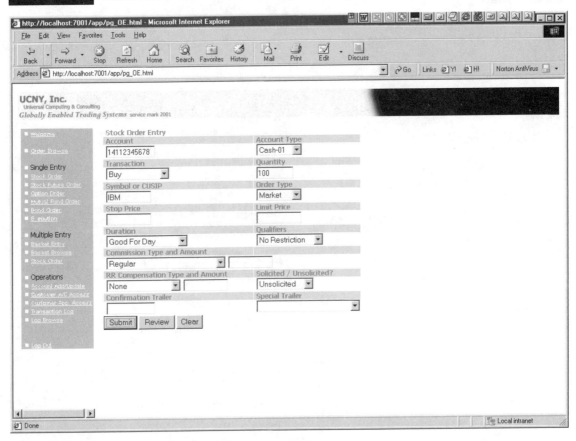

TABLE 11-5 Controls on the Trading Page

Controls	Description
Account	The customer's Account number Valid values: This is from the Customer Information System CIS system
Account Type	The valid values are: Cash/Margin/Short
Transaction	Side of the transaction Valid values: B/SL/SS/Buy Cover
Quantity	How many shares of the security Valid values: Numeric/integer > 0
Symbol of CUSIP	Security identifier/symbol or CUSIP Valid values: Symbol checked against warehouse security table

TABLE 11-5 Controls on the Trading Page *(continued)*

Controls	Description
Messages	Green or Red based upon the result. Green is success; red is problematic
Submit button	Process the data and exit the form
Review button	Review and exit the form
Clear button	Cancel the data entered and exit the form

Figure 11-15 shows the stock Order Browse screen, where account or a transaction side, i.e, B for Buy or S for Sell, or a symbol is entered and then you click Find The Orders. All of the buy orders are shown here.

FIGURE 11-15 Equity trade Order Browse screen

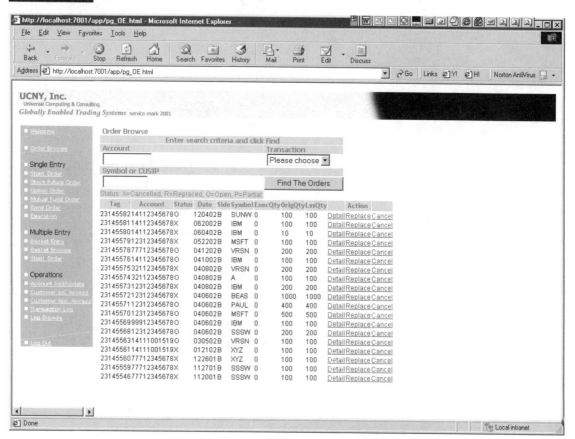

Figure 11-16 shows a class diagram that identifies and defines the relationships among the classes.

FIGURE 11-16 Class diagram for equity trade Order Browse screen

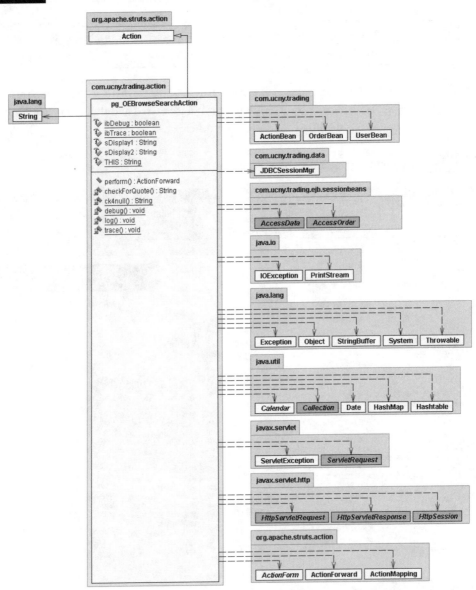

Trade Application Packages

After all of the application components are completed and the application is ready for deployment, a package diagram(s) can be used to describe associations among the component classes. Figures 11-17, 11-18, and 11-19 show package diagrams for *com.ucny.trading, com.ucny.trading.ejb.sessionbeans, com.ucny.trading.data*, and *com.ucny.trading.action*, which ties together all of the components (JSPs, EJBs, Java beans, and so on).

Trade Application Implementation Infrastructure

After the application is deployed, a component diagram(s) can be useful for describing associations among the hardware and software components and the system functionality. Figure 11-20 shows the hardware and software involved in the trade process flow.

Figure 11-21 shows the hardware and software involved in the security pricing process flow.

FIGURE 11-17   Package diagram for com.ucny.trading

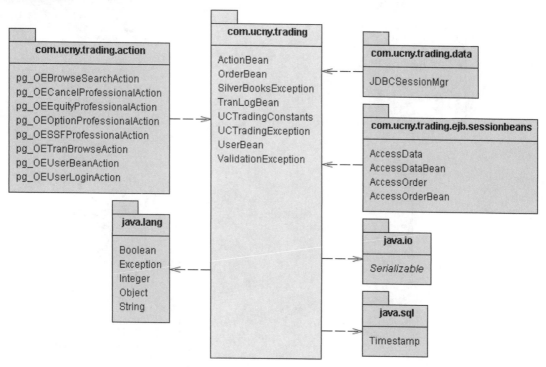

FIGURE 11-18 Package diagram for com.ucny.trading.ejb.sessionbeans

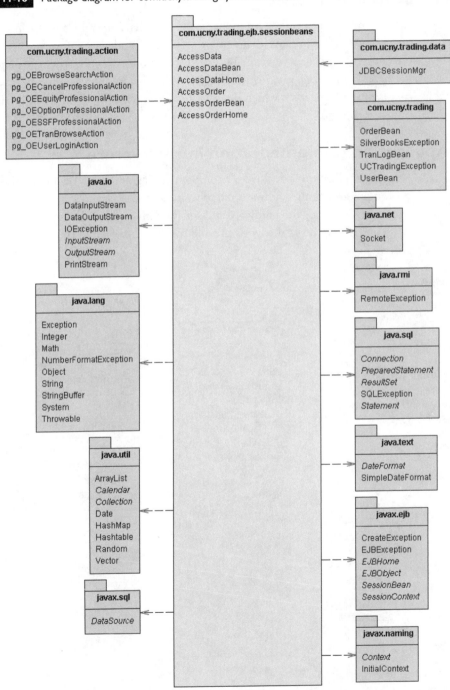

FIGURE 11-19 Package diagram for com.ucny.trading.data

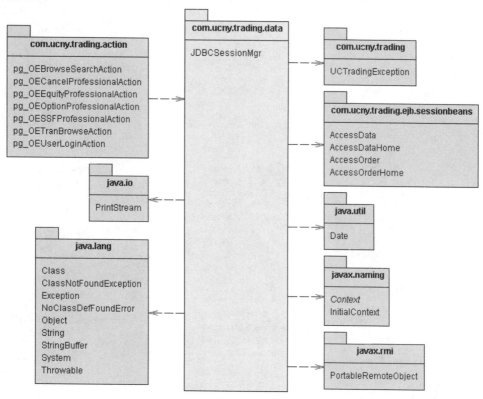

FIGURE 11-20

Hardware and software involved in the trade process flow

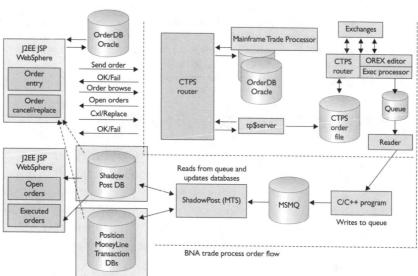

FIGURE 11-21 Hardware and software involved in the security pricing flow

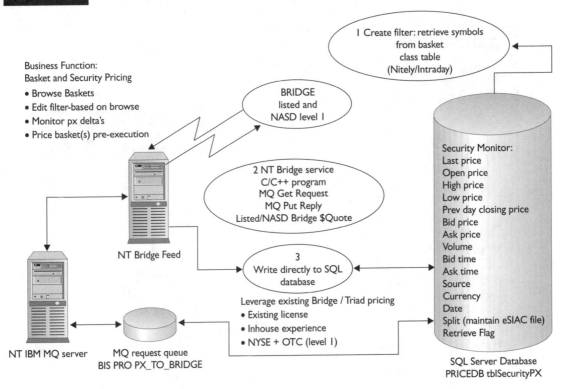

CERTIFICATION SUMMARY

This case study is an example of a real-world application. As architects, and for the purposes of the exam, you will create use cases, sequence diagrams, component diagrams, and other types of diagrams to provide a clear picture of the functions of an enterprise application. Its infrastructure, functionality, and deployment particulars can be illustrated using UML in conjunction with other diagramming and text descriptions to help users and others to evaluate and understand the application.

Glossary

Access Control The way by which interactions with resources are limited to collections of users or programs for the purpose of enforcing integrity, confidentiality, or availability constraints.

ACID The four properties that are guaranteed by a transaction: atomicity, consistency, isolation, and durability. Atomicity exists when either all of the changes are committed or, if for any reason the transaction cannot be completed, all of the changes are rolled back to their prior state. Consistency means that a transaction starts with data in a consistent state and ends with data in a consistent state. The data is said to be in consistent state when it conforms to a set of invariants or rules, such as no duplicate keys or a column not allowing nulls. Isolation means that any given transaction must appear to be running all by itself on the database. The effects of any concurrent transaction are not visible to this transaction, and the effects of this transaction are not visible until the transaction is actually committed. Durability means that once a transaction is committed, its effects are guaranteed to continue even after the recovery of a subsequent system failure.

activation The process that transfers an EJB from secondary storage to memory. This is the complementary process to passivation.

applet A Java component that executes in an application or device, usually a web browser, that supports the applet programming model.

applet container A container that supports the applet programming model.

application assembler Combines components into a deployable application unit.

application component provider Writes the business and application logic for the application by providing JavaServer Pages (JSP), Java classes, and the required deployment descriptors.

authentication The process used by callers and service providers that proves that they are to be "trusted." Authentication establishes the caller's identity and proves that they are "authenticated" instances of an identity. The three types of authentication required on the J2EE platform are basic, form-based, and mutual. The J2EE platform also supports digest authentication.

authorization   The mechanism that controls caller access and interaction with application resources or components. The caller's credentials (identity), which can also be anonymous or arbitrarily set by the caller, can be determined via authentication contexts that are available to the called component. Access can then be determined by comparing the caller's credentials with the access control rules for the required component or resource.

basic authentication   The web server authenticates a principal using the user name and password obtained from the web client via its built-in authentication mechanism. Refer to Section 11.1 Basic Authentication Scheme in the HTTP specification at *http://www.w3.org/Protocols/HTTP/1.0/spec.html#BasicAA* for more details.

BMP (bean-managed persistence)   The enterprise bean provider is responsible for creating the code for all of the database access. Consequently, this technique provides much more control over how data is accessed.

BMT (Bean-Managed Transaction)   A transaction boundary defined and controlled by an enterprise bean.

business logic   The code that implements the required functionality of an application.

caller principal   The principal that identifies the caller of the enterprise bean method.

client certificate authentication   A client authentication mechanism that uses a X.509 certificate to establish its identity.

CMP (container-managed persistence)   The Enterprise Bean Provider delegates the specifics of data access to the EJB container.

CMT (container-managed transaction) A transaction boundary defined and controlled by the EJB container.

component An application-level unit that is configurable at deployment time and supported by a container. The four types of components for the J2EE platform are enterprise beans, web components, applets, and application clients.

connector A standard extension mechanism that lets a container provide connectivity to enterprise information systems.

container An entity that provides lifecycle management, security, deployment, runtime, and component-specific services to components.

CORBA (Common Object Request Broker Architecture) The distributed object model defined by the Object Management Group (OMG).

credentials The security attributes of a principal.

deployer Installs modules and applications into the operational environment.

deployment The process of installing modules and applications into an operational environment.

deployment descriptor An XML file that accompanies each module or application, it describes specific configuration requirements that need to be resolved for the module or application to be installed successfully.

destination A JMS administered object that is either a queue for a point-to-point messaging model or a topic for a publish/subscribe messaging model.

digest authentication An authentication mechanism in which a web client authenticates by sending the server a message digest as part of the HTTP request. This message digest is calculated by taking pieces of the message along with the client's password and passing them though a one-way hash algorithm.

durable subscription   In a JMS publish/subscribe messaging system, known subscribers receive the messages when they are connected to the topic. If a known subscriber is not connected, JMS retains the messages until the subscriber reconnects or until they expire.

EAR (Enterprise Archive) file   An archive that contains a J2EE enterprise application. An EAR file comprises WAR, EJB JAR, RAR, and JAR files.

EJB container   A container within an EJB server or a J2EE application server that implements the runtime environment for enterprise beans, including security, concurrency, lifecycle management, transaction, deployment, naming, and other services provided by the J2EE platform.

EJB container provider   A vendor that supplies an EJB container.

EJB context   Allows the enterprise bean (EJB) to use services provided by the EJB container and in doing so obtain information about the invoker of a client-invoked method.

EJB home object   Provides the lifecycle operations (create, find, and remove methods) for an enterprise bean. The EJB home object, which is generated by the container's deployment tools, implements the enterprise bean's home interface. Any client wishing to use an enterprise bean will first locate its EJB home object via JNDI. Then it will call the lifecycle operations (methods) provided by the EJB home object to reference the EJB object (remote reference to the enterprise bean).

EJB JAR (Java Archive) file   An archive file that contains an EJB module.

EJB object   An object that implements the remote interface of the enterprise bean. Clients of an EJB reference an EJB object and do not reference an enterprise bean instance directly.

EJB server   A server that can host one or more EJB containers.

EJB server provider   A vendor that supplies an EJB server.

enterprise bean   A component that implements either a business function or a business entity. The component can be an entity, session, or message-driven bean.

enterprise bean provider   The person or vendor that creates enterprise bean classes, remote and home interfaces, and deployment descriptor files, and then packages them into an EJB JAR file.

enterprise information system (EIS)   The applications that maintain data for an enterprise. These applications offer a well defined set of services that are exposed to callers as local and/or remote interfaces. Some examples of EIS are legacy mainframe transaction processing and database systems.

Enterprise JavaBeans (EJB)   Component architecture for development and deployment of distributed, object-oriented, enterprise-level applications. EJBs are scalable, secure, and transactional.

entity bean   An enterprise bean that represents data, uniquely identified by a primary key, which is persisted and maintained by a database. The entity bean is able to manage its own persistence (BMP), or it can leave this function to the EJB container.

form-based authentication   An authentication mechanism that allows for the use of a custom HTML form as the user interface for capturing the authentication information.

handle   An opaque, long-lived, and serializable reference to an enterprise bean instance.

home handle   An object used to obtain a reference to the home interface.

home interface   An object that provides the management or lifecycle operations (create, remove, find) for an EJB. The home interface of a session bean has create and remove methods, and the home interface of an entity bean has create, finder, and remove methods.

HTML (HyperText Markup Language)   A file format for creating hypertext documents on the web.

HTTP (HyperText Transfer Protocol)   A web protocol based on TCP/IP that is used to fetch hypertext objects from remote hosts—for example, web pages, images, and binary files.

HTTPS   The HTTP protocol layered over the Secure Socket Layer (SSL) protocol. This provides a more secure transfer of data using encrypted data streams.

IIOP (Internet Inter-ORB Protocol)   A protocol used for communication between CORBA object request brokers (ORBs).

J2EE application server   Provides EJB and/or web containers to support the runtime environment of a J2EE product.

J2EE product provider   A vendor that supplies a J2EE product implemented as per the J2EE platform specification.

J2EE role   The function performed by a party in the development and deployment phases of an application developed using J2EE technology. The roles are Application Component Provider, Application Assembler, Deployer, J2EE Product Provider, EJB Container Provider, EJB Server Provider, Web Container Provider, Web Server Provider, Tool Provider, and System Administrator.

JAR (Java Archive) file   A file format that allows several files to be stored in a single file. Compatible with zip archives.

JavaBeans component   A portable, platform independent, reusable component model that can be manipulated in a visual builder tool and coded into applications. To make this possible, JavaBeans must adhere to defined property and event interface conventions.

JavaMail   Provides a standard and independent framework for Java client applications to use electronic mail. This provides the ability to do the following:

- Compose messages, including multi-part messages with attachments
- Send messages to particular servers
- Retrieve and store messages in folders

JDBC   Provides a database-independent connectivity between Java and a wide range of data sources.

JMS (Java Message Service)   Provides a common way for a Java application to create, send, receive, and read an enterprise messaging system's messages.

JMS provider   An enterprise messaging system that implements the Java Message Service along with administrative and control functions.

JNDI (Java Naming and Directory Interface)   An API that provides naming and directory functionality for Java classes.

JSP (JavaServer Page)   JavaServer Pages use template data, custom elements, scripting languages, and server-side Java objects to return dynamic content to a client typically within a web browser. A JSP is a combination of HTML syntax and Java syntax that is executed at runtime to create content for web-based clients dynamically. More advanced JSPs can use templates and custom tag libraries to further enhance their functionality and reuseability.

JTA (Java Transaction API)   An API that allows applications and J2EE servers to use transactions.

JTS (Java Transaction Service)   Defines the implementation of a transaction manager, which supports the Java Transaction API (JTA) and implements the Java mapping of the Object Management Group (OMG) Object Transaction Service (OTS) specification.

MDB (message-driven bean)   An enterprise bean that consumes messages asynchronously. A client invokes MDBs by sending messages to the destination to which the MDB is listening.

ORB (Object Request Broker)   Enables CORBA objects to locate and then communicate with one another.

OS principal   A principal that exists for the operating system on which the J2EE platform is executing.

OTS (Object Transaction Service)   Defines the interfaces that permit CORBA objects to participate in transactions.

passivation   The process that transfers an enterprise bean from memory to secondary storage. This is the complementary process to activation.

persistence   Protocol for moving the state of an entity bean between its instance variables and a persistent store (a database).

point-to-point messaging model   A messaging model that uses queues. In JMS, clients can write messages to a queue and can read messages from a queue.

primary key   An object within a home that uniquely identifies an entity bean.

principal   The identity assigned to a user that has been authenticated.

privilege   A non-unique security attribute that can be shared by many principals, such as a group.

publish/subscribe messaging model   A messaging model that uses topics. In JMS, clients can publish messages to a topic and multiple clients can subscribe and receive messages from a topic.

queue   Destination used in point-to-point messaging model.

realm   A string passed on HTTP request during basic authentication. This specifies the protection domain to be used for authentication.

remote interface   Enterprise bean interface that defines the business methods a client can invoke.

resource adapter   System-level software used by an EJB container or a client to connect to an EIS.

resource manager   Provides shared access to a set of resources. It participates in transactions that are externally controlled and coordinated by a transaction manager.

RMI (Remote Method Invocation)   A distributed object model that allows an object running in one Java Virtual Machine (JVM) to invoke methods on an object running in a different JVM.

RMI-IIOP   An RMI implementation that uses CORBA's IIOP protocol. RMI-IIOP allows developers to code using the RMI APIs while the interprocess communication actually involves the IIOP protocol instead of the JRMP protocol with which RMI is usually associated.

role mapping   Associating groups and/or principals known to the container to security roles specified within the deployment descriptor. Before installing the component on the server, these security roles need to be mapped (associated) by the deployer.

security attributes   Set of properties associated with a principal via an authentication protocol and/or a J2EE product provider.

security constraint   The declarative way of protecting web resource collections. A security constraint consists of these parts: a web resource collection, an authorization constraint, and a user data constraint.

security context   An object that encapsulates the shared security state between two entities.

security permission   A mechanism used by the J2EE platform to convey the programming restrictions imposed upon application component providers.

security role   An abstract logical grouping of users defined by an application assembler. When an application is deployed, roles are associated to security identities that actually exist in the deployment environment, such as principals or groups.

security view   A set of security roles created by the application assembler.

server principal   The operating system principal that the server is executing as.

servlet   A Java program that generates dynamic content and interacts with web clients using a request-response model.

servlet container   Also called a web container. Provides services that facilitate the requests-responses model. It also decodes requests and formats responses. All servlet containers support HTTP and can optionally support other request-response protocols such as HTTPS.

servlet context   An object that contains information about the web application that the servlet is executing as a part of. Through this object, a servlet can log events, obtain URL references to resources, and set and store context attributes for other servlets within the same context.

session   Object used by servlets to track user interaction with a web application across multiple HTTP requests.

session bean   An enterprise bean that performs operations for a client. A session bean is created by a client and typically exists only for the duration of a single client-server session. A session bean can be either stateful, in which it maintains conversational state across methods and transactions, or stateless.

SQL (Structured Query Language)   The standardized relational database language for defining and maintaining database objects and manipulating the data within them.

SQL/J   Standards that include specifications for embedding SQL statements within the Java programming language and for calling Java static methods as SQL stored procedures and user-defined functions.

SSL (Secure Socket Layer)   Protocol that provides communication between a client and server to be encrypted for privacy. Servers must be authenticated and clients are optionally authenticated.

stateful session bean   A session bean that maintains a conversational state.

stateless session bean   A session bean that does not maintain conversational state. All instances of the same stateless session bean are identical.

system administrator   The individual responsible for configuring, administering, and maintaining computers, networks, and software systems.

topic   Destination used in the publish-subscribe messaging model.

transaction   An atomic unit of work that changes data from one state to another. A transaction can comprise one or more changes, all of which will either complete or roll back. Transactions allow several users to access the same data at the same time (concurrently).

transaction attribute   A value defined in the deployment descriptor of an enterprise bean module. It tells the EJB container how to control the transaction scope when the enterprise bean's methods are invoked. The following are the possible values for a transaction attribute: *Required, RequiresNew, Supports, NotSupported, Mandatory, Never.*

transaction isolation level   The degree to which the intermediate state of the data being modified by a transaction can be seen by other concurrent transactions; also the data being modified by other transactions can be seen by it.

transaction manager   Provides the management functions and services required to support synchronization, transaction demarcation, transaction context propagation, and transactional resource management.

URI (Uniform Resource Identifier)   A compact string of characters that identifies either an abstract or physical resource. A URI is an abstract superclass of the URL or URN concrete subclasses.

URL (Uniform Resource Locator)   A standard way for referring to an arbitrary piece of data on the web. Each URL is in the form *protocol://host/localinfo,* where *protocol* specifies the protocol to use, such as HTTP or FTP; *host* specifies the remote host where the resource exists; and *localinfo*, which is often a file name, is passed to the protocol handler on the remote host to actually find the resource.

URL path   URL passed in a HTTP request to invoke a servlet. It consists of a Context Path, a Servlet Path, and PathInfo. Context Path is the path prefix associated with the servlet context. Servlet Path, which starts with a slash (/) character, is the path section that corresponds to the servlet container mapping that activated the request. The PathInfo is the part of the request path that is neither part of the Context Path nor the Servlet Path.

URN (Uniform Resource Name)   A unique identifier for an entity that does not specify where the entity is actually located. A URN may be used to attempt to find an entity locally before looking it up on the web. The URN allows the web location to change, while still allowing the entity to be found.

WAR (Web Archive) file   A JAR archive that contains a web application.

web application   An Internet application, including those that use Java technologies such as JavaServer Pages and servlets, as well as those that use non-Java technologies such as CGI and Perl.

web component   A component that can be either a servlet or a JavaServer Page, and that provides service by responding to requests.

web container   A container provided by a J2EE or web server that implements the J2EE web component contract. This defines the runtime environment and services for web components including concurrency, deployment, lifecycle management, security, transaction, and other services.

web module   A unit that consists of one or more web components along with a web deployment descriptor.

web resource collection   A list of URL patterns and HTTP methods that describe a set of resources that are to be protected via a security constraint.

web server   Software that provides services to access the network (Internet, an intranet, or an extranet). The web server hosts web sites, supports HTTP (and possibly other protocols), and executes server-side programs such as servlets. On a J2EE platform, a web server provides services to one or more web containers.

XML (eXtensible Markup Language)   A markup language that evolved from Standard Generalized Markup Language (SGML), and that allows the definition of tags (markup) needed to identify the content, data, and text in XML documents.

A

About the CD

The CD-ROM included with this book comes complete with MasterExam, and the electronic version of the book. The software is easy to install on any Windows 98/NT/2000 computer and must be installed to access the MasterExam features. You may, however, browse the electronic book directly from the CD without installation. To register for a second bonus MasterExam, simply click the Bonus Exam link on the Main Page and follow the directions to the free online registration.

System Requirements

Software requires Windows 98 or higher and Internet Explorer 5.0 or above and 20MB of hard disk space for full installation. The Electronic book requires Adobe Acrobat Reader. To access Online Training from LearnKey you must have RealPlayer Basic 8 or Real Plugin, which will be automatically installed if you purchase on-line training.

Code on the CD

Included on the CD in the root directory is a zip file containing the code examples for Chapters 5, 6, 7, 8, 9, and 10. A readme.txt file, located in the \sceaj2ee\code\support\Weblogic directory within the zip file, explains the contents and gives directions on how to compile, deploy, and execute the code in a Windows-based environment. To download this file, browse to the root directory of the CD-ROM and in Windows, use a utility, e.g. WinZip, to extract or copy the files to your hard drive. From a non-Windows (or Windows) computer with the JDK installed, use the Java Archive (JAR) command to extract the contents of the zip file to the file system. Here is the command line to do this:

```
jar xvf sceaj2ee.zip
```

Installing and Running MasterExam

If your computer CD-ROM drive is configured to auto run, the CD-ROM will automatically start up upon inserting the disk. From the opening screen you may install MasterExam by pressing the *MasterExam* button. This will begin the installation process and create a program group named "LearnKey." To run MasterExam, use START | PROGRAMS | LEARNKEY. If the auto run feature did not launch your CD, browse to the CD and Click on the "RunInstall" icon.

MasterExam

MasterExam provides you with a simulation of the actual exam. The number of questions, the type of questions, and the time allowed are intended to be an accurate representation of the exam environment. You have the option to take an open book exam, including hints, references, and answer(s), a closed book exam, or the timed MasterExam simulation.

When you launch MasterExam, a digital clock display will appear in the upper left-hand corner of your screen. The clock will continue to count down to zero unless you choose to end the exam before the time expires.

Electronic Book

The entire contents of the Study Guide are provided in PDF. Adobe's Acrobat Reader has been included on the CD.

Help

A help file is provided through the help button on the main page in the lower left hand corner. Individual help features are also available through MasterExam.

Removing Installation(s)

MasterExam is installed to your hard drive. For BEST results removing programs, use the START | PROGRAMS | LEARNKEY | UNINSTALL options to remove MasterExam.

Technical Support

For questions regarding the technical content of the electronic book or MasterExam, please visit *www.osborne.com* or e-mail *customer.service@mcgraw-hill.com*. For customers outside the 50 United States, e-mail: *international_cs@mcgraw-hill.com*.

LearnKey Technical Support

For technical problems with the software (installation, operation, removing installations), and for questions regarding LearnKey Online Training and MasterSim content, please visit *www.learnkey.com* or e-mail *techsupport@learnkey.com*.

LearnKey Online Training

The **LearnKey Online Training** link will allow you to purchase online training from *Osborne.Onlineexpert.com*. Courses may also be purchased directly from *www.LearnKey.com* or by calling 800 865-0165.

The first time that you run Training, you will be required to Register with the online product. Follow the instructions for a first time user. Please make sure to use a valid e-mail address.

Prior to running Online Training you will need to add the Real Plugin and the RealCBT plugin to your system. This will automatically be facilitated to your system when you run the training the first time.

INDEX

Note: Page numbers in *italics* refer to illustrations or tables.

601

INTERNATIONAL CONTACT INFORMATION

AUSTRALIA
McGraw-Hill Book Company Australia Pty. Ltd.
TEL +61-2-9900-1800
FAX +61-2-9878-8881
http://www.mcgraw-hill.com.au
books-it_sydney@mcgraw-hill.com

CANADA
McGraw-Hill Ryerson Ltd.
TEL +905-430-5000
FAX +905-430-5020
http://www.mcgraw-hill.ca

GREECE, MIDDLE EAST, & AFRICA
(Excluding South Africa)
McGraw-Hill Hellas
TEL +30-210-6560-990
TEL +30-210-6560-993
TEL +30-210-6560-994
FAX +30-210-6545-525

MEXICO (Also serving Latin America)
McGraw-Hill Interamericana Editores S.A. de C.V.
TEL +525-117-1583
FAX +525-117-1589
http://www.mcgraw-hill.com.mx
fernando_castellanos@mcgraw-hill.com

SINGAPORE (Serving Asia)
McGraw-Hill Book Company
TEL +65-6863-1580
FAX +65-6862-3354
http://www.mcgraw-hill.com.sg
mghasia@mcgraw-hill.com

SOUTH AFRICA
McGraw-Hill South Africa
TEL +27-11-622-7512
FAX +27-11-622-9045
robyn_swanepoel@mcgraw-hill.com

SPAIN
McGraw-Hill/Interamericana de España, S.A.U.
TEL +34-91-180-3000
FAX +34-91-372-8513
http://www.mcgraw-hill.es
professional@mcgraw-hill.es

UNITED KINGDOM, NORTHERN,
EASTERN, & CENTRAL EUROPE
McGraw-Hill Education Europe
TEL +44-1-628-502500
FAX +44-1-628-770224
http://www.mcgraw-hill.co.uk
computing_europe@mcgraw-hill.com

ALL OTHER INQUIRIES Contact:
McGraw-Hill/Osborne
TEL +1-510-420-7700
FAX +1-510-420-7703
http://www.osborne.com
omg_international@mcgraw-hill.com

LICENSE AGREEMENT